114
155
280.

302

CIRCUITS

302 CIRCUITS

Elektor Electronics (Publishing)
P.O. Box 1414
Dorchester DT2 8YH
England

British Library Cataloguing in Publication Data
A catalogue record for this book is available from
the British Library

ISBN 0 905705 25 4

First published in the United Kingdom 1985
Reprinted 1987, 1988, 1991, 1992, 1994

© Elektuur BV

Printed in the Netherlands by Tulp BV, Zwolle

WARNING: electricity is dangerous

The projects in this book are, to the best of the Publisher's knowledge and belief, both accurately described and safe. None the less, great care must always be taken when assembling electronic circuits that carry mains voltages: the Publishers cannot accept responsibility for any accidents that may occur.

Because electricity is dangerous, its use, application and transmission are subject to rules, regulations and guidance. These are laid down in numerous laws, Electricity Generating Board regulations, British Standards and recommendations of the Institution of Electrical Engineers (IEE). Some of these may be obtained from your local electricity showroom, but most, if not all, should be available for reference in your local library.

contents

RF & video

test & measurement

001 microcomputer power supply protection

When the 5 V and/or 12 V part of a computer's power supply breaks down it can mean one of two things: the supply will be either too high or too low (generally zero volts). When the voltage drops the consequences are generally limited to the RAM memory being erased or corrupted. The effects of the voltage rising, due to a faulty voltage regulator, for example, are far more serious. The chances of all the 40 000 to 100 000 transistors in the microprocessor surviving something like that are quite slim. That is more than enough reason to find a place for this supply protection circuit in any computer.

This circuit disconnects the computer's power supply from the mains when its output voltage becomes too high or if it detects a short circuit. If, for example, the voltage on the 5 V line increases for some reason zener diode D1 will start conducting at about 5.6 V. This causes thyristor Th1 to conduct and short the offending supply line to ground. (It is essential for this method of operation that the computer's power supply is current-limited). This causes transistor T1 to switch off with the result that the relay drops out and takes the mains supply with it.

The 12 V supply is protected in much the same way. When the voltage reaches about 12.7 V thyristor Th2 conducts and shorts the 12 V line to ground. The supply to the coil of the relay is then cut off so Rel once again

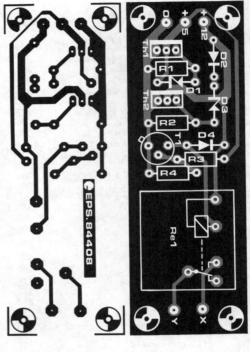

falls out. If there is a short-circuit within the computer itself the effect is the same, except, of course, that our circuit does not have to provide the 'short'.

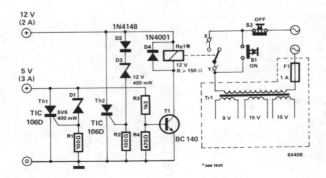

Parts list

Resistors:
R1,R2 = 100 Ω
R3 = 1k2
R4 = 470 Ω

Semiconductors:
D1 = 5V6 400 mW zener
D2 = 1N4148
D3 = 12 V 400 mW zener
D4 = 1N4001
T1 = BC 140
Th1,Th2 = TIC 106

Miscellaneous:
F1 = fuse, 1 A slow blow
Re1 = 12 V relay, e.g. Maplin no. HY20W
S1 = push button, push to make
S2 = push button, push to break

When the short-circuit or fault is found (and cured) the supply can be switched on again by pressing push button S1. An 'off' button has also been provided, which should be of particular interest to ZX users as these computers do not have an on/off switch. Constructing this circuit is aided by the availability of the printed circuit board shown in figure 2. It is principally intended for use with the microcomputer power supply published elsewhere in this issue and it can be connected directly to that circuit's +5 V and +12 V outputs. If you wish to use this protection with a computer with no 12 V supply line the 12 V section can simply be left out. The relay will then have to be changed so that a 5 V type is used instead of 12 V and it then has to be connected to the 5 V supply line.

002 three-state TTL logic probe

Regular readers of *Elektor* will know that we often publish various items of test gear. The design shown here is nothing really unusual but it is none the less worth considering because it is very handy. The end product is about the size of a thick felt-tip marker but this marker comes with built-in 'intelligence'.

One of the three LEDs in the circuit will light depending on the voltage measured at the test point (TP). This voltage is first of all fed to two comparators (A1 and A2). A reference voltage is fed to the other input

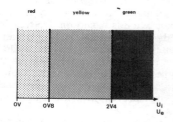

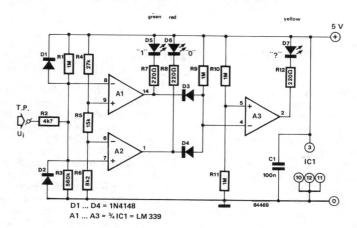

D1 ... D4 = 1N4148
A1 ... A3 = ¾ IC1 = LM 339

of each comparator from voltage divider R4/R5/R6. The values chosen give thresholds at 0.8 and 2.4 V as the range between these two levels is a 'forbidden area' for TTL. If the voltage at TP is lower than 0.8 V the output of A2 goes low and causes the red LED (D6) to light. If the measured voltage is higher than 2.4 V the output of A1 will be low so the green LED (D5) will light. Sometimes, of course, the voltage will be between 0.8 and 2.4 V and then neither the output of A1 nor the output of A2 will be low. When TP is not connected to anything the same thing applies due to the action of R1 and R3. The inverting input of A3 is then pulled high via R9 so the yellow LED (D7) lights.

As we have already suggested, the completed circuit can be made into a very attractive finished product. All the components can be mounted in a line on a narrow piece of veroboard, as the photo shows, and this can then be slipped into some sort of tube. Ideally this should be transparent to enable the LEDs to shine through.

003 2N3055 sunswitch

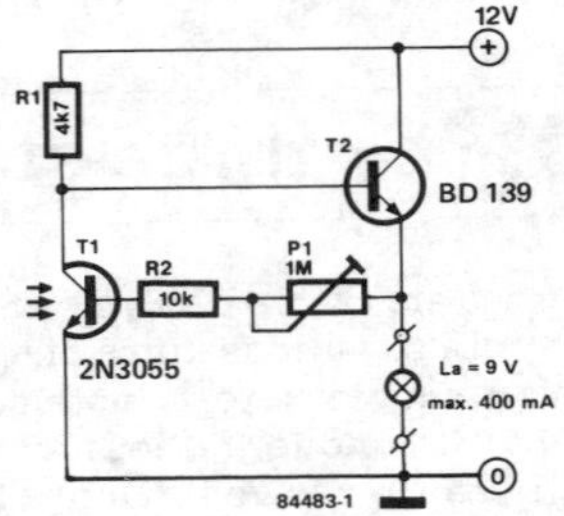

The 2N3055, strange though it may seem, can operate very well as a phototransistor, as the circuit here shows. The power transistor must be made light sensitive, of course, and this is done by cutting off the top of the case. The light-sensitive area revealed is quite large enabling the 'new' photo transistor to operate very effectively. The sunswitch is based on two transistors, the decapitated 2N3055 (T1) and a switching transistor, T2. As long as no light (or not enough) falls on T1 this transistor does not conduct. Resistor R1 then provides a base current for T2, which conducts and lights the lamp at the output of the circuit.

When enough light falls on T1 it conducts and earths the base of T2 so the lamp extinguishes. The two transistors are coupled

via R2 and P1 to improve the switching behaviour. The light intensity at which the circuit switches is set by means of preset P1.

from an idea by H.J. Hooft

004 guitar preamplifier

The output signal level provided by many electric guitars is not high enough to overdrive a valve amplifier. This overdriving is an essential part of the final guitar sound. The preamplifier circuit shown here boosts the guitar signal so that the input stage of the guitar amplifier is guaranteed to clip. As an aid to this the gain can be selected between 8 dB and 20 dB.

The layout of the circuit is very simple. A single LF 356 provides the amplification, which is decided by the ratio of $(R_2 + R_3 +$ $P1)/(R_3 + P1)$. The input impedance of 1 M is defined by R1 as the opamp has FET inputs. This is a suitable impedance for most guitar pick-ups. A 9 V battery provides the power supply which is converted to a symmetrical ± 4.5 V for the opamp by R4, R5, C3, and C4. Current consumption is about 5 mA.

The circuit complete with battery can easily be fitted into a small case. If a socket and plug are mounted in the case, as the photo shows, the preamp can simply be plugged

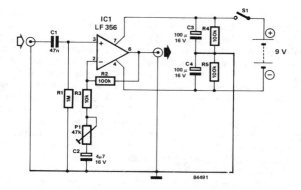

into the guitar. If this is done, preset P1 can be replaced by an ordinary potentiometer so that the amplification can be controlled by means of a knob on the case.

005 energy-saving porch light

This circuit forms a switch that can be triggered on (or off) at the onset of darkness and remain active for a period that is vari-able from thirty minutes to five hours. The main design consideration was that of keeping power consumption to a minimum

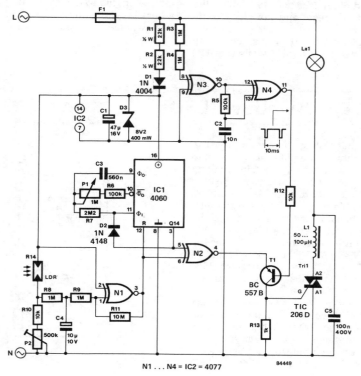

N1 . . . N4 = IC2 = 4077

84449

while retaining a fair degree of versatility. The primary purpose was to provide an economical porch light but the circuit can obviously be used for any short-term switching application that is referenced to ambient light levels.

In spite of its simplicity the circuit is relatively sophisticated. The basis of the circuit is a 14-stage ripple counter with an internal clock oscillator contained in the 4060 (IC1) which does most of the work. The frequency of the oscillator is determined by C3, R6, and potentiometer P1 which enables the frequency to be adjusted. The clock is started when a logic 0 reaches the reset input of IC1. This is achieved by the light-dependent resistor R14 and the components associated with gate N1. When the ambient light level drops, the resistance of the LDR increases and causes the output of N1 to revert to logic 0. The point at which this occurs can be determined by the setting of P2. It is worth noting that, although not desirable for this particular application, if the ambient light level increases again for any reason for a period of not less than 10 . . . 20 s, the counter will be reset and the clock oscillator will stop.

In the normal course of events, the output of gate N2 will be at logic 1 while the 4060 continues to count up and transistor T1 will be controlled by the output of gate N4. The two gates N3 and N4 together form a simple, but effective, mains zero crossing point detector. This results in the output of N4 providing a short pulse at each zero crossing point of the mains cycle. It is this pulse that is used to trigger the triac via transistor T1 when the output of N2 is logic 1. It will be apparent that the triac will therefore only be switched on when the mains power supply is at zero potential — an ideal situation!

The light La will thus be switched on until such time that the count cycle of IC1 causes its Q14 output to change to logic 1. This will then halt the clock oscillator via diode D2 and maintain the high logic level at the Q14 output.

At this time, gate N2 will find a '1' at its pin 5 input and a '0' at pin 6. The output of N2 will therefore return to a low level and switch the light off.

Power levels up to 100 W can be switched by a TIC 206D unaided. However, if higher power levels (up to 500 W) are contemplated, the triac must be provided with a heatsink, for instance, an SK13.

The switched time period is adjustable by P1.

006 'window' LEDs

It is often interesting (if not required) to know whether an amplifier is going into saturation, or whether certain limiting values (thermometer, power supply, etc.) are being exceeded. It is, however, not always feasible to use a fully-fledged window discriminator and in those cases the circuit presented may be of interest.

When the level of the input voltage lies between 3.5 V and 8.5 V, transistors T1 and T2 conduct (T3 and T4 are cut off) so that LED D1 lights to indicate that the input signal is 'in range'.

When the input level rises above about 8.5 V, T2 and T3 conduct (T1 and T4 are cut off) which causes LED D2 to light indicating that the input level is 'above range'.

Finally, when the input signal drops below about 3.5 V, T1 and T4 conduct so that LED

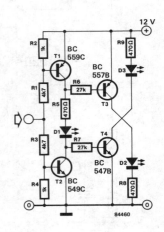

D3 lights indicating that the input is 'below range'.

The current consumption is for all practical purposes governed by the LED currents which are 20 mA maximum: it may briefly rise above this value during switch-over. When the input (junction R1/R3) is disconnected, the input voltage equals about half the supply voltage (6 V) so that LED D1 will light.

007   RS 232 analyser

To be able to use a computer properly, you need a number of relevant peripheral units. These units are often connected to the computer via a serial interface V24 or RS 232. If anything goes wrong, or is suspected of having gone wrong, the analyser described here may prove to be very useful. It is simply connected in series with the relevant line. The additional load on the line is so small that true on line testing is possible.

The circuit consists of two transistor drivers for two LEDs: red/red or red/green. With positive levels, in the range of about 4.5 ... 5.5 V, T1 conducts and D1 lights.

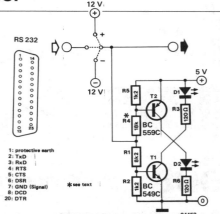

1: protective earth
2: TxD
3: RxD
4: RTS
5: CTS
6: DSR
7: GND (Signal)
8: DCD
20: DTR

✳ see text

84452

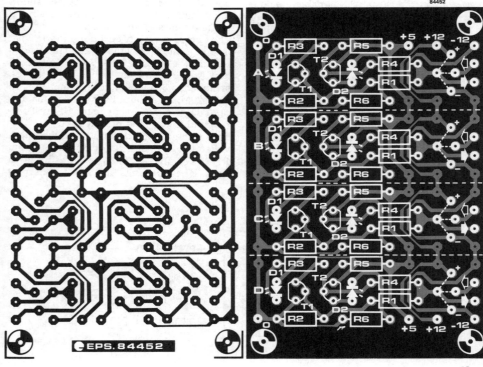

Parts list
(components for one circuit)

Resistors:
R1 = 8k2
R2,R5 = 1k2
R3,R6 = 120 Ω
R4 = 18 k

Semiconductors:
D1,D2 = LED, red
or
D1 = LED, red
D2 = LED, green
T1 = BC 549C
T2 = BC 559C

With negative levels, of the order of −5.5 . . . −7.0 V, T2 conducts and D2 lights. If R4 is reduced to about 15 k, the circuit becomes active at about −3.5 . . . −5.0 V. It should be noted here that in the RS232 negative levels correspond to logic 1, and positive levels to logic 0!

The printed circuit board can house four of these circuits, so that one board can monitor, for instance, signals RxD, TxD, RTS, and CTS which are, in the majority of cases, the most important. If you want to, or must, monitor more signals, all you have to do is to build more boards. The wire bridges make it possible to hold certain signals at a fixed level during testing. If the boards are fitted into a case, it is, of course, possible to replace these bridges by switches mounted at the front of the case.

Current consumption in each circuit amounts to 150 μA under no-signal conditions, and to 27 mA with signal. In most cases, the supply can therefore be taken from the +5 V line in the computer.

The wiring layout of the plug is shown for the computer side of the connecting cable.

008 photoelectronic relay

Motorola ICs 3040 and 3041 enable the construction of a simple electronic relay that in spite of its simplicity has some interesting characteristics. For instance, the ICs have an internal zero crossing detector that saves quite a few external components. Moreover, the ICs have an isolation voltage of not less than 7.5 kV which enables the relay to be connected to any circuit operating from mains voltage.

The ICs may be compared with a normal opto-coupler in which the usual phototransistor has been replaced by a phototriac (100 mA/400 V at 25°C). The advantage of this is that virtually all types of silicon-controlled rectifiers (SCRs) may be used in the circuit, which would not be possible if a phototransistor were used.

The choice of type of SCR depends on what is to be switched by the relay. If the load is resistive, a TIC 226D/400 V will do fine. If, however, inductive loads have to be switched, a 600 V SCR, for instance, a type TIC 226M, is needed. Bear in mind that the operating voltage of capacitor C1 must correspond to the type of SCR used.

The value of R1 depends on the input voltage, U_i, and is calculated from $R1 = 1000 \, (U_i − 1.3)/I_{oc}$ where U_i is in volts, R1 is in ohms, and I_{oc}, the current

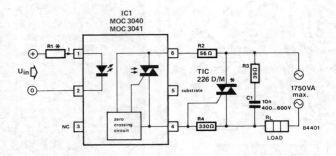

14

through the LED in the opto-coupler, is in mA.

Assuming $U_i = 12$ V, and $I_{oc} = 30$ mA (as in the MOC 3040), the calculated value of R1 = 356 Ω for which a standard 330 Ω should be used. In the MOC 3041 I_{oc} is only 15 mA, so that the practical value of R1

would be 680 Ω.

The maximum current the electronic relay can switch is about 8 A.

Motorola application

009 blown fuse indicator

This circuit, as the name suggests, indicates when a fuse has blown. As long as the fuse is good the LED lights continuously, but when it blows the LED flashes. If the values given in the diagram are used the circuit is suitable for 12 V operation but it can easily be made suitable for 6 or 24 V by simply halving or doubling the values of all the resistors.

The indicator consists of an astable multivibrator (T1 and T2) and a LED driver stage (T3). The whole circuit, with the exception of R5, is connected before the fuse in the supply. The output of the multivibrator, which is always active as long as the supply is present, is connected, via D2, to the input of the LED driver stage (the base of T3). As long as the fuse is intact, the base current for T3 is always provided via R5 and D1, with the result that the LED lights continuously. When the fuse blows the base current is only provided by the AMV and, as this is not continuous, the LED flashes.

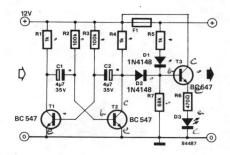

The current consumption of the circuit is about 30 mA, most of which is drawn by the LED. If the indicator is fitted to some battery-powered circuit it is worth while to use a high-efficiency LED for D3 and to change the value of R6 to suit the lower LED current.

E. Neefjes

010 combining 4017 counters

The well-known CMOS IC type 4017 is a decade counter which offers an excellent means of sequentially scanning small matrices. However, it may also be used as a programmable frequency devider.

There are occasions when one counter or divider is not enough to provide the required function. One way of resolving this difficulty lies in combining a number of 4017s as shown in the accompanying diagram. The AND gates, N1, N3, ..., together with inverters N2, N4, ..., ensure that the output level at Q9 of each of the counters is retained at their own output terminal. The length of the counter/divider

chain is determined simply by a jump connection (with S1 closed). When switch S1 is closed momentarily, the chain will cycle through just once if A is connected to pin 11 of ICn.

The counter chain may also be used as the basis of a simple waveform generator. For that application the outputs of the counters are each applied via different value resistors to the inverting input of a type 741 opamp.

V. Johnson

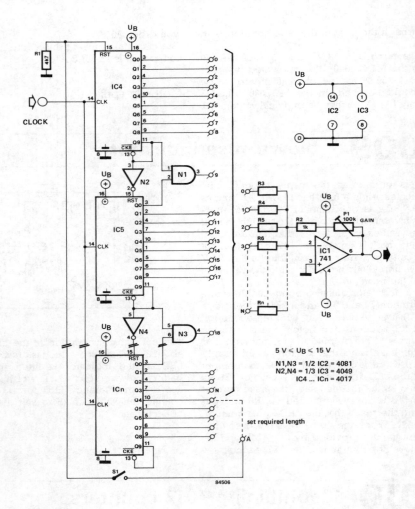

5 V ≤ U_B ≤ 15 V

N1,N3 = 1/2 IC2 = 4081
N2,N4 = 1/3 IC3 = 4049
IC4 ... ICn = 4017

84506

011   musical doorbell

Although we would not like to make a habit of it, going back to an old design when new components become available is sometimes very rewarding. And so it is in this case of the musical doorbell with the introduction of a new IC, or rather quartet of ICs, the UM 3481/82/83/84 series.

As could be expected, the principal part of the circuit is contained in the IC: oscillator, frequency divider, drive ROM, a ROM with 512 musical notes, tone generator, rhythm generator, timbre generator, modulator,

run-off control, and pre-amplifier.
Apart from the IC, the circuit comprises an a.c. operated power supply with voltage regulator, a push-pull amplifier for driving the loudspeaker, and a number of associated components.

Resistors R1, R2, potentiometer P2, and capacitor C2 are the frequency-determining elements for the on-chip oscillator. Preset P2 is for adjusting the run-off speed, that is, the speed at which the tune is played.
Resistor R7 and capacitor C4 ensure opti-

16

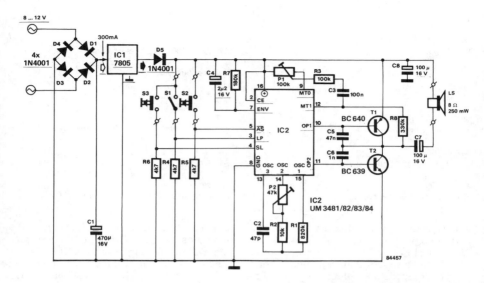

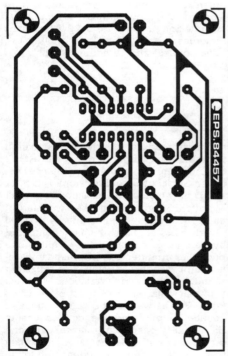

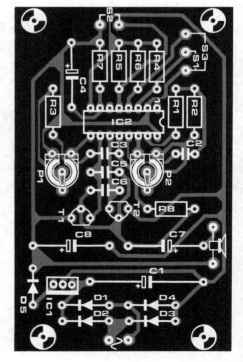

mum performance of the internal modulator.

Resistor R3, preset P1, and capacitor C3 form a volume control which controls the on-chip pre-amplifier.

The circuit is operated by S1 ... S3 and R4 ... R6. Switch S2 is the normal bell-push. If you want to pre-program a given melody,

Parts list

Resistors:
R1 = 820 k
R2 = 10 k
R3 = 100 k
R4,R5,R6 = 47 k
R7 = 180 k
R8 = 330 k
P1 = 100 k preset
P2 = 47 k preset

Capacitors:
C1 = 470 μ/16 V electrolytic
C2 = 47 p
C3 = 100 n
C4 = 2μ2/16 V electrolytic

C5 = 47 n
C6 = 1 n
C7,C8 = 100 μ/16 V electrolytic

Semiconductors:
D1 . . . D4,D5 = 1N4001
T1 = BC 640
T2 = BC 639
IC1 = 7805
IC2 = UM 3481 . . . UM 3484 (see text)

Miscellaneous:
S1 = SPST
S2,S3 = spring-loaded push-button,
press-to-make
LS = loudspeaker, miniature, 8 Ω, 250 mW

an additional push-button may be connected in parallel with S2.
With S1 closed, all melodies stored in the ROM will be sounded in sequence; when it is open, only the one selected by S3 will be played.
A particular melody is chosen by closing S1 and pressing S2 continuously, while S3 is pressed repeatedly until the wanted melody has been reached.
Until now, four ICs in the series have become available and these differ only in the melodies stored. The UM 3481 contains eight Christmas carols and the UM 3484 the sounds of Big Ben striking one to twelve in ascending order. The UM 3482 has twelve tunes, among which "Frère Jacques, frère Jacques", "Happy Birthday to you", and "Cradle Song", while the UM 3483 contains melodies like "The Last Rose of Summer", "The Lorelei", and "Wedding March".

012   bird imitator

Perhaps it is a longing for nature in our technological society that prompts so many readers' requests for 'electronic birds'. And who are we to disappoint them? Since our knowledge of ornithology is rather restricted we would not like to say on which bird the present circuit is modelled, but it sounds exotic!
The circuit consists of three relaxation oscillators and a decade counter. The oscillators are astable multivibrators, AMV1 . . . 3, each of which is based on two inverters.
Oscillator AMV1 operates at a frequency of a fraction of a hertz, which is used to clock counter IC2. As long as the counter is triggered, a logic 1 travels across outputs Q0 . . . Q9 in rhythm with the clock.
Oscillator AMV2 may be compared with the throat of a bird: it generates an audible high-frequency tone.
Oscillator AMV3 provides a range of frequencies with which the output of AMV2 is modulated, so that the final output sounds

like a bird and not like the time signal on the radio. The output frequency of AMV3 depends on the value of resistance between capacitor C4 and resistor R4, in other words on which of the resistors R8 . . . R11 is switched into circuit. The switching of these resistors is effected by CMOS switches ES1 . . . ES4, which are controlled by various combinations of counter outputs. This arrangement ensures that the final output is not a monotonously repeating sound, but is full of rich variations. Note that you may change the value of resistors R8 . . . R11 as well as the combinations of counter outputs and the connections to ES1 . . . ES4: our circuit shows only one possible layout. It is, however, important that all outputs of IC2 are connected to the switches. If more than one output is connected to a switch, suitable diodes should be connected in series as shown to prevent short-circuits.
Apart from the trigger pulses for the coun-

18

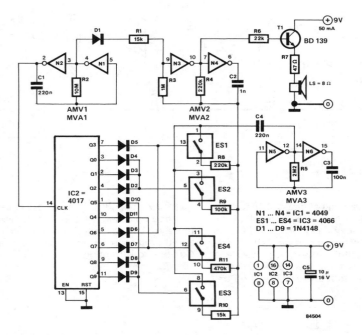

ter, AMV1 also generates pause pulses for AMV2. When the output of N1 (pin 4) is high, a current flows to pin 9 of N3 via diode D1 and resistor R1. This causes AMV2 to cease oscillating and the bird is quiet for a little while.

A PP3 battery (9 V) is perfectly suitable as power supply.

Finally, note that a small resonant loudspeaker can produce quite a volume of sound!

P. Ruopp

013 scratch and rumble filter

The purpose of this filter is to attenuate very low and very high audio frequencies as signals in these frequency ranges generally do more harm than good for the total audio signal. Another way of considering this circuit is to see it as a very wide bandpass filter for the band containing the most important part of the audio spectrum.

The layout is quite simple as it consists of two filters in series, a high-pass followed by a low-pass. Each filter consists of a pair of cascaded second-order filter stages to achieve a very steep characteristic of 24 dB/octave. The cut-off frequencies are at 11.8 Hz and 10.7 kHz with the component

values given here. The suitability of these points depends on the application and it is not at all difficult to change them. The 11.8 Hz cut-off can be shifted up by reducing the value of capacitors C1 ... C4, or it can be lowered by increasing the capaci-

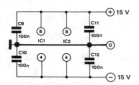

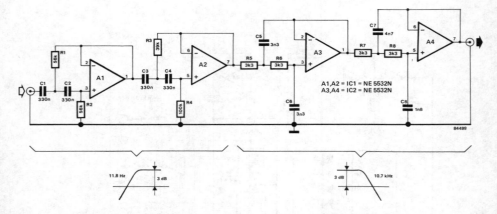

tance. These capacitors must all have the same value. The cut-off frequency of the low-pass filter can also be modified by changing the value of resistors R5 . . . R8. Like the capacitors, these four resistors must all have the same value but this value can be reduced to increase the cut-off fre-

quency or raised to lower the frequency. The opamps used are a low-noise type and there are two in each IC package. Two ICs are therefore required for each channel. Current consumption per channel is about 20 mA.

---

014   LC meter

An LC meter is undoubtedly indispensable to anyone involved in h.f. techniques. The present design accepts the unknown inductance, L_X, or capacitance, C_X, in a two-transistor oscillator circuit, of which the output voltage is kept constant between 30 and 40 mV by a regulator.

When, in the oscillator circuit, C_X is connected in parallel with capacitor C_0, or L_X in series with inductor L_0, the frequency of

the circuit diminishes. This diminution is measured by a frequency-to-voltage converter, T3/T4. The consequent output voltage of emitter follower T5 is used to actuate meter M1.

Meter M1 is connected at the diagonals of a bridge circuit, so that it indicates zero in the absence of C_X or L_X.

The meter is set to full-scale deflection (f.s.d.) by P2 when either $L_X = L_0$ or $C_X =$

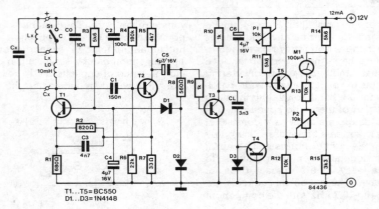

C_O is inserted into the oscillator circuit. The tolerance of frequency-determining capacitor C_L in the frequency-to-voltage converter is balanced out by P1. It is therefore necessary to switch in a different 10 k preset for each measuring range, and whenever that is done the f.s.d. should be set afresh with P2.

The values given in the circuit for L_O and C_O are valid for an f.s.d. of 10 nF or 10 mH. A maximum of nine measuring ranges may be provided by means of a 4-wafer, 9-position rotary switch. The values of L_O, C_O, C_L, and the resulting frequency, without L_x or C_x and at full-scale deflection, are given in the table. The accuracy of the measurements, given careful calibration, is about 3 per cent.

Graduation of the scale is near enough equal for all ranges, but is 'stretched' by a factor of about 3 for low readings. This needs, of course, an appropriate correction.

Calibrating the scale may be carried out

Table.

meter range	f.s.d.	L_O mH	C_O nF	C_L nF	f_O kHz	f_x at $C_x = C_O$ or $L_x = L_O$ kHz
1	100 pF	1	0.1	0.1	502	355
2	1 nF	1	1	0.33	158	112
3	10 nF	10	10	3.3	15.8	11.2
4	100 nF	10	100	10	5.02	3.55
5	10 μH	0.01	10	0.1	502	355
6	100 μH	0.1	10	0.33	158	112
7	1 mH	1	10	1	50.2	35.5
8	10 mH	10	10	3.3	15.8	11.2
9	100 mH	100	10	3.3	5.02	3.55

with a table compiled with the formula $n_i = n_m (1-f_r)/(1-f_c)$, where

n_i = number of scale divisions indicated
n_m = number of scale divisions at f.s.d.
f_r = relative frequency
f_c = lowest relative frequency
Total current consumption amounts to about 12 mA at 12 V.

ITT Application

---

015   40 watt main amplifier

The amplifier described here is intended for applications with a relatively modest output power requirement.

The output stage contains two type 2N3055 power transistors: proven, reliable components. At first sight it appears that the output stage is not symmetrical because transistors T15 and T16 are NPN types but a second look will show that it is: the top half consists of NPN 'supertransistor' T11/T13/T15, while the lower half comprises PNP 'supertransistor' T12/T14/T16. These 'supertransistors' are complementary: as their emitters are connected together via R25...R27 and R28...R30, the output stage is symmetrical.

The remainder of the amplifier is also constructed symmetrically: a double differential amplifier, T1/T2 and T3/T4, current sources T5 and T6, followed by driver stages T7 and T8.

The output power is 40 watts into 8 Ω or 60 watts into 4 Ω for a distortion not greater than 0.01% over the frequency range 20 Hz...20 kHz. Maximum power at the onset of clipping is 45 watts into 8 Ω and 65

watts into 4 Ω. The input sensitivity is 800 (850) mV$_{eff}$ for 40 (45) watts into 8 Ω and 700 (725) mV$_{eff}$ for 60 (65) watts into 4 Ω. The frequency characteristic is within 1 dB from 15 Hz to about 100 kHz.

Partly because of the high current amplification (not less than 200 000) the output stage has a low quiescent current (which is not critical) of 25...50 mA. Even with P1 set for minimal resistance, a spectrum analyser connected to our prototype showed a cross-over distortion of a very small magnitude. The quiescent current is set by P1, with a universal meter (dc-mV range) con-

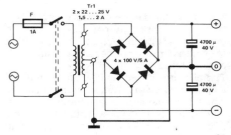

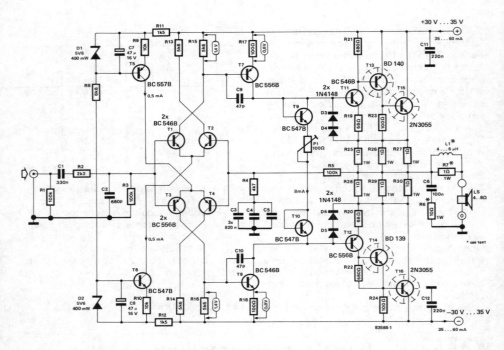

nected between the emitter of T15 and the collector of T16, that is, across the series-connected resistor chain R25...R30. A voltage of 33 mV corresponds to a current of 50 mA. There is no printed circuit board available for this project, but it can be constructed using Vero board. It is advisable to arrange the layout as much as possible in line with the circuit diagram. A common heat sink of 1.5...2°C/W is required for T15 and T16, not forgetting the mica washers! T13 and T14 should each have a separate heat sink of about 12°C/W. Although the

output stage, as far as quiescent current is concerned, is virtually unaffected by temperature, T9 and T11, as well as T10 and T12, may be thermally coupled, that is, they can be glued together by their flat vertical surfaces.

L1 is constructed by winding 2 × 10 turns of 0.8...1 mm dia. enamelled copperwire around resistor R7.

The power supply is quite normal. Current consumption amounts to 1.0 (1.06)A for 40 (45) watts into 8 Ω and 1.75 (1.81)A for 60 (65) watts into 4 Ω.

016 touch-pad potentiometer

Touch-pad keys normally use a simple digital memory, but they can be operated to give an analogue output voltage as is shown here in an inexpensive circuit that is easy to build.

The circuit is based on IC1, an operational amplifier with very high input impedance, which is connected as an integrator. When touch-pad Se1 is touched with a finger, capacitor C2, an MKT (metallized plastic foil)

type, charges via the skin resistance, which causes the output voltage of IC1 to drop linearly to zero. When the other touch-pad, Se2, is touched, the opposite happens: the output potential of IC1 will then rise linearly until it reaches the level of the supply voltage. The beauty of the circuit is that when you take your finger from the pad, the value of the voltage then present at the output of IC1 is maintained by the charge on C2. Owing to unavoidable leakage currents in the capacitor, the output voltage will, however, drift by about two per cent per hour towards zero or towards the supply voltage, depending on which of the key pads was touched last. To keep these leakage currents small, it is necessary to keep the circuit well away from moisture or humidity, which should be borne in mind when choosing a case.

The range of applications for this circuit is wide: it may be used anywhere there is a potentiometer that can be controlled by a variable voltage.

If you prefer to use normal push button switches instead of touch-pad types, figure 1b shows how to connect these in the circuit. Resistors R3 and R4 simulate the skin resistance; switches S1 and S2 provide the input voltage for IC1. Pressing the

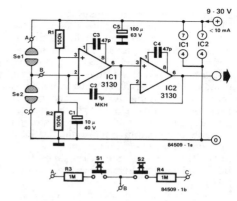

switches simultaneously has no effect. Capacitors C3 and C4 obviate any tendency of the operational amplifier to oscillate.

017 multi-channel analogue-to-digital converter

The use of a microprocessor system as control computer often makes it necessary for a large number of analogue signals to be monitored. If a certain degree of accuracy is expected from these signals, a number of suitable A/D converters will be needed.

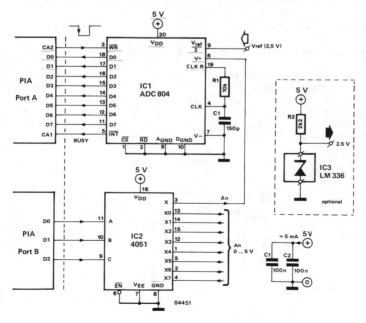

And that is not exactly cheap . . .

The circuit presented here offers the facility of connecting eight analogue signals to a CD 4051 multiplexer. The channel select inputs, A, B, and C, select the signal being monitored at the time: at binary 000, channel AN0; at binary 001, channel AN1; at binary 010, channel AN2; and so on. The selected analogue signal (which must lie between 0 and +5 V) is passed straight through to the output (pin 3) of the CD 4051. The channel select inputs may be controlled by, for example, three lines from port B of a peripheral interface adapter (PIA).

The actual A/D conversion is carried out by a CMOS IC type ADC804. This transforms the analogue signal into an eight-bit data word within 100 μs. The on-chip clock needs an external RC network (pins 4 and 19). Pin 9 must have a reference voltage which lies exactly in the centre of the measuring range. The conversion process commences at a leading edge on pin 3 ($\overline{WR}$) and simultaneously the voltage on pin 5 becomes 5 V at the trailing edge. After 100 μs pin 5 becomes 0 V and the 8-bit data word is then available at the port A inputs (D0 . . . D7). As there are 256 possible combinations, and the measuring range is five volts, each step is 19 mV 'wide'.

The circuit may be used with practically any microprocessor system which has a port available (PIA 6520-21; PIA 6820-21; VIA 6520; VIA 6522; Z80-PIO; 8255; etc.). Programming is dependent upon the requirement. For relatively slow operations, such as heating control, alarm systems, weather stations, and similar, BASIC may be used with PEEK and POKE instructions. With on-line controls, and maybe even with model railway control, it will normally be necessary to use a machine code program which is much faster.

018   power supply monitor

This monitor circuit is based on the MC 3424 power supply supervisory IC. It provides two-channel overvoltage crowbar protection, which is very useful for floppy disk systems, and overvoltage and undervoltage monitoring of the +5 V line, which is particularly important in microprocessor supplies.

Each channel in the MC 3424 has an input and an output comparator. Channel 1 is the undervoltage monitor, while channel 2 provides crowbar overvoltage protection.

The input comparators sense the regulated supply line (pins 3 and 15). Each of them provides a common-mode range of 0 . . . (V_{CC}−1.4 V) volts. The source resistance of the inverting inputs determines the amount of hysteresis.

An on-chip generated reference voltage of 2.5 V (available at pin 1) is permanently connected to the non-inverting input (pin 2) of comparator 1 and to the inverting input (pin 14) of comparator 2.

When the voltage on the supply line drops below about 4.2 V, the input comparator of channel 1 (pins 2 and 3) changes state which causes a low logic level at pin 6 and the red LED, D1, lights. The LED could be

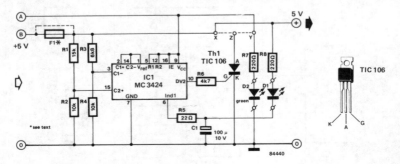

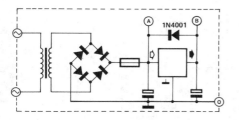

Parts list

Resistors:
R1 = 15 k
R2,R4 = 10 k
R3 = 6k8
R5 = 22
R6 = 4k7
R7,R8 = 220

Capacitors:
C1 = 100 μ/16 V

Semiconductors:
D1 = LED, red
D2 = LED, green
IC1 = MC3424
Th1 = TIC106

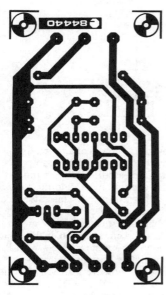

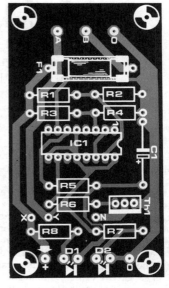

replaced by an interrupt routine in the computer to safeguard stored data and to switch over to the back-up battery.

When the supply line rises above about 6.2 V, the input comparator in channel 2 (pins 14 and 15) changes state and pin 10 of IC1 becomes logic low. The silicon-controlled rectifier (SCR), Th1, then fires and short-circuits the supply to earth. Depending on whether the stabilized 5 V or the unstabilized line (A) is connected to the anode of Th1 (wire link XZ or YZ), the supply is cut off either by fuse F1 in the 5 V line blowing or the short-circuit across the smoothing capacitor in the protected

power supply. Note that the 1N4001 diode in the protected supply is essential to safeguard the stabilizer.

If the protected power supply is already fitted with a fuse, a wire bridge should be soldered on the pc board instead of fuse F1. Furthermore, in that case Z is linked to Y. If fuse F1 is used, however, Z is linked to X.

A ready-etched printed-circuit board is not available for the monitor, but a pcb may be made by yourself from the track layout given on the pc board pages.

Finally, please note that IC1 should be powered *before* the protected supply.

019   interior temperature control for cars

The single most important part of any car is its driver and it stands to reason that the better the driver, the better the overall stan-

dard of road safety will be. Of course, we could just leave the car to its own devices with a bit of help from a computer, but we

25

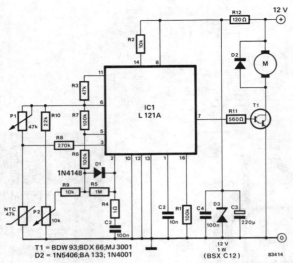

T1 = BDW 93; BDX 66; MJ 3001
D2 = 1N5406; BA 133; 1N4001

12 V
1 W
(BSX C12)

83414

all know what computers can do...! No, there are some things better left undone. The alternative is to help the human driver to do a better job. This circuit is not a design to produce perfect drivers but it does aim to improve the environment in a car.

Basically, the circuit enables the desired temperature in the car to be set between two limits. The ambient temperature is sensed by an NTC (negative temperature coefficient) thermistor with a nominal value of 47 kΩ at 25°C. The value of the thermistor at any time is used to set the level at one of the inputs of an opamp in the L121. This opamp sets the triggering level of the internal logic which drives the IC output stage. Potentiometer P2 controls the second input of the same opamp and is used to adjust the temperature at which the circuit operates.

When the temperature inside the car increases the resistance of the thermistor

decreases and the voltage on pin 3, the non-inverting input of the opamp, also decreases. After a period of time the level set by P2 is reached and the logic control circuit in IC1 is triggered. This drives transistor T1 causing it to conduct and switch on the coolingfan motor. Cool air is then blown into the car. As soon as the temperature falls to a certain level, set with P1, the circuit switches the fan off again.

The circuit is powered directly by the car battery but zener diode D3 is needed as a protection against the spikes that always occur on car voltage supply lines. Note that the thermistor must be mounted in a suitable location in the car (best found by trial and error).

SGS Application

020   low-power switching regulator

The low-power switching regulator type 4193, which is housed in an 8-pin miniature DIL package, is designed specifically for battery operated equipment. A regulated power supply can be constructed for such equipment with just eleven components: five resistors, two capacitors, one diode, a choke, a 4193, and a 2.4...9.0 V battery.

The output of this supply will remain near-constant at 9 V until the battery has decayed to a terminal voltage of 2.4 V. A practical circuit is shown in figure 1.

The 4193 has an internal reference circuit of which the control current, I_C, is set externally by resistor R1 connected between the battery and the I_C pin (6). This current can vary from 0.5 μA to 100 μA without affecting the operation of the chip. The value of R1 is given by

$$R1 = [(U_b - 1.3)/I_c] \text{ k}\Omega$$

where U_b is the battery voltage in volts and I_c is in mA.

In addition to setting bias currents throughout the chip, the reference voltage is used for the low-battery detector circuit, and to set the threshold for the input of an on-chip regulation loop for comparison with a feedback voltage, U_f (pin 7).

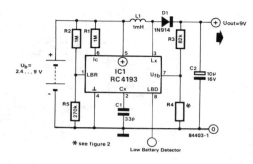

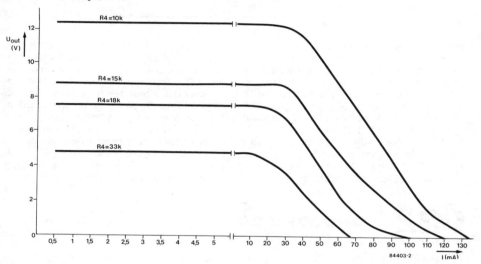

The low-battery indicator voltage level, U_d, is programmed by means of resistors R2 and R5. The value of R2 is given by

$$R2 = [10^3(U_d - 1.3)/5] \text{ k}\Omega$$

The internal regulation loop turns off the chip when the feedback voltage drops below 1.3 V.

Capacitor C1 is the frequency determining component for the internal sawtooth oscil-

lator in the regulation loop.

The output voltage, U_o, is given by

$$U_o = [1.3(R3 + R4)/R4] \text{ volts}$$

and is plotted (figure 2) against the output current, I_o, for various values of R4 (with R3 = 82 kΩ), and an input voltage of $U_o/2$.

Raytheon application

021 infra-red wireless receiver

This circuit is the receiver to match the transmitter featured in circuit 067. Together these two form a very simple, but effective, wireless transmission system for any audio signal.

The signal is transmitted by the infra-red

LED in the transmitter. The receiver converts this IR signal into a rectangular waveform in which the width of the pulses corresponds to the audio information. The signal obtained after amplification and filtering has to be integrated only to retrieve

27

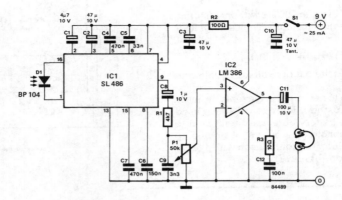

the audio information. What could be simpler?

The SL 486 IC is a suitable single-chip receiver for the receiver as it contains, among other things, a regulated amplifier and a filter section. The signal picked up by the infra-red photodiode, D1, is fed to the input (pins 1 and 16) of IC1. The output at pin 9 is applied to a.f. amplifier IC2 via an integrator circuit consisting of resistor R1 and capacitor C9. IC2 brings the audio signal to a suitable level for the headphones.

In its basic format the receiver contains no form of filtering so there is quite a lot of interference from ambient light and this makes the final audio signal very noisy. Fortunately this effect can be greatly reduced by shielding the photodiode from ambient light, or, even better, by fitting a lens in front of it. This last idea is particularly interesting as by experimenting with a lens you can increase the range from the original 5 . . . 10 metres to 20 . . . 50 metres. That is really quite good for such a simple circuit.

---

022 stroboscope

WARNING! The circuit of the stroboscope is connected directly to the mains and experiments on the opened unit are therefore highly dangerous. Even after the unit has been disconnected from the mains, some capacitors may still give you a lethal shock! Preset P1 must have a nylon spindle and be fitted so that none of its metal parts can be touched: ignoring this may be lethal.

The heart of the unit is, of course, the gas-discharge tube, which is U-shaped and filled with xenon (Xe - one of the inert gases). The tube is fitted with an anode and cathode at either end, and an ignition grid. Diodes D1 and D2, together with capacitors C1 and C2, form a voltage doubler which raises the direct voltage to about 600 V. This voltage is applied to the anode and cathode

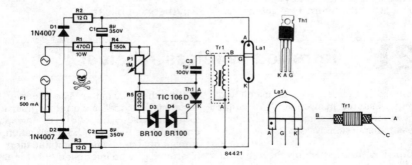

of the tube.

Normally, xenon (and other gases) is a poor conductor of electricity but the electric field resulting from the 600 V potential across the anode and cathode causes ionization of molecules and atoms in the immediate vicinity of these electrodes. The gaseous ions are attracted to the charged electrodes and a small preconducting current flows. A grid potential of 5 . . . 10 kV is required to fire the tube, which means causing the gas to break down so that a large current flows across the tube. The relatively high grid potential is obtained from ignition transformer Tr1. To cause a high potential across the secondary, the current through the primary should be interrupted very rapidly and this is done by a silicon-controlled rectifier, Th1.

Capacitor C3 charges because the voltage across C2 is 300 V and the primary of Tr1 is low-ohmic. As soon as the threshold of the two trigger diodes, D3 and D4, is reached, Th1 conducts. Capacitor C3 then discharges rapidly via the primary winding of Tr1 which induces a very high voltage in the secondary and this in turn causes the xenon tube to fire.

The setting of preset P1 determines the charging rate of C3 and therefore the firing rate of the discharge tube.

Resistor R1 is connected in the neutral line to serve as a current limiter, because when the discharge tube is firing it is a virtual short-circuit; without R1 fuse F1 would blow instantly.

The discharge tube, which should be of the 60 W/s type, is normally provided complete with ignition transformer. The anode is usually indicated by a red dot.

023   remote shutter release

It is true, of course, that it has been possible for many years to release a camera shutter remotely. But that is normally done by a (too) short cable, which can be a nuisance, and which is invariably too expensive for what it does. It seems therefore a good idea to release the shutter optically: the only prerequisite for this is that the camera is provided with an electronic shutter-release facility.

The proposed circuit (see figure 1) is built into a small case (see figure 2) which is fitted with a flash connector enabling it to be fixed to the camera instead of the flash unit. The little case may be made from the screening can of an RF or IF transformer. The simple circuit is based on a type

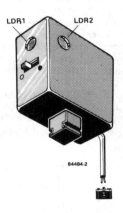

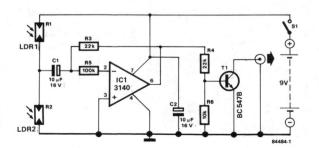

CA 3140 opamp which has been connected as a differentiator. To drive transistor T1, the inverting input of the CA 3140 must be fed with a short negative pulse. This is obtained from quick changes in the light incidence onto either of the light-dependent resistors (LDRs), R1 and R2. Two LDRs are needed to provide the difference potential to which the IC reacts.

It does not matter whether this difference is caused by a shadow falling onto R1 or a flash of light onto R2. The CA 3140 does not react to slow changes in incident light because of C1. Ambient light, which falls equally and simultaneously onto both LDRs, has no effect.

The negative pulses are inverted by the opamp and then used to switch on transistor T1 for an instant. The consequent short burst of current is sufficient to release the camera shutter. If you use a flash of light to operate the camera, you may be quite a distance away from it, particularly in the dark.

The circuit may be matched to a variety of cameras. The onset of conduction of T1 is dependent on the value of R4, while the sensitivity of the circuit may be augmented by increasing the value of R3.

Current consumption depends on ambient brightness and lies between 1.5 and 5 mA.

P. Becker

024   digiLED

This design is a somewhat unusual test aid for digital circuits. Most such circuits are usually tested in a static state to provide time to look at the logic levels at various points by making d.c. measurements. This is often not good enough, however, considering the various clock signals, resets, and trigger pulses that make a circuit 'tick'. What this really demands is a tester that can also detect single pulses.

As the circuit diagram shows, either CMOS or TTL can be catered for and the supply is taken from the circuit under test. The tester indicates clearly by means of a pair of LEDs (D5 and D6) whether the logic level examined is '0' or '1'. The input is fed into the noninverting input of a schmitt trigger comparator (IC1). The inverting input of this 3130 is fed from one of two fixed reference levels depending on whether CMOS or TTL is selected. The hysteresis inherent in a schmitt trigger ensures that a 'dead zone' must first be passed before the circuit reacts to the change in input level. This means that when a change of level is indicated there is absolutely no doubt that the transition has taken place. The exact switching points measured in our prototype

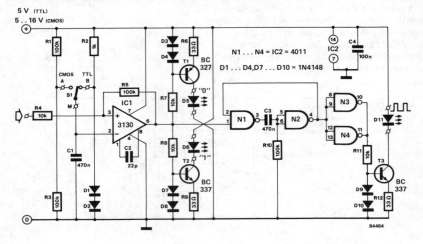

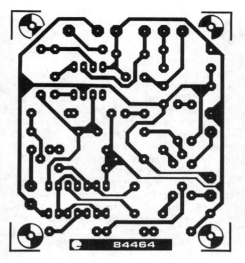

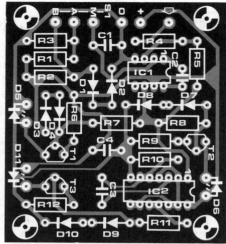

Parts list

Resistors:
R1,R3,R5,R10 = 100 k
R2 = 1 k
R4,R7,R8,R11 = 10 k
R6,R9,R12 = 33 Ω

Capacitors:
C1,C3 = 470 n
C2 = 22 p
C4 = 100 n

Semiconductors:
D1 . . . D4, D7 . . . D10 = 1N4148
D5,D6,D11 = LED
T1 = BC 327
T2,T3 = BC 337
IC1 = 3130
IC2 = 4011

Miscellaneous:
S1 = single pole toggle switch

are given in the table.
Pulses are detected by the section consisting of N1 . . . N4, T1, and the associated components. The monostable consisting of N1 and N2 (and C3 and R10, of course) reacts to a high to low transition at the input and lights LED D11 for a certain length of time (long enough for it to be noticed). Pulse trains also cause D11 to light but, in this case, continuously as the monostable time bridges the pulse interval. At the same time LEDs D5 and D6 also light and if both are the same colour a comparison between the brightness of the two will give a rough idea of the duty factor of the pulse train. Frequencies of up to about 400 kHz can be processed by the circuit. The current consumption of the tester is about 50 mA. Building this circuit is simplified by using the printed circuit board we have developed. The design is given here but it is not available through the EPS service. This is not, however, a major drawback to making this simple but useful logic tester.

025 valve simulator

Nostalgia is becoming ever more of a 'big business'. This is understandable as we all have a tendency to remember 'the good old days' when life was simpler, less complicated, and everybody was happy. In reality, of course, it was quite different but we often prefer to let our minds play tricks on us so we only remember the good things. Part of the nostalgia for many electronic hobbyists has to be the original valve radios. They were a breed apart, with the way they looked and the sounds they made, and it was impossible not to be taken in by their magic. Many attics still hide these radios, which no longer work, so we thought it would be interesting to fit a transistor radio into one of these old cases and add a bit of 'magic' of our own. Then your modern radio is guaranteed to make genuine 'antique' noises and it even takes a while to warm up just like valves always do.

The circuit is based on two operational transconductance amplifiers (OTA), one of which, IC1, generates the 'valve hum' while the other, IC2, provides the audio signal that goes to the final amplifier. The outputs of the two OTAs are connected together so that the amplifier they feed receives a mixture of two signals. The volume of the hum, which is taken from the transformer's secondary winding, can be set with preset P1 and the signal level is set with P2. The gain of each OTA is determined by the bias current applied to pin 5 of the IC. The actual 'valve' sequence of silence — loud hum — reducing hum — growing sound is generated by two monostable multivibrators.

When the supply is switched on, MMV1 is triggered via R1 and C1, with the result that the Q output goes high. At the same time, transistor T1 prevents any bias current from

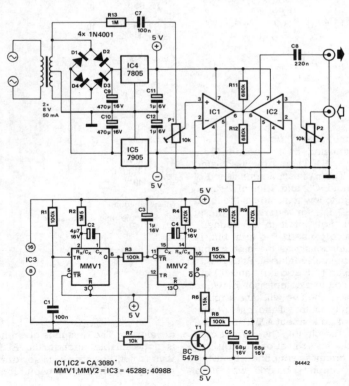

IC1,IC2 = CA 3080
MMV1,MMV2 = IC3 = 4528B; 4098B

84442

32

being passed to IC2 so no audio signals are generated by this OTA. The Q output of MMV2 is still low so IC1 receives no bias current and no sound is heard. After about seven seconds the Q output of MMV1 goes low again so MMV2 is triggered. Its Q output goes high causing the bias current fed to IC1 via the R5/C5 combination to increase gradually. Even though T1 is no longer conducting, the '0' level at the $\overline{Q}$ output of MMV2 prevents IC2 from generating the audio signal for the time being. After about five seconds the output of MMV2 changes so that Q becomes '0' and

$\overline{Q}$ becomes '1'. The amplification of IC1 then drops slowly and that of IC2 rises slowly. Because of this the hum reduces gradually and the sound (music, or whatever) increases gradually until it finally drowns out the hum.

The symmetrical power supply for the circuit is based on a pair of voltage regulators, IC4 and IC5. Current consumption is less than 10 mA so the circuit could be powered from the existing supply in the radio. If this is done do not forget the connection from the secondary winding of the transformer to provide the hum.

026   switch-on delay

There is no doubt about the value of a switch-on delay for a power amplifier. We all know the irritating (and potentially damaging) pop heard from the loudspeakers when the power amplifier is switched on or off. The circuit described here provides a technically simple, but none the less satisfactory, solution to this problem. A relay is used to isolate the loudspeakers until the switch-on surge has passed, as this is what causes the loudspeakers to pop. Switching off an amplifier may also cause loudspeakers to pop but this circuit prevents this by switching the speakers out of circuit just before this happens.

As the diagram shows, we have kept the circuit as simple as possible. Because of

this the circuit is both inexpensive and easy to build. One slight disadvantage of this design is that it can only be used with a power amplifier that has a symmetrical power supply (with a maximum of ± 60 V). This is not really such a big problem as most modern power amplifiers have a symmetrical supply.

The operation of the circuit is perfectly straightforward. The a.c. voltage is tapped directly from the amplifier transformer and half-wave rectified by diode D1. The voltage divider resistors, R1 and R2 must have suitable values so that the maximum voltage on C1 is about 5 V higher than the relay voltage. The values given in the diagram are suitable for a U_b of 45 V and a relay voltage of 24 V. If different specifi-

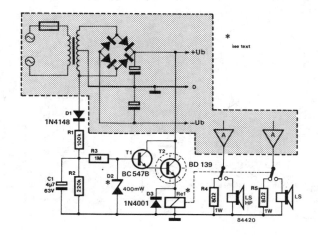

cations are chosen the values of the components must, of course, be suitably adapted. The relay voltage is particularly important as this must be at least 2 V lower than U_b. It should also be remembered that the relay must be able to switch a large current; something of the order of 10 amps is not unusual (depending on the power of the amplifier).

When the power amplifier is switched on, C1 is charged via R1 to about 29 V (in our example). Transistors T1 and T2 follow the capacitor voltage until the zener voltage of D1 is reached ($U_{zener} = U_{relay} + 1.4$ V). The voltage is now sufficient to actuate the relay, and with it the loudspeakers. The value of C1 stated ensures a delay of about 5 seconds before this actually occurs,

which is time enough to allow the amplifier to stabilize so no pop is heard. This time can be made longer or shorter by changing the value of C1.

When the power amplifier is switched off the same thing happens, in principle, but in the opposite order and much more quickly. The voltage drops as C1 discharges via R2. The circuit is 'tuned' so that the voltage across C1 falls quite quickly below the relay voltage and the relay drops out. The loudspeakers are then certain to be switched out of circuit before the pop is heard.

Finally it should be noted that even with good cooling T2 must never dissipate more than 5 W
$[P = I_{re}(U_b - U_{re})]$.

027 Wien bridge oscillator

The Wien bridge oscillator is a commonly used circuit, which is not surprising considering that it has low distortion and its resonant frequency can quite easily be made adjustable. This resonant frequency depends on a pair of resistors (each = R ohms) and a pair of capacitors (each = C farad) and is defined by the formula $f = 1/2\pi RC$. In the circuit shown here R consists of R1 + P1a (or R2 + P1b) and C is either C1, C2 or C3 (or, C4, C5 or C6). The oscillator proper consists of these components together with IC1, IC2 and their associated components.

Part of the output signal from IC2 is fed to

the regulating attenuator consisting of IC3 and T1. This FET, used here as a variable resistor, is part of the feedback loop of IC2. The gain of this opamp is thus made voltage dependent and can be changed by altering the control voltage of T1 with P2. This potentiometer must be set so that the circuit oscillates stably. The range of the oscillator, with the component values shown, is about 20 Hz...22.5 kHz and distortion is no more than approximately 2%.

B.G. Lindsay

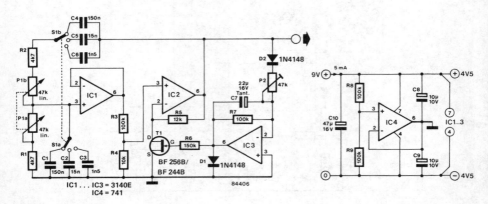

028 overvoltage protection

Although the circuit described uses an SCR (silicon-controlled rectifier) as protection device, it does not depend on direct crowbar action: instead the SCR causes a fuse to blow.

A 723 voltage regulator, used as locked comparator and SCR driver, provides an internally generated reference voltage of 7.15 V at pin 6. This voltage is divided by 2 (R4/R5) and applied to the inverting input (pin 4) of the comparator.

The voltage to be protected (at point A) is divided in R1, P1, and R2 and then applied to the non-inverting input of the comparator (pin 5). The trigger level may be set between 4.5 . . . 17 V with P1.

Points B, C, and D are all connected to the unregulated power supply line. Note that the voltage at pin 12 of the 723 should not be less than 9.5 V. If the unregulated line is lower than this value, pin 12 (point B) must be connected to an auxiliary voltage of not less than 9.5 V.

When the voltage at point A exceeds a value predetermined by P1, pins 9 and 10 of the 723 become logic high and the SCR (a type TIC 106 or equivalent) fires. This creates a virtual short-circuit between the positive terminal of C1 and earth which causes fuse F1 to blow. The time lapse between the overvoltage occurring and the trip action is 1 . . . 2 μs.

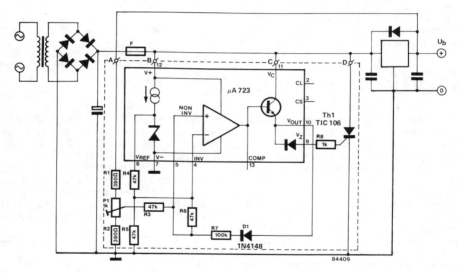

029 alarm timer

A periodic alarm signal has many applications in daily life: 'lights off' indicator in cars, water level indicator, alarm clock, memory aid, limit indicator, and calling signal are but a few.

The circuit begins to operate as soon as its input level becomes '0'; after about 30 seconds the buzzer sounds four times at one-second intervals. This happens every

thirty seconds until the input goes logic high again.

The circuit is based on a 14-stage CMOS binary counter and oscillator type 4060. The oscillator frequency, f, is determined by $f = 1/4R3C1$, where f is in Hz, R3 in ohms, and C1 in farad.

The oscillator is internally connected to the clock input of the counter. As soon as the

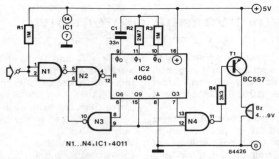

reset input (pin 12) is logic low, the counter begins to operate. Because at the onset outputs Q4, Q7, and Q10 are logic '0', pin 12 goes low when the input to N1 is '0'. After about 30 seconds, Q10 becomes '1'. The 1 Hz signal on Q4 is then applied to the base of transistor T1. This transistor therefore conducts in rhythm with the 1 Hz signal and switches the buzzer on and off at the same frequency. After four seconds output Q7 (pin 6) also becomes logic '1'. As both inputs of NAND gate N3 are now logic high, its output becomes '0'. This level ensures that the reset input (pin 12) of IC2 briefly goes high, so that the counter resets all outputs. If the input to the circuit is still '0', the process starts anew; otherwise the alarm stays quiet.

R. Rastetter

030 transistor polarity tester

There are not too many transistor testers which can independently differentiate between n-p-n and p-n-p types. True, the making of such a distinction is not often called for, even though in many a component drawer the two types are thoroughly mixed up. Normally, the data sheet or a list of comparative types quickly gives the answer. If these, however, are not available or there are other reasons why this method cannot be used, the tester described here will prove very useful.

Operation is very simple: the test transistor is placed in the socket and push-button S1 is pressed. If the transistor pins correspond to pins B-C-E of the socket, it is an n-p-n transistor which is optically indicated by LED D1. If LED D2 lights, it indicates that the transistor pins correspond to pins (B)-(C)-(E) and that therefore the transistor is a p-n-p type.

How does it work? Transistors T1 and T2, together with associated resistors and capacitors, form an astable multivibrator (AMV), the frequency of which can be set with potentiometer P1. The test transistor is connected to one of the outputs (collector of T2) of the AMV via protection resistor R6. If the test transistor is an n-p-n type, it conducts when T2 is cut off. At the same time, T3 conducts so that D1 lights.

If, however, the test transistor is a p-n-p type, it conducts when T2 does, and this cuts off T3. As the collector potential of T1 is then high, T4 conducts and D2 lights. Terminals 1 and 2 have been added as an

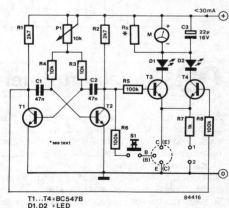

T1...T4 = BC547B
D1, D2 = LED

84416

36

aside and may, for instance, be used to test the continuity of conductors. This is possible, because when the terminals are short-circuited both LEDs light. The terminals may also be used to determine the anode and cathode of a diode: the LEDs remain extinguished when the cathode is connected to 1, but light with the anode at this terminal.

Meter M indicates the current flowing through the test transistor: capacitor C3 smoothes the rectangular pulses from the AMV. If you do not want this metering circuit, simply connect the anodes of the LEDs to the positive supply line via Rs = 330 Ω. The supply voltage should be not higher than 6 V to prevent the emitter-base reverse potential exceeding the maximum permissible level of 6 V should the emitter and base connections be accidentally reversed.

G. Gerhardt

031   time signal receiver

A very accurate time signal is available by tuning in to the Rugby MSF transmitter. This is not, however, the only such signal emitted into the air waves. A similar service is provided by the French long-wave station 'France Inter'. This transmitter is somewhat unusual as it transmits speech and music as well as the second-pulses. Its carrier frequency is exactly 10.2^{14} Hz (163 840 Hz) which can quite easily be divided to obtain the time-base signal required. The time code transmitted by France Inter every minute contains binary information encoded by a series of single and double pulses. This system makes it easier for a modified radio to process the signal.

The circuit described here can be used to receive the France Inter time signal almost anywhere in West Europe. The receiver was designed in such a way that it can be used for direct control of a time-clock. The input signal picked up by the aerial coil is first amplified before being fed to a mixer.

Here it is combined with the signal from a 6553 kHz crystal oscillator whose frequency is divided by 40. The mixer's output signal, which has a frequency of about 60 Hz, passes to a PLL (phase locked loop) where a phase detector compares it to a 60 Hz VCO (voltage-controlled oscillator) frequency. The difference between the two frequencies is taken as a correction signal that is subsequently used to control the VCO via a low-pass filter. The differences in question are the result of modulation of the input signal. Modulation of speech or music causes small frequency differences which are suppressed in the low-pass filter. The control signal for the VCO is therefore almost entirely due to the pulse-time modulation. This information is easily extracted by amplifying the signal, filtering it and then applying it via a trigger circuit to an MMV. Here the pulses are suitably shaped for the time clock.

All the parts of the block diagram are easily

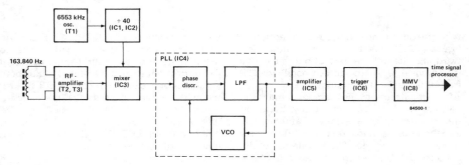

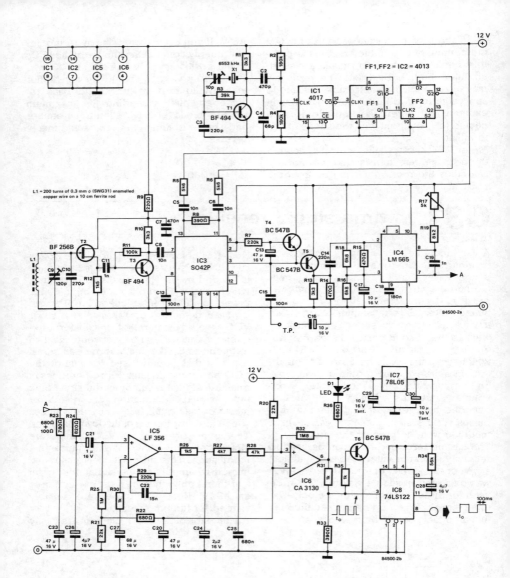

recognised on the main circuit diagram of figure 2. Building the circuit is straightforward and the only remark about this is that it is advisable to screen the oscillator (T1) from the rest of the circuit.

After construction the receiver must be calibrated. Start by temporarily breaking the connection between pins 4 and 5 of IC4 and then connecting a resistor of about 1 kΩ from pin 4 to ground. The frequency of the signal at pin 4 is then compared with that at

the test point (marked TP). This can be done by using sensitive headphones to listen to the frequency and trimming preset R17 and/or trimmer capacitor C1 until both signals sound exactly the same. All that remains then is to set C9 so that the second-pulses heard at TP sound as loud as possible. Assuming everything else in the circuit is correct, LED D1 will now light each time a second-pulse is received.

032 FM pocket radio

To the best of our knowledge this is the simplest FM radio that can be made. Not only that, but it also works quite well, even if the sensitivity does not seem very good. The principle of this receiver may appear somewhat unusual to some. It is based on an oscillator, consisting of transistors T2 and T3, that is synchronized with the received frequency by T1. This transistor operates as a wide-band VHF preamplifier. In principle this stage could be omitted and the aerial connected direct to capacitor C4, but the sensitivity would then be greatly impaired. The oscillator is tuned to 87...108 MHz by capacitor C5. Due to the synchronization mentioned, the oscillator output has the same frequency variations as the signal

picked up by the aerial. These variations are caused by the audio information. The frequency-modulated signal appears across P1 + R5. Low-pass filter R6/C6 extracts the audio signal, which is then amplified in T4...T6 and fed to the output terminal via C9.

The winding details for the coils are indicated in the diagram. The radio is tuned to different stations by means of tuning capacitor C5. Potentiometer P1 should then be set to give the best possible reception of the transmitter. Combined with a loudspeaker and amplifier this circuit can easily be made into a very compact pocket radio.

P. Engel

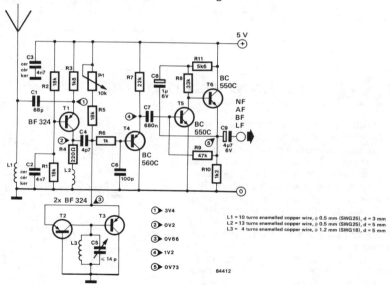

L1 = 10 turns enamelled copper wire, φ 0.5 mm (SWG25), d = 3 mm
L2 = 13 turns enamelled copper wire, φ 0.5 mm (SWG25), d = 5 mm
L3 = 4 turns enamelled copper wire, φ 1.2 mm (SWG18), d = 5 mm

84412

033 hi-lo pulse rate discriminator

The circuit described here gives a visual indication whether the rate of an incoming pulse train is above or below a predetermined value. Based on a type 74LS123 dual retriggerable monostable multivibrator (MMV) with clear, it should find ready application in microcomputer systems operating with more than one clock, for instance a TRS80 with speed-up modification. The reference rate, f_r, is determined by the time constant R1C1, which with the values as shown amounts to 0.45 µs to give

$f_r = 2.2$ MHz.

When the rate of the input signal, f_i, applied to $\overline{A1}$ of MMV1 lies below f_r, output $\overline{Q1}$ is able to follow the input signal. Input B2 of MMV2 goes high at the leading edge of the trigger pulse, so that MMV2 accepts the negative edge trigger on input $\overline{A2}$. Output $\overline{Q2}$ then goes low, which causes D2, the 'low' rate LED, to light.

When f_i is higher than f_r, MMV1 is retriggered before its internal pulse period has lapsed. This causes output $\overline{Q1}$ of MMV1 and input B2 of MMV2 to be held at low logic level. Output Q2 of MMV2 then remains low and Dl, the 'high' rate LED, lights.

An error pulse of about 5 ms occurs on MMV2 when the circuit is switched on and

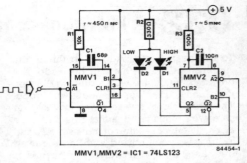

MMV1, MMV2 = IC1 = 74LS123

84454-1

this is indicated by D2 lighting. This 'reaction' pulse is necessary because the circuit needs at least one clock pulse to start up.

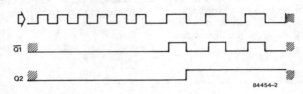

84454-2

034 audio preamp buffer

The circuit is simply what the title suggests, a buffer between an audio preamplifier and an output stage. It does have the added facility however, of being able to drive more than one output amplifier simultaneously.

The preamp load is standard at 100 pF in parallel with 47 k. To be fully versatile it was considered that the opamp used must be capable of driving similar loads at a level of 10 V without a problem. The LF 356 shown here can manage this.

The amplification factor is adjustable between 1 and 5 with the preset in the feedback loop of the opamps. These amplifiers also serve to balance the output levels of the two buffer stages. If required, the balancing can be achieved very easily by means of a 50 Hz signal source and an ordinary multimeter. The 50 Hz is applied to both inputs of the buffer circuit and one preset is adjusted to provide the required gain factor. The multimeter, switched to a suitable a.c. range, is then placed between the two outputs. The second preset is now adjusted to produce a zero reading on the meter.

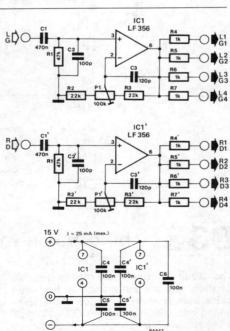

035 versatile timer

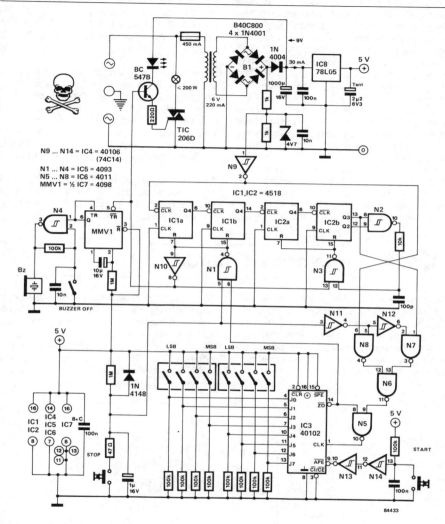

The timer described uses few components but has, none the less, a relatively wide timing range which may be programmed by BCD (binary coded decimal) thumbwheel switches. The circuit may be modified to cater for even longer periods than shown, up to years if required.

The circuit consists basically of a clock generator and a presettable BCD down counter. The master clock is derived from the output of the bridge rectifier. This voltage is stabilized at 5 V by a zener diode and then applied to schmitt-trigger N9 to produce a pulse train of 100 Hz. The pulse train is first divided by 100 in IC1 and then by 60 in IC2 to give a final clock of 1 pulse/min.

Counter IC3 counts down from a number set by the BCD switches at a rate of one step per clock pulse. Ordinary SPST switches may be used instead of the BCD ones, but the binary code for the required time inter-

41

val must then be remembered.

When the start button is pressed, the parallel data from the switches is loaded into the counter, the $\overline{ZD}$ output of IC3 goes high and releases the inhibit on the clock input via N5. At the same time the reset is removed from IC1 and IC2 via N1, N10, and N3. The output of N10 also switches on the triac which in turn switches on the load. The counter is then counting down from the preset number.

When the counter reaches zero, it stops counting, its $\overline{ZD}$ output goes low, the clock stops, IC1 and IC2 are reset in preparation for the next timing cycle, and the load is switched off.

The output of N10 also triggers monostable MMV which then switches on a simple oscillator based on N4 and the buzzer sounds, provided the switch is closed.

The circuit is self-setting, that is, when power is switched on, it automatically resets to the stop condition in preparation for the forthcoming timing cycle. To this end, the 100 Hz signal at the output of N9 is passed to the clock input of IC3 which counts down to zero very rapidly. The $\overline{ZD}$ output (low) subsequently resets IC1 and IC2.

Pressing the stop switch to abort a timing cycle has the same effect as power on.

The timing range may be expanded or shortened by adding or omitting one or more 4518 counters. The count-down cycle may be fixed permanently to a specific time lapse by replacing the BCD thumbswitches with hard-wiring at the J inputs of IC3.

As there are a lot of spikes in this circuit, good decoupling is essential. A 100 n capacitor should be provided directly across the supply pins of each IC.

036   one-armed bandit

This new game might be described as a sort of electronic one-armed bandit. The good news is, however, that you don't have to put money into it; the bad news is that you cannot win money from it either. So, for the stakes, you'll have to come to an agreement with your playing partners.

The circuit is based on a type 4024 seven-stage binary counter/divider. At the beginning of the game it is reset by spring-loaded press-to-make switch S2. The counter outputs, Q1 . . . Q7, are then logic low, and the LEDs, D1 . . . D5, are out. The output of NAND Schmitt trigger N2 is high and

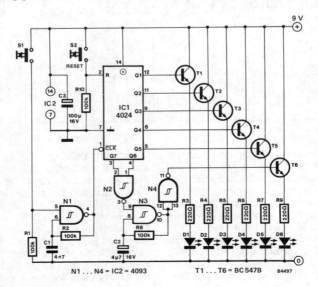

N1 . . . N4 = IC2 = 4093   T1 . . . T6 = BC 547B   84497

switches on relaxation oscillator N3. The oscillator signal is inverted in N4 and this turns on amplifier T6 so that LED D6 lights. The game is started by pressing another spring-loaded push-to-make switch, S1, when oscillator N1 is turned on and clocks the counter. As soon as S1 is released, N1 ceases to oscillate and the counter stops at a random output combination. One or more of the LEDs D1 ... D5 will be alight at that time and each of these is awarded a point or points as you may decide. Note the number of points before S1 is pressed anew. When outputs Q6 and Q7 of the counter are both high, N3 ceases to oscillate and LED D6 goes out. This is the signal for the next

player to try his or her luck. If D6 does not extinguish (because Q6 and Q7 are not high) the same player has another go.

The player who has amassed the largest number of points at the end of the game is the winner or the loser, depending on how you play this game of chance.

The circuit needs a power supply of 4.5 ... 9 V. The current consumption is dependent mainly on the bias resistors R3 ... R7: with values shown, the current through each of the LEDs is about 30 mA. The size and colour of LEDs D1 ... D5 may be chosen to your own preference.

H.J. Walter

037 baudrate generator

Most asynchronous receiver/transmitters (generally known as UARTs) operate at a clock frequency which is sixteen times the transmission rate. There are special ICs available that are dedicated to this particular timing function but they are neither freely available nor cheap. The classic switchable oscillator/divider circuit is, however, a good substitute. The clock frequencies provided in the design shown

here correspond to the standard transmission rates of 1200, 600, 300, 150, 110 and 75 baud.

The oscillator is based on inverters N1 and N2, in combination with the 1 MHz crystal. Its signal is fed, via N3, to the first 4024. A bistable, consisting of N9 and N10, is included in the reset line to this divider to ensure that the reset is perfectly synchronized with the clock signal. The output signal

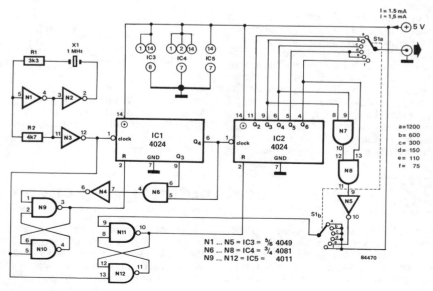

from IC1 feeds the clock input of the second 4024, which can be programmed by S1 (a double-pole six-way wafer switch). The reset pulse for this seven-stage binary counter is provided by N5, N7, and N8 and travels via a second synchronizing bistable (N11/N12), which is, once again, clocked by the oscillator signal. Switch S1 can be replaced by a pair of wire jumpers in the appropriate places if one baudrate is continuously selected.

The table here indicates the frequencies measured in our prototype corresponding to the various baudrates. The exact frequencies are also given to show that the error is negligible in all cases.

The circuit could quite easily be extended

to make it suitable for a different crystal than the one stated. It will then be possible to make use of an old crystal instead of having to buy one.

Table

baud-rate	exact frequency (Hz)	measured frequency (Hz)	error
1200	19200	19229	0.15%
600	9600	9614	0.15%
300	4800	4807	0.15%
150	2400	2404	0.15%
110	1760	1748	0.68%
75	1200	1202	0.15%

038 fatigue tester

The human eye has a certain built-in delay. This fact is used for films, TV sets, and fluorescent lights, as above a certain flash frequency the eye does not notice any lack of continuity. It has now come to light that the highest flash frequency a person can detect is adversely affected by tiredness and alcohol consumption. A very small circuit is all that is needed to determine exactly what this frequency is at any time of the day or night.

As the diagram shows, the circuit is very simple. It is based on an old favourite, the 555 timer, which is connected here as an astable multivibrator. Its output is connected to a LED that flashes at a certain frequency. This frequency can be varied between 20 and 50 Hz with potentiometer P1. The highest frequency that most people can detect is between 30 and 40 flashes per second, but one test we conducted on a Monday morning produced a startling number of blank stares accompanied by

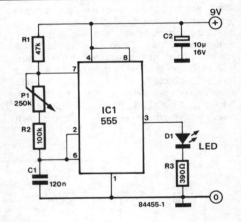

the question 'What LED??'.

Given the nature of the circuit, it is not surprising that the current consumption is only about 25 mA so a 9 V battery is all the power that is needed.

039 economical motor driving circuit

Oh, for the good old days, when if you wanted to run a motor for two minutes you switched on the power for two minutes. Now we have computer-controlled robot arms, electronic mice, and all manner of

technological advances. For all this, however, many people still shy away from the idea of something like a motor-driving circuit. As the drawing here shows, such a circuit is quite straightforward, especially

44

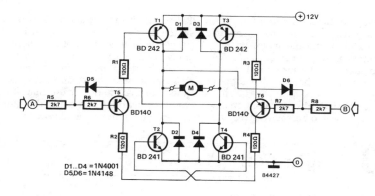

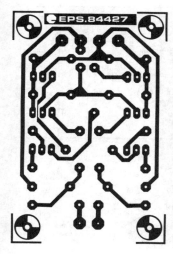

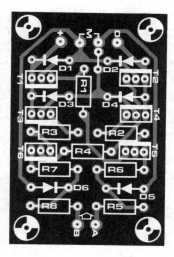

Parts list

Resistors:
R1 . . . R4 = 120 Ω
R5 . . . R8 = 2k7

Semiconductors:
D1 . . . D4 = 1N4001
D5,D6 = 1N4148
T1,T3 = BD 242
T2,T4 = BD 241
T5,T6 = BD 140/BD 136

as we have even gone so far as to design a printed circuit board for it.

The circuit has two inputs and if both are '1' (+12 V) nothing happens. As soon as the voltage on one of the inputs, A, for example, becomes '0', driver transistor T5 conducts. This causes both T1 and T4 to conduct and the motor turns in a particular direction. This brings us to the stage where we must explain why the circuit is economical.

It will not have escaped your notice that each pair of transistors in the bridge is controlled by a single driver transistor. This not only saves components, but also saves the energy that would otherwise be used by two driver transistors. When T5 is made to conduct T1 will conduct. At the same time a current flows from T1 via T5 to the base of T4 so this transistor also conducts. This

means, in effect, that we are using the base current of T1 and T3 to drive T4 and T2 respectively, giving us a common driving circuit.

There are two other components that merit a few lines of explanation, namely D5 and D6. These ensure that nothing untoward happens if both inputs are earthed at the same time. If, for example, input A is at zero volts both T1 and T4 conduct and the anode of D6 is connected to the +12 V line. If input B is now earthed, T6 (as well as T2 and T3) cannot conduct because its base is kept positive. Input B can only be actuated, therefore, after the voltage at A goes high, and vice versa.

Pulse-width modulation could be used to control the speed of the motor. What this means is that the signal fed to input A or B is not continuous but a string of pulses whose width can be varied. The narrower the pulses are, the faster the motor turns.

If heavier motors are to be driven, T1 ... T4 may be replaced by darlingtons that are rated high enough to handle the higher current.

The inputs to this circuit are intentionally active low to enable it to be easily driven by TTL logic. The outputs of TTL gates can switch a few milliamps to earth but can supply very little current themselves, certainly not enough to drive a transistor. If the supply for the motor is greater than 5 V the TTL gates must have open-collector outputs. The maximum current that the motor can draw is about 1 amp and the quiescent current consumption is almost nil.

040   light-pen

A light pen is a tool that allows the coordinates of a point on the screen to be entered into a computer. It is based on the principle of sending a pulse to the screen control circuit at the precise moment it sweeps the spot just in front of the lightpen. In the case of the Elektor VDU card the screen is controlled by a 6845; when this IC's LPEN input (pin 3) goes from '0' to '1', it loads the address of the character it is writing into registers 16 and 17. We will see later what can be done with this information.

The sensor in the light-pen is a partly covered light-dependent resistor (LDR), the exposed part of which forms a window the same size as a character on the screen. When the electron beam in the screen passes in front of this window the LDR's resistance reduces drastically. This causes transistor T1 to conduct, followed by T2, with the result that a pulse suitable for the LPEN input of the CRTC (cathode ray tube circuit) appears at the collector of the BC 559. As soon as this transistor saturates, T3 switches off and the LED extinguishes, indicating that the light-pen is correctly pointed at the character. For correct operation of the light-pen, preset P1 must be calibrated. This is done by placing the LDR, which is screened as shown in the sketch, in front of a character and then trimming the preset until the LED is extinguished. Registers R16 and R17 in the 6845 CRTC store the address of the character indicated by the light-pen. This address is somewhere in the range from 0000 to 3FFF$_{HEX}$, which is the 16 K of screen memory addressable by the 6845. All that then remains is to convert this address into usable information.

It could be considered as an index specify-

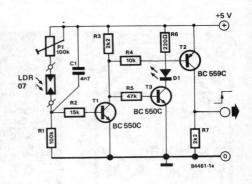

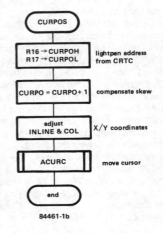

= size of a character on the screen

84461-1b

ing the offset relative to the display start address. When these two are added, the address indicated by the light-pen is obtained and could have a character POKEd to it. Another possibility is to move the cursor to this point. The information provided by the CRTC must then be converted to X and Y coordinates (vertical and horizontal) which are used to modify pointers COL (vertical) and INLINE (horizontal). The ACURC routine (see the listing in Paperware 3)* is called to move the cursor to this address. As the flow chart indicates, the in-

formation provided by the CRTC must be corrected because in the Elektor VDU card the DEN and CUR signals in the CRTC are delayed by bistables FF1 . . . FF4 to compensate for the delay inherent in the data handling chain.The character indicated by the light-pen is therefore not in the address indicated by the CRTC but in the one immediately following it.

*Available from Elektor Publishers.

041   stereo doorbell

The stereo is on, playing loud enough to do justice to your favourite rock record. The doorbell rings but in your ecstacy you don't realize it, even if you had been able to hear it. It doesn't take long before the would-be guest gets fed up and decides to protect his

(or her!) gentle ears by going someplace quieter, like a heavy metal concert. That leaves you with two options: cut the mains lead of the stereo or fit a more effective doorbell.
The circuit here is a combination of the two

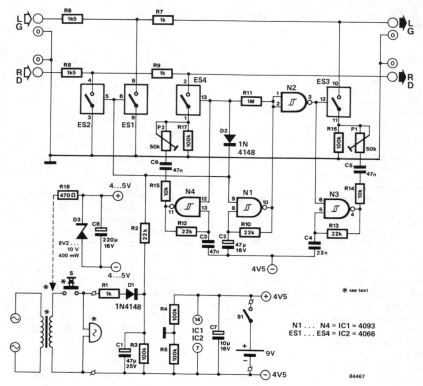

but we guarantee it is less destructive than the first. It cuts the volume of the stereo's output drastically when the bell is operated. Then to make sure the message is received, the bell gives a number of tones of different frequencies switching from one channel to the other.
The operation of the circuit is quite simple. When the bell button is pressed, there is a voltage across the bell which is rectified by diode D1 to provide a logic '1'. This causes a number of things to happen, the first of which is that electronic switches ES1 and ES2 are closed. The outputs of both left and right channels are then greatly attenuated. At the same time the rhythm generator based on N1 starts working. This controls oscillators N3 and N4 and ensures that the signals they provide are fed to the left and right channel respectively. The tone in the left channel is about 800 Hz, while that in the right channel has a frequency of about 400 Hz.

The current drawn by this circuit is quite small; less than 5 mA. The supply voltage could be provided by a battery or it could be taken from the bell transformer. Note that the signal earth is taken from the centre of voltage divider R4/R5.
The volumes of the bell tones are set by presets P1 and P2. Be very cautious about setting the volume too high as the rectangular waveforms of the bell tone signals contain many high-frequency harmonics that could cause tweeters to become terminally dead.
The circuit should be connected in the audio system preferably between preamplifier and power amplifier. This point is often accessible by a preamplifier output/power amplifier input connection. A second possibility is to connect the inputs of the circuit to the tape recorder outputs and the circuit outputs to the recorder inputs. Then set the amplifier to tape playing.

042 70/90 watt amplifier

Characteristics:

output power (f = 1 kHz, d = 0.5%): 75 W
  into 8 Ω (97 W into 4 Ω)
offset voltage: 40 mV
quiescent current (set with R16): 50 mA
input impedance: 10 kΩ
input sensitivity: 760 mV (600 mV for 4 Ω)
harmonic distortion
  (at $P_{max.}$ and 1 kHz): 0.01%
intermodulation distortion
  (at $P_{max.}$ and 1 kHz): 0.02%
frequency range
  (−2 dB, reference level 10 dB under $P_{max.}$
  at 1 kHz): 10 Hz . . . 60 kHz
signal to noise ratio (P = 50 mW)
  − weighted A curve IEC 179: 83 dB
  − unweighted curve: 75 dB

This is an amplifier with a very simple layout that none the less produces quite a high output. Power isn't everything, however, so it is backed up in this case by the other characteristics which are quite good.
A symmetrical supply was chosen to avoid the problem of having to use an electrolytic capacitor at the output. Consequently a differential amplifier is used at the input. The

input signal is fed to the base of transistor T1 and feedback is taken from the base of T2. The current through the differential stage is kept at a constant 1 mA by the action of current source T3. The amplified input signal is taken from the collector of T1 to darlington T4/T8, which, in combination with current source T5, forms the class A driver stage for the power transistors. The current through the driver stage is quite small (about 7 mA) because T6 and T9 are power darlingtons.
The class AB quiescent current for the power transistors is made less subject to temperature fluctuations by mounting T7 on the same heat sink as T6 and T9. This current is set by trimming R16. The amplifier's a.c. stability is improved by the inclusion of RC networks in the output stage and in the feedback loop. If it is considered necessary, overload and short-circuit protection is provided by the circuit shown in figure 2. This should be mounted in the space indicated by the dotted lines in figure 1.
The amplifier is designed to provide a power of 70 W into 8 Ω, but if the component values given in brackets are used it

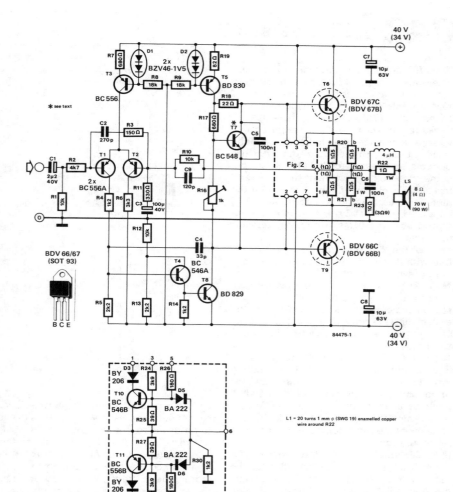

L1 = 20 turns 1 mm ⌀ (SWG 19) enamelled copper wire around R22

84475-1   40 V (34 V)

84475-2

can be connected to 4 Ω loudspeakers and then provides a maximum of about 90 W. The protection circuit of figure 2 must also be modified if a 4 Ω load is used. The values of R24 and R28 are then 3k9, R26 and R28 are 220 Ω, and D5, D6 and R30 are removed altogether.

The power supply (not indicated) need only consist of the usual transformer, rectifier and smoothing capacitors. The electrolytic capacitors should be about 5 000 to 10 000 μF each. The rectified voltage for the 70 W/8 Ω version should be ±40 V with the load; with no load this corresponds to about ±47 V. At 4 Ω these values are ±34 and ±40 V respectively. Don't underestimate the transformer requirements! It must be able to provide 1.4 A for the 70 W/8 Ω version (mono) and 2.2 A for the 90 W/4 Ω version. It is strongly recommended that a fuse be included in both positive and negative supply lines; 2 A for 8 Ω or 3 A for 4 Ω.

Finally, a word about the cooling requirements of T6 and T9. In the 8 Ω mono amplifier the heat sink for these transistors must be rated at 3.4°C/W maximum; for stereo this is 1°C/W. These values become 2.5 and 0.5°C/W for the 4 Ω version.

49

043   2716 versus 2708

The 2708 EPROM has become virtually obsolete, and with good reason. It needs three supply voltages for its capacity of 1024 × 8 bits whereas its immediate successor, the 2716, uses the same 24-pin package but only needs a single supply voltage for twice the memory capacity (2048 × 8 bits). Furthermore, the 2708 has become so difficult to find that it has become more expensive than the 2716, and that alone is reason enough to consider the modifications needed to substitute a 2716 for a 2708. Fortunately, few changes are required as the address decoding remains the same.

Most of the 2716 pins are directly compatible with those on the 2708, but the following are worthy of note:

■ Pin 21 (−5 V on the 2708) must be connected to +5 V for the 2716.

■ Pin 20, incorrectly called $\overline{CS}$ (chip select) on the 2708 while its function is actually $\overline{OE}$ (output enable), retains the same function.

■ Pin 19 (+12 V on the 2708) becomes address input A10 for the 2716. Depending on the logic level on this pin either the first or second 1 K block is selected. A switch could be used for this so if the EPROM contains a monitor, for example, two different versions of the same software could be stored in the same IC.

■ Pin 18, which is connected to ground for the 2708, need not be changed for the 2716 ($\overline{CE}$, chip enable); note in passing that the 2716 will then never achieve the minimum power dissipation of 132 mW (stand by current).

There are several different ways of carrying

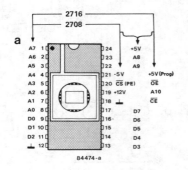

84474-a

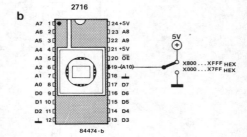

84474-b

out these modifications. An intermediary IC socket could be used with the pins that are to be changed not inserted into the socket but wired separately. If preferred, the same thing could be done without using a socket. The method we recommend, however, is to modify the printed circuit board by cutting the appropriate tracks. Be especially careful if this is done with a double-sided board.

Note: See also circuit 096.

044   EPROM eraser

All that's required to erase an EPROM is basically an ultraviolet (UV) lamp which radiates the EPROM window at the right distance (about 2 ... 3 cm) for a period which depends on the manufacturer (normally 10 ... 40 minutes). As we don't think you'll want to sit around gazing at your wristwatch while all this is going on, we

have designed a timer which automatically ensures the correct radiation time and indicates the end of the erasure period.

The counter-IC, type 4060, has an internal oscillator the frequency of which is determined by R2, R3, P1, and C3. When the supply is switched on, IC2 receives a reset pulse from C5 which makes it start count-

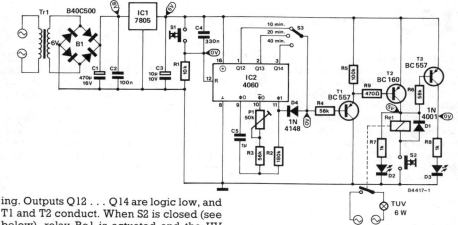

ing. Outputs Q12 . . . Q14 are logic low, and T1 and T2 conduct. When S2 is closed (see below), relay Re1 is actuated and the UV lamp is switched on. In addition, red LED D2 lights. The base of T3 is connected to the positive supply line via T2 so that T3 is cut off. After the time set by S3 has lapsed, the relevant output of IC2 goes high. Transistors T1 and T2 are then cut off, the relay switches off the UV lamp, and LED D2 extinguishes. The base of T3 is connected to earth via the relay coil and S2: transistor T3 conducts and green LED D3 lights to indicate the completion of erasure.

A tip: fit the UV lamp in a suitable case with open underside as shown in figure 2. Pushbutton S2 should be mounted in a way which ensures that it closes when the case is laid flat on an even surface, but opens as soon as the unit is lifted; the relay Re1 then ceases to operate and switches off the UV lamp. *This is absolutely necessary as ultraviolet light is extremely harmful to your eyes.*

The clock frequency may be set by P1 in two ways: (1) with the aid of an oscilloscope or frequency counter to 6.85 Hz, or (2) by measuring the time taken for output Q12 of IC2 to become logic 1 after reset switch S1 has been pressed: this should be exactly 10 minutes.

Note that the relay contact must be rated for switching 240 V a.c.! The relay itself may be of the pc board type.

The mains power supply may be any well-regulated type giving 6 V d.c. The current consumption without the relay is about 5 mA.

Using the eraser is fairly easy: lay the EPROM on a flat surface and place the case over it after having set S3 to the required erase time (10, 20, or 40 minutes). Lighting of the red LED indicates that erasure is in progress. A push on S1 ensures that the correct erasure time will be run through: this is necessary as the counter begins to count as soon as the supply voltage is switched on.

045 fridge alarm

As we all know, it is important that doors of fridges and freezers are normally closed. An alarm to tell you that it isn't is the subject of this article. It is based on a light-dependent resistor (LDR). As soon as the door of the fridge, or freezer, being guarded is opened, light falls onto the LDR: the circuit is then actuated and a warning tone is sounded until the door is closed again.

The circuit may also be used to monitor other doors (for instance, to prevent heat loss, or as a precaution against a fire spreading), but because of the ambient light it is of course impossible to use an LDR. This can therefore be replaced by a microswitch, in which case the alarm will sound when the switch is closed. Note that this requires a switch which closes when the door is opened.

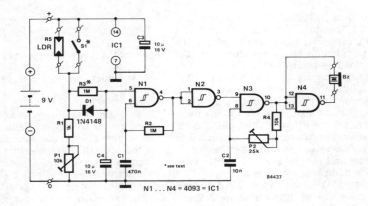

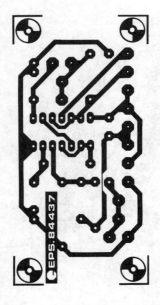

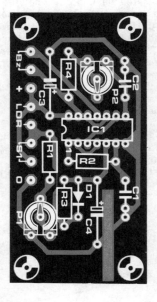

Parts list

Resistors:
R1 = 1 k
R2,R3 = 1 M (value of R3 may be reduced: see text)
R4 = 10 k
R5 = LDR
P1 = preset 10 k
P2 = preset 25 k

Capacitors:
C1 = 470 n
C2 = 10 n
C3,C4 = 10 μ/16 V

Semiconductors:
D1 = 1N4148
IC1 = 4093

Miscellaneous:
S1 = door (micro) switch
piezo electric buzzer
PP3 (9 V) battery with clips
case 100 × 50 × 40 mm
printed circuit 84437

A delay of about 10 s between the opening of the door and the sounding of the alarm is provided by the time constant R3C4. If faster reaction of the circuit is required, the value of R3 may be reduced to 220 k.
At the moment the threshold of N1 is exceeded, the gate commences to oscillate at a frequency of a few hertz. Each consequent rectangular pulse at the output

(pin 3) of inverter N2 fires oscillator N3 which generates pulse trains whose rate amounts to a few kilohertz. The pulse trains are fed to inverter N4 which causes the piezo buzzer to emit a tone.
Without N2, oscillator N3 would work continuously when N1 is not being triggered: the output of N1 would then be high, and the logic 1 at pin 8 of N3 would cause the oscillator to function.
Inverter N4 serves to amplify the output of the buzzer. If the buzzer would simply be connected between the output of N3 and earth, the membrane would merely move from its rest position to one side. By connecting the buzzer across an inverter, its polarity is constantly reversed and this causes a doubling of the alternating voltage across it. Preset P2 provides further optimization of the volume by tuning N3 to the resonant frequency of the buzzer.
Preset P1 determines the sensitivity of the alarm: the smaller its value, the less sensitive the circuit is.
The alarm is most conveniently constructed on the printed-circuit board shown in figure 2.
Current consumption in the quiescent condition is of the order of 0.5 mA and when the alarm operates about 4 mA.

from an idea by W. Groot Nueland

046   6502 bootstrap

During its initialization procedure, the 6502 processor starts by getting the start vector which is located at addresses $FFFC and $FFFD in ROM. This is a fixed instruction that cannot be changed, and it points to a memory zone in PROM, which, in most computers, is very difficult for the user to access. The circuit described here makes it easy to reroute the 6502 to a start address chosen by the user: $XFFC/$XFFD where X is any hexadecimal value. At this address the CPU will find the appropiate vector pointing to the start routine written by the user (in EPROM) instead of the standard routine written by the manufacturer.
The only hardware change required to achieve this is to connect the circuit shown between the 6502 and its bus. Now every

time the CPU emits an address between $FFF8 and $FFFF (the address decoding is a little less precise than is necessary for only re-routing the processor when it outputs addresses $FFFC and $FFFD), the bus receives an address between $XFF8 and $XFFF, where X is determined by the user by four switches (or four wire links). If S4, for instance, is switched to +5 V, A15' is equal to A15, but if the other position is selected, A15' = $\overline{A15}$. To use this circuit, lines A3 ... A15 on the bus must be fed to N1 and the link between outputs A12 ... A15 of the 6502 and the system bus must be broken. These lines are then connected to lines A12' ... A15' of the detour circuit. Each of lines A12 ... A15 is connected to one of the inputs of AND gates

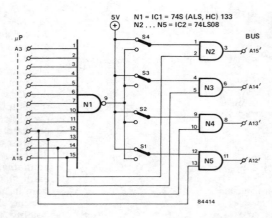

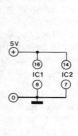

N2 ... N5. The second input to each of these gates is fed by the logic level set by the user with the switches. The resultant binary word constitutes the hexadecimal value of X in the destination addresses $XFFC and $XFFD.

In most cases this memory zone will be found in an EPROM which, apart from the RESET vector, will probably also contain the initialization routine. Note that the change described here implies that the IRQ and NMI vectors (XFFE/XFFF and XFFA/XFFB respectively) and the corresponding routines are modified accordingly.

047 power switches for µPs

It is not enough simply to own a micro computer, you must also know what to do with it. Having found an interesting field of application the next question will be 'how should it be done?'. The answer usually involves programming input/output circuits, or designing them. This can strike fear into the hearts of many users of computers that have rudimentary, or non-existent, input/output facilities. Fortunately, this fear is groundless and, as the circuit here shows, it is not at all difficult to use a computer to drive relays, electronic switches, and all sorts of lamps, motors, or whatever. The basis of this circuit is formed by the eight bistables contained in IC1. These are controlled by a positive pulse (for the 74LS373) or a leading edge (74LS374) and ensure that the output logic levels remain stable. The control signal applied to pin 11 could be obtained in several ways, such as via a programmable output port or by address decoding*. The eight data entries D0 ... D7 should be connected either directly to the processor's bus or to a second programmable output port. Each of the outputs, Q0 ... Q7, controls a darlington (T1/T2) which can switch up to 60 V at up to 1 A. The power dissipation is then low

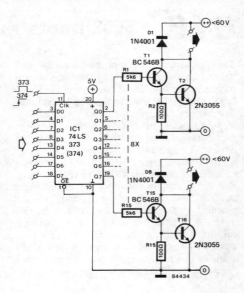

enough to obviate the need for a heat sink. The darlington saturates as soon as a high logic level appears at the corresponding output of IC1, and it switches off when the output is low. If voltages lower than 45 V are to be switched, a BC 547 can be used in place of the BC 546. A diode, D1, has been included as a protection against voltage spikes.

This circuit is very flexible. If you do not want to use all eight outputs of IC1, the same IC is used but the number of darlingtons is reduced. Similarly, a number of ICs may be cascaded, with each IC driving up to eight outputs. In this case they could be controlled by two output ports, with port A, for example, serving as a common data bus to all the flip-flops and port B being used to select the appropriate device. This would enable up to 64 darlingtons to be controlled via two programmable output ports.

* See, e.g., the articles on this subject in the January and February 1984 issues of *Elektor*

048 coffee temperature indicator

You've just finished a hard day's work and are heading home, looking forward to a relaxing evening and sitting in your favourite chair while your faithful dog brings your slippers and paper. The crowning glory is, of course, the cup of hot coffee . . . But sometimes it doesn't work quite like that! The dog has to be pried out of what is also his favourite chair, and it takes almost all your effort to coax him, grumbling and growling, to reluctantly fetch your slippers and paper. You put on the slippers and your feet begin to feel decidedly damp, the rain has made the ink in the paper run, and then to top it all the coffee is too cold. Before you chuck in the towel . . . read on; we may not be much good at canine psychology, but we do have some ideas about coffee.

There is little dispute that the best temperature for coffee is at least 80 degrees centigrade. That is the temperature where your tongue just begins to . . . but let's not go into that here. Because coffee has also become a common prescription for the ailment known as 'Mondaymorning', we decided that it would be better to remove all traces of guesswork from this question of 'how hot is it?'.

As the diagram shows, there is not very much involved in this circuit. A voltage regulator, a temperature to voltage converter, a comparator, a couple of transistors and LEDs, and a handful of resistors and capacitors, is the total component count. The operation is also straightforward. If the coffee is at less than the correct temperature, the output of IC3 is low, keeping T1 switched off. The other transistor, T2, therefore conducts and the red LED lights to show that the coffee is too cold. As soon as the temperature is high enough (above 80°C), the green LED lights.

What actually happens is this: the temperature, which is measured by IC2, is converted to a voltage. The idea is that the LM35 should hang in the coffee, so the three connections to the IC must be

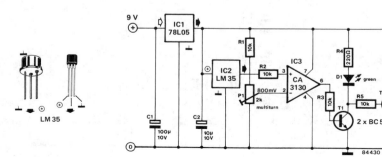

isolated. This can be done by fixing the temperature sensor in an old ballpoint pen, or by sealing it with some non-poisonous two-component glue, or in a heat-shrink sleeve.

The output voltage of IC2 increases by 10 mV for every degree centigrade rise in temperature. The reference voltage at the inverting input of IC3 must be set to 800 mV with P1. As soon as the voltage on the non-inverting input also reaches 800 mV, the output of the comparatorswitches to '1'. This causes T1 to conduct, switching T2 and the red LED off. The green LED will now light to show that the coffee is at the right temperature. Incidentally, a clever handyman could probably adapt this circuit to indicate if the dog is in a good or a bad mood!

049 VHF/AM air band converter

Many enthusiasts would be interested in listening to what goes on in the VHF air band of 108 . . . 132 MHz were it not that receivers covering those frequencies are fairly expensive. Fortunately, air communications use amplitude modulation and if you therefore have a good short-wave receiver it is pretty straightforward to connect a suitable converter to it. And that's what this article is all about . . .

The converter actually covers the frequency range of about 106 . . . 150 MHz so that apart from the air band it covers a small part of the broadcasting band (up to 108 MHz, but that's mainly FM) and the 144 . . . . 146 MHz (that is, the 2 m) amateur band.

The converter consists of a VHF amplifier, a mixer, and an oscillator. After it has been amplified in T1, the input signal is applied to a MOSFET mixer where it is combined with the output of crystal oscillator T3. Three tuned circuits between the aerial input and mixer ensure good selectivity and good image rejection. The difference-frequency output of the mixer is taken from

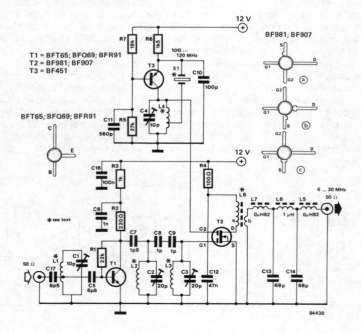

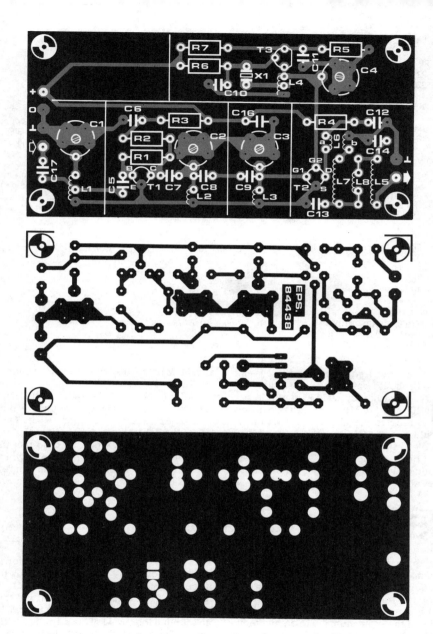

its drain and fed to a 50 ohm output via a filter consisting of L7, L8, L5, C13, and C14. Tuning is carried out at the short-wave receiver between 6 and 30 MHz.

The bandwidth of the tuned circuits is, of course, not sufficient to cover the whole range of about 106 . . . 150 MHz. At around 106 MHz the bandwidth is some 3 MHz; at 150 MHz it is about 12 MHz. Once you have chosen the band you want to listen in, tune the crystal and circuits L1-C1, L2-C2, and L3-C3 to the centre frequency of that band. The crystal frequency, f_x, is equal to the difference between the input frequency, f_i,

57

Parts list

Resistors:
R1 = 22 k
R2 = 220 Ω
R3 = 1 k
R4 = 100 Ω
R5 = 27 k
R6 = 1k5
R7 = 18 k

Capacitors:
C1,C4 = 10 p trimmer
C2,C3 = 20 p trimmer
C5,C17 = 6p8
C6 = 1 n ceramic
C7 = 1p8
C8,C9 = 1 p
C10 = 100 p
C11 = 560 p
C12 = 47 n
C13,C14 = 68 p
C15 = 3p3
C16 = 100 n

Semiconductors:
T1 = BFQ69, BFR91, BFT65
T2 = BF907, BF981
T3 = BF451

Inductors:
L1 = 7 turns with tap at 3 turns
    from earth   ⎫ enamelled copper
L2 = 3 turns   ⎬ wire SWG 20
L3 = 3 turns   ⎪ close wound on
L4 = 4 turns with tap at 1 turn   ⎭ pencil
    from earth
L6a = 4 turns enamelled copper   ⎫ together on ferrite
      wire SWG 36   ⎬ bead 3 × 8 mm
L6b = 4 turns enamelled copper   ⎭
      wire SWG 24
L5, L7 = 0µH82
L8 = 1 µH

Crystal 100...120MHz, fifth overtone

available from
IQD Limited
North Street
Crewkerne
Somerset TA18 7AR

PC Board 84438

and the output frequency, f_o: $f_x = f_i - f_o$, where f_o should be as high as permitted by the crystal frequency which should lie between 100 and 120 MHz. For instance, if you want to receive the 117 ... 119 MHz band, f_x could be 100 MHz (to keep f_o as high as possible) and the short-wave receiver would be tuned between 17 and 19 MHz. If you select the 2 m amateur band, the short-wave receiver could be tuned between 28 and 30 MHz so that the crystal frequency would be 116 MHz [(144 ... 146) — (28 ... 30) MHz]. Air coils L1 ... L4 may be wound on a pencil and L6 on a ferrite bead, while L5, L7 and L8 are available ready made. Note that the printed circuit is double-sided so that the component side is an earth plane to which the various RF screens shown in figure 2 should be soldered.

---

050 auto duty factor

It is quite a common practice to use a schmitt trigger to generate a rectangular waveform from some other signal. The duty factor and frequency at the output depend on the input signal but, other than that, the shape of the input signal is relatively unimportant. The one essential requirement is that the signal must exceed, or at least reach, the triggering threshold of the schmitt trigger. With the circuit shown in figure 1 that is not necessarily so.

To be able to process smaller signals a.c. coupling may be used and the signal need then only be greater than the hysteresis.

The peak value of asymmetrical signals must, however, be larger than this or the upper or lower threshold may not be reached. The signal in figure 2a will thus produce an output whereas there will be no output if the signal of 2b is applied to the input. The circuit illustrated always retains the same sensitivity irrespective of the shape of the input signal.

The ideal input to this circuit is a small signal fed to the schmitt trigger inverter via capacitor C1. The value at the output is averaged by R2/C2 and fed back to the input. The d.c. setting at the input is thus

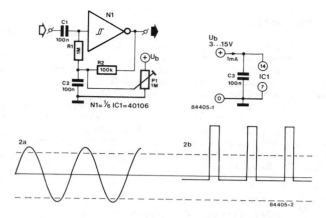

N1 = ⅙ IC1 = 40106

84405-1

84405-2

'tailored' to the peak value of the input signal, with the result that any signal whose magnitude is larger than the difference between the schmitt trigger's thresholds (the hysteresis) will cause a rectangular waveform to appear at the output. The sensitivity of the circuit can be set by preset potentiometer P1.

Unfortunately, as in so many things, there is a small cloud wrapped around this circuit's silver lining, namely that when there is no signal at the input the circuit acts as a free-running oscillator. To prevent this happening when there *is* a signal present, the frequency of oscillation must be at least ten times lower than the frequency at which the circuit is used (100 Hz with the values shown). It is then an ideal auto-trigger for an oscilloscope, for example. A disadvantage of the circuit is that it is not very suitable for signals with a very short duty factor as small differences in peak value then produce broken pulse trains at the output.

051 temperature reading on a multimeter

A multimeter is the most common item of test equipment used by electronic hobbyists. This is with good reason, considering how useful it is, but, of course, its abilities are fairly limited. Ask it about amps or volts or ohms and it is in its element. Broach the subject of degrees, however, and all you are likely to get is the multimetric equivalent of a blank stare. The versatility of a multimeter can easily be improved by adding the temperature-to-voltage converter shown here.

The temperature sensor used is an LM 335 which has a linear temperature characteristic of 10 mV/K. During manufacture this device is calibrated so that it gives an output of 2.73 V at 0°C (273 K). The LM 336 in the diagram is a very stable 2.5 V zener diode whose output is fed to IC2. The amplification of this CA 3040 can be varied

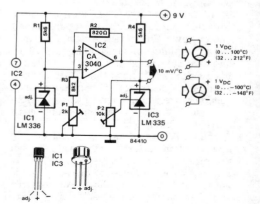

84410

between 1.08 and 1.10 times, by P1, so this potentiometer must be adjusted to give 2.73 V at the output of IC2 when IC1 is at

59

0°C. The circuit is now calibrated at freezing point.

Calibration at 100°C is carried out by comparison with an accurate thermometer. When the LM 335 is at this temperature, P2 must be adjusted to give a reading of 1 V between the output terminals of the circuit.

The accuracy of the temperature reading given with this circuit depends to a certain extent on the multimeter used. The greater the resolution the better the accuracy. The connections to the meter must, of course, be reversed to read temperatures below

0°C.

This circuit can also be used to enable temperatures to be measured in degrees Fahrenheit. In this case the freezing point adjustment is made at 32°F (2.73 V at the output of IC2). At 212°F, P2 is adjusted to give 0.9 V between the output terminals. One degree Fahrenheit is then represented by 5 mV, so a meter with 1 V f.s.d. will read from 32 . . . 232°F.

The current consumption of the circuit is about 10 mA.

---

052   linear opto-coupler

The MOC 5010 opto-coupler may be used to isolate a circuit from the mains, as audio interface, in medical electronics, and in many other applications.

Because of its high isolation resistance (10^{11} ohms), the MOC 5010 is eminently suitable for applications where a circuit is connected directly to the mains, as, for instance, in most TV receivers. It can therefore be used to give enhanced performance to the *TV sound interface* described in the April 1982 issue of *Elektor*. With a bandwidth stretching from 5 Hz to well over 100 kHz, there is no need to worry about the audio response as there was in earlier opto-couplers.

Basically, the MOC 5010 converts a variation in input current into a variation of output voltage. Input voltages are first transformed into currents. The circuit shown in figure 1 has an amplification factor of about 0.75. Its input should not exceed 2 V_{rms}, while the bandwidth is 118 kHz at the -3 dB points.

Field-effect transistor T1 functions as a voltage/current converter: its slope is about 3 . . . 4 mA/V. The quiescent drain-source current is about 10 mA.

Amplifier A has a transfer resistance of around 200 mV/mA so that the total gain is of the order of 0.6 . . . 0.8 (-4.5 . . . -2.0 dB). The output impedance of the amplifier is not greater than 200 ohms. An external amplifier may be connected to pin 4 of the IC. When the input voltages lie above 2 V_{rms}, a potentiometer should be used as a voltage divider as shown in figure 2. If the overall gain is too small, a transistor

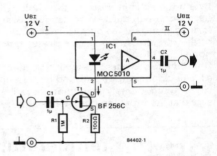

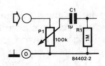

should be used instead of the FET (also with 10 mA quiescent current), but the circuit then virtually reverts to that published in April 1982!

It is important to note that two separate power supplies are required: not only the two $+12$ V terminals, but also the two '0' lines must be kept isolated from one another! In many cases it should be possible to obtain the $+12$ V for the transmitting end of the circuit from the TV set: this is, of course, easily found out if you have the service manual or even a circuit diagram of the set.

053 twin door-bell

The present circuit is particularly useful where two families share one house, and where therefore two doorbells are a godsend, but where for one reason or another two push-buttons cannot be fitted. The only solution is then to operate the two bells with one push-button.

When the button, S1, is pressed briefly, bell 1 sounds, and when it is pressed for a longer time, bell 2 will ring. Pressing the button triggers monostable multivibrator (MMV) IC1. The consequent logic 1 at the output (pin 3) causes T1 to conduct and this connects the clock input (pin 11) of D-type bistable IC2 to earth. This state does not last long, however, because as soon as the output of IC1 returns to logic 0, transistor T1 cuts off, and the clock input of IC2 goes high.

When S1 is pressed for an instant only, that is, it is open again at the trailing edge of the output of the MMV, the D input of IC2, and consequently the Q output, goes high. The Q output (pin 13) is applied to one of the inputs of AND gate N1. The other input of N1 receives a high signal from IC4 (pin 3) and

this lasts longer than the Q output of IC2. The output of N1 is then logic 1 which causes T2 to turn on and this results in triac Tri1 firing: bell 1 then rings.

When the button, S1, is pressed for a longer time, it is still closed at the trailing edge of the output of IC1. Consequently, the D input of IC2 is low, and the $\overline{Q}$ output is high. This output is applied to one of the inputs of AND gate N2. The other input of N2 is in parallel with the second input of N1. From here on the circuit action is similar to that described above, but in this case T3 conducts to turn on triac Tri2 and this causes bell 2 to ring.

The width of the pulses caused by the closing of S1 is preset by P1, while the duration of the signal, and therefore of the ringing, is determined by P2.

The two triacs make it possible for a standard bell transformer to be used.

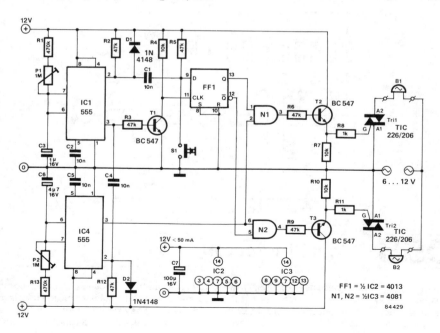

FF1 = ½ IC2 = 4013
N1, N2 = ½ IC3 = 4081

84429

054 switch indicator

It is sometimes necessary to generate a pulse as soon as a mechanical switch is operated. The circuit proposed here does just that and only needs a small number of components. Furthermore, it can easily be expanded for more contacts. The circuit diagram shows the layout for a six-way switch. An important feature of the circuit is that it works with both make-before-break and break-before-make switches.

A couple of XOR gates (N1 and N2) are used to detect when switching takes place; N1 handles positions 1...4 and N2 takes care of positions 5 and 6. A number of LEDs (D1...D6) indicate the switch position selected. Every time the position is switched the level at the output of N2 changes, thereby triggering the monostable multivibrator consisting of N3, R1 and C1. With the values stated, this causes a 200 μs pulse to be output at pin 8 of N3.

When building this circuit it must be remembered that the inputs of N1 and N2 have pull-up resistors (R2 . . . R4) so there is always a defined level present. The value of

the resistors is not at all critical. The LEDs with their resistors may be left out if a visual indication of the switch position in not desired. Extra XOR gates will have to be included if the number of switch positions is higher than six. These are added in the same way as N2 (so with 8 inputs an extra XOR is placed between N2 and the MMV, the free input to the gate is then connected to switch position 7 and position 8 only gets a LED and resistor.

Either TTL or CMOS ICs can be used for the XORs, such as 74LS86, 74HC86, 4030, or 4070. If TTL is used, the output pulse will not always have the same width as the MMV reacts at different levels of the waveform. The supply voltage for a TTL or HCMOS version is 5 V, in other cases 3...15 V is permissible. The length of the output pulse may be changed by using different values for R1 and/or C1. If CMOS ICs are used, the value of R1 can be as high as a few megaohms. The current consumption with CMOS is 10 mA, with TTL this rises to 20 mA.

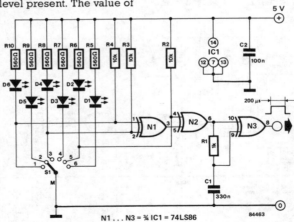

N1 . . . N3 = ¾ IC1 = 74LS86   84463

055 level indicator

Compact cassettes, because of their low cost and easy availability, have been the mainstay memory in personal and hobby computers for almost as long as these have

been available. These cassettes convert digital computer data into audio signals and vice versa. They can, however, not prevent drop-outs caused by wrongly set signal

62

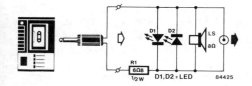

(audible as two quite distinct tones), or whether the cassette content is between two programmes (when only a slight hiss is heard).

The indicator is connected to the ear-piece socket on the recorder by the jack plug and the cassette interface input via the coaxial socket. Most cassette interfaces need a signal level of 2 V_{pp}. When the signal provided by the recorder is at about this level, the LEDs begin to flicker; if the level is too high, they light continuously.

If the loudspeaker volume is too high, connect a 100 Ω preset in series with it, so that the volume may be adjusted to personal requirement.

levels. The present level indicator can help to prevent these mishaps.

All that's needed to build the indicator is a 3.5 mm jack plug, two LEDs, a resistor, small loudspeaker, and a jack socket. The LEDs are connected in anti-parallel. The loudspeaker serves as a monitor to indicate whether the recorder is emitting signals

056 fast analogue to digital converter

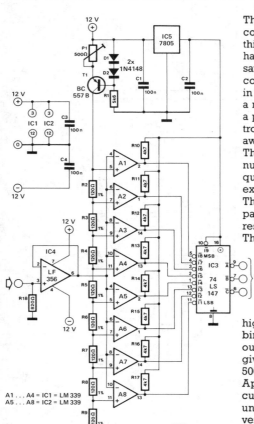

The design for a fast analogue to digital converter shown here clearly shows that this type of circuit does not necessarily have to be complicated. Instead of the usual sawtooth generator + comparator + counter + oscillator, we have used a system in which a fixed reference voltage is fed to a number of comparators. This is known as a parallel converter. The delay normally introduced by the counting process is done away with so the whole process is very fast. The disadvantage of this set-up is the large number of components as each step requires a comparator, but in the three-bit example here that is not a problem.

The reference voltages for the various comparators are generated by a series of 1% resistors and a current source based on T1. The conversion factor is set with P1 ($U_{ref} = 1.5 \ldots 9$ V). The analogue input voltage is fed via buffer stage IC4 to the inverting inputs of A1 . . . A8. A priority encoder is used for the conversion to binary code. It achieves this by translating the number of the highest comparator actuated into a three-bit binary code which appears (inverted) at the output of IC3. With the component values given, the circuit will operate up to about 500 kHz.

Apart from the usual applications, this circuit can also be used, for instance, to make unusual effects in a video signal or to convert a black and white picture to colour, when used with a video combiner. If a PAL

63

or SECAM signal is applied to the circuit, an extra 4.43 MHz notch filter must be added at the input. The circuit can be matched to the normal 75 Ω video cable by connecting an 82 Ω resistor in parallel with R18, with the 4.43 MHz filter between the two resistors.

057 microcomputer power supply

The attraction of this power supply is based on two of its characteristics. First of all it is extremely compact and secondly it supplies three, or strictly speaking four, voltages: +5 V/3 A, +12 V/2 A, and a symmetrical ± 12 V/250 mA. The credit for the compactness is due to the fact that only one transformer is used for the three voltages. It is a toroidal transformer made by ILP (they call it a 4T344) and has three secondary

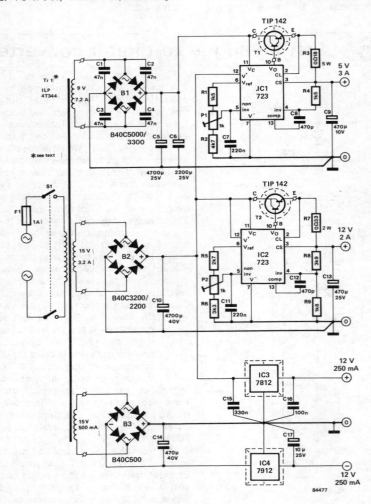

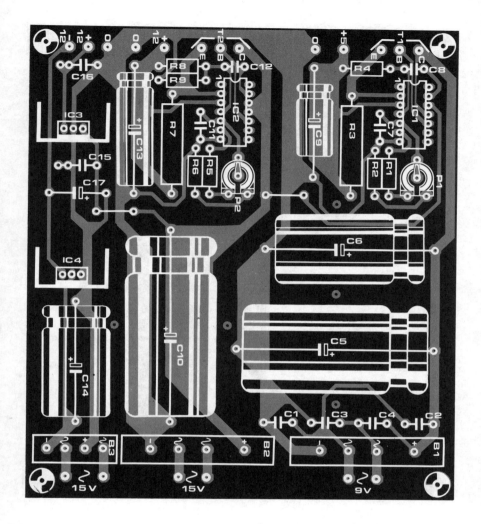

Parts list

Resistors:
R1,R4 = 1k5
R2 = 4k7
R3 = 0R18/5 W
R5 = 2k7
R6 = 3k3
R7 = 0R33/2 W
R8 = 3k9
R9 = 1k8
P1,P2 = 1 k preset

Capacitors:
C1 . . . C4 = 47 n
C5 = 4700 µ/25 V
C6 = 2200 µ/25 V
C7,C11 = 220 n
C8,C12 = 470 p
C9 = 470 µ/10 V
C10 = 4700 µ/40 V
C13 = 470 µ/25 V
C14 = 470 µ/40 V
C15 = 330 n
C16 = 100 n
C17 = 10 µ/25 V

Semiconductors:
B1 = bridge rectifier, 5 A/40 V, e.g.
  B40C5000/3300
B2 = bridge rectifier, 3.2 A/40 V, e.g.
  B40C3200/2200
B3 = bridge rectifier, 500 mA/40 V, e.g. B40C500
T1,T2 = TIP 142
IC1,IC2 = LM 723
IC3 = 7812
IC4 = 7912

Miscellaneous:
F1 = fuse, 1 A slow blow
Tr1 = toroidal transformer, ILP no. 4T344
Heat sink for T1 + T2, max. 1.5°C/W
2 off heatsink for IC3 and IC4, max. 15°C/W
S1 = double pole mains switch

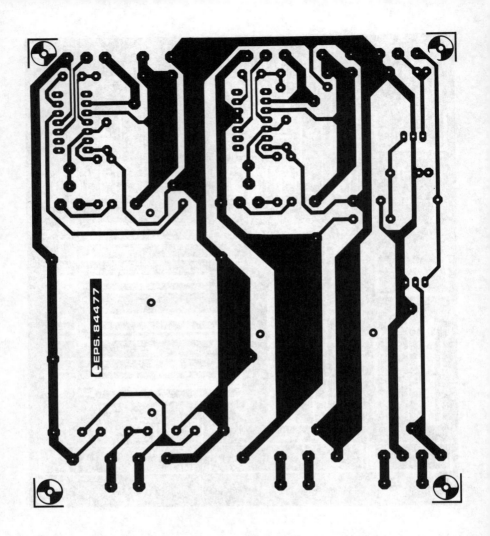

EPS.84477

windings of 9 V/7.2 A, 15 V/3.2 A, and 15 V/0.5 A. It could, of course, be replaced by three separate transformers but then the circuit would lose a lot of its charm.

We felt no need to re-invent the wheel as regards the voltage regulating circuitry. A pair of 723s followed by TIP 142s to do the heavy work are used for the 5 V and 12 V. The symmetrical ± 12 V is provided via a 7812 and a 7912 (IC3 and IC4). Thanks to the printed circuit board of figure 2, building this power supply is straightforward. It is important to mount transistors T1 and T2 on a heat sink. This should have a temperature rise of a maximum of 1.5°C/W and can be

common to both transistors. Each of the transistors must, of course, be fitted with a mica washer between it and the heat sink. Voltage regulators IC3 and IC4 must each be provided with a heat sink of 15°C/W. The noise suppression in this power supply proved very good when we tested the prototypes. At full load there was barely a ripple to be seen on the oscilloscope even when it was set to 10 mV per division. The stability was also shown to be excellent. Switching from full load to no load gave a voltage difference of only a few millivolts. Two final remarks. As we have already said, the toroidal transformer can be replaced by three separate ones. In this case the minimum needed is one 9 V/5 A transformer, one 15 V/3.2 A, and one 15 V/0.4 A. If you wish to protect this supply against overvoltages and short-circuits this can easily be done by adding the *microcomputer power supply protection* described in circuit 1.

058 stereo balance indicator

Mechanical deficiencies that affect the sound reproduction in a stereo amplifier are perhaps the last you think about when problems are encountered. And yet, they play a larger role than is generally known. True, their effects are normally so small that few of us notice them, or ascribe them to something else.

Most of such deficiencies can be traced back to the stereo volume control, in which the two resistance tracks are often out of step. The consequent difference in volume between the two channels can normally be evened up by the balance control.

If you wish to determine the exact difference, the present stereo balance indicator should be right up your street! Simply connect this to the left-hand and right-hand loudspeaker output terminals of the amplifier and feed equal signals — preferably sinusoidal — to the two input channels of the amplifier. If then the signals at the two loudspeaker terminals are of exactly the same level, the centre-zero meter in the

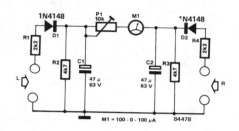

M1 = 100 - 0 - 100 μA   84478

balance indicator will not deflect. If, however, the level of the signal in the left-hand channel is higher than that of the signal in the right-hand channel, the meter will deflect towards the left (or to the right in the opposite case). The balance control can in that case be adjusted till the meter reads zero again: the effect of the volume control tracks being out of step has then been eliminated.

Preset P1 in the balance indicator should be adjusted for full-scale deflection of the meter when only one channel is operating.

059 three-state indicator

The circuit presented here was designed primarily for 6502 users. It indicates which of the following signals occurred last
RESET = $\overline{RES}$ = 0
INTERRUPT REQUEST = $\overline{IRQ}$ = 0
NON-MASKABLE INTERRUPT = $\overline{NMI}$ = 0
This information is particularly helpful in the event of failure of a 6502 microprocessor system. It is equally useful during the handling of specific software for such a system.

The circuit effectively forms a three-state indicator and consists of three NAND gate latches. Each latch is set by one of the three signals mentioned above. When that happens, the latch in question resets the other

two latches via the relevant diodes. At the same time the high Q level causes the relevant transistor to conduct and this in turn makes the appropriate LED light. This LED will remain on until one of the other two latches is set.

An auto reset is also provided but this should be omitted if the particular 6502 system has an automatic reset circuit. In the latter case, it is, of course, the very task of the present circuit to indicate that RES was the last (and first!) of the three signals. If the auto reset is fitted, it will ensure that the LEDs are switched off when the circuit is first switched on.

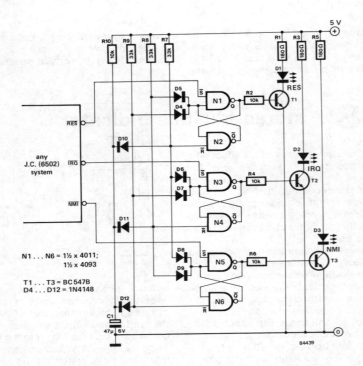

060 self-switching battery charger

This is a charger designed specially for batteries that are not used for long periods, e.g. those of motorcycles that are laid up for the winter. You then take the battery from the vehicle and connect it permanently to the charger, which is switched on one or two times during a week. The battery is charged and when it has reached nominal voltage, the charger switches itself off. It remains on standby, however, and when the battery voltage has dropped below the nominal value, it switches itself on again.

Suppose that the battery in the circuit diagram has a voltage below its nominal value. As soon as the charger is switched on, a current flows through D3 to the gate of silicon-controlled rectifier (SCR) Th1. The SCR conducts and a charging current flows through the battery that is indicated by ammeter M. The battery voltage increases gradually and with it the potential across R1/P1. Capacitor C1 then charges and at a given level of voltage across it, zener diode

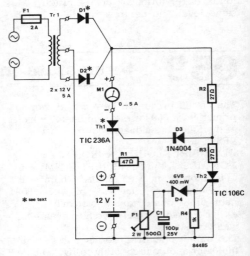

D4 starts to conduct. A current then flows to the gate of Th2: this SCR conducts and causes the gate current to Th1 to drop

68

below the holding value. When that happens, Th1 cuts off and switches the charging current to the battery off: the ammeter then reads 0. When after some time the battery voltage drops below its nominal value again, the gate current to Th2 drops. SCR Th2 then cuts off, the gate current to Th1 increases, that SCR conducts, and a charging current flows again to the battery.

The charger is calibrated by connecting a fully-charged battery in the circuit and adjusting P1 so that just no current flows through the ammeter.

Note that the transformer must not be called upon to deliver more than 5 A charging current. This is because when Th1 con-ducts its only load is formed by the transformer secondary and the battery.

For security of operation, Th1 should be able to switch currents of up to 10 A: the TIC 236A and TIC 246A, for instance, meet this requirement. The same applies to the silicon rectifier diodes for which the SKN26/04, SD25, BYS24-90, for instance, are suitable. The maximum forward current of these diodes should not be below 8 A!

General Electric, Auburn, N.Y., U.S.A.
Notice 630.15

061   VHF dipper

Way back when electronics was still young (shortly after the stone age) when grids, anodes, and cathodes were all the rage, this device would have been called a grid dipper. Now it is more likely to be called a dip meter or a transistor dipper. No matter what it is called, it is still the same instrument, and in the handy transistorized form shown here it is an indispensable aid for any HF handyman.

Before we start describing the circuit, we must first establish exactly what a dip meter is. A dip meter could be considered as a sort of frequency meter whose purpose in life is to define the resonant frequency of LC circuits. The circuits do not have to radiate.

To see how the meter works we can best go straight to the circuit diagram. The parts that make up a dip meter are always the same: a tuneable oscillator, a rectifier, and a moving coil meter. The oscillator here is based on T1 and T2, and is tuned by capacitor C1 and coil Lx. This coil is fitted outside the metal case into which the circuit must be built, and must be easily exchangeable for a different coil to enable the range to be changed.

When the dipper is switched on, the oscillating voltage generated is rectified (by D1 and C2) and is then passed to the meter via P1, which adjusts the meter reading. Nothing unusual so far, but now comes the interesting bit. If Lx is inductively coupled to the coil of some other LC

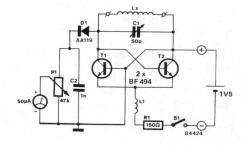

L1 = 10 turns of 0.5 mm enamelled copper wire on 5 mm ⌀ without a former
Lx = see text

circuit, whose resonant frequency is the same as the oscillator frequency of our dipper, this other coil will draw energy from the oscillator coil. The result is that the voltage across the meter drops and the reading is reduced.

What happens in practice is this: the dipper is switched on and P1 is adjusted so that the meter gives maximum, or almost maximum, deflection. The coil of the LC circuit to be measured is now placed close to Lx and C1 is adjusted until the meter reading shows a clear 'dip'. The frequency can now be read off from the graduated scale on C1.

This graduation is where Murphy gets his hand in. A second, graduated, dip meter or — even better — a frequency meter is needed for this. With the layout shown here and a free wound coil (without a former) of 2 turns of 1 mm (SWG 19) copper wire with

69

a diameter of about 15 mm, the range of the dip meter is about 50 ... 150 MHz. A coil could be wound on a DIN plug and a DIN socket mounted in the case of the dip meter to facilitate easy changing of the inductor. A few points to note. The BF 494 transistors in the oscillator can only handle up to about 150 MHz. If higher frequencies are contemplated, these transistors must be replaced by another type, such as the BFR 91 which allows up to 250 MHz. Capacitor C1 could be the 50 pF capacitor from the Jackson C804 range, but a cheaper solution is to use two 100 pF mica capacitors con-

nected in series. Another possibility is to get hold of an (old) four-gang FM tuning capacitor and link the four sections, each of which is about 10 to 14 pF, in parallel. Finally: any dip meter, including this one, can, in principle, also be used as an absorption meter or field strength meter. To use it as such, leave the voltage supply of the meter off and look not for a dip but rather for the maximum reading on the moving coil meter.

P. Engel

062 electronic key-set

This electronic key-set, although similar to its mechanical counterpart (switching, interlocking, reciprocal release, and so on) has one important advantage over it: when two or more keys are pressed simultaneously, all contacts remain open, which is by no means guaranteed with a mechanical set. The latter may actually allow several contacts to close at the same time, which can have disastrous consequences.

The circuit is simplicity itself: five standard or miniature push-button switches, two ICs, four resistors, six diodes, and five LEDs.

The heart of the circuit is IC2, a BCD-to-decimal decoder type 4028. This guarantees that whatever the input information only one of its outputs is logic high (= switch closed).

To start at the beginning: inputs A ... D of IC2 are at low logic level via resistors R3 ... R6 and the 0 output is therefore logic 1. This is inverted by N1 which causes D1 to light. If then, for instance, S1 is pressed, input A goes high while the other inputs remain low. The decoder then switches from output 0 to output 1. The high level output at pin 14 is fed back (inter-

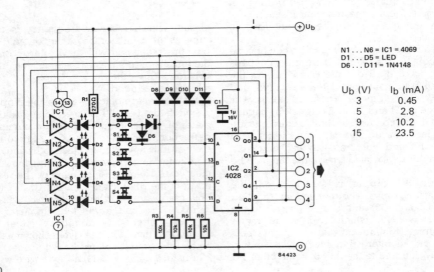

N1 ... N6 = IC1 = 4069
D1 ... D5 = LED
D6 ... D11 = 1N4148

Ub (V)	Ib (mA)
3	0.45
5	2.8
9	10.2
15	23.5

84423

locked) to input A via diode D11 so that a stable situation ensues and this continues even after S1 has been released. The level on pin 14 is also inverted by N2 so that D2 lights.

To activate output 3, switch S3 should be closed briefly. As input A is still high when C becomes high, the input information to the decoder is briefly 0101 (decimal 5), and IC2 therefore activates output 5 which has not been connected. As output 1 then goes low, the feedback to input A disappears and pin 10 becomes logic 0. Only input C is then high and IC2 switches on output 3. The interlock now lies across D9 to input C. Simultaneously, the level on pin 1 is inverted by N4 which causes D4 to light. The operation is similar when the other push buttons are pressed.

Because only decimal outputs Q0 ... Q4

and Q8 of IC2 are terminated, only the corresponding binary inputs can change the state of IC2. This is, however, only so if just one switch is pressed. When more are operated simultaneously, IC2 receives input information that activates non-terminated decimal outputs. The terminated outputs are logic low as long as the switches are pressed, and all LEDs remain off.

Switch S0 activates output 0: the input information to IC2 is then 1001 (decimal 9) As the corresponding output is not terminated, there is no interlock to the input, so that inputs A ... D go low as soon as S0 is released.

H.J. Probst

063 automatic reserve warning light

Warning lights fulfill an undeniably important role in many technical installations. However, even in the best of equipment, these lamps can fail. A glowing filament was never intended to have an indefinite lifespan. The circuit here cannot prevent the filament from failing, but it ensures that if the warning lamp cannot light, for whatever reason, a reserve light is automatically switched on. This secondary bulb, moreover, will only light when it is absolutely necessary, that is, to indicate a fault in the equipment.

Apart from the two lamps, the total component count for this circuit is just two transistors and two resistors. The principle of the circuit is very simple: assuming there is a fault in the equipment, lamp La1 lights and a small part of the lamp's current flows to the base of T1, causing this transistor to conduct. As a result of this, the base of T2 is effectively shorted to earth and this transistor cannot conduct. No current flows through the reserve light (La2) in the collector line of T2, so La2 is not lit.

As soon as La1 goes out, owing to a bad contact, for example, or because the bulb is blown, the base current to T1 is cut off so this transistor immediately switches off. The current that flows through R2 then

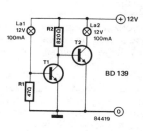

causes T2 to conduct and the reserve lamp lights.

Lamps which need a higher voltage than the 12 V given in our diagram can, of course, also be used in this circuit configuration. The components must then, however, be modified to suit the new situation.

ITT application

064 simple regulated power supply

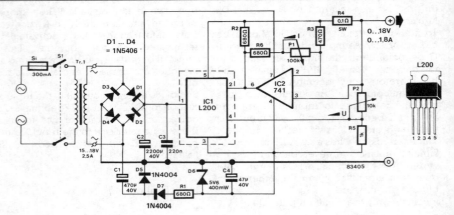

If you compare the expense and the rating of this power supply you will get a surprise, because the output voltage and current are fully adjustable between 0...18 V and 0...1.8 A respectively and costs have still been kept very reasonable. Refering to the circuit diagram: the input comprises a mains switch, fuse, transformer, bridge rectifier, and smoothing capacitor (C2). Diode D5 and capacitor C1 produce a negative auxiliary voltage, which is stabilized by zener diode D6 and capacitor C4. The negative voltage provides the negative supply for the two ICs.

All this is necessary to enable the output voltage to be adjusted down to zero volts. During the construction of this part of the circuit bear in mind that the positive lead of electrolytic capacitor C4 is connected to earth!

Regulation is provided by IC1 and IC2. Capacitor C3 suppresses any residual tran-

sients at the input of IC1 and it should therefore be connected as closely as possible to IC1 (similary C4 and IC2).

The reference level output from pin 4 of IC1 goes to the voltage divider made up of R5 and P2 (this pot sets the value of the output voltage). IC2 is connected as a differential amplifier and compares the signals at its two inputs. The difference between the inputs is the voltage drop across 'current' sensor R4. This IC feeds the current sensing input (pin 2) of the L200. P1 in the feedback loop of the 741 is used to vary the output current of the circuit.

IC1 must be mounted on a suitable heat sink as it dissipates nearly all the power of the circuit. The power supply can quite easily be built into a case and a voltmeter and ammeter mounted on the front panel. In view of the accuracy of the circuit these should ideally be digital meters, but virtually any type will do.

065 funny bird

Birds of all sorts are lovingly owned by many people, but most of them have, unfortunately (?), not yet learnt to communicate with us (or we with them?). Our bird has taken a step in the right direction: when you whistle at it, it chirps back.

The necessary circuit has been split into

two sections. The first is constructed around opamps A1 ... A4. The incoming whistle received by the microphone is amplified in A1 the gain factor of which can be set between 20 and 500 by P1.

To ensure that the bird really reacts to a whistle, the input signal is filtered in A2. It

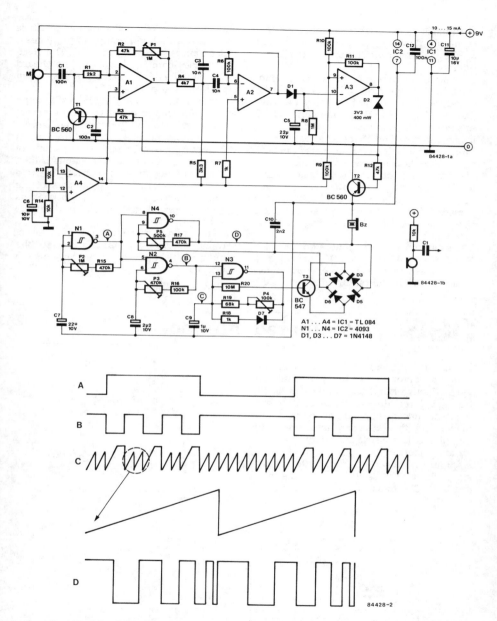

84428-2

is then rectified by D1 and decoupled by C5. Opamp A3, fundamentally a trigger with hysteresis, functions here as a monostable multivibrator (MMV). Its output (with an incoming whistle) remains logic 0 until C5 has discharged via R8 to such an extent that the voltage across it lies below the hysteresis threshold of A3. As long as the output (pin 8) is logic 0, p-n-p transistor T2 conducts and connects the earth return of the supply to the second section of the circuit.

As opamps A1 ... A3 require a symmetrical supply, impedance inverter A4

73

produces a voltage whose level is half that of the supply voltage, and which is applied to the non-inverting inputs of the other opamps.

As long as the output of A3 is low, T1 conducts and consequently short-circuits the microphone, which is necessary to avoid positive feedback. Delay network C2/R3 ensures that T1 continues to conduct for an instant after A3 has changed state.

The response of the bird emanates from the second section of the circuit, more precisely a voltage-controlled oscillator (VCO) formed by N4, D3 . . . D6, T3, and associated components. If the base of T3 is provided with a sawtooth pulse train at a rate of a few hertz, a chirping noise is produced.

The sawtooth signal is generated by gates N1 . . . N3. NAND gate N1 provides a square wave to oscillator N2, which functions only when the output of N1 is logic 1

(see figure 2). When the output of N2 is logic 1, sawtooth generator N3 produces a pulse train as shown in figure 2C. The ensuing noise cannot, however, be heard because the VCO is blocked by the output signal of N1 at pin 8 of N4.

As soon as the output of N2 becomes logic low, N3 ceases to oscillate and its output voltage tends to rise to the positive supply level. It is because N2 and N3 oscillate at different frequencies that a totally arbitrary sawtooth signal ensues. That signal is then pulse-frequency modulated by N4 to drive the piezo buzzer. The frequencies of the oscillators may be varied with P2 . . . P5 as appropriate, so that a range of bird sounds can be produced.

When a two-terminal instead of a three-terminal electret microphone is used, the input circuit should be altered as shown in figure 1b.

066   µP infra-red interface

In general the normal connections between a computer and its peripherals are very effective but these cables can hardly be considered decorative. A cable carrying serial information can, however, be replaced by this infra-red interface even though it only consists of a simple transmitter and receiver.

As figure 1 shows, the transmitter uses a single BC 557B transistor to drive the infrared LED. The transistor is itself controlled

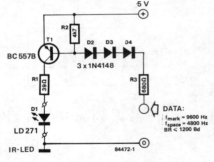

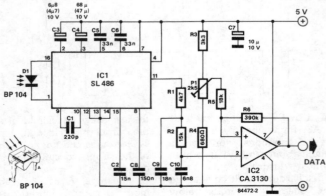

by the microprocessor so a short program is required to make the computer generate the transmitter signals needed. The frequencies used here are 4800 and 9600 Hz and the maximum baud rate at these frequencies is 1200.

The receiver, seen in figure 2, makes use of an IC (the SL486) especially developed for infra-red applications. This contains several gain stages, a pulse-width expander, and a voltage regulator. The receiver diode (D1) is connected directly to the IC. The stretch output, pin 11, is connected to the low-pass

filter made up of R1, R2, C9, and C10 and this, in turn, feeds schmitt trigger IC2. The decoded data is then available at the output of this IC.

When fitting the components to the printed circuit boards shown in figure 3 it is important to remember that the leads for the receiver diode should be kept as short as possible. The 5 V supply for the boards can be taken from the computer or peripheral device. The only calibration needed concerns preset P1 which must be trimmed so that the data is received with no errors.

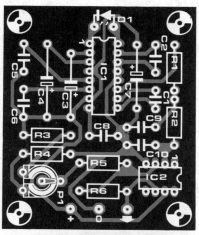

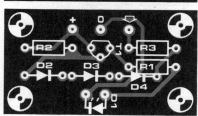

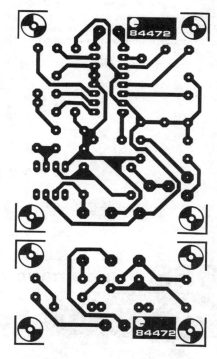

Capacitors:
C1 = 220 p
C2 = 15 n
C3 = 6µ8 (4µ7)/10 V
C4 = 68 µ (47 µ)/10 V
C5,C6 = 33 n
C7 = 10 µ/10 V
C8 = 150 n
C9 = 18 n
C10 = 6n8

Semiconductors:
D1 = infra-red detector, e.g. BP 104
IC1 = SL 486
IC2 = CA 3130

Parts list

— Receiver

Resistors:
R1 = 4k7
R2 = 15 k
R3 = 3k3
R4 = 680 Ω
R5 = 18 k
R6 = 390 k
P1 = 2k5 preset

Parts list

— Transmitter

Resistors:
R1 = 39 Ω
R2 = 4k7
R3 = 680 Ω

Semiconductors:
D1 = infra-red LED, e.g. LD 271
D2 . . . D4 = 1N4148
T1 = BC 557B

067 infra-red wireless transmitter

This circuit is intended for use with the receiver described in circuit 021 to form the simplest infra-red wireless system imaginable. It uses pulse width modulation (PWM) which, although unsuitable for critical hi-fi applications, gives a reasonable quality and has an acceptable range.

The transmitter is based on an LM 567 tone decoder IC. The layout is somewhat unusual but the chip's internal VCO and switching stage combine to give much better linearity than could be achieved with, for example, a simple circuit based on a 555 timer IC.

The operation of the circuit is quite straightforward. The audio signal (at least 50 mV$_{pp}$) is amplified by transistor T1 and is then used to modulate IC1. Pin 6 of the 567 is the trigger input so that the audio signal is superimposed on an HF (about 50 kHz) triangular signal. This causes the rectangular output signal to be pulse width modulated. The remainder of the IC is used as a buffer so that the 567 can drive infrared LED D1 direct (at a peak current of at least 100 mA) without the need of any external components. The transmission frequency can be set between about 25 and 40 kHz by preset P2.

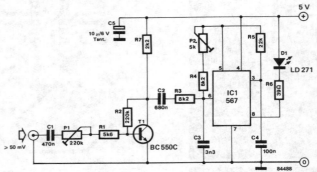

068 automatic cloakroom light

This circuit should put an end to your guests fumbling for the light switch in the cloakroom. It ensures automatically that the light is switched on as soon as someone enters the cloakroom and is switched off again when that person leaves.

The principle of the circuit is fairly simple. The bistables in a 4013 CMOS IC are connected in series. One, FF2, is arranged as an R-S latch to debounce the switch. This switch, S1, must change over as soon as the door is opened and is therefore best located in the door-frame. When the door is opened, FF2 is set and its output (pin 13) goes therefore high. This clocks FF1 on pin 3 and this bistable toggles: its output goes high and this switches on transistor T1. The transistor current actuates a relay

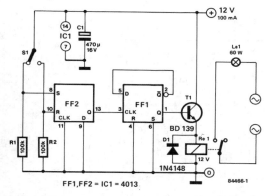

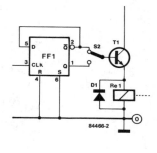

FF1,FF2 = IC1 = 4013

84466-1

84466-2

and the light is switched on. When the door is closed, nothing happens because FF2 is reset and its output on pin 13 goes low. It's only when the door is opened again that FF1 changes state: pin 13 then goes high and this causes FF1 to toggle. The output at pin 1 then goes low and cuts off the transistor so that the relay is deenergized and the light goes out. The relay should operate from voltages between 5 and 15 V.
Because the door may be opened and closed without anyone entering, it is possible that the light gets out of step with requirements. This can, of course, be remedied by opening and shutting the door again, but a better way is to connect a second switch, S2, as shown in figure 2. This switch reverses FF1 and brings matters back into step.
The circuit diagram in figure 1 shows S1 in position 'door open' and bistable FF2 is then set.

069   'lights on' warning

Who has not at one time or another forgotten to switch off his car's lights on a murky morning? That is not much of a problem when colleagues or passers-by are kind enough to draw your attention to it. But if there are no such friendly souls about, you may at the end of the day find that your battery is as flat as a pancake. Some modern cars have a factory-fitted warning unit, others have their wiring arranged such that when the ignition is switched off only parking lights can be left on. The majority of cars, however, are not protected against such an oversight and it is for those that we have developed the present warning circuit. This has an advantage over other similar circuits in that you can switch on your headlights when the ignition is switched off.
The circuit is based on two astable multivibrators (AMVs) of which the first is formed by NAND gates N1/N2 and associated components. It operates as a clock with a frequency of about 20 Hz. The

second AMV, based on N3/N4, operates as a tone generator at a frequency of about 3300 Hz.
The clock and tone generator are controlled by a transistor-relay logic circuit which obtains its data from the car's electrical system.
The warning unit is connected to the car's electrical system at terminals 15, 58 (56), and M in the circuit diagram. These are DIN designations used in the majority of cars; if yours is an exception, 15 is the ignition coil terminal, 56 is the centre contact of the dip switch, 58 is the parking light terminal, and M is the earth. The broken lines in the circuit indicate parts already fitted in the car: L is the lights switch, Z is the ignition switch with underneath it the ignition coil and contact breaker.
When with the ignition switched on, the lights are turned on, transistor T1 conducts. At the same time, relay Re is actuated and short-circuits the collector-emitter junction of T1. Although this connects the +12 V

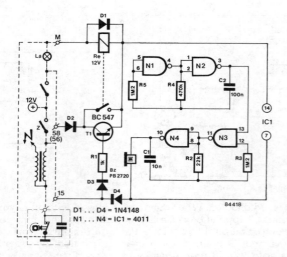

line to pin 14 of IC1, the AMV does not yet operate because pin 7 is not connected to earth. There is therefore no alarm tone from the buzzer.

If now the ignition is switched off, the relay remains actuated and the +12 V line connected to pin 14 of IC1. Pin 7 of the IC is then connected to earth by the contact breaker or other load via diode D4. Both generators now function and the buzzer

emits a warning note. If the lights are then switched off, the relay is no longer actuated, and the +12 V line is removed from pin 14 of IC1, which stops the generators. If the lights are required to remain on, the lights switch can simply be turned on: the alarm will then not be activated.

H. Braubach

070 sync separator

This little circuit can separate the synchronization section from the rest of a video signal. When supplied with a composite video signal of at least 0.5 V_{pp}, the circuit outputs quite a respectable (9 V_{pp}) synchronization signal. This is eminently suitable for use with the video effect circuit no. 56.

The basis of the circuit is a comparator consisting of two transistors, the inverting input (T2) of which is connected to a fixed d.c. voltage. When the input signal at the non-inverting input (the base of T1) falls below the voltage set at the base of T2 (about 3.6 V), transistor T1 switches off and T2 conducts. If a video signal is applied to the in-

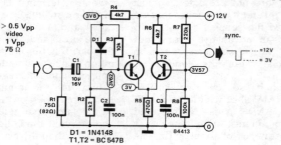

put, the d.c. voltage setting of T1 will be slightly higher than that of T2. On top of this the base setting circuit of T1 contains a clamping diode which will only allow a very small change in the negative direction (roughly 0.4 V). The result of all this is that the video signal at the base of T1 will never fall below about 3.2 V. This limiting of the lower values means that only a small part of the input signal (provided it is larger than the minimum value) will affect the output signal. In the positive direction T1 simply conducts all the more and T2 remains switched off (the output is then about 12 V). During the sync section, however, T1 will switch off so the sync pulses appear, amplified, at the output.

The current consumption of the circuit is only a few milliamps.

071 switching delay

It is sometimes required that one of two parallel-operating units is switched on just after, and switched off just before, the other. An example is in film or camera work where the lights must be switched on just before the camera, and switched off just after it. The present circuit provides such a delay. Because the IC we used contains four NAND schmitt triggers, of which only two are needed for the delay circuit, we took the opportunity of providing a de-bouncing latch.

In the circuit diagram, N1/N2 form the de-bouncing latch, and N3/N4 the delay circuit. Suppose that switch S1 is in the off position. The output of N2 is then low, capacitors C1 and C2 are discharged, and the outputs of N3 and N4 are high. The base potential of p-n-p transistors T1 and T2 is then almost equal to the emitter voltage so that the transistors are cut off and the relays,

Rel and Re2, are at rest.

When S1 is turned on, the output of N2 becomes high, and C2 is charged instantaneously via D3. The output of N4 goes low and consequently the base of T2 becomes more negative than the emitter. This transistor then conducts and Re2 is actuated.

At the same time, capacitor C1 charges also, but more slowly, via D2 and R2; the output of N3 does not go low until the voltage across C1 has reached the threshold value of the gate. When the level on pin 4 of N3 is low, T1 conducts, and Rel is actuated.

When S1 is switched off again, C1 discharges instantaneously over D1, so that Rel returns to rest at once. Capacitor C2 on the other hand discharges more slowly over R3 and D4 so that there is a noticeable delay before Re2 is deenergized.

The delay at switch-on depends on the time constant R2/C1, and that at switch-off on

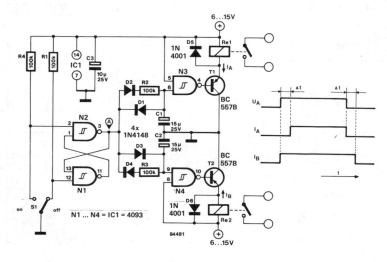

R3/C2. With the values shown, both are 2 . . . 3 seconds.

The circuit requires an operating voltage of 6 . . . 15 V; the current depends on the relays used. The maximum current through a BC 557 should not exceed 100 mA, and the relays should therefore be chosen with that in mind. It is, of course, possible to use transistors which allow a larger current.

from an idea by B. Willaert

072 sawtooth generator

Sawtooth generators are required in electronics for many purposes. Typical examples are found in music electronics where the rectangular output of a single octave divider must be converted into a sawtooth-shaped signal, or in measurement technology to provide the control signal for an analogue-to-digital converter.

In spite of its modest configuration, the circuit provides a perfectly usable output signal. The (external) clock pulses are applied to a 7-stage binary counter, a CMOS type 4024 IC. The output signals of the IC, Q0 . . . Q6, are applied together with the clock signal to an opamp which has been connected as a summing integrator. Resistors R1 . . . R8 are so arranged that the value of each is half that of the preceding one. In other words, R2 = ½R1, R5 = ½R4, and so on. The effect of this is that the gain of the opamp doubles for each successive Q output of IC1. For instance, the amplification of output Q2 is two times that of Q1. Since the frequency is halved at each successive Q output, this means that the higher the pulse rate, the lower the amplification as is shown in figure 1. If high stability resistors are used, the resulting steps in the output will be symmetrical; with the values shown small deviations from linearity in the step will occur.

The time/voltage characteristics show clearly how the stepped waveform is built up. For convenience's sake, the inversion in the opamp has been ignored: what is important here is the mathematical relation between the various waveforms. In reality, the stepped waveform would be a descending rather than an ascending one. Where an ascending waveform is required,

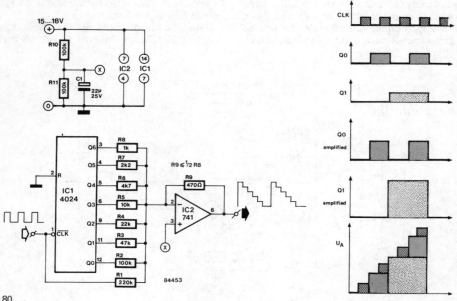

a second opamp with unity gain should be connected to the output.

The output waveform has 256 steps; this number may be halved by omitting R8, halved again by omitting R7, and so on. Resistor R9 must be made about half the value of the last resistor used, as otherwise the height of the output signal will be halved. The fundamental frequency of the sawtooth signal is the same as that of the finally used output of the IC.

The clock signal should have a frequency 256 times the required output frequency. If fewer divider stages are used, the clock frequency may be halved (compound!) for each omitted stage. The height of the clock pulses at Q0 . . . Q6 should preferably be the same to prevent asymmetry of the stepped waveform.

Power requirements are 15 . . . 18 V with a current consumption of about 12 mA.

073 electronic pocket-pinball

This portable pocket-pinball game may not exactly be a substitute for its big brothers in the amusement arcades, but it still provides a lot of fun.

The circuit is relatively simple: three CMOS ICs, nine LEDs, six resistors, one capacitor, one pushbutton and a 9 V battery. Together with R1, R2 and C1, NOR gates N1...N3 form a clock generator whose signal is applied to decimal counter IC3. For as long as the player presses pushbutton S1, clock

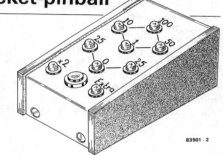

83501 - 2

pulses are counted. When the button is released, the counter is inhibited for the incoming clock signals and only one of LEDs D1...D7 will light. The carry output of the decimal counter toggles bistables FF1 and FF2 which are connected as 2-bit binary counters. Depending on the counter status, the player is entitled to a free ball (LED D8 lights) or he can double the score (LED D9 lights).

Obviously, this simple circuit is not equipped with a points counter. The points gained by each player must therefore be noted on a piece of paper. The values are indicated next to the corresponding LEDs on the circuit diagram. If only one of LEDs D5...D7 lights, the ball is out of play; with "0" it was through the middle, and with "25" to the right or left. It is then the turn of the next player. If, however, D8 lights in addition to the "25" LED, the player has gained a free ball. He can try his luck again.

With a little care, the front panel can be designed with the LEDs positioned in such a way that the game resembles the full-scale pinball machine (figure 2).

H.J. Walter

074 stereo noise suppressor

Weak VHF/FM signals, particularly stereo broadcasts, are normally received against a background of noise. When the receiver is then switched over to mono, much of the noise disappears, but so, unfortunately, does the stereo effect. The present circuit reduces the noise drastically, but does not eliminate the stereo effect. A potentiometer allows selection of the best compromise between noise and channel separation. The circuit is simply inserted between the tuner and the amplifier.

Inputs and outputs are isolated from direct voltages by coupling capacitors C1, C2, C5, and C6. The input impedance is of the order of 100 k due to resistors R3 and R4 which also provide a direct voltage to operational amplifiers IC1 and IC2. This voltage is half the supply voltage due to voltage divider R1/R2 which is decoupled by C3.

The opamps function as impedance inverters with unity gain. Their outputs are taken to a stereo potentiometer, the minimum value of which is limited to 3k3 by resistors R5 and R6. The output terminals of the two sections of the potentiometer are shunted by capacitor C4 when switch S1 is closed. This capacitor causes frequency-dependent cross-talk between the channels and the consequent decrease in channel separation provides a reduction in noise. The capacitor therefore acts as a low-pass filter. The frequency response of the composite signal is not affected by the action of C4: the difference signal (the stereo component) is, however, attenuated at a rate of 6 dB/octave. The cut-off frequency of the low-pass filter may be set between 1.3 kHz and 5.1 kHz with P1.

The suppressor is switched on and off by S1: with this switch open, the input signal

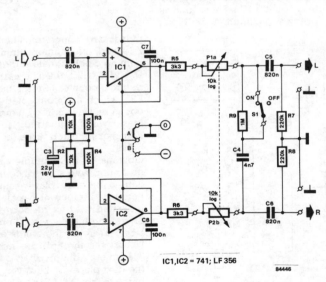

IC1,IC2 = 741; LF 356

Parts list

Resistors:
R1,R2 = 10 k*
R3,R4 = 100 k
R5,R6 = 3k3
R7,R8 = 220 k
R9 = 1 M
P1 = 10 k log. stereo potentiometer

Capacitors:
C1,C2,C5,C6 = 820 n
C3 = 22 μ/16 V*
C4 = 4n7
C7,C8 = 100 n

Semiconductors:
IC1,IC2 = LF 356

Miscellaneous:
S1 = SPST switch
* see text

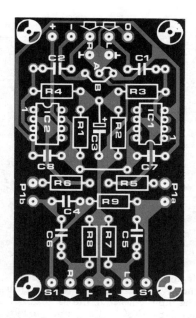

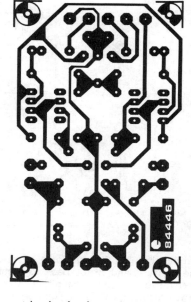

appears unchanged at the output. The output impedance of the circuit depends on the setting of P1: its maximum value is about 14 k.

Current consumption amounts to about 10 mA. As is shown in the circuit, the power supply may be symmetric or non-symmetric: in the latter case the supply voltage may be 9 ... 30 V, when wire bridge A on the printed circuit should be fitted. When a 5 ... 15 V symmetrical supply is used, wire bridge B should be fitted, R2 should be replaced by a wire bridge, and R1 and C3 are omitted.

075 dissipation limiter 1

Most mains power supplies nowadays make use of a voltage regulator IC. These circuits undoubtedly simplify the design and result in a more compact unit. This applies to fixed output as well as to variable output devices. The latter have, however, one unfortunate characteristic: at high input voltage, low output voltage, and low load current, the dissipation in the regulator is maximum.

This loss can be minimized with little additional effort and cost as can be seen from the circuit diagram. In this, the additional components are connected between the bridge rectifier and capacitor C1.

Immediately after switch-on, a zener voltage, U_Z, develops across D5 which causes T1 to conduct. The current through T1 then flows to the gate of silicon-controlled rectifier (SCR) Th1. The SCR then conducts and the consequent current charges C1 via R4. It is only when C1 is charged that the regulator, IC1, provides an output voltage, U_O, whose level is preset with P1.

What happens next becomes clearer from figure 2. Once C1 has been charged to its maximum voltage, U_{C1}, the current through Th1 drops below the holding value and the SCR blocks. Power to the load is now supplied only by C1 which naturally discharges. The rate of the discharge depends on the value of the load current, I_L. When U_{C1} drops below the level of $U_O + U_Z$, T1 and Th1 conduct again so that C1 is charged afresh. And so the process continues ...

The moment T1 and Th1 are turned on, the

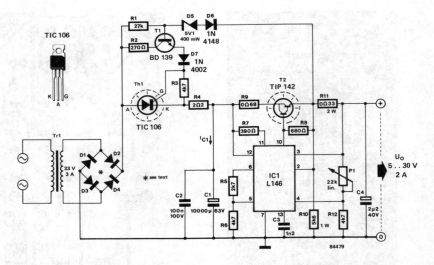

current through C1 suddenly increases (see figure 2) and drops back to nominal when these devices are cut off. The current surges through C1 (or, if you prefer, the switching on of T1 and Th1) occur every half-cycle, or every fourth half-cycle, or whenever, of the pulsating direct voltage (shown in dotted lines in figure 2) at the junction D2-D4. The time when they occur is dependent only on the value of the load.

Because of the surges, diodes D1 . . . D4 should be 10 A types, e.g., SKN 26/04. The input voltage to the regulator IC must not exceed 80 V: the output voltage may then be preset between 5 V and 50 V. Obviously, the transformer, D1 . . . D4, and C1 must be rated to cope with these values.

SGS, Technical Note 145

076 LED current sensor

It is sometimes necessary, or at least desirable, to be able to detect relatively large a.c. currents. One way of doing this is to use a LED in a network with resistors and/or 1N4001 diodes. This is, however, not such a good idea as there will always be a certain amount of voltage 'lost' across the LED if nowhere else.

From a technical point of view there are better ways of detecting the current, such as using current transformers. The advantages of this method are that the current to be measured can be converted to a value that better suits the measuring equipment and the transformer provides a distinct separation between the value that is measured and the measuring equipment. This latter point is particularly important as the measured value is often extremely high.

Moving on to the practical side of things; we have been talking about a current transformer but what we actually used is a normal mains transformer. The low-voltage winding is connected in series with the current that is to be defined. The primary winding is now free to have the LED(s) or other measuring equipment connected to it. When choosing a transformer, bear in mind the maximum current that is expected in the secondary winding and the maximum permitted LED current. Consider this example: the current to be detected is 0.6 A so the low-voltage winding must be able to handle at least this. Assuming that a current of 30 mA is the maximum for the measuring circuit we choose a 240 V/12 V transformer to give us approximately the right ratio (600/30).

The voltage loss across the winding in the

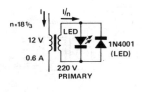

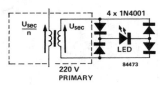

primary circuit is relatively small. In the ideal case the resistance and leakage of the transformer are small enough to be ignored so the voltage loss is only the LED voltage divided by the transformer ratio.

The transformer secondary must always be connected to a load, for both positive and negative half-cycles. This is the reason for adding a second LED or a diode in the circuit. Without this load the primary winding would act as a normal coil which would result in a higher voltage drop across the primary and a higher voltage at the secondary. This diode or LED also protects the LED against high reverse voltages.

077 super simple bell extension

This has got to be one of the simplest electronic bell extension circuits ever designed. In all it contains just seven components and none of them is even slightly unusual. They are the kind of parts that most electronic hobbyists will probably have lying around somewhere.

The telephone bell operates on an a.c. voltage so this must be rectified by the four 1N4148 diodes to make it suitable for the d.c. buzzer. Obviously, the voltage across the buzzer cannot be allowed to rise too high so a resistor is connected in series with the rectifier and a zener diode across the buzzer. The values used give a voltage of about 5 V across the buzzer, but, depending on the type selected, this can

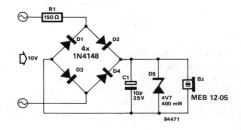

quite easily be changed. Furthermore, if the input voltage is more than about 10 V a.c. the value of the series resistor will have to be increased according to Ohm's law ($U = RI$). Take care not to exceed the buzzer's maximum permitted current.

078 small high-power amplifier

The TDA 2030, made by SGS Ates, is a complete amplifier contained in a single IC with a five-pin pentawatt package. Its class AB output stage can provide a power of 14 W into 4 Ω at a supply voltage of ± 14 V. The amplifier has a built-in short-circuit and overload protection, and also a thermal shutdown. This means that it is not so easy to destroy the IC as long as the supply voltage is kept below the absolute maximum of ± 18 V.

Combining two 2030s with a few inexpensive power transistors forms an amplifier

that can provide quite a lot of power into a load of 2 to 4 Ω. As the diagram shows, the circuit is a standard bridge amplifier so there is little to be said about it. Each half of the bridge consists of a TDA 2030 driving two complementary power transistors. The diodes, D1 . . . D4, are needed to protect the transistors from the loudspeaker coil's inductive voltage. The gain of the whole amplifier is defined by:

$$A = 20 \log_{10} [1 + (R2/R5) + (R8/R5)] \text{ dB.}$$

With the values stated this works out at 32 dB. If the gain is to be changed it must

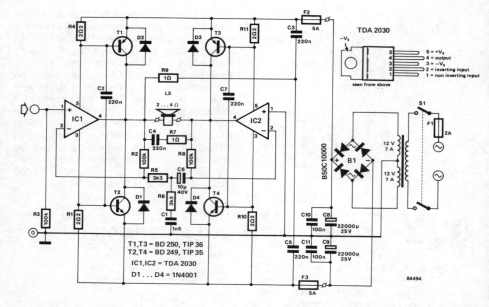

T1,T3 = BD 250, TIP 36
T2,T4 = BD 249, TIP 35
IC1,IC2 = TDA 2030
D1 . . . D4 = 1N4001

TDA 2030

5 = +V_s
4 = output
3 = −V_s
2 = inverting input
1 = non inverting input

seen from above

be remembered that R2 and R8 must have the same value.

The load on the amplifier may also be 2 Ω rather than the more normal 4 Ω if the power transistors stated are used. With a suitable power supply the amplifier can then provide up to 200 W. Large heat sinks are essential, especially in this latter case. The only characteristic we will quote is the distortion, which, at less than 1%, is quite acceptable.

079 electronic mousetrap

This mousetrap is not intended to kill a mouse with the aid of electronics, but rather to imprison it in a gentle way. Afterwards, it may be given its freedom in a suitable area.

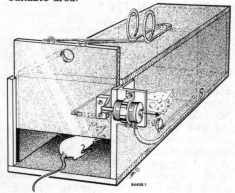

The principle of the trap is the age-old trap-door up-dated by being operated electronically. Figure 1 shows the construction of the device. In this, a small wooden box is divided into two chambers: the larger one is fitted with the trap-door, while the smaller one contains the electronic circuit and power supply.

In spite of the modern construction, some bait is still required, and as of old a piece of bacon or cheese is best for this. On its way to the bait the little rodent breaks the beam of a light barrier and this causes an electromagnet to release the trap-door which then blocks the way out. The distance between the trap-door and the light barrier must be longer than the length of a mouse otherwise the animal's tail will be caught.

How the trap-door is released is shown in figure 1. The light barrier consists of a light-emitting diode, LED D1, and a light-dependent resistor, LDR. When the LDR is illuminated by the LED, it is low-ohmic, and the latch N1/N2 is not set. When the beam of light is broken, the latch changes state, and the consequent logic 1 at the output of N2 triggers monostable multivibrator (MMV) N3/N4 which then imparts a pulse to driver T1/T2. The width of this pulse is about one second which is sufficient to actuate the electro-magnet which then releases the trap-door. Latch N1/N2 ensures that once the circuit is triggered, it does not react to further breaks in the light barrier caused by the mouse moving inside its prison.

The electro-magnet should be home-made,

preferably by using the coil of a spare relay or doorbell. Also suitable are electromagnets as used in cassette and tape recorders.

The required power may be provided by any transformer which has a secondary voltage of 8 . . . 12 V at a current of not less than 100 mA: it may be a bell transformer or of the type used in a battery eliminator. If the device is used only occasionally, a PP3 battery may be adequate. Before placing the mousetrap in position, make sure that it operates satisfactorily. The trap is reset by a spring-loaded push-button, S1. The state of readiness is indicated by the lighting of LED D2.

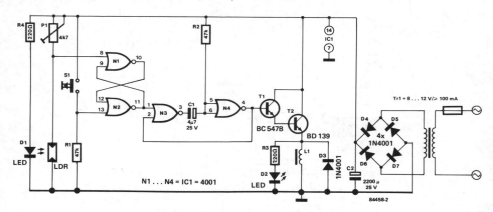

080 alarm clock for cars

The circuit is based on the MM 5387A, a relatively new (though readily available) IC which drives LED displays direct.

For use in a car, a quartz controlled time base is provided around IC2/IC3. The crystal frequency of 3.2768 MHz is divided to a final clock frequency of 50 Hz. If mains operation is used, this part of the circuit may be omitted and the mains frequency used as clock (the mains must, of course, be isolated from the circuit by, for instance, an opto-isolator).

The circuit around IC4 is basically a regulator which controls the brightness of the displays. It should be noted that only one of the cathodes of each display needs to be connected. Diodes D4 and D5 form the

flashing colon between LD2 and LD3. Because the clock is operated in the 12-hour mode, diodes D2 and D3 indicate morning (a.m.) and afternoon (p.m.) respectively.

The car battery voltage is stabilized by R3, L1, C4, and C5, while zener D1 protects the CMOS-ICs. In mains operation, the rectified voltage may be applied directly across C4 (transformer to be used: secondary 12 V, 400 mA; R3, L1, and C5 may be omitted).

The alarm is built around N1 . . . N4. A 1 kHz signal is taken from oscillator IC3 (pin 1) and modulated with a 1 Hz signal from IC1 (pin 39) in N4. The ALARM OUT switches the alarm on and off via N3.

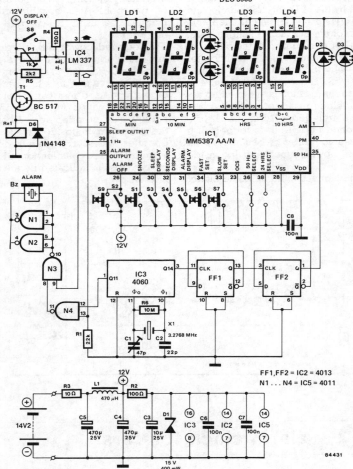

LD1...LD4 = MAN 8440; DLO 3903

FF1,FF2 = IC2 = 4013
N1...N4 = IC5 = 4011

84431

The SLEEP output is buffered by T1 and relay Re so that, for instance, a radio can be switched on and off via a relay contact.

Setting up

Switch on the supply; the display should then flash.

Setting the time: ensure that switches S1...S8 are open. The time can then be set with S6 (fast) and S7 (low).

Setting the alarm: set as time but with S5 closed in addition. Make sure that the switches are opened again after setting, and remember a.m. and p.m.

Setting sleep time: close S3 when the

display will read 00:59. This time may be shortened by pressing S6 and/or S7. As long as S3 is closed, relay Re is actuated until either the indicated time has lapsed or S1 is pressed.

Indicating seconds: close S4.

Alarm: when the alarm goes off, it may be stopped with S9 or S2. Keeping S2 closed disables the alarm permanently. Pressing S1 stops the alarm temporarily: after 8...9 minutes it goes off anew. If the alarm is not switched off manually, it stops automatically after 59 minutes.

If the clock is used without a crystal time base, an external 1 kHz signal must be pro-

88

vided for N4, otherwise the alarm does not work.

To reduce power consumption (particularly in cars), it is possible to switch off the display with S8. This switch may be combined with the ignition switch. Current consumption with the display on is about 200 mA, dropping to about 20 mA when the display is switched off.

081   pace counter

For a change, here is a circuit which is primarily intended for sports people: it can count steps or jumps. From now on, whenever you go through a skipping session in training, this circuit can tell you precisely and at any moment how many jumps you have made.

All you need is a cheap LCD (liquid crystal display) pocket calculator, a small piezo buzzer, a type 4066 CMOS IC, and a few other components.

First, the buzzer has to be prepared as it will serve as the measuring detector. Carefully cut away a strip of the plastic housing and glue a small piece of relatively heavy metal (lead or iron) onto the brass membrane (see figure 2). Because of the increased inertia of the modified membrane it bends at every step or jump. The consequent piezo voltage generated by the buzzer is applied to the input of the circuit.

The piezo signal is amplified by darlington pair T1 and T2, the gain of which is preset by P1. When the signal arrives at T3, it is converted into rectangular pulses which are used to control electronic switches ES1 and ES2. These switches form a monostable multivibrator whose delay is preset with P2. Any pulses arriving during the delay period have no effect whatever so that, for instance, noise pulses are effectively suppressed.

Now comes the question, of course, how to get to the memory of the calculator. To that end, one of the keys of the calculator is connected in parallel with a third electronic switch, ES3. Which key of the calculator is taken depends on the calculator. With many calculators it suffices to input a constant by which the counter position is increased when the + or the M+ key is pressed. With yet other calculators, first the 1 and then the +, or M+, keys are pressed. If you buy a pocket calculator specially for this purpose, make sure that it is possible to increase the memory, and thus the LCD, with one key, by 1 (that is, the constant).

The circuit is very economical as far as current consumption is concerned and can therefore be powered by the calculator battery (normally +3 V).

The counter is best constructed on a small piece of wiring (Vero) board which, after completion, is screwed to the back of the calculator. The buzzer is fitted similarly. Holes need to be drilled in the case for passing the wires to the battery and from ES3.

As far as the setting of the presets is con-

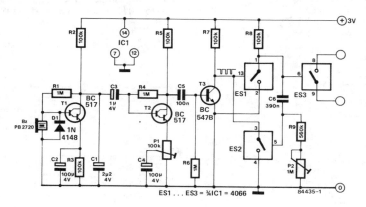

ES1 . . . ES3 = ¾IC1 = 4066   84435–1

cerned, you will have to try what is the best setting, as this will depend on the required sensitivity of the circuit in combination with the particular calculator. The whole assembly is so small that it can easily be slipped into a trouser or breast pocket; it is also possible to hang it round your neck or fix it to one of your legs.

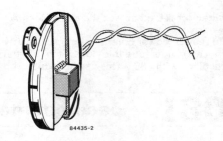

84435-2

082   parallel/serial converter

Parallel/serial converters have numerous applications in computer technology, for instance, in interface circuits for printers with a serial input, or as adapter for a keyboard with parallel output when the computer has one or more serial, but no more parallel, interfaces available.

The circuit is based on four LSTTL ICs: a four-bit synchronous binary counter, IC1, a parallel-load eight-bit shift register, IC2, a quad two-input NAND gate, IC3, and a quad two-input NOR gate, IC4. As the circuit contains neither time-dependent nor discrete elements, you'll have to take care of its control by the system yourself.

In the quiescent state, the binary counter is set to 1010 (decimal 10). This condition is decoded by NAND gates N1 . . . N3 and NOR gate N7 into a stop signal for the counter (the output of N3 = ENABLE in-

put — pin 10 — of IC1 = logic 0). The output of N3 is logic 1 for all other input combinations to N1 and N7.

The shift register is inhibited by the logic high level on output Q_D (pin 11) of IC1. A logic low input at input $\overline{LD}$ ($\overline{XMT}$) actuates the conversion process. The counter is then switched to binary input 1110 (decimal 14) and at the same time the register shifts the data to output Q_H (pin 9).

After $\overline{LD}$ has become high again, the leading edge of the next clock pulse switches the counter to 1111 (decimal 15). The CRY (carry) output (pin 15) of the counter then goes high which causes the serial output, SO, to become logic 0 via N5 and N6. At the following clock pulse the counter proceeds to 0000 and this condition is retained during the next eight clock pulses, that is, until the counter is switched to 0111 (decimal 7); output Q_D is logic 0 during this time. In this period IC2 releases the parallel-loaded data serially, that is, one bit per clock pulse.

At the ninth clock pulse, the counter proceeds to 1000 (decimal 8) and output Q_D

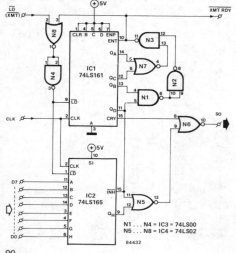

N1 . . . N4 = IC3 = 74LS00
N5 . . . N8 = IC4 = 74LS02

84432

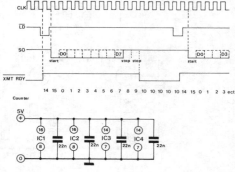

90

becomes logic high again. The two following clock pulses cause N5 and N6 to pass the two stop bits (logic 1). The next counter position is 1010 (decimal 10) and the converter is back in the output condition. The output is logic 1 because of the start bit which is logic 0.

The $\overline{\text{XMTRDY}}$ signal is identical to the output level of N3 and is applied simultaneously with it to one of the inputs of N8. This gate together with gate N4 forms an OR

function. As the level of $\overline{\text{XMTRDY}}$ is logic 1 during the data transfer, $\overline{\text{LD}}$ pulses during that time have no effect whatever.

The circuit works equally well with 8-bit or 7-bit plus parity bit information. If only 7-bit information is to be used, input D7 should be made permanently logic high: a third stop bit should not affect most systems one way or another.

The current consumption of the converter amounts to about 70 mA.

083 transformerless mains power supply

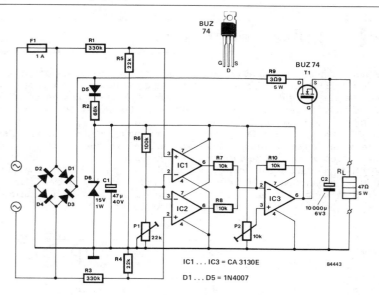

BUZ 74

IC1 ... IC3 = CA 3130E

D1 ... D5 = 1N4007

84443

Warning! This circuit needs to be constructed and wired with the greatest care as the full mains voltage is present at several points.

The pulsating direct voltage provided by rectifier D1 ... D4 has a peak value of 310 V. This voltage is applied to the drain of power MOSFET T1 via limiting resistor R9. A control circuit ensures that the MOSFET only conducts during the short times just before and after the mains voltage goes through zero. During these times the momentary value of the pulsating direct voltage does not exceed 5 V. In the same short times

smoothing capacitor C2 is charged: during the remainder of the time it provides the output current. Consequently, this capacitor has a very high value: 10 000 μ. The load-current pulses have a peak value, if only for a brief moment, of the order of 4 A! The stability of the output voltage is essentially dependent upon the load. The output current may be 110 mA maximum. The supply for the control circuit is provided by resistor R2, capacitor C1, and diodes D5 and D6. The control circuit is a window comparator constructed from three opamps. Correct calibration of the control circuit is therefore very important. Before

91

the mains is applied for the first time, set P1 to the centre of its travel and turn P2 so that its wiper is at earth potential. Then connect the mains and check the operating voltage of the circuit. Next connect a voltmeter (10 V dc range) at the output and adjust P2 until the meter just begins to deflect. Finally, adjust P1 for a meter reading of 4.8 . . . 5 V.

Applications of the circuit are restricted. It is evident that it cannot be used with equipment which should be electrically isolated from the mains. It is equally unsuitable for use with equipment that is allergic to mains spikes and noise. It is, however, eminently suitable where there is no space for a mains

transformer. The unit should only be used for powering equipment that is contained well-insulated in a plastic case. Any equipment powered by the present unit should not be connected to other equipment by cable. Such connections, if necessary, should be by opto-coupler only.

Heat dissipation in T1 and R9 amounts to only about 3 W so that even if the circuit is fitted in a small case there should be no heat problems. During assembly the usual precautions relevant to mains operated circuits should be observed scrupulously.

Siemens application note

084 pulse generator 1

The generator presented is based on two 555-timer ICs and provides rectangular pulse trains (waves) of which the pulse width and the pulse rate are variable.

The first timer, IC1, is connected as an astable square-wave generator. Symmetry of waveform is maintained to within a few per cent by a stereo potentiometer and two diodes. Bear in mind that a square wave, by definition, is a rectangular wave with a 50 per cent duty factor, that is, its pulse width must be equal to half the pulse

spacing. The frequency range is determined by switch-selective capacitors: with values as shown, it lies between 1 Hz and 100 kHz. Maximum output current of IC1 is 100 mA.

The trailing edge of the output pulses from IC1 is used to trigger the second 555 which is connected as a monostable. This stage enables the pulse width to be varied between 10 μs and 100 ms by switch-selective capacitors. Maximum output current of IC2 is also 100 mA.

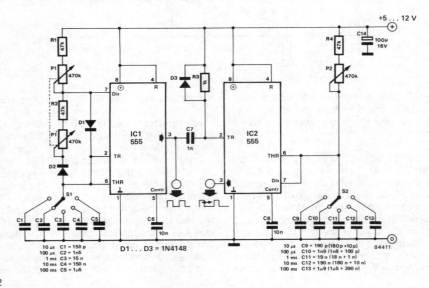

Switches, potentiometers, and capacitors C1 ... C5 and C9 ... C13 may be replaced by single, fixed components if a pulse generator with predetermined parameters only is required.

The supply voltage may be between 5 ... 12 V; the off-load current is about 10 mA.

It is advisable to use good-quality capacitors if optimum performance of the generator is to be realized.

085 flashing telephone light

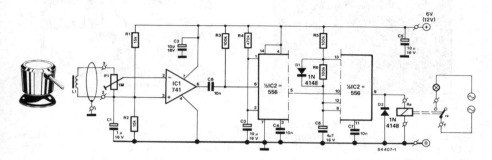

In many instances it is not only the hard of hearing who are unable to hear the telephone ringing: even with normal hearing it is often impossible to detect it above the noise from the vacuum cleaner or the radio. The present circuit enables the ringing of the phone to be seen with the aid of a flashing lamp. It is perfectly feasible to put a number of lamps in parallel and place them in different locations.

Inductor L1 is attached to the telephone by a suction pad: it may be necessary to try out several positions on the telephone to obtain best results.

A reference voltage of about 4.8 V is provided by potential divider R1/R2 and applied to the non-inverting input of opamp IC1 direct and to the inverting input via L1/P1. The preset is adjusted to give equal levels of direct voltage at both inputs of the opamp: the output of IC1 is then logic low. When the telephone rings, an alternating

voltage is induced in L1, causing the potential at the non-inverting input of IC1 periodically to exceed that at the inverting input. This results in a rectangular pulse train at the output of the opamp. The trailing edges of these pulses trigger one half of IC2 via C8. This half of the IC operates as a monostable multivibrator (MMV), the output of which is low during time-out. When a pulse arrives at pin 6, the timer is triggered and the output (pin 5) goes high. As long as the output is high, subsequent pulses at pin 6 have no effect: only when the MMV has reset does the next pulse at pin 6 trigger the timer. The output pulse has a width of about five seconds, which is determined by the values of R4 and C3.

The second half of IC2 functions as an astable multivibrator producing rectangular pulse trains when its reset input (pin 10) is high, which is as long as the MMV is triggered. The pulse repetition fre-

Parts list

Resistors:
R1 = 15 k
R2 = 10 k
R3,R5,R6 = 100 k
R4 = 470 k
P1 = 1 M preset

Capacitors:
C1 = 1 μ/16 V
C2,C3,C5 = 10 μ/16 V
C4,C7,C8 = 10 n
C6 = 4μ7/16 V

Semiconductors:
D1,D2 = 1N4148
IC1 = 741
IC2 = 556

Miscellaneous:
L1 = telephone pick-up coil with suction pad
Re = relay, see text

93

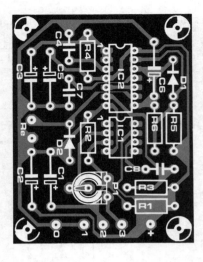
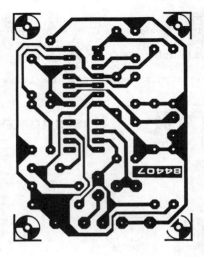

quency is determined by the values of R5, R6, and C6. The output signal on pin 9 of the AMV switches relay Re on and off. As the pulse spacing is just about one second, the relay, and therefore the lamp(s) connected to it, is switched on and off five times. The quiescent current consumption of the

circuit is about 10 mA at 6 V.
In selecting the relay, its operating voltage as well as the power rating of the lamps should be taken into account.
The printed-circuit board for this circuit is not available ready-etched.

086   single-button code lock

The disadvantage of almost every available code lock is that some sort of keyboard must be mounted at the door for keying in the (secret) code to open the lock. These keyboards attract attention with the result that all sorts of undesirables are likely to be found tapping on the buttons.
The circuit here uses the normal doorbell push button to feed in the secret lock code. The code consists of a series of long and short pulses, just like a sort of Morse. At the centre of the circuit is an eight-bit shift register (IC1). The outputs of this IC are connected, via switches S1 . . . S8, inverters N3 . . . N10, and diodes D1 . . . D8, to the base of transistor T1 which controls the lock relay. This transistor can only conduct if there is a '1' on the cathodes of all the diodes. In all other cases the base current supplied by R3 will be carried away by one or more diodes. The switches are used to select normal or inverted output from the
94

register. This is how to set the secret code, which in the diagram here is 00110011.
When the bell button is pressed Re1 closes and the bell rings. At the same time the second relay contact switches the bistable consisting of N1 and N2. The output of N2 provides the clock signal to IC1 and N1 triggers monostable multivibrators MMV1 and MMV2. The data read into the shift register is produced by MMV1 but it is only shifted after N2 supplies a rising clock pulse, which happens when the bell push button is released. The monostable time of MMV1 is short: about a half second. If the button is released within this time, a '0' is read in; any longer time produces a '1' as $\overline{Q}$ of MMV1 has become '1' again. In this way the shift register can be filled with the correct code. The second MMV serves as a protection by resetting the shift register if no pulses come for five seconds. The lock then closes again (or remains closed). The

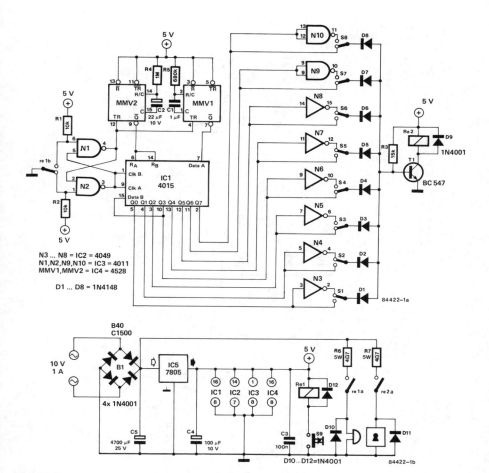

N3 ... N8 = IC2 = 4049
N1,N2,N9,N10 = IC3 = 4011
MMV1,MMV2 = IC4 = 4528

D1 ... D8 = 1N4148

pulse times and the reset time can be changed by modifying the values of R5 and R4 respectively.

The circuit is powered via a 5 V regulator and the current consumption is determined by the type of relay used.

T.G. Tio

087 central heating monitor

One of the largest annual expenses for most home owners is the fuel for the central heating. Apart from keeping the house temperature as low as comfort will allow there is not very much we can do about this bill. We just set the temperature and let the room thermostat and central heating boiler get on with it. The circuit shown here is designed to go one step further by allowing us to see what the boiler and thermostat are doing at all times.

The circuit indicates various conditions by means of three LEDs. They show when the thermostat requests more heat (D1) and whether the boiler is then on (D2) or off (D3). We will see how this is achieved by referring to the diagram of figure 1, and beginning with the request for more heat.

95

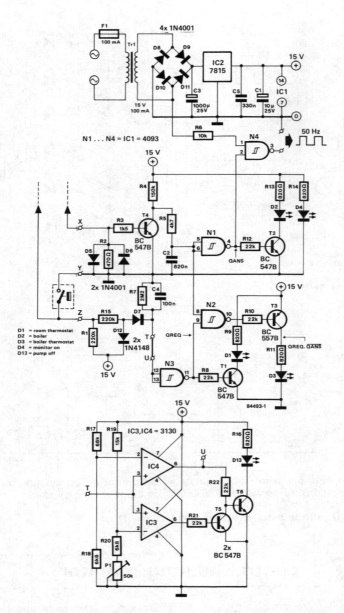

The relevant LED, D1, will not light if the input of N3 is '1'. This is the case if there is 24 V a.c. across the open contacts of the room thermostat (RT). This voltage is rectified by R15, D7, R7 and C4 before being passed to N3. The input of N3 will also be '1' if the 24 V is not present because the maximum thermostat (MT) in the boiler is open. In this case the external resistance between points Y and Z is extremely high so voltage divider R7/D7/R15/R1 keeps pins 12 and 13 of N3 high.

The purpose of diodes D5 and D6 is to act as a current sensor, with the result that transistor T4 conducts every half-cycle of the mains during which the burner operates.

Capacitor C2 is then discharged, via R5 and T4, more quickly than it is charged via R4 and R5. The inputs of N1 are both '0' so D2 lights. The situation is slightly different for LED D3. If the burner remains off when more heat is requested both inputs of N2 will be '1' so its output will be '0' and the LED will light.

A stream of 50 Hz pulses is constantly fed to one input of N4. These will be passed to the output if the second input is '1'. This is the case whenever the burner is operating so this output could be used as a measure of the central heating system's fuel consumption.

The circuit for a central heating burner is very often similar to that shown in figure 2. An optional pump switch is also indicated. A 10 μF capacitor (C6 = 6.8 μ and 3.3 μ in parallel) is added to prevent the monitor from permanently indicating a request for heat because if C6 were not included there would always be an external resistance due to the primary opto-coupler circuit in the pump switch. Four diodes, D14 . . . D17, are needed to compensate for the raised threshold in the same opto-coupler (due to D5 and D6). It is worth noting that in some cases the voltage dropped across the wire running from the boiler to the thermostat is greater than the optocoupler's threshold voltage.

If a pump switch is included in your central heating system, another LED, D13, can be added to the monitor. Replace the T-U link in figure 1 by the window comparator cir-cuit based on IC3 and IC4. The LED will then light whenever the pump switches on, if this is not a result of the thermostat requesting more heat, and then switches off again. The burner circuit is then on stand-by and there are only a few volts across the contacts of the room thermostat.

This central heating monitor is best mounted close to the room thermostat. To install it, first cut one of the two wires entering the thermostat (it doesn't matter which one), and connect this to X. One of the thermostat's terminals is now 'free' and should be linked to Y. The other terminal must be connected to Z by a length of wire.

If the central heating system contains a pump switch, capacitor C6 and diodes D14 . . . D17 must be included. It is strictly forbidden for any unauthorized person (i.e. you!) to make any changes within the central heating burner circuit. The monitor described here takes account of this and even when it is switched off it does not affect the working of the central heating system, because it is a totally passive circuit.

The behaviour of the central heating system can be changed with this monitor as it makes it possible to determine for how long the burner is on and off. The output of N1 when used as a clock signal for the event counter described in circuit 215 enables the number of burner on/off cycles to be counted over a long period of time. On the basis of these two figures it is then possible to set the thermostat to its optimum value.

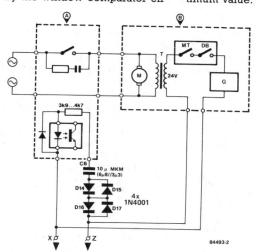

A = pump switch
B = central-heating boiler
M = pump
T = boiler transformer
G = gas block
DB = boil dry protection
MT = maximum thermostat (boiler thermostat)

84493-2

088 mini signal cleaner

A problem well known to personal computer users is the difficulty of swapping cassette tapes containing software. One of the main reasons for this is the setting of the read/write head in the cassette recorder. This should be at 90° with respect to the tape but in practice this is not always the

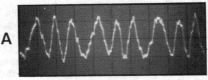

84510-2a

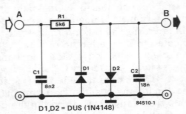

D1,D2 = DUS (1N4148)
84510-1

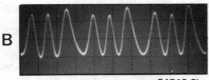

84510-2b

case, with the result that loading a program from a strange tape causes problems. With the use of FSK (Frequency Shift Keying), the signal cleaner provides a very marked improvement. The time spent searching for the correct signal level is then greatly reduced. As the filter requires only five components, there should be no problem finding a space for it within the case of any computer.

The layout of the circuit is not at all complex. The signal passes first through the

low-pass filter, consisting of R1 and C2, which has a cut-off frequency of about 1600 Hz. In frequency shift keying a '0' or '1' is recorded on the tape as a sinusoidal signal (with frequencies of 1200 and 2400 Hz respectively) so this filtering removes all the rough edges (figure 2a) from the signal. The result is shown in figure 2b. The two diodes limit the peak value of the output signal to about ±600 mV.

089 frequency meter

Intersil IC type 7226B is just the right counter for a simple but reliable frequency meter which covers a range of 9 MHz. The circuit of the meter divides into four functional sections:
- input stage, T1, T2, N2, N3;
- multiplier, FF1, FF2, IC3, IC4;
- counter, IC5;
- display, Ld1 . . . 6

In general, the circuit is a standard design, much of which has been described in past issues of *Elektor*. The primary function of the input stage is converting the input signal into rectangular pulses that are fed to the counter either direct or via the multiplier. The stage can handle input voltages of up to 50 V r.m.s. which is sufficient for most measurements. Diodes D1 and D2 conduct when the input voltage is

above about 600 mV so that the input impedance is determined primarily by the value of R2, that is, around 1 M.

The multiplier (× 100) is particularly important for the measurement of frequencies between 5 Hz and 1 . . . 2 kHz.

The counter, the Intersil 7226B, contains a crystal oscillator, a time base, a counter, a seven-segment decoder, a multiplexer, and a number of drivers for the direct control of the LED display.

In our prototype a 1 MHz crystal was used for driving the on-chip oscillator, but if D5 is omitted a (cheaper) 10 MHz crystal may be used.

The LED display is the popular type MAN 4640A.

The function of the switches is:
- S1a connects the input stage to the

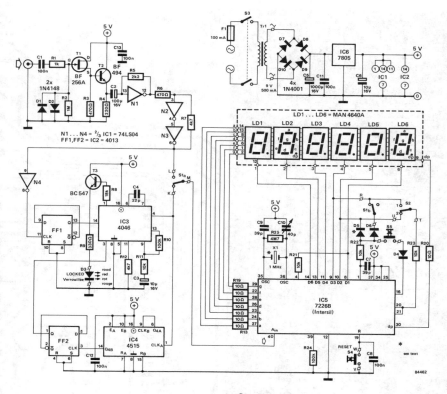

Parts list

Resistors:
R1 = 1 k
R2 = 1 M
R3,R6 = 470 Ω
R4 = 220 Ω
R5 = 2k2
R7,R12 = 4k7
R8 = 18 k
R9 = 330 Ω
R10,R24 = 100 k
R11,R21 . . . R23 = 10 k
R13 . . . R20 = 10 Ω
R25 = 4M7

Capacitors:
C1,C8,C11 . . . C13 = 100 n
C2 = 100 μ/16 V
C3,C6 = 10 μ/16 V
C4 = 22 p
C5 = 1000 μ/16 V
C7,C9 = 39 p
C10 = 40 p trimmer

Semiconductors:
D1,D2,D4 . . . D6 = 1N4148 (for D5 see text)
D3 = LED (red)
D7 . . . D10 = 1N4001
T1 = BF 256A
T2 = BF 494
T3 = BC 547
IC1 = 74LS04
IC2 = 4013
IC3 = 4046
IC4 = 4518
IC5 = 7226B (Intersil)
IC6 = 7805
Ld1 . . . Ld6 = MAN 4640A (common cathode)

Miscellaneous:
S1 = double-pole change-over switch
S2 = single-pole change-over switch
S3 = DPST switch
S4,S5 = spring-loaded push-button press-to-make switch
X1 = 1 MHz or 10 MHz crystal (HC18 or HC25 holder) (see text)
Tr1 = mains transformer, secondary 9 V/500 mA
F1 = fuse, 100 mA, delayed action
printed circuit 84462 (frequency meter less display)
printed circuit 80089-2 (for the display)

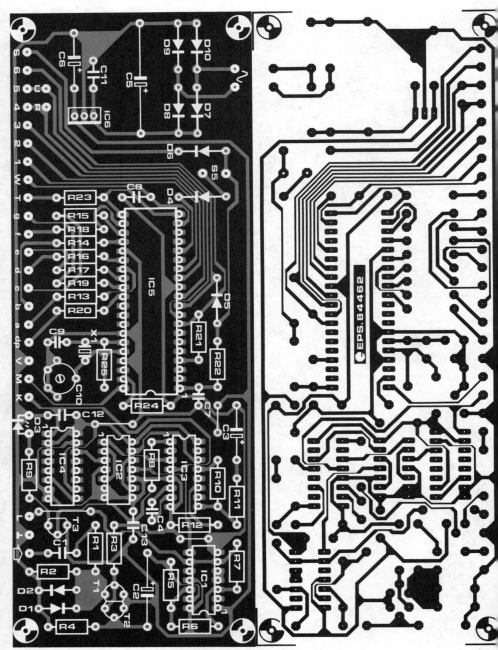

counter either direct or via the multiplier (as shown);

■ S1b ensures the correct position of the decimal point when the multiplier is in circuit;

■ S2 normally determines the position of the decimal point, that is, whether the display reads kHz or MHz;

- S3 is the mains on/off switch;
- S4 is the reset switch;
- S5 serves to test the display: when it is pressed, all segments should light.

Finally, note that printed circuit 84462 for the meter has no provision for the display; this may be fitted on board 80089-2 originally designed for the Junior Computer.

090   twin RS 232

The D-type connectors generally used for RS 232 interfaces are quite robust and are well able to take the wear and tear that comes with frequently being inserted and removed. The human computer user can, however, get a bit frayed around the edges when he has to change his computer's RS 232 lead from one peripheral to another for the umpteenth time. This is not helped by the fact that, for aesthetic reasons, the RS 232 port is almost invariably located out of sight at the back of the computer. Fortunately, many people never have this problem but none the less it does crop up fairly often: e.g., when a computer, terminal, and printer are used together, or one computer and two printers, or two computers and one printer.

In answer to an unspoken plea for a cure

for this situation we have designed what is, in effect, an RS 232 single-pole two-way switch. The interesting part of the circuit is the two high-efficiency LEDs connected to four of the interface's data transfer lines. The (red or yellow) LED corresponding to the channel in use flickers when data is passing through the lines so that would be a bad time to switch to the other channel. After the LED stops flickering, data transfer is over so the other channel can be selected and its LED will light immediately. You may be wondering why the LEDs are needed and why it is not possible simply to switch from one channel to the other at any time. To see why we have a look at what happens if the switch is opened, even momentarily, while data transfer is under way. The logic levels are then undefined

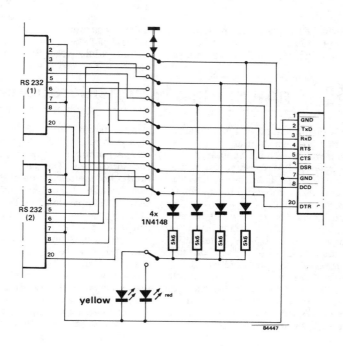

for a short period of time, which is clearly a very bad idea. Many RS 232 interfaces are fortunately fitted with MC 1488/1489 ICs which always have a defined logic level at the inputs even when any of the inputs is connected to nothing (floating).

The numbering indicated in the diagram corresponds to a 25-pin D-type connector. The designations of the RS 232 lines can be found on *Elektor infocard 64*, if you feel the need to refresh your memory.

091 audible ohmmeter

It is sometimes useful to have a small instrument that can give a quick indication of the approximate value of a resistor.
The present circuit enables an unknown resistor to be compared with a number of known resistors and in that way indicate between which two values the unknown resistor lies.
The circuit is based on the well-known 555 which is connected as an oscillator (astable multivibrator). The output of the oscillator is used to drive a piezo electric buzzer.
The frequency of the oscillator is inversely proportional to the value of Rx (the unknown resistor) and is determined from

$$f = \frac{1}{\ln2\left[\,R1 + 2(R2 + \dfrac{R3Rx}{R3+Rx})\,\right]C2} \ Hz$$

where $\ln2 = 0.6931$, all resistors are in ohms, and C2 is in farads.
By substituting one or two of the known

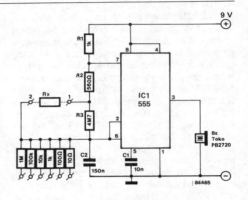

resistors for Rx, the note emitted by the buzzer should give a fair indication of the approximate value of Rx. Of course, if you have perfect pitch, you do not need the known resistors . . . In that case, we'll tell you that if Rx = 0, the frequency is about 4500 Hz, while when Rx = ∞, it is 2 Hz.

092 power supply considerations

In its standard application, the 723 voltage regulator provides an output of 2 . . . 37 volts but in many cases it is necessary to be able to go down to 0 V. To do so, an auxiliary negative voltage is required: in the present circuit this is provided by an LM337 negative regulator (IC2).
It is not sufficient just to connect an additional circuit onto the same transformer as the positive supply: to get a negative voltage, there MUST be a load on the positive supply. This is provided by R5/T2, which ensures that a current flows at all times when the mains is switched on.
The circuit provides adjustable current limiting which is effected by applying a voltage of 0.6 V between pin 2 (CL = cur-

rent limit) and pin 3 (CS = current sense). This voltage is the sum of the drops across R8 (proportional to the output current, I_o) and across P3. The latter voltage is the product of the resistance of P3 and the current through T1. Further stabilization of the base of T1 is provided by T2. In spite of this double stabilization there remains a small ripple (0.3 per cent) on the current into CL. Voltage stabilization is provided by IC1: hum and noise are less than 1 mV at an output of 15 V at 150 mA.
The output voltage increases linearly with the resistance of P2. Maximum output level can be preset with P1.
The negative supply has a longer time constant than the positive section so that when

102

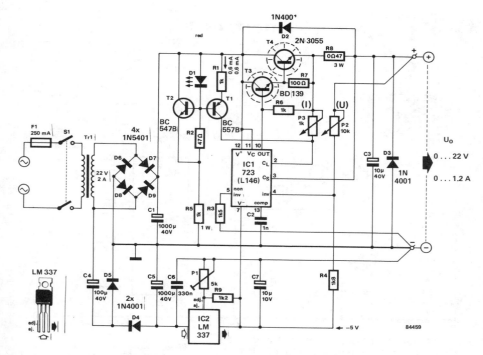

the mains is switched off, it remains active slightly longer. If this were not arranged, the output might momentarily rise (which could damage the equipment being powered) owing to the inability of the 723 to go down to zero without an auxiliary voltage.

The 2N3055, provided it is mounted on a suitable heat sink (2 °C/W), can dissipate 30 ... 40 watts. At a transformer voltage of 22 V, this means that well in excess of 1 A can be handled.

The choice of transformer is fairly critical, because strictly speaking 24 V is already slightly too high for the 723 which tolerates just about 36 V. It is therefore better to use the L146, an improved version of the 723 which can handle up to 80 V. Note, however, that even then the transformer secondary voltage should not be much higher (a few volts) because otherwise the maximum rated voltages of the electrolytic capacitors and transistors will be exceeded.

Some further points worth bearing in mind:
■ The transformer secondary voltage should be about equal to the required maximum output voltage, at least, that is, if this lies above 20 V.

■ Always ensure that the current rating of the transformer is at least 1.4 times the output current.

■ The output voltage is equal to $P2U_{neg}/R4$ volts; U_{neg} should be set at about -5 V with P1. By adjusting P1 (and therefore U_{neg}) slightly, the maximum output voltage can be set precisely to 22 V. If the required maximum output voltage is quite different from this value, R4 has to be adapted so that U_{neg} still remains about -5 V.

■ The maximum output current is determined by R8 and is equal to $0.6/0.47 = 1.28$ A.

■ Do not allow the 3055 to dissipate more than 40 W continuously!

Finally: the earth return is intentionally shown as three parallel lines to give a clear point of reference where the voltage or current, in the final instance, is constant. Owing to the unavoidable voltage drops across the earth returns, regulation will always be inferior when the returns are not kept separate.

W. Vogt

093 joystick interface 1

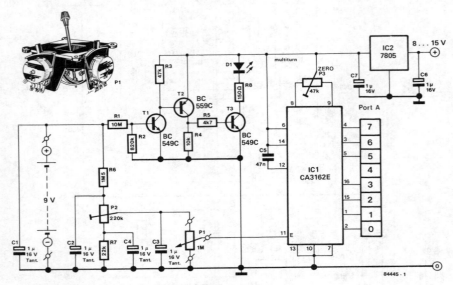

84445 - 1

Just as it is very easy to implement an 'all or nothing' control (four positions identified by two bits, or eight positions identified by three bits), it is very difficult to realize an inexpensive proportional control. When a reader suggested using an analog to digital converter, such as a 3162, to convert the voltage at the wiper of a joystick potentiometer into a single binary word we recognized the potential of the idea. The IC used is more than just a normal analog to digital converter as it provides a multiplexed BCD output (4 bits: pins 2, 1, 15 and 16). The information needed for multiplexing is supplied to three pins: 4, 3, and 5, in descending order of significance. The software controlling the input port must be able to interpret this information and the main points which should be borne in mind when writing this software can be gleaned by studying the flowchart in figure 2. A '0' appears on port A bits 7, 6 and 5 in turn, indicating that the BCD code on bits 0 . . . 3 (which can be from 0000 to 1001) corresponds to the most significant nibble (four bits), next significant nibble, and least significant nibble respectively. The position of the wiper of preset P2, which is part of the voltage divider connected to joystick potentiometer P1, determines whether the

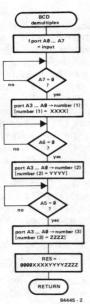

84445 - 2

output values range from 0 to 255 (which can be transmitted as a single hexadecimal byte — FF_{HEX}) or from 0 to 999 (three BCD digits).

104

The power for the circuit may be provided either by the microcomputer to which the interface is connected, or by a voltage regulator supplied with a voltage of 8 ... 15 V. The voltage reference applied to voltage divider R6/P2/R7 must, however, be very stable so it cannot come from the circuit's supply. A small 9 V battery is therefore included and this is quite sufficient for the few microamps it will have to supply. Naturally enough, there will come a time when the battery voltage is too low but we have included a circuit to indicate this condition. When the voltage drops below 8 V, T1 switches off, speedily followed by T2 and T3. The LED, D1, then extinguishes. When the input port has been programmed, all that remains is to calibrate the interface, as follows:

■ move the wiper of P1 completely towards ground and then trim P3 to get an output of zero (000 or 001);

■ move the wiper of P1 as far as possible towards P2 and then trim this latter preset to get the maximum value (either 254 or 255, or 998 or 999).

The values set during calibration may be altered somewhat if necessary in order to prevent any possibility of the upper or lower limits being passed. This is done by selecting, for example, 005 as the lower limit and 250 or 994 as the upper limit. Then there is little need to worry about the stability of the battery voltage.

P. Palisson

094   sonic deterrent

Most of us will agree that rats and mice are generally not the most welcome visitors to our homes. At the same time, many of us are definitely averse to killing these animals. For them, the present unit may be a godsend, although house pets may not agree. This is because the unit emits a fairly high note from a loudspeaker to frighten away our unwanted visitors.

A 4047 CMOS IC is arranged to operate as a relaxation oscillator whose frequency may be set between 5 kHz and 30 kHz with preset P1. Outputs Q and $\overline{Q}$ are each applied to a type 4050 non-inverting driver, IC2 and IC3. The six stages contained in these ICs are connected in parallel to enable direct driving of T1/T2 and T3/T4 respectively. Either T1 and T4 or T2 and T3 conduct simultaneously. These transistor pairs are capable of driving a low-cost piezo tweeter.

A simple mains power supply may be built as shown.

Unfortunately, we cannot vouch for the effectiveness of the circuit. We would, however, advise you to change the frequency from time to time to prevent the little animals getting used to the sound. But, as we said, we don't know how your cat, dog, or canary is going to like all this . . .

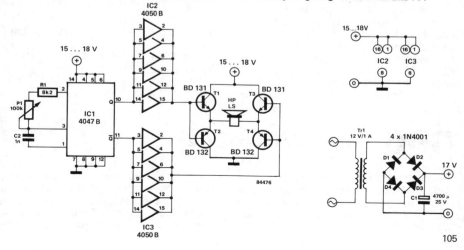

105

095 amplification selector

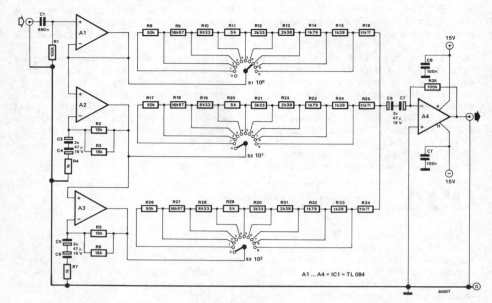

An amplification selector is an accurate measuring instrument that is inserted into a signal path and then allows the gain of that signal to be set precisely between 0 and 999 in unit steps.

Amplifier A1 functions as a (unity gain) buffer for the test signal which is subsequently applied to a chain of resistors, R8 ... R16, and then to amplifier A4.

Amplifiers A1 ... A3 are connected in cascade. Whereas A1 has unity gain, amplifiers A2 and A3 have a gain of ×10. Each of them is followed by a similar chain of resistors as A1, R17 ... R25, and R26 ... R34 respectively. The signal is also applied from the chains to A4. The gain depends on the setting of switches S1 ... S3. You will see from the circuit diagram that the resistor chains, together with R35, are part of the negative-feedback loop of A4. The result is a mixing amplifier with a conversion gain between 0 and 999. The total resistance of each of the resistor chains is 100 k. If then, for instance, the three switches are in position 1, the total amplification is

$$R35/R8 + \ldots + R16 = 1$$
plus
$$10R35/R17 + \ldots + R25 = 10 \text{ (gain in A2!)}$$
plus
$$100R35/R26 + \ldots + R34 = 100$$
$$\text{(gain in A2 + A3!)}$$
$$= 111$$

096 2 × 2716 = 2732

Almost everybody who builds micro-computer projects will notice sooner or later that he has been stockpiling certain often-used components. A case in point is the 2716 EPROM, which is so commonly used that it is wise always to have a couple on hand. In spite of the fact that the 2716 is so common, EPROMs with double this capacity (2732 = 4096 × 8 bits) are also very popular. This doesn't mean, of course, that

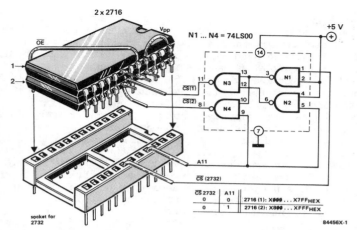

everybody should throw away all their 2716s. Quite the opposite, in fact, we thought it would be interesting to have a 4 K memory consisting of a pair of 2716s.

All the lines intended for the 2732 are used directly by the two 2716s except for A11, $\overline{CS}$, and V_{pp}. Every pin on the 2716s is common to both ICs with the exception, of course, of $\overline{CS}$. The enable signals for this pin are taken from the outputs of the 74LS00. One of the EPROMs [referred to here as 2716 (1)] is ad-

dressed for the first 2 K block of the 2732, and A11 is then logic low. The second 2716 is enabled when the second 2 K block is being accessed (A11 is then logic high). Remember to apply the appropriate logic levels for the $\overline{OE}$ and V_{pp} pins: pin 21 must be connected to +5 V and pin 20 to earth. The method of construction and fitting of this circuit should be carefully considered to cause the minimum of disturbance on the printed circuit board.

097   reversing buzzer

Almost every new car manufactured in the world today is fitted with reversing lights. Great idea! Not only do they help you see where you are reversing in the dark, but they also make your intentions clear to

anybody behind the car. In some Asian countries it is even a legal obligation for every car to have an externally audible reversing indicator. The one problem with these ideas is that the car driver does not

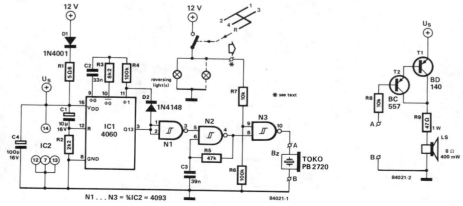

directly benefit from them.

It is an undeniable fact of human nature that we often forget or neglect the care and caution instilled into us while learning a new skill. Nowhere is this more obvious than in driving a car. We frequently tend to do what is convenient rather than what is correct.

Just one small, but common, fault is starting the car in gear with the clutch depressed. Then you only have to release the clutch and away you go...But in which direction? It can prove very surprising, to say the least, when you expect to move smoothly forwards but instead find the driver of the slightly shortened car behind you tapping on your window to express his opinion of your character in a somewhat heated manner.

The circuit here also gets excited when you start the car in reverse gear but all it does is buzz at you in displeasure.

When the ignition is switched on, the car battery voltage is applied to the circuit and the oscillator around N2 starts. This provides one of the inputs to N3. If the car is in reverse gear, the second input of N3 is taken high via R7, and this causes the buzzer to sound.

Simultaneously, pin 12 of the CD 4060 is taken high and this chip is reset. This IC is a 14-stage binary counter and oscillator, the frequency of which is set by external components (C2, R3 and R4). After a certain time (about six seconds), the Q13 output (pin 3) of IC1 goes high and stops oscillator N2 by taking its input (pin 5) low via N1. This, of course, stops the buzzer and ensures that it does not sound every time the car is put into reverse gear, which would be very annoying.

An alternative to using the buzzer is the small circuit shown in figure 2, consisting of a loudspeaker driven by a darlington pair. Transistors T1 and T2 may also be replaced by a single-package darlington such as a BC 516.

098   tape contents detector

The circuit proposed makes it possible to ascertain whether a digital cassette has been written into or not. It has been tested on a Commodore computer, with a ZX81, and with a Junior Computer. Not only does it enable you to distinguish between blank and recorded tape, but also, by alternate switching between play-back and fast forward wind — or rewind — to find the beginning of a program on the tape.

When used with the Commodore or Junior Computers, the circuit shows by means of

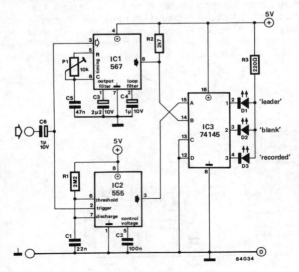

three LEDs whether the tape is blank (D2), contains a leader (D1), or has been recorded (D3). The leader, or pilot tone, is a signal which precedes the recorded information, or, in the Commodore, is interjected between the program coding (name, length, and so on) and the actual recorded data.

The leader is not available with the ZX81 which in itself is a serious disadvantage. On the other hand, it makes the construction of the detector a lot easier, as shown below. The input of the detector (see figure 1), is connected to the output of the cassette recorder. The signal from the recorder is taken via C6 to the input (pin 3) of a tone decoder, IC1, and to the input (pin 2) of a monostable, IC2. There are three possible states:

■ No signal. The output of IC1 (pin 8) is then logic 1, and that of IC2 (pin 3) is logic 0. The signal at the inputs (pins 12, 13, 14, 15) of the BCD*-to-decimal decoder, IC3, is then a binary signal 0010 (as 12 and 13 are connected to earth which is logic 0). This causes the output (pin 3) for the decimal number '2' to be actuated, that is, to become logic 0. A current then flows through R3 and LED D2 into this pin; the LED lights to indicate that the cassette is blank.

■ Leader present. The constant frequency of the pilot tone is recognized by IC1, causing its output to go low. At the same time, IC2 receives a stream of trigger pulses, which causes its output to go high. The binary number at the inputs of IC3 is then 0001, which makes pin 2 go low. A current then flows through R3 and LED D1: the

LED lights to indicate 'leader present'.

■ Data present. The output of IC1 remains logic high, because the input frequency lies outside the bandwidth of the tone decoder. The monostable remains triggered, so that its output remains logic 1. The binary number at the inputs of IC3 is 0011 causing pin 4 to become logic 0. The LED D3 then lights to indicate 'data present'. The centre frequency, f_c, of IC1 is determined by P1 and C5 and can be calculated from $f_c = 1/P_1C_5$ (Hz) where P_1 is the *preset* value of P1. The bandwidth, B, of the tone decoder is calculated from $B = 1070 \sqrt{U_i/f_cC_4}$ Hz., where U_i is the r.m.s. value of the input signal in volts, C_4 is the value of C4 in μF, and f_c is the centre frequency in Hz. It should be noted that U_i should be smaller than 200 mV.

When the ZX81 is used, D1, IC1, P1, R2, and C3...C5 can be omitted. Pin 14 of IC3 is then connected to the positive supply line. This section need not be read by ZX81 users, as in their case there is nothing to be calibrated. Otherwise, connect your home computer to the cassette recorder and write a program of a few dozen single figures (as close together as possible) onto the tape: this gives you a leader on the cassette. Rewind the tape, and then play back. Starting from centre setting, adjust P1 slowly until LED D1 lights for 2...10 seconds for each leader.

M. Hafner

*BCD = binary coded decimal

099 tolerance indicator

This useful circuit helps to match resistors by comparing their values and indicating any difference between them. This enables tolerances as low as 0.25% to be calculated with accuracy. The circuit does not even need to be calibrated! The tolerance indicator can serve all sorts of purposes: it can measure resistances for voltage dividers in synthesizers and other electronic instruments, power supplies, measuring devices, and D/A converters.

The advantages of the circuit speak for

themselves. Although calculating tolerances by measuring resistors is a pretty straightforward job, it is of course much more practical to be able to compare values with a constant reference.

Now it can be seen at once whether the resistor under test is the right one or not, without having to resort to tedious calculations. In most cases, this method will afford a great deal more accuracy than the use of digital multimeters.

The tolerances are indicated immediately

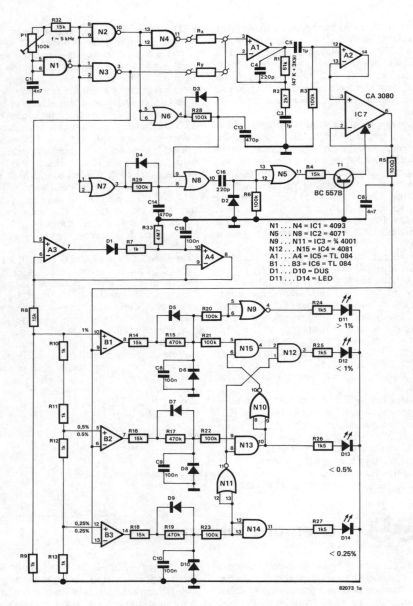

and there are no problems with drift. The circuit does not require any high-precision resistors and/or reference voltage sources. A single preset serves to calibrate the unit, which, by the way, is very cheap to build, since it does not need any special components and the display consists of just four LEDs.

One way to find out whether two resistors are identical is to connect them in series with a reference voltage source and measure the voltage at the junction between them. If they have the same value, the voltage at the junction will be half the reference voltage. A reference voltage of 10 V, for example, will give a result of 5.00 V. If

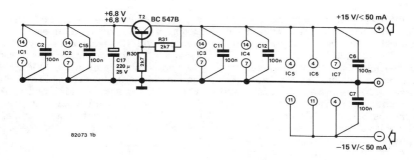

82073 1b

the level measured does not coincide, the difference can be calculated by a straightforward subtraction, and we're left with the tolerance.

A far less complicated solution involves the circuit in figure 1.

A CMOS IC, type 4093 (IC1) acts as an oscillator and generates two rectangular pulses that are phase shifted by 180° with respect to each other and have a frequency of 4...5 kHz. These pulses are passed to the two resistors under test, R_x and R_y. The other ends of the two resistors are connected to the positive input of opamp A1. Let us assume that the resistors are identical. This means the positive input of A1 will receive a constant DC voltage, since, according to the principle mentioned in the previous paragraph, the sum of the pulses is equal to half the total voltage across R_x + R_y. If, on the other hand, the resistors are not identical, a pulse will reach the non-inverting input of A1, for the voltage here will either be smaller or greater than half the total voltage. The gain of A1 is set at about 20x. In the case of 1% tolerance, a rectangular pulse will be generated with a value of 25 mV_{pp}. Consequently, the output will produce a rectangular signal with a value of 500 mV_{pp}. Its DC component is filtered out by C5R3, after which the signal is coupled to the buffer A2 before reaching OTA (operational transconductance amplifier) type CA 3080.

The OTA operates as a sample-and-hold circuit to eliminate any interference from the input signal. It does this by sampling the input signal and storing it in C8. The control signal for the OTA is extracted from the direct and the inverted oscillator signals. The control *current* for the OTA circuit is derived via integrators R28/C13 and R29/C14, differentiator C16/R6, and transistor T1. Gates N5...N7 act as buffers. N8 links the

two input signals so that they form a control pulse lasting about 22 μs. As a result, there will be a clean rectangular pulse across the storage capacitor for the comparators B1...B3.

The non-inverting inputs can be connected to the reference voltage for the following tolerance levels: 1%, 0.5%, and 0.25%. The reference voltage is not a very precise DC voltage, but is derived directly from the peak value of the oscillator voltage. Together, A3 and A4 constitute a peak value rectifier. This only requires a relatively small storage capacitor, because of the buffer, A4, which follows real rectifier D1. The capacitor discharges very slowly due to the 4M7 input resistance. The feedback across the two amplifiers prevents the forward voltage of the rectifier diode from having any effect. Thus, the peak value of the square wave signal will always reach the rectifier output, irrespective of its absolute value.

Any change in the peak value of the voltage across the resistors under test, in other words, any change at the input of A3, will exert a direct influence on the level of the reference voltage. This means that the comparator voltages will always be in the same proportion to the input (test) voltage. The circuit therefore adjusts itself, so to speak. As a result, even fluctuations in the power supply voltage will have no effect whatsoever on the stability of the tolerance indicator, so that the circuit can operate from a non-stabilized ± 15 V power supply.

What about the display circuit? The reference voltage is divided by R8/R9 and is fed to comparator B1 direct and to B2 and B3 via R10...R13. The comparators toggle as soon as the voltage at the inverting inputs reaches or exceeds the reference voltage levels at the non-inverting inputs. Integrating networks R15/C8, R17/C9, and R19/C10 shape the switching signals for the logic circuits following them. The latter makes sure only the LED that is valid at any particular moment lights.

Tolerances less than 0.25%, however, will continue to be indicated by the 0.25% LED. The other LEDs represent 0.5%, 1%, and >1%, respectively. The >1% LED lights when the test terminals are open.

The circuit is very easy to calibrate. Pl is adjusted for an oscillator frequency of 5 kHz. An oscilloscope or frequency counter would, of course, be ideal here, but it can also be verified with a multimeter. Use two resistors with the same value, say, 10 k, for R_X and R_Y. Set Pl in the centre position. Connect a multimeter in the 10 V range to the junction of the two resistors and check whether the voltage at this point is about 3.4 V. If not, turn Pl until that value is reached. If you do not possess any of the meters mentioned, set Pl in the centre position.

100 electronic dog whistle

Some time ago a piezo tweeter came onto the market accompanied by an enormous amount of publicity such as 'over 300 W' and 'without a crossover network', etc. The 'Hallelujah Chorus' of the advertising fraternity was convinced that it would take the world by storm. The tweeter did not in fact receive the universal acclaim expected and as result they are still relatively cheap and easily available.

This article is certainly not going to argue the pros and cons of this tweeter, although for certain applications it is ideal.

The main difference between normal dynamic horns and the piezo is its construction. The latter has a membrane driven by a small plate of piezo ceramic material. The result is a horn with a very small dynamic mass. Incidentally, the same principles are employed in certain ceramic cartridges and in cigarette lighters.

The impedance curve of a piezo tweeter is shown in figure 1. This type of tweeter has a very high efficiency and it can, therefore, be driven by a battery powered circuit and made to reproduce very high frequencies. Just right for the dog circuit!

Have you ever wondered why your dog pricks up its ears from time to time when no sound is audible? As most of you will know, dogs are able to hear audio frequencies outside the human hearing spectrum. The average person will not hear a frequency of 20 kHz (there are exceptions) irrespective of the volume. On the other hand, animals, and in particular dogs, are sensitive to these tones and will react instantly; unless they are asleep or just lazy. Anyway, whistles producing such frequencies are useful, allowing dogs to be called from great distances without waking up the whole neighbourhood. Mind you, even using one will not guarantee that fact because dogs are not the only ones able to

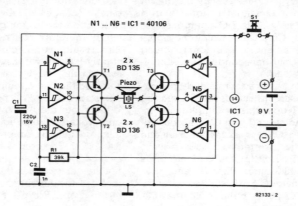

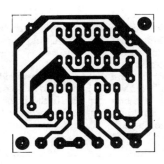

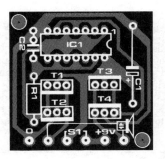

Parts list

Resistors:
R1 = 39 k

Capacitors:
C1 = 220 μ/16 V
C2 = 1 n

Semiconductors:
T1,T3 = BD 135, BD 137, BD 139
T2,T4 = BD 136, BD 138, BD 140
IC1 = 40106

Miscellaneous:
Piezo tweeter KSN 1001A, KSN 1005A (Motorola)
S1 = pushbutton
Battery: 9 V transistor battery

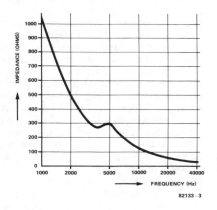

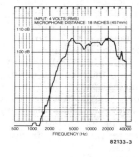

hear it! Canaries, young children, and some adults are likely to hear it as well! There is also the probability that all the dogs in the neighbourhood will respond and land on your doorstep.

The high frequency tone required is generated the circuit illustrated in figure 2. A rectangular pulse instead of a sine wave is used to keep battery consumption as low as possible. The tone is produced by N1...N3, R1, and C2, which constitute an astable multivibrator. Because the piezo horn forms a capacitive load, the wave forms of the signal will have high peaks. That is why Schmitt trigger inverters N1...N3 and N4...N6 (all 6 inverters are contained in the 40106 IC) have been connected in parallel and supplied with an output stage, con-

sisting of T1/T2 and T3/T4 respectively. N4...N6 invert the signal coming from N1...N3. In this way a 'power oscillator' is constructed. When fed by a 9 V battery, this 'power oscillator' supplies an alternating voltage with a peak value of 15 V_{pp} and a frequency of approximately 21 kHz. Could not be better for our needs!

Figure 3 shows the frequency response of the piezo tweeter. We are mainly interested in the 20 kHz range and fortunately the horn reaches its maximum efficiency at this frequency. This curve was recorded with a controlled voltage of 4 V_{rms} and a microphone held at a distance of 457 mm from the horn. The Elektor dog whistle supplies a voltage of 15 V_{pp}. The rms value of this voltage is approximately 6.5 V, because we are dealing with a rectangular voltage with a slightly unsymmetrical duty factor. When the distance between horn and microphone is 1 m, the same voltage results in a sound pressure of 101 dB above threshold intensity.

Care should be taken when using the whistle. Even though the user may not be able to hear it, the sound produced may give somebody or other a headache because it is similar to sitting in front of the speakers of a 1000 W disco system for a few hours.

Bear in mind that the long term side effects of all this are not known, so to be on the safe side it is better to accept the possibility that it could 'damage your health' (like smoking).

101 automatic squelch

A squelch ensures that a receiver amplifier does not get inundated by unwanted noise when the transmitter signal is not present. Such a device is essential for communications equipment, since the transmitter is switched off between transmissions. If the receiver does not possess a squelch circuit, the noise literally bursts out of the loudspeaker during these breaks.

Besides the straightforward construction and calibration, a major advantage of the automatic squelch circuit described here is that you do not have to be an expert to install it into the audio section of the receiver. The audio bandwidth in communications equipment is almost always relatively narrow, as only speech and telegraph (morse) code has to be transmitted. Consequently, the bandwidth is usually in the order of 1.5...4.5 kHz.

It is normal for the transmitter to be switched off immediately after the information has been sent. The noise which builds up during the breaks can be suppressed with the aid of a squelch circuit. Basically, there are three different types of squelch systems: carrier squelch; noise squelch; and signal-to-noise squelch. The carrier squelch circuit derives its information from the presence or absence of the transmitted carrier wave. It is evident that this system cannot be used with single sideband (SSB) or double sideband (DSB) transmissions as the carrier wave is suppressed. The noise squelch circuit checks whether or not the transmitter is active by examining the amount of noise present outside the audio pass band, since a strong noise signal is produced when no transmitter signal is present. The last system is the signal-to-noise squelch circuit which determines the relationship of the detected signal to the amount of noise present continuously. The audio signal is not passed on to the amplifier stages if the signal-to-noise ratio drops below a certain level.

The major drawback of this system is that it is a rather extensive and complicated circuit compared to the other systems.

At the beginning of this article we mentioned the bandwidth of communications equipment. This will be our starting point,

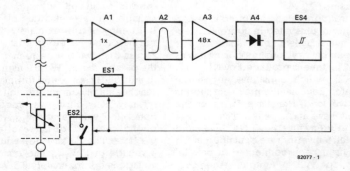

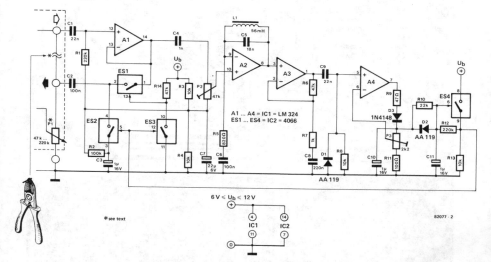

6V ≤ Ub ≤ 12 V

*see text

since we are going to describe a fully auto-matic noise squelch circuit.

This circuit is primarily intended for narrow band FM receivers (such as CB equipment). It examines the level of noise present in the audio stages within a small frequency band and just outside the audio spectrum. The signal path between the demodulator output and the audio input is broken as soon as the noise exceeds a pre-determined level. Consequently, the loud-speaker will fall silent until the signal is substantially stronger than the noise.

The block diagram of the automatic squelch control circuit is illustrated in figure 1. The output signal from the demodulator is fed to a buffer amplifier, A1. The output of this buffer is fed back to the audio input via electronic switch ES1. However, the buffer output is also fed via band pass filter A2 to amplifier A3 and rectifier. The DC output of the rectifier stage determines whether or not electronic switch ES4 is open or closed. The latter in turn controls electronic switches ES1 and ES2.

When the noise level is below the predetermined value, switch ES1 is closed and switch ES2 is open. Therefore, the output signal from the demodulator is passed directly to the audio input. On the other hand, when the noise level is excessive, switch ES1 will be open and ES2 will be closed. This effectively breaks the signal path and shortcircuits the input to the audio

stages. The combination of ES1/ES2 is included to eliminate any disturbing switching sounds from the output amplifier. The circuit diagram of the automatic squelch control is shown in figure 2. The connection to the hot end of volume control P1 is broken inside the receiver. This lead is then connected to the input of buffer amplifier A1. The output of the buffer amplifier is then connected to the hot end of P1 via ES1.

As the circuit is powered by a single supply rail, the opamps have to be biased artificially. This is accomplished by poten-tial divider R3/R4, resistor R1, and preset P2. Consequently, the non-inverting inputs of A1 and A2 receive approximately half the supply voltage.

The output of A1 is also fed to the input of opamp A2, which forms the band pass filter, via capacitor C4 and preset P2. The LC tuned circuit connected between the inverting input and the output of A2 deter-mines the centre frequency of the band pass filter. The centre frequency can be changed quite easily by altering the value of the inductor, L1, and/or the capacitor, C5. With the values indicated, the centre frequency is around 5 kHz. The signal level fed to the input of the band pass filter can be set by P2.

On its route to the rectifier stage con-structed around A4, the output signal from the band pass filter is amplified by opamp

115

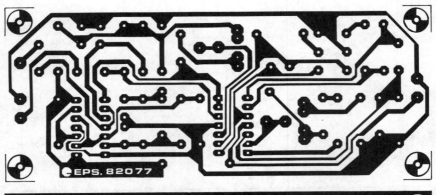

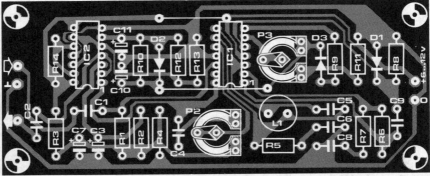

Parts list

Resistors:
R1,R12 = 220 k
R2 = 100 k
R3,R4,R8,R13 = 10 k
R5 = 820 Ω
R6,R14 = 47 k
R7 = 1 k
R9 = 47 Ω
R10 = 22 k
R11 = 100 Ω
P2 = 47 k preset
P3 = 2k2 preset

Capacitors:
C1,C9 = 22 n
C2,C6 = 100 n
C3,C10,C11 = 1 μ/16 V
C4 = 1 n
C5 = 18 n
C7 = 22 μ/6 V
C8 = 220 n

Semiconductors:
D1,D2 = AA 119
D3 = 1N4148
IC1 = LM 324
IC2 = 4066

Miscellaneous:
L1 = 56 mH

A3. The gain of the rectifier stage can be adjusted by preset P3.

The circuitry around electronic switch ES4 not only acts as a Schmitt trigger, but also ensures that the switch is not continuously opening and closing. When the voltage across capacitor C10 exceeds a certain value, ES4 is actuated and the full supply voltage appears across resistor R13. The combination D2-R10-R12-C11 slows down the switch when this voltage changes value, preventing short noise pulses from influencing the circuit. The junction of ES4 and R13 is connected to ES2 and ES3. The combination ES3-R14 functions as an inverter and drives ES1. Switch ES1 will be closed and ES2 will be open when the noise level is low. The output of buffer amplifier A1 is then fed to the input of the receiver audio stages. On the other hand, when a lot of noise is present, ES1 will open and ES2 will close, so that the loudspeaker will remain silent.

The printed circuit board for the automatic squelch control is given in figure 3. As the circuit is relatively straightforward, construction should not present any problems. The same holds true for the installation; the volume control is quite easy to find and there is normally sufficient room inside the equipment to install the board. If not, the squelch circuit can be mounted in a separate small box.

The supply voltage for the squelch circuit must be between 6 V and 12 V. The current consumption is only a few milliamps, therefore the receiver power supply can most probably be used.

Calibration of the circuit is straightforward. The input level to A2 is preset by P2 in such a way that the noise peaks at the output of this opamp are correctly limited. The trigger threshold of ES4 (the lowest noise level at which the squelch circuit is actuated) is set by P3. The setting of P2, although sounding complicated, is really quite simple. An incorrect setting of P2 means that the circuit switches on and off continuously, in which case P2 should be adjusted until the circuit reacts as it should.

The automatic squelch control may be used in a number of applications such as CB transceivers, the *MW receiver* (*Elektor* March 1981) and the *induction loop paging system* (*Elektor* January 1982) when used as a *babyphone* or intercom.

102   connection tester 1

The connection tester is an excellent aid for examining the quality of soldered joints and connections in an electronic circuit. The tester will indicate a 'good' connection with an acoustic signal. With a normal multimeter one must keep at least one eye on the pointer, so an acoustic indication makes testing that much quicker and easier: both eyes are free to check the circuit. The tester gives a tone when there is a connection, and remains silent when there is an open circuit or when the resistance across the connection exceeds 1 Ω. To prevent any damage to sensitive components, and for good battery life, it injects only a weak signal.

When connections are being tested, there is a fair chance that resistors, semiconductors, and other components are involved in the measurement. Moreover, it is possible that certain components cannot cope with the current and/or voltage the tester injects. For this reason, a good tester will not react to low-impedance PN junctions (diodes, transistors), and resistors. Furthermore, the device must be sensitive enough to operate with a weak test signal. The circuit shown in figure 1 meets all these requirements. Thanks to the high gain of the opamp (type 741) used in this circuit, the current and voltage for the test signal can be limited to 200 µA and 2 mV respectively. The voltage difference between the inverting (pin 2) and non-inverting input (pin 3) of the 741 is amplified considerably. The voltage drop across R2 ensures that the output of the opamp becomes negative, since the inverting input has a higher potential than the non-inverting input. The potential at the non-inverting input can be increased by turning P1, so that this input becomes more positive than the inverting one. The result is a positive voltage at the output of the opamp. The oscillator constructed around N1 will then produce a tone in the buzzer. The voltage drop across R2 is caused by a good contact between the probes of the tester. Compared to an op-

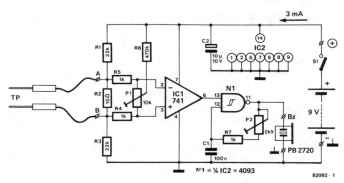

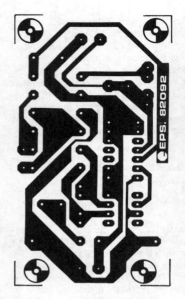
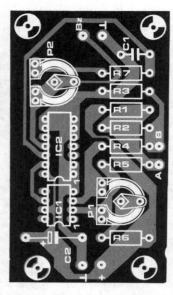

Parts list

Resistors:
R1,R3 = 22 k
R2 = 10 Ω
R4,R5,R7 = 1 k
R6 = 470 k
P1 = 10 k preset
P2 = 2k5 preset

Capacitors:
C1 = 100 n
C2 = 10 μ/10 V

Semiconductors:
IC1 = 741
IC2 = 4093

Miscellaneous:
Bz = buzzer (CIRKIT)
S1 = on/off switch
PCB 82092

tical indication, an acoustic indication is not only more convenient, but its current consumption can be lower as well. The buzzer is loudest when its resonance frequency is about 4.6 kHz. The current consumption will then be about 3 mA. The frequency, and therefore the volume, can be set with P2.

After correct calibration, only resistances of up to 1 ohm (in a connection) are tolerated. A value lower than 1 ohm either indicates a good contact or a short circuit. The calibration procedure is as follows: Place a resistor of 1 ohm (5 or 10%) between the probes and set P1 in a way that the buzzer is about to give a tone. Remove the 1 Ω resistor and cause a short circuit between the probes; again the buzzer will make itself noticeable. Volume can now be set with P2. When the short circuit is removed the buzzer must remain silent. To be certain, correct operation can be checked once more by placing a resistor of a few ohms between the probes. If the buzzer sounds now the calibration will have to be repeated.

One final remark: the supply voltage of the circuit under test must be switched off when the circuit is examined with the tester described in this article. The supply voltage could have a negative effect on the tester or even damage it.

103 safety switch for stereo equipment

Well over half the damage to homes through fire is caused by domestic equipment being left on for excessive periods of time. Stereo equipment is only one of the many items which are easily forgotten about. It is not unusual, after a hectic day (or night) to listen to a favourite record tape or radio programme for a little relaxation. This works so well that when weary listeners drift off into oblivion, the last thing likely to be on their minds is to turn off the stereo!

Another point worth noting, but not half as important as the safety aspect, is the increase in the electricity bill.

If the simple circuit described here is incorporated into the stereo equipment, or the television set for that matter, there will be no need to worry about these items being the cause for a rude, smoky awakening in the small hours. The circuit is designed to switch off the equipment after about 5 minutes of silence.

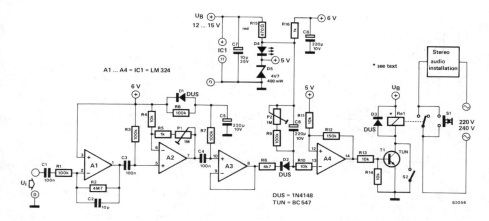

A1 ... A4 = IC1 = LM 324

DUS = 1N4148
TUN = BC 547

82056

The principle of operation is as follows: The auxiliary output signal from the amplifier is boosted considerably by opamps A1 and A2 (by at least two volts). Preset potentiometer P1 is used to adjust the gain between 23 dB and 73 dB. This provides a very wide sensitivity range, which is absolutely necessary as the equipment must not be allowed to switch itself off when the volume of the music is low.

Opamp A3 acts simply as a buffer amplifier, after which the input signal is rectified and smoothed by diode D1 and capacitor C6 respectively. Provided the voltage across capacitor C6 exceeds a certain value, the output of the Schmitt trigger, A4, will go high, transistor T1 will conduct, and the relay will be actuated. If, however, the voltage across C6 drops below the threshold of the Schmitt trigger, the output of A4 will go low, and the relay will be deactuated. The equipment is now switched off.

The rate at which the voltage across C6 drops is determined by the setting of preset P2 and corresponds to the period of silence required before everything is turned off. This interval can be adjusted between roughly 1 and 10 minutes. If necessary, the automatic switch can be bypassed by switch S2.

Once the safety switch has been turned on, the relay contacts will have to be shorted by switch S1, as otherwise the circuit will not be provided with any supply voltage and the relay will not be actuated! The supply voltage may be derived from either the tuner or the power amplifier (or the television, if practicable). A 12 V IC voltage regulator may be added if only high voltages are present inside the apparatus. The current consumption of the circuit is about 15 mA (at 12 V) when the relay is not operated.

Finally, the relay voltage must correspond to the supply voltage. Furthermore, the current rating of the relay should not exceed 100 mA, for T1's sake!

104   20°C + indicator

Temperatures above 20°C throughout the house are more than most people can afford nowadays. The trouble is, when it is snug and warm you are less inclined to notice that the heating is up too high (getting into a sweat thinking about the bill!) than when it is a little chilly and your teeth start to chatter. Heating systems that do not include thermostat regulation can now be provided with an elektronic excess temperature indicator. As a result, money and energy can be saved without your having to suffer discomfort.

An optical temperature display, in the form of a thermometer for instance, has the disadvantage that it becomes part of the furni-

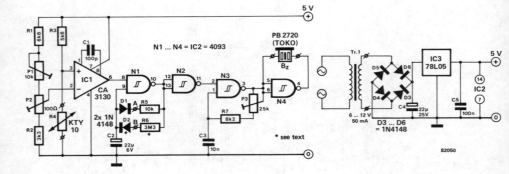

ture and therefore attracts little attention. An acoustic warning device, on the other hand, will make inmates sit up and take action (or at least bark!). The circuit in figure 1 shows how this idea can be put into practice. Resistor R4 is a KTY 10 temperature sensor which has a positive temperature coefficient (PTC) and is included in a bridge circuit that is fed with a stabilized supply voltage of +5 V. IC1 is a 3130 opamp and acts as a bridge amplifier. As long as the room temperature is below the threshold value set by P1 (coarse adjustment) and P2 (fine adjustment) respectively, the output of IC1 will be zero volts. As soon as the room temperature exceeds this value, however, the voltage at the non-inverting input (pin 3) of the opamp will be higher than the voltage at the other input (pin 2), so that the output (pin 8) will go high. This actuates the oscillator constructed around N1. Every minute, the oscillator generates a single pulse that lasts about 0.2 seconds. By way of the inverter N2, the pulse triggers oscillator N3 which then produces a warning signal. The tone has a frequency of about 5 kHz and drives the buzzer (a piezo-electric miniature loudspeaker) connected between the input and the output of the gate N4. Since the transducer provides a clear tone at about 4.6 kHz, P3 can be used to set both the frequency and the volume.

The circuit is an energy-saver in every sense of the word, for it requires very little current. Since not more than 2 mA is consumed, the power supply can be straightforward. It is best to include this, together with the circuit, in a small case. The sensor should be mounted on the outside of the case, to prevent a wrong temperature indication due to the transformer getting overheated.

Before the circuit is calibrated, the points marked 'A' and 'B' in the circuit diagram are linked. P1 is adjusted until the buzzer 'squeaks'; P3 is turned to select the desired volume.

P1 and P2 are preset for a room temperature corresponding to the required threshold value. At the right temperature level, the alarm will not sound, but as soon as this is exceeded, the buzzer will emit a high-pitched tone. Once the link A-B has been removed, the energy-saving temperature indicator will be ready for use.

105   high-impedance one-watt amplifier

A one-watt audio amplifier is nowadays easily contained on a small IC only found in portable radios and TV receivers, and cassette recorders. However, if such an amplifier offers hi-fi performance, the number of possible applications grows: for instance, it may be used for direct driving of

headphones, or as output stage in a hi-fi pre-amplifier for driving an active loudspeaker.

The circuit of the suggested amplifier consists of an opamp and a push-pull output stage. In spite of this simple configuration, some novelties in the circuit ensure good

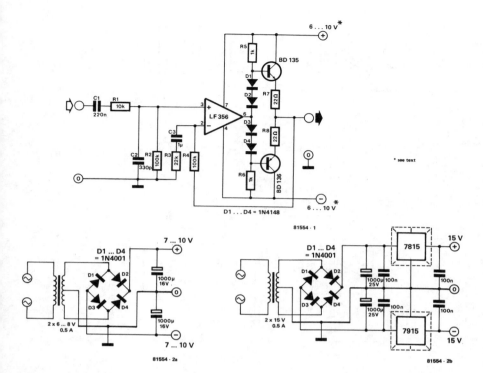

performance figures.

Low-pass filter R1-C2 at the input limits the slew rate of the input signal. In conjunction with the relatively fast opamp, this arrangement ensures very low non-linear distortion.

The quiescent current of the push-pull amplifier is fixed at 30 mA by diodes D1...D4 and emitter resistors R7 and R8: at this level of current the crossover distortion is very low. Furthermore, negative feedback keeps the overall distortion down to 0.1 per cent over the −3 dB power bandwidth of 10 Hz...30 kHz.

Feedback resistors R3 and R4 fix the overall gain at 15 dB. The maximum output is 1 watt into 8 Ω for an input signal of 500 mV$_{rms}$ High-impedance headphones as well as

4 Ω loudspeakers may also be used without any detriment.

If the two output transistors are mounted on suitable heat sinks, the amplifier will not be damaged by short circuits of the output terminals.

When driving high-impedance headphones at relatively high output is required, the supply voltage should be increased to ± 15 V. In that case, the circuit will only stand short circuits of the output for short periods.

The power supply may be of the simple, unstabilized type as shown in figure 2a. For supply voltages of ± 15 V the circuit of 2b should be used: the two voltage regulators help to prevent damage in case of short circuits at the output.

106 wind sound generator

Generating wind at professional film and television studios is a relatively simple matter: all they have to do is press a button and

a powerful fan supplies anything in the way of simulated sea breezes to gale force winds. In the home, such effects are much

1

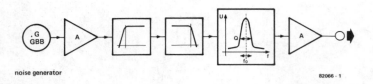

noise generator

82066 · 1

2

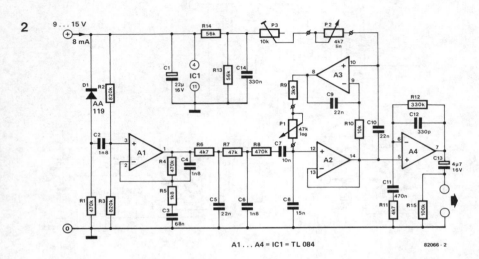

A1 ... A4 = IC1 = TL 084

82066 · 2

harder to create, and usually result in the perpetrator being thoroughly winded...

Anyone requiring a windlike sound, such as amateur photographers during a film or slide show, can make use of this portable electronic wind sound generator. A few components, a battery, and an amplifier are all that are required to produce effects ranging from a gentle breeze to a Caribbean hurricane. Just the thing for livening up a dull party!

The sound of the wind is very similar to the major headache of hi-fi enthusiasts: noise. Nevertheless, it is not sufficient to use just a noise generator to imitate gusts and gales, because the main characteristic of this is a considerable volume within a limited frequency range. The increase in volume accompanied by a howling or whistling tone is caused by diverting, compressing, and then expanding the actual wind. The slightest alteration will produce a different sound. Of course, the same principle applies to wind instruments where the column of air inside a tube is compressed and expanded to obtain the various notes of the scale.

122

We are not going to discuss electronic wind instruments here, as the majority of music synthesizers are able to imitate them. Rather, we are going to discuss an effective wind sound generator which uses a reverse biased germanium diode as a noise generator. The block diagram of the unit is given in figure 1.

The output of the noise generator is first amplified and then fed to an active bandpass filter constructed round two opamps. The bandwidth of the filter is very narrow to achieve maximum performance. In the design presented here, the selectivity and the centre frequency of the filter are variable, enabling a large variety of wind sounds to be selected.

The circuit diagram of the wind sound generator is shown in figure 2.

Germanium diode D1 and resistor R1 constitute the noise generator. The noise signal is amplified by opamp A1 which produces a noise level of about 150 mV$_{pp}$ at the output (pin 1). The amplified noise signal is then fed through a high-pass filter consisting of resistor R4 and capacitor C4 and then through a low-pass filter comprising

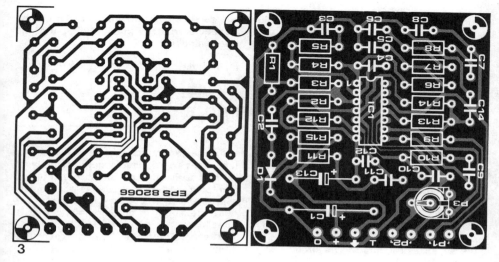

3

Parts list

Resistors:
R1,R4,R8 = 470 k
R2,R3 = 820 k
R5 = 1k8
R6,R11 = 4k7
R7 = 47 k
R9 = 3k9
R10 = 10 k
R12 = 330 k
R13,R14 = 56 k
R15 = 100 k
P1 = 47 k logarithmic
P2 = 4k7 linear
P3 = 10 k preset

Capacitors:
C1 = 22 μ/16 V
C2,C4,C6 = 1n8
C3 = 68 n
C5,C9,C10 = 22 n
C7 = 10 n
C8 = 15 n
C11 = 470 n
C12 = 330 p
C13 = 4μ7/16 V
C14 = 330 n

Semiconductors:
D1 = AA 119
IC1 = TL 084 or LM 324

Miscellaneous:
9 V battery or 9 V power supply (see text)

R6/C5 and R7/C6 to reduce the bandwidth. Resistor R8, capacitor C8, and opamps A2 and A3 form a tuned circuit with a resonant frequency that can be adjusted by potentiometer P1. The Q of the circuit can be regulated by P2 and P3. As a result, the wind force is set by the former and the volume of its whistling tone by the latter.

Opamp A2 also acts as a buffer stage and provides a low impedance output for the wind signal. The peak value at this output will only be about 1.4 mV, and this therefore needs to be amplified somewhat. This is accomplished by opamp A4: the final peak value of the wind signal is of the order of 100 mV.

Although the circuit has few components, the performance is quite surprising. All the components (apart from the potentio-

meters) are best mounted on the printed circuit board shown in figure 3.

Since the current consumption of the circuit is a mere 8 mA, it can be battery powered. A separate small power supply may also be used provided the supply voltage is adequately smoothed. A number of suitable circuits have been published in *Elektor* over the years.

Calibration simply involves the adjustment of preset potentiometer P3. With P1 and P2 set to their minimum and maximum resistances respectively, P3 is turned (starting from its minimum resistance value) until the band pass filter is just about to change frequency. In other words, the amplifier and loudspeaker should not emit the slightest breeze!

It may be advisable to connect the wind

123

sound generator to a mixer prior to the audio amplifier. This would enable the unit to be operated with maximum efficiency during slide and/or film shows, etc. The device is, of course, also suitable as a sound effects generator, in which case it can be connected directly to the line input of the audio amplifier.

H. Pietzko

107 electronic tuning aid

This article will be of special interest to those readers who enjoy music, particularly musicians. Tuning any instrument quickly and efficiently can sometimes be a problem; at the very least, it can be laborious. This article provides a quick and easy method. The use of digital technology ensures that simplicity is not achieved at the expense of accuracy. The circuit easily lends itself to be modified to suit any particular purpose.

This tuning aid will provide what a great many musicians have been looking for. There are two main problems associated with tone generators — which is all a tuning fork really is. The first is that of stability. It is obvious that the instrument being tuned can only be as accurate as the tuning source and therefore the circuit must produce the same F# in a month's time as it does today.

The second difficulty arises when the tuning source provides a number of notes. The relationship between them must of course be fixed and they must also remain stable. A look at the circuit diagram in figure 1 will show that the number of components could hardly be any less. All the

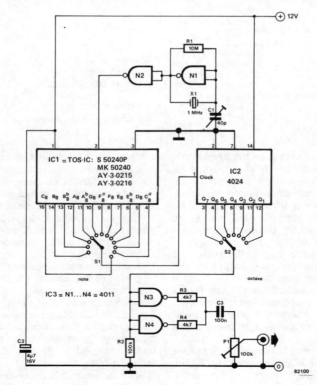

124

available tones are derived from a master oscillator. This is formed by two gates, N1 and N2, and is crystal controlled for good accuracy. This effectively takes care of the stability and long term accuracy problems. The use of a crystal keeps drift to an absolute minimum. The oscillator frequency can be trimmed by variable capacitor C1.

The oscillator frequency is fed to pin 1 of master tone generator IC1. This provides the complete set of twelve notes of an octave without any need for external components.

A 1 MHz crystal provides a frequency at pin 16 of 2092.0502 Hz.

It is a simple matter to select any one of the outputs with the aid of switch S1. However, we still finish up with just any one note of one octave. This may satisfy many requirements, but it would be very useful to be able to select any one of the number of octaves as well.

Fortunately this can be accomplished quite simply. The wiper of switch S1 is fed di-rectly to the clock input of a 7 stage counter, IC2. The seven outputs of this IC provide us with any one of seven octaves. All that remains of the circuit are the gates N3 and N4 and the surrounding components. The two gates are connected in parallel and act as buffers for the output. Potentiometer P1 is used to adjust the output level.

For precise calibration a frequency counter is needed. This is connected to the output of N2, and C1 is adjusted for a reading of 1.00012 MHz. Although originally intended as a tuning aid, the circuit has many other uses. For specific purposes one or even both switches may be dispensed with, and one or a few specific tones can be hard-wired. For instance, guitarists will require E, A, D, G, B and E. A six-way switch with taps at the right outputs will provide this very easily.

S. Akkal

108   sound cube

Cubes are attractive to the human mind, a fact well proved by the pyramids and the popularity of Rubik's cube. The cube described here contains a variable audio generator. Each face of the cube has a touch switch on its surface and contact with one or more of these will cause a sound to be produced. However, the sound will vary depending on how many and which of the faces are touched. The sound cube is quite fascinating to all ages and, once picked up, becomes very difficult to put down.

History will probably show that Rubik has done more for today's cube than all the other ancients put together and it is entirely possible that our sound cube will not reach the same degree of fame. However, it is musical and therefore not really in the same class. That is not to say that it is a musical instrument, more a musical game. In effect, the cube will produce a tone whenever a side is touched. Each side has its own individual tone but this will be changed if two or more sides are touced at the same time, when picking it up for instance. Replacing the cube on the table will immediately silence it.

This could all work out to be a very complex circuit but a glance at the circuit diagram will show this not to be the case. It will be obvious that the heart of the circuit must be an oscillator and this is formed by inverters N7 and N8. The timing components of the oscillator are capacitor C1 and the resistor chain consisting of R7 to R13. Six electronic switches (ES1 to ES6) placed across the resistors are controlled from a touch plate in each face of the cube. If touch switch S1 is bridged by a finger, ES1 will be actuated, effectively taking R8 out of circuit. The frequency of the oscillator is determined by the total value of the resistors that are in circuit. Which face operates which electronic switch is left to the constructor; some combinations may be better than others.

The output of the oscillator is fed via a buffer, N9, to our audio stage, transistor T1 and the speaker. The type of speaker used is not critical providing it is 8 Ω. The available space will probably be the determining factor!

The one essential point of the cube is that all the faces appear to be identical in order

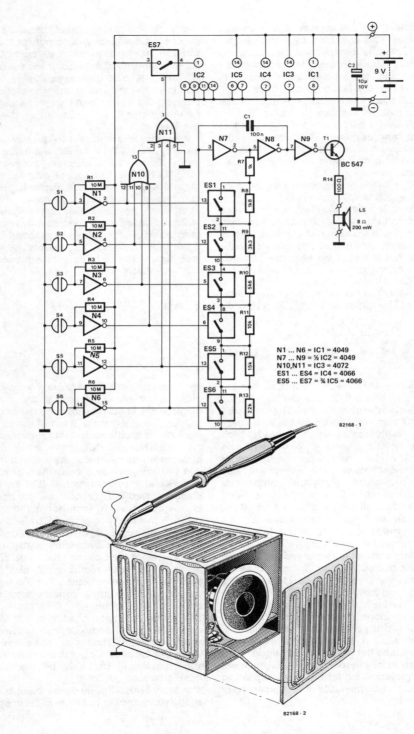

1

ES7

IC2 IC5 IC4 IC3 IC1

N11

N10

N7 N8 N9 T1
BC 547

C1
100 n

C2
10µ
10V

9 V

R7
1k

R14
100 Ω

LS
8 Ω
200 mW

R1
10 M
N1
S1

R2
10 M
N2
S2

R3
10 M
N3
S3

R4
10 M
N4
S4

R5
10 M
N5
S5

R6
10 M
N6
S6

ES1
R8
1k8

ES2
R9
3k3

ES3
R10
5k6

ES4
R11
10k

ES5
R12
15k

ES6
R13
22k

N1 ... N6 = IC1 = 4049
N7 ... N9 = ½ IC2 = 4049
N10,N11 = IC3 = 4072
ES1 ... ES4 = IC4 = 4066
ES5 ... ES7 = ¾ IC5 = 4066

82168 - 1

2

82168 · 2

that its orientation remains a mystery. This causes a major problem when a on/off switch is to be fitted. To overcome this we have included an electronic power switch consisting of gates N10 and N11 together with ES7. Briefly, if no touch switch (S1 to S6) is bridged the electronic switch ES7 becomes open circuit thus switching off the oscillator. The use of CMOS ICs ensure that power consumption is kept to a very low level: the 9 volt battery should therefore last for quite a time.

Manufacturing a cube is on a par with making four chair legs independently — only three legs will ever touch the ground at any one time. Murphy's Law definitely states that the final face of a cube will not fit its allotted space when completing the cube and you can bet your reel of solder on that! For this reason another source of cubes would be a major advantage. Toy shops for the young are a cubic paradise and should provide one or two ideas. It is well worth shopping around for ideas before aquiring your cube because a good cube is an anonymous cube and very few fit into this category. Bear in mind that each face of the cube must contain a touch switch in one form or another. Figure 2 illustrates how this can be achieved by a printed circuit type of switch. If these can be made and fitted onto each face of your selected cube your problems are almost over.

The final problem is that of getting the circuit, the speaker and the battery inside the cube — we have to leave that one to you! Don't forget to make some holes in each face to let the sound out or you will have a mute cube on your hands.

Two points that may make for a more appealing cube. The sensitivity of the touch switches can be increased by raising the values of resistors R1 to R6 to about 22 MΩ. Finally, the tone range can be varied by changing the value of C1 to taste.

K. Siol

109   stop-signal override for model railways

Model railway enthusiasts know the problem: colour light signals disconnect the supply voltage from a section of track as soon as the signal is on red. Any train approaching the signal stops on the dead section of track. It can only continue its journey when the signal indicates 'line clear' or 'reduce speed'.

The problem arises when a train approaches the signal from the opposite direction during shunting or at rural stations. This is not possible with the usual colour light signal circuit which disconnects the supply voltage, thus preventing traffic in both directions.

What is needed is a circuit that allows the signal to operate almost like a diode: in the normal direction the signal stops trains but allows trains to travel in the reverse direction.

In addition to the light signal we need two rail contacts at the two ends of the controlled section (see figure 1). These are contact A at the end and contact B at the beginning, when viewed in the normal direction of travel. The train travelling in the reverse direction reaches contact A first. The contact closes and sets bistable FF1. The Q-output of the bistable goes to logic 1 and energizes the relay via T1. The relay contact closes and bridges the circuit that was originally disconnected by the signal. The train can travel in reverse along the controlled section of track. As soon as it reaches contact B the bistable is reset and the original state is restored. A train travelling in the normal direction first reaches contact B, thus causing the bistable to be reset and enabling proper functioning of the signal.

LED D6 (drawn with dashed lines in the circuit) lights when the signal override is effective.

The power supply of the override circuit is generously rated and can power several override circuits of this type. The current drawn by one of these circuits depends on the relay used. Transistor T1 can supply a maximum relay coil current of 100 mA. Instead of using a separate transformer for

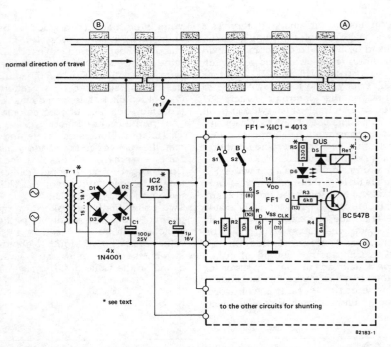

normal direction of travel

FF1 = ½IC1 = 4013

* see text

to the other circuits for shunting

82183-1

the power supply, the AC voltage can also be obtained from the lighting output of the model railway transformer.

If a 12 V relay is utilized, the AC voltage required is 15...18 V and a 7812 voltage regulator is needed for IC2. With a 5 V relay, a type 7805 regulator must be used for IC2, in which case the transformer secondary voltage should be approximately 8...12 V. With a relay voltage of 5 V, the value of R5 should be 120 Ω.

110 economical crystal time base

This time base circuit is built using normal readily available CMOS ICs and a cheap crystal. The circuit gives the constructor a choice of 50 Hz, 100 Hz, or 200 Hz time bases. The 50 Hz reference frequency is an ideal time base for the construction or cali-

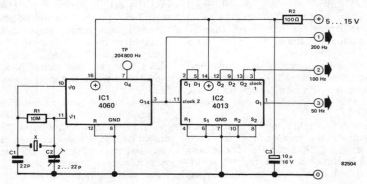

X = 3.2768 MHz

82504

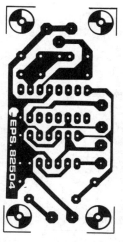

Parts list

Resistors:
R1 = 10 M
R2 = 100 Ω

Capacitors:
C1 = 22 p
C2 = 2...22 p trimmer
C3 = 10 µ/16 V

Semiconductors:
IC1 = 4060
IC2 = 4013

Miscellaneous:
X = 3.2768 MHz crystal

bration of electronic clocks, frequency meters and so on. Because of the flexible supply voltage requirement, it is also a good basis from which to build a digital clock for the car.

IC1 contains an oscillator and a 2^{14} divider. Providing the oscillator loop is correctly calibrated with C2, the output at pin 3 (Q14) will produce a 200 Hz square wave. With the help of the two bistables in IC2 this square wave voltage is then divided by two and then by four resulting in two further outputs of 100 Hz and 50 Hz, the latter from pin 1. Readers who have a frequency meter can calibrate the circuit by simply connecting the meter to pin 7 of IC1 (Q4) and adjusting C2 until a reading of 204.800 Hz is indicated. As a matter of interest, anyone without a frequency meter should not despair since setting trimmer C2 to about midway will provide sufficient accuracy for most applications.

The 100 Hz output is useful for the construction of digital counters. For this purpose we suggest that a 1 : 10 divider (like the 4518) is connected to the 100 Hz output pin. The power supply requirements are: 5...15 V at 0.5...2.5 mA.

111 DC motor speed control

The LM 1014 IC from National Semiconductor can be used to provide a constant speed control for small DC motors. A well known trick is used here. This takes into consideration the fact that when the motor current rises (owing to an increase in load) the voltage across the motor will follow suit. The reason for this is that if the motor speed drops slightly, the back e.m.f. decreases which means that the motor current (given the same supply voltage) is going to increase. It follows that raising the voltage across the motor will increase the speed.

Theoretically then, it is possible to hold the motor speed virtually constant in this way. However, in practice this system has a tendency to be unstable and the only way to keep it within acceptable limits is to allow slight speed variations in the order of a few percent (depending on load conditions).

A disadvantage of the circuit is that the value of the components required cannot be given as hard and fast. It is a circuit then that does require some experimenting with to obtain the best results. The values of resistors R1, R2, and R3 should be selected so that R1R3/5R2 is equal to the dynamic impedance of the motor. How do you find this? A good start for the calculation is to simply measure the resistance of the motor with a multimeter and start with this value. Choose R1 to be slightly on the low side from the formula and check whether or not the motor is still controllable. As long as it

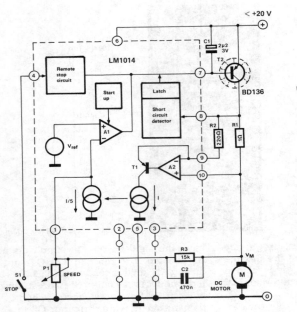

$$U_M = U_{ref} \left(1 + \frac{R3}{P1}\right) + I_M \frac{R1 \cdot R3}{5 \cdot R2}$$

82590

table

V_{ref} (V)	$\Delta V_{ref}/\Delta T$ (mV/°C)	Condition
0.95	−1.0	2/3 open
1.15	−0.3	2 gnd, 3 open
1.35	+0.3	2 open, 3 gnd
1.55	+1.0	2/3 gnd

doesn't run wild (run up to maximum speed and stay there) or start hunting, R1 can be increased in value.

The output voltage, and with it the speed, can be adjusted by P1. The formula for the output voltage is given in the diagram. Before calculations are begun, a reference voltage must be selected via pins 2 and 3. Each reference voltage has a different temperature coefficient (see table). This parameter of the motor will rarely be known and so the choice will come down to personal taste.

The value of P1 is not really critical. This potentiometer at minimum value will certainly give maximum volts supply but using too small a value will only make it impossible to slow the motor very much. The choice of R1 not only determines the dynamic characteristic of the circuit but also limits the maximum motor current. With the value shown in the diagram (1 Ω), the maximum current will be 1.4 A. The values given were actually used with a motor that was measured as follows:

dynamic resistance: 16.3 Ω
reverse e.m.f.: 3.25 V at 2000 rpm
current: 5.9 mA per mNm of moment
National Semiconductor Applications

112   power failure protection

Nothing can be worse than having even a brief collapse of the mains supply voltage when working with a system using volatile memory, like RAM.

After the interruption, no matter how small, it will be apparent that the data in the RAM has well and truly evaporated. For that reason a lot of circuits are designed to obviate the problem of mains supply failure. The circuit described here falls into the same general category.

An bridge rectifier is added to the existing power supply, together with a relay Re1 in series with resistor R1. The contact for the standby power supply of 10 – 15 V is made by Re1. The circuit must detect a mains voltage collapse as early as possible. As soon as Re1 is no longer actuated, the batteries take over. Obviously, no matter how quickly this changeover takes place, it will

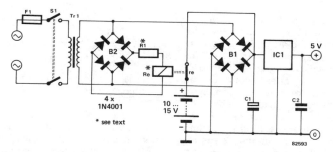

take a finite period of time, therefore capacitor C1 must be able to supply the necessary current during this period.
Any drop in voltage across this capacitor is catered for by the regulator IC1. An AC relay can also be used and, in this case, the bridge rectifier B2 can be dispensed with. When a DC type is used, the hold voltage of the relay should be about 1.2 V below that of the secondary voltage of the transformer. The following formula is used to establish the correct type of relay.

$R_S = [(2U_p/\pi - U_h - 2U_d)/I_h]\Omega$
$I_h = [U_h/R_r] A$
R_S = series resistor;
U_p = peak value of secondary voltage = 1.414 U_{rms};
U_h = hold voltage;
I_h = hold current;

U_d = forward voltage of diode = 0.6 V;
R_r = coil resistance of relay.
The relay should be sufficiently slow to bridge the gap when the voltage drops below the 'hold' level, but not too slow, otherwise C1 will get into difficulties and cause the relay to buzz. The tighter the operating tolerances, the faster the switch-over to the standby power supply.
Remember that the standby supply does not necessarily have to power the complete system, but only the RAMs. In this way the accumulator will last that much longer.
It is possible to trickle charge the battery by connecting it via a series resistor to the voltage across C1 (in parallel with the relay contacts). The value of the resistor will depend on the specific battery (NiCd) in use.

113 automatic outdoor light

The purpose of this circuit is to automatically switch on an outside light to illuminate your front door, when a visitor arrives.
The circuit uses a light detecting resistor (LDR) as the sensor. For the circuit to work, an external light source such as a lamp post is required. Needless to say, this source needs to be close by. Please remember

that the removal or repositioning of lamp posts needs the authority of the local council, so we do not recommend this circuit to anyone who has to remodel the landscape. The LDR is mounted in a tube, behind a lens, and aimed at the light source. This structure is positioned so that the person approaching the front door causes a

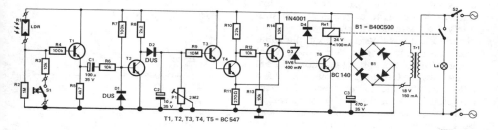

shadow to fall onto the lens. Do not forget to ensure that the tube containing the LDR is water-tight. Immediately the LDR is in shadow, its resistance will increase. This results in T1 applying a negative pulse to T2 via C1 and R6. T2 continues to conduct until this negative pulse arrives. As soon as T2 cuts off, C2 starts to charge. When the voltage across C2 rises above 2 V, the schmitt-trigger formed by T3, T4, T5, (and their surrounding components), switches on transistor T6. T6 conducts and triggers the relay, which switches on the outside light. The rate at which C2 discharges is adjusted by P1. When the voltage across C2 falls below 1.5 V, the schmitt-trigger returns to a quiescent state. T6 will cut off, switching off the relay and therefore the light.

The light will remain on for a maximum of one minute. Longer periods are possible, but then C2 will have to be replaced by a larger capacitor. Switch S1 and R3 are con-

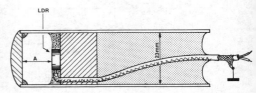

nected in parallel with R2. S1 can be a make/break contact mounted on the front door. When the door is opened, the light will switch on, going out immediately the door is shut.

For the circuit to work effectively, the tube containing the LDR (and lens) must be positioned, relative to the light source, so that the voltage measured at the junction of R1 and R2 is not less than 3 V, and not more than 20 V.

J. Bodewes

114 low octave switch

The limited five-octave range of many electronic pianos and organs can be extended by one octave at the lower end with the aid of the circuit here. It is connected between the main oscillator (input point A) and the highest octave generator (output point B). A monostable is constructed with N1, N2, C1, P1, and R4. Its period is set by P1 so that the monostable divides the frequency of the main oscillator by 2. Switch S1 provides the ability to switch between the original tone range and the lowered tone range. Diodes D1 and D2 protect the input against high level and negative input signals. The value of C1 depends on the frequency of the main oscillator, but can be found quite easily after some experimenting; the frequency of the piano or organ should suddenly be lowered by one octave when turning P1. If this does not occur, the value of C1 must be increased. When the correct value is found, the correct position for P1 is that where the frequency is lowered, plus a little extra 'tweak' to retain stability. This completes the calibration procedure. A final note: the input voltage at point A must be at least 60% of the supply voltage.

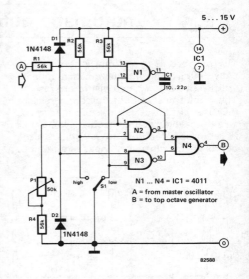

115   78L voltage regulators . . . and 79L

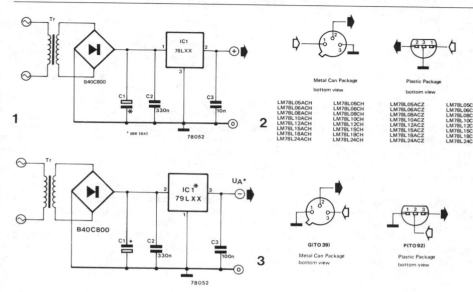

1

2

Metal Can Package
bottom view

LM78L05ACH	LM78L05CH
LM78L06ACH	LM78L06CH
LM78L08ACH	LM78L08CH
LM78L10ACH	LM78L10CH
LM78L12ACH	LM78L12CH
LM78L15ACH	LM78L15CH
LM78L18ACH	LM78L18CH
LM78L24ACH	LM78L24CH

Plastic Package
bottom view

LM78L05ACZ	LM78L05CZ
LM78L06ACZ	LM78L06CZ
LM78L08ACZ	LM78L08CZ
LM78L10ACZ	LM78L10CZ
LM78L12ACZ	LM78L12CZ
LM78L15ACZ	LM78L15CZ
LM78L18ACZ	LM78L18CZ
LM78L24ACZ	LM78L24CZ

3

G(TO 39)
Metal Can Package
bottom view

P(TO 92)
Plastic Package
bottom view

Low-power IC voltage regulators of the 78L series offer the advantages of good regulation, current limiting/short circuit protection at 100 mA, and thermal shutdown in the event of excessive power dissipation. In fact, virtually the only way in which these regulators can be damaged is by incorrect polarity or by an excessive input voltage. Regulators in the 78L series up to the 8 V type will withstand input voltages up to about 35 V, whilst the 24 V type will withstand 40 V. Normally, of course, the regulators would not be operated with such a large input-output differential as this would lead to excessive power dissipation.

A choice of 8 output voltages is offered in the 78L series of regulators, as shown in table 1. The full type number also carries a letter suffix (not shown in table 1) to denote the output voltage tolerance and package type. The AC suffix denotes a voltage tolerance of ±5%, whilst the C suffix denotes a tolerance of ± 10%. The letter H denotes a metal can package, whilst the letter Z denotes a plastic package. Thus a 78L05ACZ would be a 5 V regulator with a 5% tolerance in a plastic package.

All the regulators in the 78L series will deliver a maximum current of 100 mA provided the input-output voltage differential

4

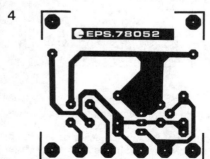

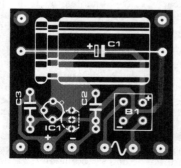

Capacitors:
C1 = see text and table
C2 = 330 n
C3 = 10 n

Semiconductors:
IC = 78LXX (see text and table)
B = 40 V/800 mA bridge rectifier
PCB 78052

Table 1   Imax. = 100 mA

Uout	type	Utr. (RMS) min.	max.	C1
5 V	78L05	6.4 V	9.6 V	1000 μ/16 V
6 V	78L06	7.3 V	10.3 V	1000 μ/16 V
8 V	78L08	9.6 V	12.0 V	470 μ/25 V
10 V	78L10	11.0 V	13.4 V	470 μ/25 V
12 V	78L12	13.1 V	15.2 V	330 μ/25 V
15 V	78L15	15.2 V	17.3 V	330 μ/25 V
18 V	78L18	17.5 V	19.5 V	330 μ/35 V
24 V	78L24	21.9 V	23.7 V	330 μ/35 V

does not exceed 7 V, otherwise excessive power dissipation will result and the thermal shutdown will operate. This occurs at a dissipation of about 700 mW; however, the metal-can version may dissipate 1.4 W if fitted with a heatsink.

A regulator circuit using the 78L ICs is shown in figure 1, together with the layout of a suitable printed circuit board. The to obtain the rated output voltage at a current up to 100 mA are given in table 1, together with suitable values for the reservoir capacitor, C1. The capacitance/voltage prod-

uct of these capacitors is chosen so that any one of them will fit the printed circuit board without difficulty.

A similar range of regulators exists for negative voltages: the 79L series. Even though the pinning is different, the same basic p.c. board layout can be used. The regulator is mounted 'backwards' in the plastic position; '+' then becomes the *negative* output, and the positive end of C1 is supply common.

116   signal strength meter

A meter of this kind is very useful for determining the radiation characteristics of directional beam transceiver aerials. It allows the user to trim the aerial accurately for an optimum transmitting radiation pattern.

An auxiliary aerial should be positioned a short way from the main transmitting one. The signal received by this is then fed to a resonance circuit formed by L1, L2, and varicap C2. This enables the meter to be accurately tuned to the particular transmitting frequency to be measured. With the coil values shown in the circuit diagram the band-width of the meter is 6...60 MHz. The RF signal is fed to diode D1, which constitutes a rectifier/demodulation stage. Finally, the signal is routed to the non-inverting input of opamp IC1. The gain of this opamp, and therefore the sensitivity of the 1 mA meter, is adjusted by P1.

The prototype was found to be extremely sensitive, and highly selective. A pair of headphones can be connected to the out-

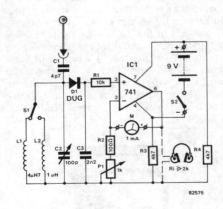

put of the opamp allowing the actual transmission to be monitored. The overall resistance of these should not be less than 2k2 otherwise an extra amplification stage will be required.

117 magic running lights

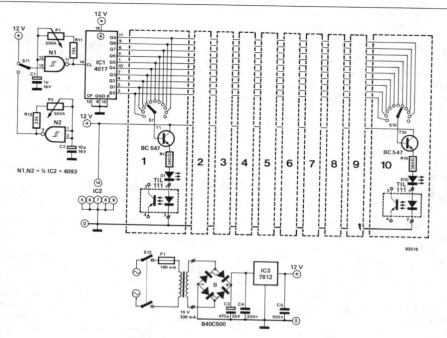

The ten-channel running lights circuit shown here is remarkable in that it has many preset facilities. Every one of the outputs of counter IC1 can be connected to any one of the ten different output drivers with the aid of ten 10-way wafers. The result is an immense variety of light patterns, running in various directions; from left to right, towards each other, away from each other, in all sorts of rhythms... The running speed is selected by S11 and is controlled by either a single oscillator (N1) or by two oscillators, in which case N1 is controlled by N2 and the result is a 'hopping' effect. Should the constructor only wish to drive LEDs, the cathodes of LEDs D1...D10 may be grounded. The circuit diagram does, however, make provision for another alternative: the use of optocouplers to drive standard coloured light bulbs. Whichever circuit you choose, it won't be a 'flash in the pan!'

118 slave flash trigger

A triggering circuit for slave flash guns ensures that the slave flashes simultaneously with the main or master gun. Apart from the commercially available units, there are quite a few circuit designs published in electronic magazines. Unfortunately most of these have one major drawback. They all need some form of power supply, such as normal batteries etc. The circuit design described in this article uses a virtually inexhaustible supply! Solar cells are applied here in an ingenious way! The flash of light emitted by the master gun will trigger the slave. The small delay which occurs is so small (in the order of 1/1000th of a second), that it is virtually undetectable by the human eye.

The circuit consists of a sensitive low powered silicon-controlled rectifier (SCR), in this case the TIC 106D (Th1), and a choke. The solar cells (which should have a minimum surface area of 100 mm²) are connected in series. They generate the ignition pulse for the SCR immediately the master flash is fired. A 68 mH choke ensures that the circuit is insensitive to ambient light. The prototype achieved an operating distance of 50 metres, between the slave and a master flash gun with a power figure of 28!

G. Kleinnibbelink

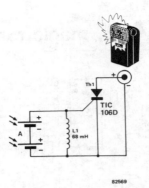

82569

119   high-speed NiCd charger

The graph in figure 1 shows what happens during a (fast) NiCd charge cycle. At first, the voltage rises very quickly from its initial discharged state to attain as much as 1.42 V with a 25% charge level. After this point, the voltage will tend to rise more gradually. Just before the fully charged level is reached, the voltage surprisingly surges once more.

As figure 1 shows, the gas produced when the battery is about 75% charged, causes a dramatic increase in the pressure and temperature inside the battery. By using the temperature curve relative to the charge, a simple procedure involving two special temperature sensor ICs serves to switch off the supply current when the temperature of the battery has risen by 5°C. As can be seen in the graph, this is fairly conservative: an almost flat battery will be charged to 50%, and even an almost fully charged battery will remain within the 20% over-charge margin.

Figure 2 shows the circuit diagram. The output of the comparator opamp IC1 goes low whenever the voltage at its negative input is equal to that at its positive input. P1 sets the voltage level at the positive input so that it is 50 mV above that of the negative input. When the operational voltage is switched on (don't connect up the battery yet!) sensors D1 and D2 must be given enough time to reach the *same* temperature. Depending on the temperature of D2, the voltage at the negative input will increase by 10 mV per degree centigrade.

As D2 is mounted on top of the NiCd (preferably tightly strapped by a rubber band), the rise in battery temperature will automatically switch off the charge current. A different voltage may of course also be set at the positive input. As illustrated in figure 1, the battery has only reached 50% of its charge level by the time the temperature has risen by 5°C, if it was initially completely discharged. However, there is a reason for this. The graph shown here cannot be taken as gospel for every battery and for all possible charge currents — and it is better to err on the safe side!

There is an alternative: you can progressively increase the temperature difference the circuit will tolerate before cutting off, until your particular type of NiCad cell proves to be fully charged. The advantage is obvious, but the risk should be equally clear...Fortunately, temperature rises quite steeply once the cell is fully charged, so the chance of getting too far off the mark

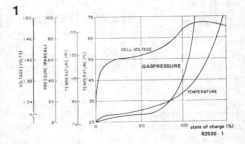

82530 - 1

136

2

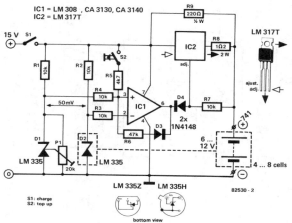

IC1 = LM 308 , CA 3130, CA 3140
IC2 = LM 317T

S1: charge
S2: top up

bottom view

is not so high. According to the graph, 12°C (120 mV) is still quite safe.

The circuit works as follows. After closing S1 and operating S2, the charger starts to pump about 1 A into the battery. The current is provided by the variable voltage regulator IC, the LM 317T, which serves as a constant-current source. If the comparator output is high, D3 and D4 will be cut off. As a result, the internal reference voltage of IC2, 1.25 V, will be across R8, enabling about 1 A current to flow into the battery. Should the comparator output be low, the cathodes of D3 and D4 will be practically grounded. The constant-current source is switched off, and only 15...40 mA maintenance current will be flowing across R9 (depending on the battery voltage). The time required to charge a battery can be derived from its rating: approximately 30 minutes for a 0.5 Ah cell for instance. In principle, the charge current should be related to the battery capacity and in practice this means that the circuit can cater for 4...8 AA penlight cells. Larger cells, such as the A and C types, can be charged if an additional current source with the same component values is connected in parallel to IC2/R7/R8. Compact 9 V batteries can be charged if R8 is increased to 6.3 Ω (4.7 + 1.5).

One further hint: The rapid charge procedure will only benefit specific battery types (as indicated by the manufacturer). The circuit may have to be modified for each type by changing the value of R8 accordingly.

National Semiconductor

120   automatic delay switch

It is often said that two heads are better than one but this numerical advantage applied to hands could also be a great asset, especially when using probes to test a complex printed circuit board. It is an absolute certainty that the test probe that you have just painstakingly connected will flip itself off at the instant the power is switched on. Further, it is a known fact that it will land with unerring accuracy on the most sensitive part of the circuit — and discharge the smoothing capacitor across the input of the circuit! How well we know the problem! The title of this circuit could well have been *frayed temper adjuster* since it is capable of just that. It allows the use of both hands to position and hold the probes while the power to the circuit is applied automatically after a short delay. It even tells you (visually) when this is about to happen.

An astable multivibrator with a frequency of about 2 Hz is formed by gate N1. Its output is buffered by two further gates, N2 and N3, in parallel to provide enough current drive

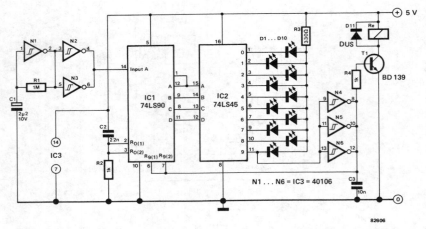

82606

for the input of the decade counter IC1. The counter is reset on power up by the C2/R2 combination before providing an output to the second IC, a binary-to-decimal decoder. The first of the ten LEDs connected to the output of this IC will light two seconds after power is applied to the circuit. It will be followed at 2 second intervals by the other LEDs until D10 lights after a total of 20 seconds.

As can be seen from the circuit diagram, the final output at pin 11 is buffered by parallel gates N4...N6. These provide sufficient base drive current to allow transistor T1 to actuate the relay at the same time that D10 lights. Power to the circuit under test is then provided via the relay contacts (not shown here) and will remain until the delay circuit is switched off. This latch is provided by the link between the N4...N6 outputs and pins 6 and 7 of IC1.

The time periods can be varied by altering the value of resistor R1: a larger value will lengthen the time. A simple stabilized supply consisting of a 7805 regulator can be used to power the delay circuit. However, the delay on switch should be placed between the regulator and the delay circuit to ensure that the initial reset works reliably.

M. A. Prins

121 smoke detector

Smoke detectors are part of any sophisticated alarm system. Most of the professionally made ones use some form of gassensor, ionization chamber, or radioactive element. The circuit described does not use any of these rather complex components but makes good use of two light detecting resistors (LDRs) and a LED. A special IC, LM1801, allows the circuit to be constructed using the minimum of components. It is an IC designed specifically for use in smoke detectors, containing, among other things, an internal supply zener, two reference voltage outputs, a voltage comparator, and a 500 mA output transistor with clamp diodes. The complete circuit is connected to the mains supply. Diode D1 rectifies the supply, R7 reducing the voltage to a workable level for the IC. Capacitor C2 smoothes this, and the internal zener of the IC stabilizes it.

The circuit uses a pair of balanced light detecting resistors. By using these in a bridge arrangement, any changes in resistance due to temperature or ageing effects are cancelled out. This bridge circuit is constructed by the network of R1, R4, the two LDRs (R12, R13), connected to one of the comparator's inputs from the junction of R4 and R13. The other inputs for the internal comparator are from the junctions of R1, R12, and the voltage divider R2/R3. This ar-

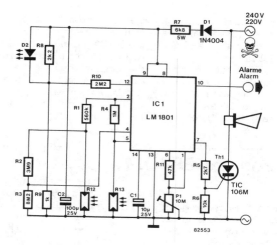

rangement ensures that both LDRs are biased at the same voltage to ensure proper tracking.

Physically, the LDRs should be situated such that smoke particles will reflect light from the LED (D2), onto R13, causing its resistance to drop. As soon as the comparator detects this drop in voltage, the IC triggers the silicon-controlled rectifier (SCR) Th1,

causing a mains powered horn to sound. P1 adjusts the sensitivity of the circuit.

The most difficult part of the construction is the placing of the LED and LDRs. Basically, the LED should be positioned exactly in the middle of the two, ensuring that there is no air flow between the LED and R12. This can be easily achieved by placing a small perspex box around R12 and the LED.

122   simple AGC

This circuit will provide an output with a fairly constant amplitude of 4 V peak to peak, from an input that may vary between 100 mV to 2 V. There was no intention of achieving hi-fi performance as the distortion figures are not exactly in that league. Nevertheless, this automatic gain control is

ideal for use when recording computer programs onto cassette tape where a constant peak value is more important than low distortion. Opamp A1 provides an output impedance that is sufficiently low to drive the attenuator formed by diodes D1 and D2. Opamp A2 is a straight-forward amplifier

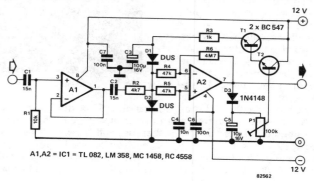

with a gain of 40 dB but its DC setting is a little unusual in that it is derived from the average of the input signal via R5 and C4. The off-set voltage of A2 cannot escape being modified to some degree but, since this is relatively stable, it should not present too much of a problem. The output includes a peak detector consisting of D3 and C5. A proportion (determined by P1) of the

voltage across C5 is passed back in the form of a feedback loop, via T1 and T2, to the D1/D2 attenuator. However, because the two transistors from a current source, it is the current through the two diodes that controls the gain of the final stage. In other words, an increase in the current across D1/D2 will result in greater attenuation of the output.

123 program EPROM. . .

After the welcome drop in prices of good quality EPROMs over the past year or so, computer enthusiasts have a great incentive for taking on more ambitious programming projects. Although normal operation calls for a 5 V supply voltage, 25 V is needed to program a 2716. In some types, the 25 V programming voltage need not be switched off while the operator checks freshly stored data. On the other hand, there are types for which the voltage has to be switched from 5 V to 25 V continously.

It therefore follows that a suitable EPROM power supply has to meet certain requirements: it needs to be straightforward, fast (often the speed is specified by the manufacturer as being, say, between 0.5 and 2 µs), accurate (no danger of overshoot or undershoot) and short proof. The well-proven 723 voltage controller IC fits the bill perfectly. As the circuit diagram shows, the 723 is at the heart of an ordinary 5 V power supply. Preset P1 limits the reference voltage (pin 6) to 5 V and feeds the signal to the non-inverting input. When transistor T1 stops conducting, the whole output voltage is fed to the inverting input (pin 4) and 5 V will therefore be available at the output. Resistor R7 limits the current.

So far so good, but what about the 25 V we said we needed? This is obtained by changing the feedback loop to pin 4. The output voltage is increased by adding a voltage divider to this section in the circuit. T1 activates the voltage divider. As soon as the base of the transistor is driven, the 723 produces the 25 V voltage. To obtain different voltage levels the values of R5, R6, and P2 will have to be changed.

Calibrate the circuit as follows: use P1 to set the output voltage to 5 V without driving T1.

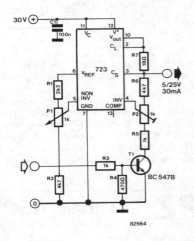

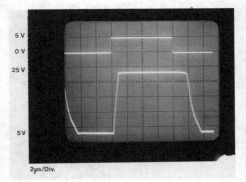

2µs/Div.

Then drive T1 by applying 5 V to R3 and set the output voltage to 25 V with P2. That's all there is to it!

The upper trace in the photograph represents the signal controlling T1 (between 0 and 5 V) and the lower trace shows the output signal. The 723 is especially fast because pin 13, the frequency compensation input, is not used here. Normally speaking, a grounded capacitor is included at this point to smooth the signal edges. Note that it takes the output signal another 2 μs to go low again once the control signal has gone low. This is because it takes tran-

sistor T1 quite a while to stop conducting. In applications where the time factor is highly critical, this may be a problem, in which case it is best to replace T1 by a CMOS switch (such as the 4066) or a V-FET (such as the BS 170), and omitting R3 and R4. Alternatively, a proper switching transistor, the BSX 20, also provides excellent results.

124   miniature amplifier

There are many ICs available today that contain all the circuitry required for various versions of power output stages. The IC presented here goes even further than that. It can be used as a complete amplifier. Obviously it is not super hi-fi but for a second (or third) amplifier it is quite good enough.

The IC contains a small power output stage and three further transistors on the same chip. This means that no further active components are required for the amplifier. The gain of the output stage is simply set by means of a capacitor and a resistor. In the circuit diagram the gain is set at 26 dB which means that pins 4 and 12 are simply left floating. If a 10 μF capacitor is connected between these pins, the gain increases to 46 dB and 34 dB if a 1k2 resistor is inserted in series with the capacitor. Transistor T1 is used as an emitter follower (high input impedance/low output impedance). This sets the input impedance of the circuit to approximately 50 kΩ. The so-called Baxandall tone control is formed by the networks R5...R8, C4...C7, and P1 and P2. Transistors T2 and T3 are the active part

of the tone control circuit and ensure a gain of 1 to 1 in this stage. The signal is then fed to the power amplifier via volume control P3. The output stage is not given in detail here, but simply as a block: IC1. The maximum output power into a 4 Ω load is about 300 mW with a distortion figure of 10%. With an 8 Ω load this becomes 600 mW again with 10% distortion. If the maximum output power is required with a 12 V supply, it is advisable to use a heat sink for IC1. A lower distortion figure can be achieved by limiting the power output to 120 mW. This presents a reasonable distortion figure of 0.2%. The minimum input voltage for maximum output is approximately 100 mV for a 4 Ω load and 150 mV for an 8 Ω load. Modifying the gain will alter the input sensitivity by a factor of 10.
When constructing the circuit a few points must be watched. Pin 18 of the IC is connected direct to the central earth connection of the circuit, in this case 0 V of the power supply. The loudspeaker must also be connected to this point.

National Semiconductor Application

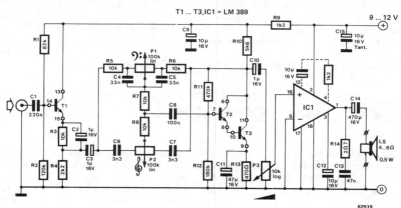

82519

125 active attenuator

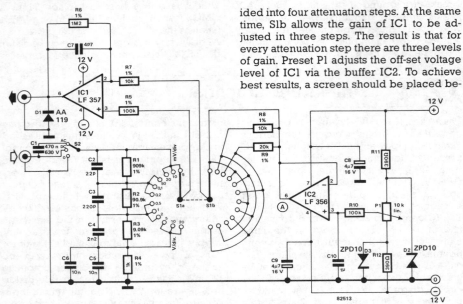

ided into four attenuation steps. At the same time, S1b allows the gain of IC1 to be adjusted in three steps. The result is that for every attenuation step there are three levels of gain. Preset P1 adjusts the off-set voltage level of IC1 via the buffer IC2. To achieve best results, a screen should be placed be-

Although countless measuring instrument preamps have been published in recent years, none of them would have served their purpose, if they could not attenuate the input signal. This is required to ensure that the full scale of the measuring instrument is utilized to the full. As a matter of interest, the attenuation, in most cases, is effected in steps of 1, 2 or 5.

The circuit described here divides the input signal into 12 steps covering a range from 5 mV (the most sensitive setting) to 20 V. Capacitors C2...C6 are included for frequency compensation. The range switch consists of two twelve way wafers, S1a and S1b.

With the help of S1a, the input signal is div-

tween the two wafers.

The result is an extremely useful input circuit for AF meters. It is ideal for hobbyists, as no special effort or components are involved. The circuit is of course equally suitable for oscilloscopes. During construction, make sure that the two switches are screened from each other and from the rest of the components, as otherwise it will be impossible to separate the tiny input signals from interference. There is no need to calibrate the circuit! If desired, the offset adjustment may be omitted. Instead, earth point A and leave out the whole offset calibration circuit, including P1 and IC2.

J. Bartels

126 pulse generator 2

With the aid of this circuit, the duty factor of a signal may be adjusted very accurately in 1% steps within the 1%...99% range. At the same time, it is possible to keep the frequency of the output signal completely independent of the duty factor setting.

dependent of the duty factor setting.

Accurate pulse generators are needed whenever a meter or a circuit that calculates the level of a signal on the basis of its duty factor and evaluates and/or pro-

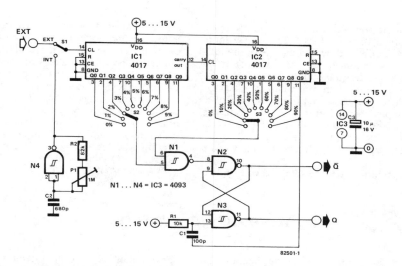

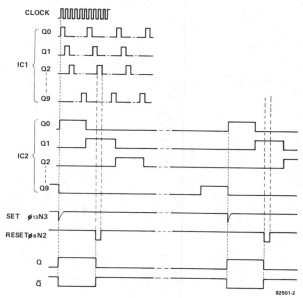

cesses the signal to be calibrated. The type of circuits in mind are remote control (PPM) and phase cutoff angle meters.

The pulse generator in figure 1 can be constructed quite easily with three CMOS ICs. The decimal counters IC1 and IC2 are connected as divide-by-tens. Bistable N2/N3 is set via R1/C1 upon the falling edge of the Q_9 signal of IC2 (which corresponds to the rising edge of Q_0!) and the Q output of the circuit goes high. The intermediate count reaches gate N1 via select switches S2

and S3. As soon as the required count is attained, N1 sends a reset pulse to the bistable and the Q output goes low.

Figure 2 shows what happens in the form of a pulse diagram. The clock signal may well be transmitted by an external device. As it is divided by ten twice, the output frequency will be 10 kHz at a maximum input frequency of 1 MHz. Alternatively, the internal oscillator may be switched on via S1, in which case an output frequency of between 20 Hz and 200 Hz, approximately

143

(variable with P1) will be obtained at an operational voltage of 12 V. The preset range may be adjusted by altering the operational voltage (within the 5...15 V range). In addition, the frequency range may be varied by selecting a different value for C2.

Back to the pulse diagram. By way of an example, a duty factor of 12% has been set here (see figure 1). Initially, the set pulse makes Q go high. But as soon as Q_2 of IC1 and Q_1 of IC2 are high, Q will go low again, etc.

Supposing we wish to set the dwell angle of a 4 cylinder engine, we will have to take the following into account: the dwell angle is defined as a certain period of time, during which the contact breaker connections are closed. This corresponds to the time interval during which the signal is low. Thus, the definition of the dwell angle is the exact opposite of that of the duty factor! What all this boils down to in this particular application is that the maximum dwell angle is 90°. This may be adjusted to, say, 54°. As a result, the variable duty factor will be:

$$[(90° - 54°)/90°]\% = 40\%$$

127   light sensitive switch

There is a wide range of applications for light sensitive switches: staircase light timers, outdoor illumination, automatic door openers by a light beam, alarm systems, and so on. Many of our readers will be familiar with the single transistor opto-switch where an LDR is placed between the base and either ground or supply depending whether a normally on or normally off function is required. This simple circuit gave way to more complex arrangements involving the use of opamps with the advent of the supercheap 741! Another, not so well-known, method of opto-detection uses a bridge circuit operating on the principle that current flow across the bridge will be zero when the bridge is in balance.

The latter principle is used in the circuit here. The opto-detector is situated in a bridge circuit and a comparator is used as a 'bridge is in balance' indicator. The comparator output fires a silicon-controlled rectifier (SCR) via a transistor. Caution must be used with this circuit, since it is not isolated from the mains supply.

Power to the circuit is derived via the

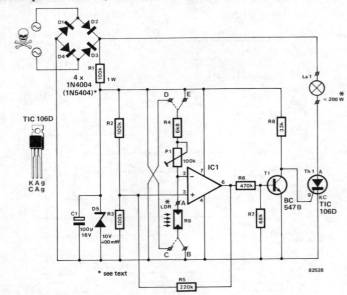

1

2

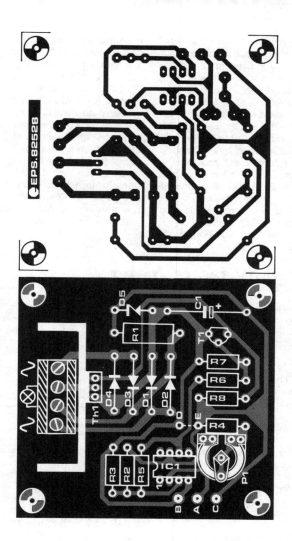

EPS.82528

Parts list

Resistors:
R1 = 100 k/1 W
R2,R3 = 100 k
R4 = 6k8
R5 = 220 k
R6 = 470 k
R7 = 68 k
R8 = 33 k
R9 = LDR 03, 05 or 07
P1 = 100 k preset potentiometer

Capacitor:
C1 = 100 μ/16 V

Semiconductors:
D1...D4 = 1N4004 (1N5404)
D5 = zener diode 10 V/400 mW
T1 = BC 547B
IC1 = 741
Th1 = TIC 106D
PCB 82528

bridge rectifier D1...D4 and is smoothed and stabilized by R1, C1 and D5. The bridge circuit may be difficult to see in the circuit diagram, but it consists of R2...R4, P1, and the light dependent resistor (LDR). IC1 is connected as comparator and its output voltage level will become approximately 1.8 V when the potential at the inverting (negative) input exceeds that of the non-inverting input. Resistor R5 creates an hysteresis of about 1 V to prevent T1 and the SCR from switching on and off (flickering) in marginal light conditions. The switching point of the comparator is adjustable by P1. With this potentiometer set to minimum resistance, the lamp will switch on at twilight. If you require greater flexibility, replace P1 by a 1 MΩ type. The LDR can be exchanged with the P1/R4 combination to provide the circuit with 'inverse law'. The lamp La1 will be extinguished at the onset of darkness. Some practical considerations: for switching higher power lamps, D1...D4 must be replaced by 1N5404 types and a heat sink must be used for Th1. With these

modifications the circuit will cater for current levels up to 3 amperes.

The maximum gate current available for Th1 is 250 μA, which means that a fairly sensitive SCR should be used.

Any LDR should be suitable. There is no apology for repeating the cautions regarding the lack of isolation from the mains supply. With this in mind it is essential that the completed circuit is housed securely in some form of plastic box. A hole can be made in the top of the box for the LDR to 'see' through. Make sure that both the input and output cables are fitted securely. These precautions will ensure that prying fingers will not come to grief.

128 duty factor meter

The duty factor of a rectangular pulse signal is normally measured by a pulse counter or an oscilloscope.

However, this can be simplified considerably by using two VMOS-FETs and a voltmeter. The FETs are switched in turn by the input pulses. The R2/C2 network combination provides an average DC level corresponding to the input waveform:

$$U_{av} = PU_b/T$$

where P is the pulse width and T is the pulse spacing.

The meter reading can be interpreted as follows: the indication of the duty factor can be expressed as a percentage (link A). For link B, a voltmeter with a centre zero is preferable.

A DVM would also do the trick, but not quite as well.

The voltage level at the input of the meter will be half the supply voltage when the duty factor is 50%. Since the other side of the meter is connected to half the supply voltage (via voltage divider R3/R4) there will be no current flow through the meter (hence a zero reading).

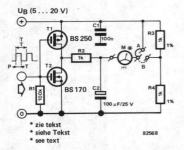

* zie tekst
* siehe Tekst
* see text   82568

The duty factor can be read directly in % if the scale is divided into 1...10 (U_b = 10 V) and the centre point (5) marked as 50%.

An important note: it is imperative to ensure that the input waveform switches abruptly between a low level (less than 0.8 V) and high (Ub −0.8 V or higher). Between these values, both FETs would start to conduct, thus causing a short circuit across the supply voltage source. Moreover, the maximum supply voltage must not be exceeded. One final remark: The internal resistance of the meter must be at least 100 kΩ.

129 an odd divider

It is often necessary to divide the frequency of some signal by a given factor. For example, several signals may be required

with frequencies that are all some fraction of a main clock signal. In this kind of situation, special-purpose divider ICs may be

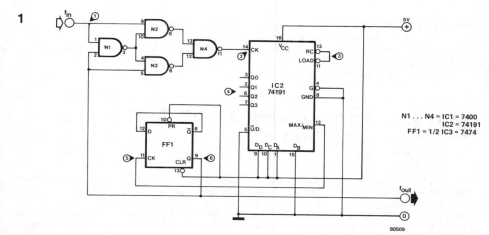

1

N1 ... N4 = IC1 = 7400
IC2 = 74191
FF1 = 1/2 IC3 = 7474

80509

used, but these have the disadvantage that they can only divide by multiples of two — even numbers, in other words. When an odd division ratio is required, some other system must be used. One of the most common is to use a counter IC: this is reset each time it reaches the count that corresponds to the desired division ratio (three, say). This system also has a disadvantage: the output signal is asymmetric, with a dutyfactor that depends on the division ratio.

The circuit described here gives an output with a 50% dutyfactor (provided the input signal is also symmetrical), and can be set to divide by any odd number between 3 and 29. The basic principle is both simple and ingenious — like all good inventions. A counter is used, as described above; however, basically it counts *half* periods of the incoming signal so that the output can be followed by a bistable while still achieving an odd division ratio.

In the circuit given in figure 1, IC2 is an up/down counter. Its clock signal is derived from an XOR circuit (gates N1...N4); basically, this inverts the input signal f_{in} when pin 2 of N1 is high and passes the signal unaltered when this pin is low. The output from the counter is passed to bistable FF1.

The circuit is best explained with reference to the pulse diagram given in figure 2. The incoming signal is shown at the top (1). The clock signal for the counter (2) is derived from this by inverting it during the positive half-period of the output signal (6) and leaving it unaltered when the output signal is zero. This clock signal is counted by IC2.

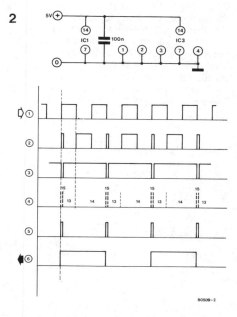

2

80509-2

The actual count is determined as follows. Each time a load pulse appears at pin 3 (this is signal 3 in figure 2, as we will see) the binary number set up at the data inputs $D_A \ldots D_D$ is loaded into the counter. In the example shown, this number is 1101 (only D_B is connected to supply common) which corresponds to 13. Starting at this number, the count proceeds up to 15 — after which a pulse appears at the ripple carry output. This is used as the load pulse! Simultaneously, an output pulse appears at pin 12,

147

clocking the bistable. As can be seen in figure 2, the output therefore changes state after 3 half-periods of the input signal. Divide-by-three, in other words!

The output frequency is determined by the number, n, that is preset at the data inputs, as follows:

$$f_{out} = f_{in}/[2\,(15 - n) - 1]$$

where n is any whole number from 0 to 13.

130 TRS 80 cassette interface rediscovered

The TRS 80 computer is a fairly good machine, but the cassette interface has already driven many an owner to the depths of despair. Why the tapes are read back so unreliably has never been worked out, and because of this there are a number of suggestions on how to improve matters. The circuit given here also produces good results, but as with so many good suggestions we do not really know why.

The TRS 80 records clock pulses and data pulses on the tape at a constant amplitude. The time interval between pulses is 2.4 ms. The logic is written by inserting a pulse be-

tween two clock pulses after 1.2 ms. If this pulse is not there this signifies a logic 0. The ironic thing now is that although the amplitude of the pulses is constant during recording, when the tape is played back the volume setting is extremely critical. One possible explanation is that one small interference pulse can easily convert a logic 0 into a logic 1. On the other hand, a drop out in the tape can convert a logic 1 into a logic 0. Matters get even worse if a clock pulse gets lost. In this case, a following data pulse may be recognised as a clock pulse, and from this point onwards

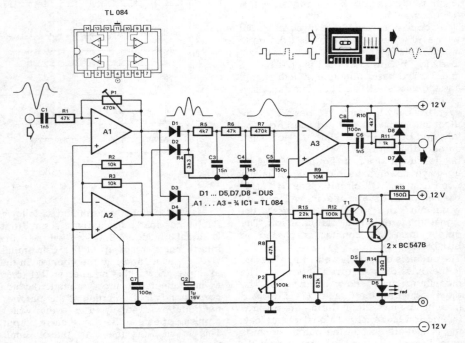

82563

the whole thing gets totally out of hand. The situation deteriorates still further when playing back commercial tapes. These are very often recorded at high speed, and this has the effect that there is not so much a pulse on the tape as a damped sine wave. In all fairness, most home recorded tapes may not appear very elegant when viewed with an oscilloscope during playback.

The following circuit attemps to solve all these problems by integrating the signal coming back from the tape recorder. This has a few advantages. Short interference pulses are filtered out by the low-pass filter R5—R6—R7—C4—C5, so they do not lead to incorrect data. Drop outs also have less effect on the circuit because, even if the pulse itself does not come out so well, the transients which follow the main pulse will still be there, and after integration will provide sufficient amplitude. To ensure that these pulses are not missed, A1 and A2 are used as a two phase rectifier. This has the added advantage that the phase of the signal coming from the cassette deck is completely unimportant. The rectified signal is passed on to the filter and also to peak detector D3/D4 and C2. When the amplitude of the cassette deck output varies a little (when an older or a different type of tape is used), no critical adjustment of the output level is required.

The filtered signal is compared in A3 with part of the peak rectified signal. In this way the comparator becomes independent of the input amplitude (within reasonable limits). This means that P2 must be used to set a suitable level so that the data arrives clean at the output. The combination C6 and R10 converts the data into short pulses with a 5 V output amplitude ideally suitable for passing to the bistable included in the TRS 80, especially for this purpose.

LED D6 is included as a simple indicator. Provided there is sufficient signal level present (in the order of a few volts), the LED will light. The gain is set by P1. The current consumption is only a few mA which can easily be obtained from the supply of the TRS 80. It should be noted that D6 can draw up to 50 mA if it is included.

131   crystal oscillator

The time base shown here uses a series resonance circuit. This achieves greater stability than parallel resonance circuits. The two main requirements of the active elements are:

1. the phase-shift between input and output must be 0°;
2. both the input and output must be low impedance, in order that the Q factor of the crystal is not affected.

It therefore follows that a CMOS crystal oscillator cannot cope with the above requirements. A TTL version, although having very little phase shift (up to a frequency of 10 MHz), comes no where near to complying with the second parameter.

The circuit described in this article meets both requirements.

The design allows frequencies of up to 30 MHz to be generated without any phase shift. Higher frequencies are possible but then T1 and T2 will have to be changed for another type (such as the BFR 91), and the values of R1...R4 will have to be reduced.

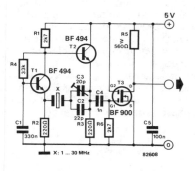

Point 2 is well taken care of by the fact that the crystal is positioned between two emitters of a push-pull stage achieving a low impedance input and output.

The MOSFET buffer in the output stage insulates the oscillator from any circuit connected to it.

132 phase sequence indicator

When making connections to a three-phase mains supply, is often essential to get the three phases in the correct sequence. Otherwise motors, for instance, have a tendency to rotate in the opposite direction — which can have surprising results. Pumps become suckers, and suckers become... forget it. In this well-regulated nation of ours, all connections of this type must be made by qualified electricians, so nothing can go wrong. End of article for those readers who are not qualified electricians. If you are still with us, the device described here can prove quite useful. In a nutshell, when its three inputs are connected to the three phases (the neutral connection isn't needed for this test), one of two LEDs will light to indicate a clockwise or anticlockwise phase sequence. In this connection (!), clockwise is defined as U, V, W (or V, W, U or W, U, V) and corresponds to the green LED. Anticlockwise, not surprisingly, is the other way 'round'; the red LED will light. The basic idea can be derived from figure 1. This is a plot of the three phases; as can be seen, at the zero-crossing of one phase the following phase is positive and the third is negative. This is quite easy to detect! To simplify the connections, an artificial neutral is created at the R1/R2/R3 junction. Only two of the phases are then used in the actual measurement; their value with respect to the artificial neutral is detected, and used as follows.
At each negative-going zero-crossing of the voltage at the U input, the bistable (FF1) clocks in the value at the W input as data. If the phase sequence is correct (clockwise),

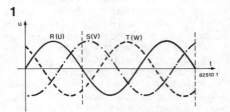

the W input should be negative at this point — as can be seen in figure 1. This means that T1 is blocked, so that a logic 1 is applied to the D input of the bistable. The actual clocking of the bistable is done in a similar way by T2. When the logic is clocked through to the output, T4 will conduct. This causes the green LED to light. If the phases are inverted (anticlockwise), T2 will be conducting at the negative-going zero-crossing of U. This means that a logic 0 is clocked into the bistable. T3 will then conduct, and the red LED will light. Obviously, swapping any two phase connections will convert one phase sequence into the other.
The two zener diodes (D1 and D2) protect the transistors — both against excessive base drive and against negative base voltages.
Two final notes. For safety reasons, the complete unit must be mounted in an insulating (plastic) case; the switch must also be a safe type! Furthermore, battery supply is a must: try to imagine what might happen with a mains supply!

F. op 't Eynde

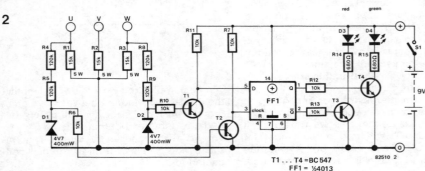

T1 ... T4 = BC 547
FF1 = ½ 4013

133   push button interface

The circuit here extends the effectiveness of the simple push-to-make switch by enabling it to be used as either a 'one-shot', with clean, debounced edges, or as a push-on/push-off latch. These functions remove the problems associated with any switch, that of electronic noise. Resistor R1 and capacitor C1 debounce the switch and provide a positive edge to trigger monostable FF1. This generates pulses (in anti-phase) at its Q and Q̄ outputs. The pulse width is determined by R1, R3, and C2. The positive pulse (Q) is fed to an OR gate consisting of D2, D3, and R5. The trailing edge of the negative pulse is used to trigger bistable FF2. The normal (or stable) state of FF1 is with its Q output low and its Q̄ output high. If, in this condition, the switch is closed briefly and then released, the J and K inputs will be low when the triggering edge arrives. In this case FF1 will ignore it and stay reset.

If, however, the switch is held closed until the monostable times out and FF2 is clocked, the J input is taken high, K low and the bistable changes state. Now Q and the output (via the OR gate) are high, and consequently, so is K. If the bistable is trig-

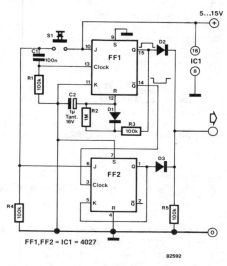

gered with K high and J low, it will revert to its reset state. Holding the switch closed will not affect the circuit action, for with both J and K high, FF2 will change state on the arrival of a clock edge.

J. Ritchie

134   12 dB voltage-controlled filter

Since their introduction in the 1970s, operational transconductance amplifiers (OTAs) have become popular components in voltage-controlled filters. This is particularly true of the dual OTA type 13600, because this already contains the necess-

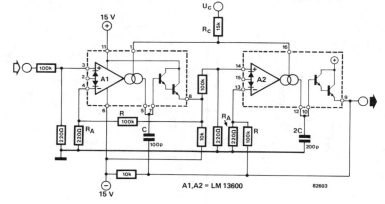

ary buffer stages. It offers excellent synchronous operation, which makes it ideal for second-order filters. Figure 1 shows the circuit diagram of a Butterworth low-pass filter based on the 13600.

The -3 dB cut-off frequency, f_c, of the filter depends on the transconductance, g_m, of the 13600, on the values of resistors R and R_A, and on the value of capacitor C (farads):

$$f_c = [g_m R_A/2 \pi C (R + R_A)] \text{ kHz}$$

The value of the transconductance in siemens (S) at room temperature is $g_m = [19.2 I_c]$ S where I_c is the current flowing into pins 1 and 16 of the OTA. The voltage

at these pins is about 1.2 V more positive than the negative supply line, i.e., -13.8 V with a ± 15 V supply. The transconductance is then

$$g_m = [19.2 (U_c + 13.8)/2R_c] \text{ S}$$

With values as shown, this gives a control characteristic (transconductance) of about 2 kHz/V. Values of f_c for various levels of U_c are:

$f_c = 28$ kHz when $U_c = 0$ V;
$f_c = 1.5$ kHz when $U_c = -13.5$ V;
$f_c = 40$ kHz when $U_c = +6$ V.

All these values can, of course, be modified by changing the values of R, R_A, R_c, and C.

135 voltage-controlled filter

The circuit diagram shows a *National Semiconductor* application of the type 13600 operational transconductance amplifier used as a state-variable filter. It offers a selective band-pass output, u_1, and a low-pass output, u_2. Both the centre frequency of the band-pass filter and the cut-off frequency of the low-pass filter are dependent on the level of control voltage U_c. Integrating capacitors C determine the range over which these frequencies can be varied.

The cut-off frequency, f_c, of the low-pass filter, and the centre frequency, f_c, of the band-pass filter are both given by

$$f_c = [g_m/21 \ C] \text{ Hz} \tag{1}$$

where g_m is the transconductance in siemens (S) and C is in farad. At room temperature, g_m

$$g_m = [19.2 \ I_c] \text{ S} \tag{2}$$

where I_c is the current flowing into pins 1 and 16 of the LM 13600. Since $I_c = U_c/2R_c$,

$$g_m = [19.2 \ U_c/2R_c] \text{ S} \tag{3}$$

Substituting formula (3) into formula (1) gives

$$f_c = [U_c/2.18 \ R_c C] \text{ Hz}$$

which clearly establishes the direct relation between f_c and the control voltage, U_c.

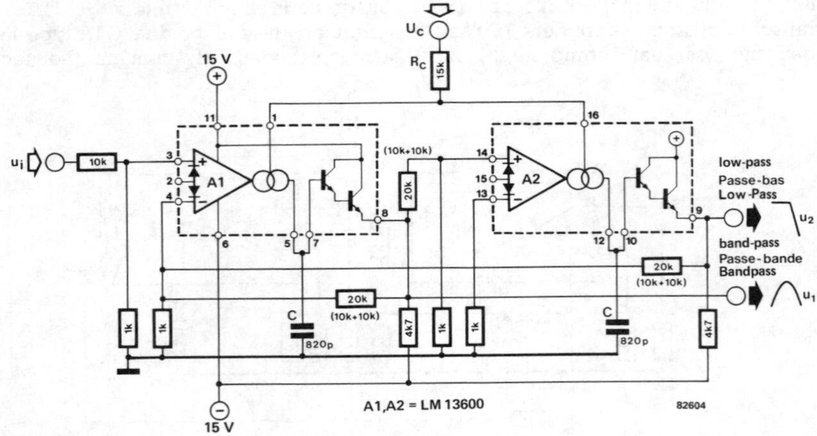

A1,A2 = LM 13600   82604

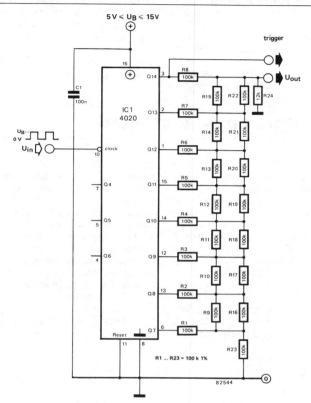

This circuit produces a logarithmic sweep output by digital means and has been designed for use with the voltage controlled waveform generator described in circuit 159.

The circuit diagram shows a 14-bit binary counter of which the clock input is connected to the sync output of a waveform generator. The eight highest outputs of the 4020 are connected to a resistor network that converts the digital code into an equivalent DC voltage level. Consequently, the DC level ranges from 0 V to approximately 0.2 U_b in 256 steps. The lower outputs are not connected (more about this later) which means that the DC voltage level at U_o increases by one step after 128 clock pulses. This output can be connected to the sweep input of a voltage controlled waveform generator. The frequency supplied by the generator (and therefore the frequency at the sync output) increases every time the control voltage rises. This means that the DC voltage and frequency increase almost exponentially, which is exactly what we need to obtain a logarithmic sweep.

When connecting U_o of the voltage controlled waveform generator to U_i of the sweep generator described here, resistor R9 at the input of IC2 must be replaced by a wire link. Consequently, there will no longer be a logarithmic voltage at U_o, but only at the output of IC2. So, the operation remains as described.

The combination sweep circuit and voltage controlled waveform generator may be calibrated in the following manner. Temporarily connect the reset pin of the 4020 to the supply voltage (+12 V). Then set the frequency at pin 11 of the XR 2206 to 80 Hz.

153

Now connect the reset pin back to 0 V. On initial switch-on, the sweep frequency (the clock frequency of IC1) will begin at the lowest point (80 Hz) and remain there for almost one second. After this, the frequency will increase by one step and so on. The process continues until 20 kHz is reached.

The sweep speed can be doubled by connecting resistors R1...R8 in the sweep circuit to the Q6...Q13 instead of the Q7...Q14 outputs. Connecting these resistors to Q5...Q12 increases this frequency by a factor two again. The initial clock speed can even be multiplied by eight by connecting them to the Q4...Q11 outputs.

J. Meijer

137   true r.m.s. converter. . .

A true r.m.s. converter is a very complex circuit that requires high tolerance components and precision calibration. It is fair to say that such a circuit gives a very high performance. The r.m.s. converter here, however, consists entirely of readily available components and yet provides a very acceptable performance.

The circuit diagram shows that the r.m.s. converter really is an automatic gain control (AGC) amplifier circuit, which is constructed around 2 ICs, the well-known XR 13600 (A1, A2) and the XR 1458 (A3, A4). The circuit adjusts its gain so that the AC power output of amplifier A1 remains con-

stant. This output level is monitored by the squaring amplifier formed by A2 and the average value is compared to a reference voltage with the aid of A3. The output of this amplifier provides the diodes of A1 with bias current via a 2 kΩ resistor and transistor T1 to attenuate the input signal. As mentioned before, the output power of A1 is held constant: therefore the r.m.s. value remains constant as well. Obviously the attenuation is directly proportional to the r.m.s. value of the input voltage and the diode bias current.

This leaves only the function of A4 to be discussed. This amplifier adjusts the ratio of

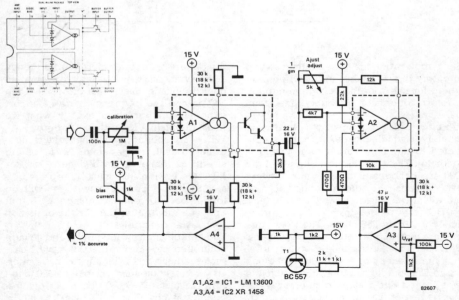

A1,A2 = IC1 = LM 13600
A3,A4 = IC2 XR 1458

82607

current flow through the diodes, so that they are equal. Consequently, the output voltage of A4 corresponds to the r.m.s. value of the input voltage.

Last, but not least, the calibration control should be set so that the output reads the correct value for a sinusoidal input; this may be compared with an ordinary multimeter.

EXAR application

138   solid state tachometer

Only a handful of components are needed to produce this tachometer that is useful both in the car and on machine tools that require a speed indication. The visual indication is by a row of LEDs in a vertical or horizontal column (or even a 270° arc). The number of LEDs lit at any one time corre-

spond to the measured rotational speed at that time.

IC1 is a frequency-to-voltage converter. If used in a car, its input can be connected (via R1) to the contact breaker terminal of the coil (commonly marked CB).

The output of IC1 is fed to the inputs of both

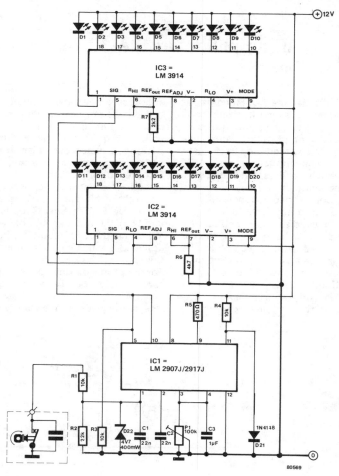

80569

IC2 and IC3. These two IC's are cascaded, that is, the ten LEDs controlled by each IC form a single line. In this case, the LEDs from IC3 will form the first ten in the line. The cascading link is between pin 6 of IC3 and pin 4 of IC2. At input voltages of up to about 1.2 V all the LEDs driven by IC3 will light; above this input level, those driven by IC2 will also light.

The relation between the input frequency and the number of LEDs lit can be varied by potentiometer P1. This will, of course, depend on the maximum number of revs required. For a four stroke four cylinder car engine, the maximum is normally in the region of 6000 rev/min. In this case the twentieth LED should light at around this figure.

If a bell transformer with a secondary voltage of 3...5 volts is temporarily connected to the input, the LED indication will be equal to 1500 rev/min and the LEDs up to and including D5 will light. It is a simple matter to adjust P1 to ensure this is so.

A spot indicator (or a single LED lit as opposed to a row) is also possible with a few minor modifications. For this pin 9 of IC3 must be connected to pin 1 of IC2 (and not to +12 V). Similarly, pin 9 and 11 of IC2 are linked together (and not to +12 V). A 22 kΩ resistor is then wired across D9.

The brightness of the LEDs can be adjusted by altering the values of R6 and R7. It may be useful to use different coloured LEDs for the varying degrees of warning signified by the length of the LED row.

---

139 RF amplifier for the 10 meter amateur band

The VN66AF manufactured by Siliconix has quite a few advantages over its rivals: good value for money, in terms of price per watt, high dielectric strength, and exceptional gain. It also has a low tendency to oscillate. The most common application for VMOS FETs is in power amplifiers, but that is not a reason to discount them for any other use. They have been used successfully in preamps and RF amplifiers. In this particular case it is used as an RF amplifier for the 10 metre amateur band (26...30 MHz). Small transmitters of around 200 mW can be transformed into reasonably powerful ones delivering between 2 and 3 W by using the circuit described here.

The design is fairly straightforward. The fixed filter network positioned at the output

suppresses noise by as much as 55 dB.

If the coils are constructed to the specifications outlined in the parts list, the filter will not require calibration. Obviously, experienced hands may wish to change the specification and the design is sufficiently flexible to allow this. The amplifier is suitable for most types of transmission since the drain current of the FET can be varied by P1. For linear applications (AM and SSB), the drain should be set to 20 mA. When used for FM and CW, P1 should be adjusted so that no quiescent current is flowing.

For the proposed design the quiescent current should be between 200 mA and 300 mA.

The ready-made printed circuit board en-

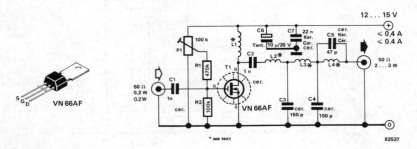

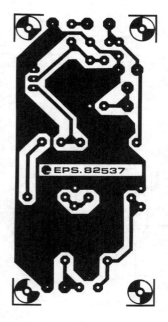 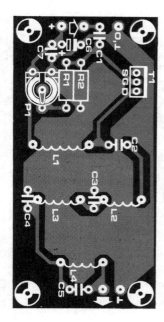

Parts list

Resistors:
R1 = 470 k
R2 = 100 k
P1 = 100 k preset

Capacitors:
C1,C2 = 1 n ceramic
C3,C4 = 150 p ceramic
C5 = 47 p
C6 = 10 μ/35 V tant.
C7 = 22 n ceramic

Semiconductors:
T1 = VN66AF (Maplin, Watford Electronics)

Coils:
L1 = 12 windings 0.6 mm dia enamelled copper wire
L2 and L4 = 5 windings of 1 mm dia enamelled copper wire
L3 = 8 windings 1 mm dia enamelled copper wire

sures speedy and accurate construction. The coils should be wound onto formers with a diameter of 9 mm. Care should be taken to lay the windings close together without any apparent gaps.
It is advisable to use a heat sink for the FET.

140   class A B amplifier

Class A amplifiers are well-known in the audio world for their low distortion and low efficiency. Manufacturers have for years tried to design a class A amplifier with much better efficiency, but have only recently come up with realistic prototypes. The amplifier described here draws on this pioneering work.

The circuit diagram shows a normal power amplifier (left-hand side) with an input stage consisting of a TDA 1034. The final stage (T1...T4) operates in class A. This dissipation remains low, because the final stage is fed by ± 5 V. However, this supply voltage is much too low for the amplifier to deliver enough power. For this reason, the zero of the symmetrical 5 V supply is connected to the output of a second power

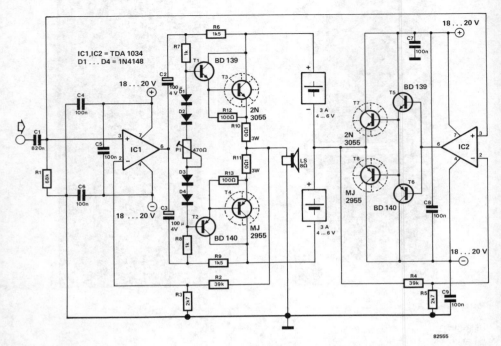

82555

amplifier consisting of IC2 and T5...T8. This amplifier operates in class B mode and is fed with the same input signal as the first amplifier. The main difference is that it operates with a higher supply voltage: ± 18 V. The amplification factor of the second amplifier equals that of the first. The loudspeaker is connected between the output of the first amplifier and the zero of the 18 V supply. The zero of the 5 V supply is connected to the output of the second amplifier.

Any input signal will now drive both amplifiers simultaneously. This means that a voltage is added to the zero of the 5 V supply by the output of the second amplifier, which has the correct value and polarity for the first output stage to deliver the desired power to the loudspeaker. During the positive swing of the signal waveform, the collector of T3 is at the necessary output voltage plus 5 V. When it swings negative, the collector of T4 is at the required negative output voltage minus 5 V. In this way the amplifier operates in class A, but the dissipation remains nearly the same as that of a class B amplifier, as the supply voltage 'runs along' with the input signal.

When this method is used, it is a must that the input amplifier (IC1) can be driven to the high supply voltage. Therefore, IC1 is supplied with ± 18 V. Furthermore, the 5 V supply must deliver a current that at least equals the peak current flowing through the loudspeaker. The power supplied by this amplifier is approximately 15 W into 8 Ω (class A).

When constructing the circuit, make sure that the 5 V supply is isolated from the 18 V supply. Use a mains transformer with two completely separated secondary windings with a centre tap, or even better, use two transformers. Only the zero of the 18 V supply serves as ground for the circuit and the loudspeaker.

141 converter for varactors

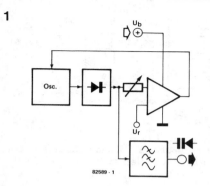

82589 - 1

The performance of varicaps is improved when the voltage across them is increased. Besides better intermodulation rejection, a 30 V circuit has a considerably higher Q than an 9 V version for the same capacitance variation. However, with battery-powered circuits, high voltages can only be realized with the aid of a converter. The circuit diagram shows the design for a converter especially constructed for this purpose. The LM 10C, from National Semiconductor, which contains two opamps and an internal reference source, is ideal for this particular application.

The oscillator is constructed around a dual-gate MOSFET (type BF 900) and operates at a supply voltage of only 1.5 V. The output voltage of the converter is controlled via the supply voltage of the oscillator. Unlike most converters, this one does not have to be

switched, so there will be no distortion. The oscillator frequency is approximately 28 kHz. An AFC (automatic frequency control) voltage can be connected to one of the opamp inputs via a series resistor; which of the two inputs depends on the polarity of the AFC voltage. With the values indicated in the circuit diagram, the output voltage can be varied between 1 and 30 V by means of the 220 k potentiometer. The supply voltage can range from 3 to 16 V.

2

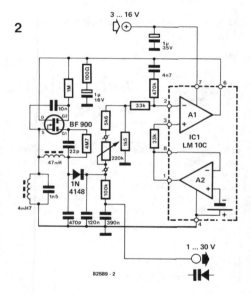

82589 - 2

142 simple frequency converter

During the last few years the TBA 120 has become one of the most frequently used ICs in RF techniques. Although designed as IF amplifier/FM demodulator, the TBA 120 can be used for a wide range of applications. This converter circuit is just one example.

The initial requirements for a converter are a mixing stage and an oscillator. The multiplier in the IC suits the needs of a mixing stage perfectly well. The oscillator can

be realized by a selective (positive coupling) feedback of the amplifier section of the TBA 120 by the resonance circuit L1/C1. The oscillator will operate at a frequency of 46 MHz with the values indicated in the circuit diagram. Consequently, we are dealing with a circuit that converts an input signal of 35.3 MHz into 10.7 MHz (46 — 35.3 = 10.7 MHz). This can be used to convert the IF signal of a TV tuner into the intermediate frequency of an FM receiver.

Obviously the circuit can also be used at other frequencies, by modifying the oscillator circuit (L1/C1) and the output filter (L2/C2) accordingly.

When the oscillator frequency is considerably lower than 46 MHz, the values of R1 and C3 have to be increased slightly. However, their value is not critical and can be determined quite easily after some experimenting.

The construction of the converter is straightforward, due to the fact that only a few components are required. However, some attention has to be paid to the common basic rules for RF circuits, such as:

- try to retain as much 'ground plane' as possible, when etching the printed circuit board;
- keep the tracking and wiring as short as possible;

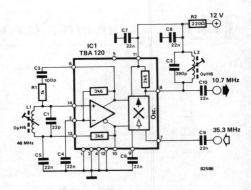

- use the shortest distance from the point to be decoupled to the ground for the decoupling capacitors C4...C8.

R. van den Brink

143 stabilized 10 . . . 350 volt power supply

There are probably many of our readers who possess high voltage valve power supplies which could do with some renovation and modernization. With the wide choice of high voltage transistors available nowadays it becomes a relatively simple matter to update such supplies. The BU 111 was used here, but the BU 126 or BUY 76 can also be used satisfactorily.

Usually, the transformers used in this sort of supply have a number of high voltage tappings. In addition, there is nearly always a

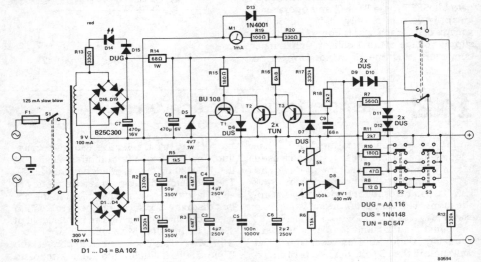

low voltage winding available. In this particular case a 300 V tapping was used for the high voltage side and a 9 V winding served to supply the stabilization circuit. The latter is very simple and needs no explanation.

About 420 V AC is produced by rectifying the secondary (300 V) voltage in D1...D4. This is a rather inconveniently high value, which is why two 350 V electrolytic capacitors are connected in series for smoothing purposes. Two parallel resistors (R1, R2) ensure that the voltage drops across the capacitors are equal. Resistor R5 reduces the dissipation of T1 and, together with a second RC network (R3, R4, C3, C4), provides the collector of T1 with a smoothed input voltage of about 350 V. Transistors T2 and T3 may be ordinary BC 547s, since they do not have to deal with high voltages and currents. Diode D7 protects the base of T3 against excessive negative voltage peaks.

Four different current thresholds may be preset with only two 6 pole pushbutton switches: 1 mA (nothing closed), 5 mA (S2 closed), 15 mA (S2 and S3 closed), and 50 mA (only S3 closed). At full load a voltage of 2.8 V is developed across resistors R8...R11. This is fed to the base of the regulator transistor T3 via D9...D12, so that this transistor turns off when the current exceeds the preset threshold value. The same voltage is also used to monitor the current with the aid of a 1 mA moving coil meter. Switch S4 enables the meter to be switched for voltage measurement.

Current is limited when it exceeds the preset threshold value by about 10%. The output voltage can be adjusted with P1 to between about 10...350 V. Fine adjustment for calibration purposes is possible with preset potentiometer P2. The supply is sufficiently protected against lengthy short circuits.

W. Seifried

144 high quality tape playback pre-amp

This circuit was designed to meet the demand for a low cost tape playback pre-amp. It is constructed around a new, low cost IC from National Semiconductor, which was designed specifically for tape playback applications. The IC is very interesting due to its low noise, wide voltage supply range, and low power consumption properties. It also requires very few external components to construct a complete circuit. The distortion factor is less than 0.1% at frequencies ranging from 20 Hz to 20 kHz, at an output of 1 V_{rms}. The printed circuit is quite small and can be mounted easily onto any cassette chassis. A power supply delivering approximately 10 mA at a voltage of anything between 10 and 16 V is sufficient. The LM 1897 is a dual gain pre-amp for any application requiring optimum noise performance. It combines the qualities of low noise and high gain with good power supply rejection (low hum) and transient-free power up. The absence of power-up transients is due primarily to the omission of coupling capacitors. This eliminates the 'click' or 'pop' from being recorded onto the tape during power supply cycling in tape playback applications. The omission of these capacitors also allows a wide-gain bandwidth with unlimited bass response. The external components in the feedback loops determine the gain and form an equalization circuit. With the values shown in the diagram (figure 1), a gain factor of 200 is achieved at a frequency of 1 kHz, corresponding to an output level of 100 mV_{rms}. Most available tape heads should give results of this kind. The equalization time constants are 3180 and 120 μs for ordinary low noise cassettes. For all other types of tape, such as ferro chrome and chromium dioxide, the time constants are 3180 and 70 μs, in which case the two R4 resistors are replaced by 33 kΩ ones. Constructors not wishing to use the muting option can leave out switch S1 and the two R7 resistors.

Screened two or four way cable should be used to connect the circuit to the tape heads. The choice is up to you, but please keep in mind that if two way cable is used, the screening sleeve is to be connected to the ground of the printed circuit board.

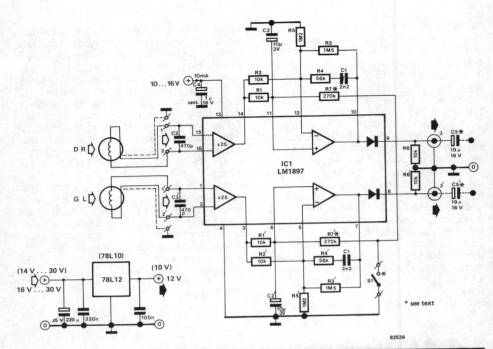

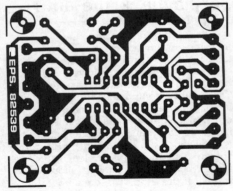

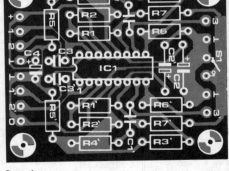

82539

Parts list

Resistors:
R1,R1',R2,R2',R6,R6' = 10 k
R3,R3' = 1M5
R4,R4' = 56 k (33 k)
R5,R5' = 1M2
R7,R7' = 270 k

Capacitors:
C1,C1' = 2n2
C2,C2' = 10 μ/3 V
C3,C3' = 470 p
C4 = 1 μ/16 V tantalum
C5,C5' = 10 μ/16 V (see text)

Semiconductor:
IC1 = LM 1897

A good ground connection between the printed circuit board and the drive chassis is also essential!

An unstabilized, filtered DC voltage of between 10 and 16 V will be sufficient for the circuit thanks to the high power supply rejection (low hum), of the IC. Batteries can also be used successfully. A voltage regulator such as the 78L12 is required only when the available supply is unfiltered or likely to be noisy.

The output of the pre-amp has not been decoupled since virtually every power amplifier contains some type of input coupling capacitor. Constructors who are in doubt about this fact can insert capacitors C5 and C5', as shown in the circuit diagram. The pre-amp has a low output impedance. This should not present any problems as the input impedance of most amplifiers and other hi-fi equipment is around 1 kΩ.

145 FET field strength meter

A field strength meter is necessary for checking the power output and aerial of transmitters. With this circuit it is possible to measure the energy radiated by the aerial. This is useful not only for hams, but also CB enthusiasts and radio control modellers.

For various reasons, this type of meter must be very sensitive. First of all, there should be a distance of as many wave lengths as possible between the measuring instrument and the transmitter. Secondly, other people will not be jumping in the air for joy when you are calibrating the aerial with a strong carrier signal. A weak signal will suffice when a sensitive field strength meter is used. Thirdly, many transmitters have a weak output power only (for example, 500 mW).

These are three of the main reasons why our field strength meter is equipped with an RF amplifier stage consisting of a dual gate MOS-FET, T1. The amplification factor

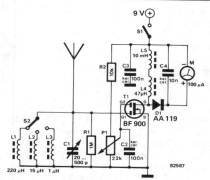

is set with P1. Switch S2 enables one of three ranges to be selected:
480 kHz...2.4 MHz (L1);
2.4...12 MHz (L2) and
12...40 MHz (L3).
A rod of approximately 30 cm will be enough to serve as aerial.
As with all RF circuits, care during construction is necessary!

146 low voltage stabilizer

Depending on their condition, 1.5 V batteries supply a voltage of 1.2...1.7 V. This circuit ca be very useful when a project has to be fed with a low constant voltage. With an input voltage of 1.2...1.8 V this stabilizer produces a relatively constant voltage of 1.15 V at a maximum load current of 5 mA.

T2 cuts off at a minimum battery voltage of 1.2 V at a load current of 5 mA. The output voltage tends to increase with a higher battery voltage, causing T2 to conduct and reducing the base current of T1 and T3 (indirectly), so that the output voltage will remain 1.15 V.

The internal impedance of this low voltage

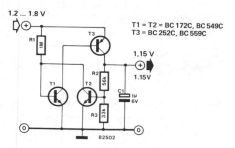

supply is 1 to 2 Ω. The output voltage will be reduced by 70 mV only when the battery voltage is changed from 1.8 V to 1.2 V.

(ITT application)

147 telephone bell

To many adults it is surprising how much pleasure the youngest members of the house can derive from a toy telephone. In children's eyes the use of a telephone is aking to being grown-up. This is a point for debate and the psychology is a little out of our province but we can add to the realism attached to this adult behaviour (?) pattern. Normally the toy telephone just sits, waiting for any one of a vast number of callers (including Santa Claus, the pet dog, and even the Queen on occasion) to ring with some vitally important information that, seemingly, only our youngest and dearest can cope with. The problems that arrive at this pretend office are quite beyond the comprehension of adults but we can help to ensure that these strife-torn folk do ring a little more often.

The circuit here produces a ringing tone similar to the modern telephone. This occurs every few minutes and stops when the hand set is removed from the receiver cradle. Schmitt-trigger gates are used in the construction: Gates N3 and N4 constitute the tone generator while N2 creates the ringing tone interval. The frequency of calls is left to gate N1 and with the component values shown this will be about every six or seven minutes. Of course, if this is not frequent enough for your own miniature tycoon, the value of C1 can be reduced to up the pace of business. This is also applicable to calls from grandparents.

Whenever the phone rings, it can only be stopped (like any other phone) by lifting the handset. This closes switch S2 (a

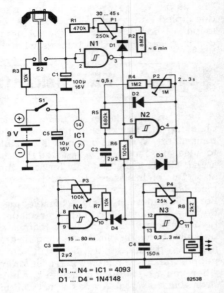

N1 ... N4 = IC1 = 4093
D1 ... D4 = 1N4148

82538

microswitch in the cradle) and halts both the tone generator and tone interval timer via N1. It also resets the call interval timer of course.

The siting of on/off switch S2 really depends on the particular telephone used but anywhere will do provided it does not conflict with the appearance of the real thing.

One final word in the interests of the real world. Have you noticed that the children never seem to get a wrong number...a crossed line...and they can raise directory enquiries in seconds...!

148 economical battery tester

Battery testers are used to get a decisive answer concerning the condition of a battery. Obviously, the test circuit most not form a considerable additional load during the measurement. This particular battery tester consumes a negligible amount of energy. A brief single flash of the LED indicates that the voltage level of the battery in the portable radio, cassette tape recorder, and so on, is still sufficent. This flash is produced as a result of capacitor C1 discharging across LED D1, which is only possible when the battery supplies enough voltage.

Depressing switch S1 will cause transistor T1 to conduct, so that C1 can discharge across the LED via the current-limiting resistor R3. The minimum battery voltage required is determined by voltage divider R1/R2. The values for R2 and R3 are calculated as follows:

$$R2 = [6 \times 10^4/U_{b(min)} - 0.6)]\ \Omega$$
$$R3 = [5U_b - 1.4)]\ \Omega$$

For instance, with a minimum battery voltage of 6.5 V (9 V battery), R2 = 10 k and R3 = 39 Ω.

The value for R4 has to be between 10 k and 1 M. The tester becomes even more economical with higher values, but a check will take longer. The battery can be tested over a period of approximately 10 seconds when R4 = 100 k.

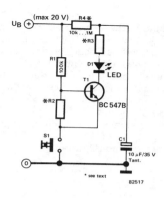

149   RS 232 interface

A microcomputer is usually connected to a peripheral device, such as a terminal, printer or teleprinter by an RS 232 interface. This normally requires a positive voltage between +5 V and +15 V (logic '0') and a negative voltage of −12 V to −5 V for logic '1'. The positive supply for the RS 232 interface can easily be derived from the unstabilized 5 V voltage of the computer. However, very often the negative supply voltage cannot be obtained from the computer because modern EPROMs and dynamic RAMs do not require a negative supply. If the device to be connected (for example a printer) is already equipped with an RS 232 interface, then a negative supply can be found at pin 3 of the RS 232 connector in the standby mode. Capacitor C1 charges via diode D1 and supplies the transmitter (T1) with a negative voltage.

T2 converts the negative level of the RS 232 transmission into a positive 5 V level for the computer again.

Obviously, the circuit will not work when it is used at both ends of the RS 232 connection (i.e., both at transmitter and receiver).

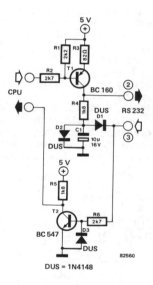

150   555 pulse generator

This circuit may look familiar to many readers since it is one of the many variations of circuits on the 555 timer theme. This does not detract from its usefulness however since a versatile pulse generator with a variable duty factor, n, is an excellent aid for the workshop.

Unlike the standard circuit usually

adopted, the resistance between pins 6 and 7 consists of P1, P2, R2, D1 and D2. A closely defined charging time for capacitor C1 is obtained by diodes D1 and D2. This would normally lead to a duty factor of 0.5, if were it not for P2. In this case the duty factor depends on the relation between P1 and P2: n = 1 + P2/P1.

The frequency, f, is approximately

$$f = [1/1.45C1 (2P1 + P2 + 4.7)] \text{ Hz}$$

where P1 and P2 are in ohms and C1 is in farads.

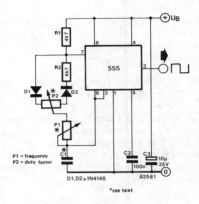

P.C.M. Verhoosel

151   a good-fidelity receiver

Some popular broadcasting stations can, in some areas, only be received on MW or LW. The reproduced sound quality of these transmissions is normally quite low. Nothing like hi-fi is normally possible because of the limited bandwidth of transmissions. However, a greatly improved sound quality is possible with the use of just a few widely available components. The improvement is so remarkable that it can be noticed distinctly. The outstanding feature of this receiver is its unconventional concept. The tuning stage of the receiver also serves as an active aerial, which can be favourably placed to get the best possible reception. Furthermore, it is completely separated from the rest of the receiver, that is, from the demodulator supplying the AF output. This part can be inserted into a separate housing, and placed next to an amplifier or the hi-fi equipment. The interconnection between the two parts should be made with standard coaxial cable. This cable feeds the RF signals and the tuning voltage (which is the operational voltage of the aerial) to the modulator. The plastic

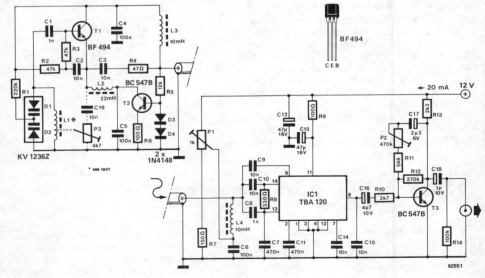

aerial housing contains an aligned input circuit, consisting of a ferrite rod (L2), and double varicap. The aerial signal is coupled to the tuning stage by an emitter/follower transistor (T1), ensuring that a high impedance output signal is fed to the modulator. This improves the selectivity. T2 together with its surrounding components forms a current source for T1. The received signal is not amplified in the active aerial stage, but in part of the TBA120 IC which forms part of the modulator. L2 serves as an emitter decoupler for T1. L3 decouples the supply and tuning voltage thereby short proofing the RF output of the active aerial. L4 effectively does the same for the demodulator. P1 can either be a trimming potentiometer allowing preset tuning of a particular station or a multi-turn type for normal variable tuning. TBA120 IC is the amplifier and quasi-synchronous-demodulator for the signal fed from the active aerial. Apart from the unusual method used for demodulation, the receiver follows the standard straight-through principles giving a good signal-to-noise ratio.

Unfortunately, the main disadvantage of this design is that it suffers from bad selectivity and low sensitivity. Consequently, the constructor should not expect the receiver to work miracles, especially during the evening hours or when tuned to distant stations. However, for most local stations it will perform well.

Potentiometer P2 sets the gain of T3, which allows the output level to be matched to the input requirements of any amplifier. Should the constructor desire to improve the selectivity, we suggest inserting a positive feedback loop with its associated components as shown by the dotted lines (see the circuit diagram). Except for L1, standard chokes can be used for the coils. L1 consists of 250 windings of 0.2 mm enamelled copper wire for LW and 80 turns of 0.3 mm enamelled copper wire for MW, wound onto a ferrite aerial approximately 20 cm in length with a diameter of 10 mm. The positive loop should be connected by tapping into the coil approximately a quarter of the way up from the earthed end. Keep all interconnecting wires and links as short as possible. The length of the coaxial cable is not critical.

152   omnivore LED

Ordinary LEDs have a rather monotonous diet: they will only consume DC current with the right polarity, in which case a series resistor cuts down the current appetite to a moderate 10...30 mA. This type of provision has a drawback in that the value of the series resistor must be calculated for each separate supply voltage, and that fluctuations in the supply can only be handled within a limited range.

Substituting a FET for the series resistor affords a number of advantages. When the gate and source are linked, the transistor forms a current source without the need for any additional components. In the type used here, the BF 256C, the constant current is roughly between 11 and 15 mA, with a wide supply range of 5...30 V. A universal silicon diode, such as the well known 1N4148, will provide polarity protection when connected in series with the LED. As a result, the LED can be driven with AC voltages in the 5...20 V range as well. At

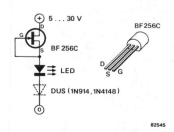

the normal 50 Hz mains frequency, the LED will barely flicker but that its brightness will be a little dulled owing to the half-wave rectification, compared to that at an equivalent DC voltage level.

153   RTTY converter

RTTY stands for radio teletype, in which data is transmitted in various codes, one of the most important being the baudot code. For the reception of teletype messages transmitted in the baudot format, a RTTY converter is needed, such as the one described here. This contains a single IC, the TL 084, and a few external components. The IC incorporates a set of four opamps, around which the filters and limiter stages are constructed.

Figure 1 shows what the receiver chain of a baudot RTTY printer usually looks like. The converter constitutes the life-line between the receiver and the teletype printer. It serves to convert signals picked up by the receiver into digital output data.

If you have no baudot teletype printer but a computer with a video interface you can receive and convert RTTY signals in the manner shown in figure 2. In addition to the RTTY converter, a baudot ASCII converter (in the form of the Junior Computer, for instance) and a video terminal (such as the Elekterminal) are required. In other words, a computer can take over the 5 bit baudot to 7 bit ASCII conversion, with one proviso — the incoming program must be adapted to serial signals. The program must ensure that serial signals consisting of 5 data bits; 1 start bit; and 1 stop bit are received at a transfer rate of 45; 50; 75, or 110 bauds.

A full description of the software required to make the Junior Computer function as a baudot ASCII converter would take us beyond the scope of this book. Instead, the article will be confined to detailing the hardware for the RTTY converter.

The block diagram in figure 3 shows how the RTTY converter works. The converter input is connected in parallel to the loudspeaker (or headphones) of the short wave receiver. The two tone frequencies for mark and space (pulse and pulse interval) are fed to a limiter amplifier that limits the speaker signal to ± 5 V. The mark and space filters following the amplifier filter the relevant frequencies from the limited signal mixture and rectify them. The rectified signals applied are to an adder which also operates as a limiter. The decoded RTTY signal is then available at the output of the adder which can drive a baudot

168

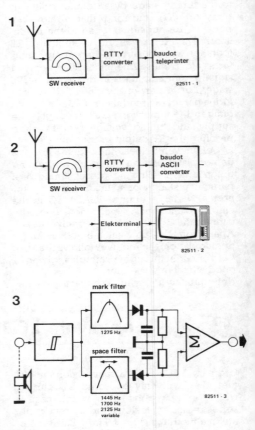

teletype printer direct.

The mark filter has a fixed IF of 1275 Hz. In the space filter the IF may be converted from 1445 Hz to 2125 Hz via 1700 Hz. As a result, the frequency shift between the mark and space filters is 170 Hz, 425 Hz or 850 Hz respectively, depending on the selected IF frequency. An additional range has now been provided within which the frequency may be varied continuously between 170 Hz and 1000 Hz. For the majority of RTTY transmitters to be received well, a frequency shift of 425 Hz is normally required. Figure 4 shows the complete RTTY converter circuit diagram. The circuit is constructed around a quad opamp. The limiter amplifier at the input is built around opamp A1. Zener diodes D1 and D2 limit the

4

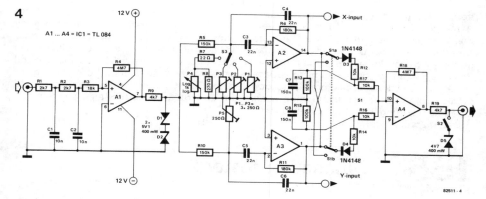

A1 ... A4 = IC1 = TL 084

82511 - 4

signal. The mark filter (opamp A3) is preset to a frequency of 1275 Hz by preset P5. The space filter (opamp A2) is provided with a variable multiple feedback loop. As a result, the circuit can be calibrated to 1445 Hz, 1700 Hz and 2125 Hz by presets P1...P3 respectively. Preset P4 adjusts the frequency shift in the 170 Hz...1000 Hz range. The outputs of the two filters can drive the X-Y inputs of an oscilloscope direct. The converter is set to optimum reception when a lissajous figure as shown in figure 5 appears on the oscilloscope screen. After being filtered, the signals are rectified by diodes D3 and D4. They are fol-

5

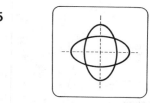

82511 - 5

lowed by low-pass filters R12/C7 and R14/C8. Opamp A4 adds the rectified signals. Switch S1 enables the mark/space signal to be inverted, if the computer interface hooked up to it requires negative logic. If switch S2 is closed, zener diode D5 limits the output signal to TTL level.

154 double alarm

Most alarm systems can be divided into two main categories. They are normally activated by closing, or interrupting, a circuit loop. One of these basic principles is used irrespective of the electronic method adopted, (micro-wave, infra-red, photocells, contacts, etc.).

Today's burglar is not the simple-minded individual normally portrayed in comic strip cartoons. The professional certainly keeps up to date with the latest technological advances in alarm systems, and keeping him out is difficult. Even part-timers know something about electronics and alarm systems. Whatever, the average burglar can easily and quickly determine what principle the system uses and will try to deactivate it. This is sometimes made easier for

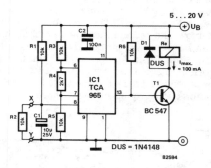

DUS = 1N4148

82594

the thief, as the connection wiring is in sight.

The circuit described here should pose the criminal a more difficult problem. It is intended to protect a single door, window or item of equipment — a TV set, for instance. A resistor, R2, is mounted inside the item that is to be protected and two leads are brought out (via break contacts or even an audio plug) to the alarm circuit proper. Resistor R2 and the connections to capacitor C1 form a make or break loop. If the loop is interrupted or the two connection wires bridged (shorting out the hidden switch) the alarm will sound.

The circuit uses a window discriminator TCA 965. The operation of the alarm is fairly simple. When pin 8 receives a higher voltage than pin 6, or a lower voltage than pin 7, the IC will drive T1. T1 conducts and actuates relay Re. A high frequency mains driven horn connected via the relay should be enough to panic the thief.

M. Prins

155 connection tester 2

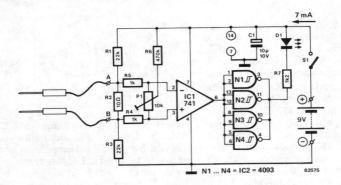

N1 ... N4 = IC2 = 4093   82575

Circuit 102 is a contact tester with acoustic indication. The circuit here gives an optical indication. The function of the present circuit is identical to that of circuit 102 so we will restrict ourselves to recapping the calibration procedure.

Place a 1 Ω resistor between the probes and adjust P1 until the LED is just about to light. Remove the resistor and create a short circuit between the probes. The LED should now light. To make sure that calibration is correct, place a resistor of only a few ohms between the probes. If the LED lights, the calibration procedure will have to be repeated. After correct adjustment, only resistances of up to 1 Ω will be tolerated. A value lower than this will either indicate a good contact or a short circuit. Keep in mind that the supply voltage of the circuit under test should be switched off, otherwise the tester could be damaged.

As long as the LED is allowed to remain lit for short periods only, the consumption of the tester will not exceed 8 mA. The battery should last at least a year.

P.C.M. Verhoosel

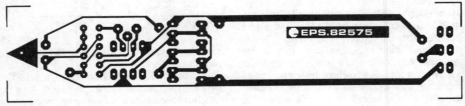

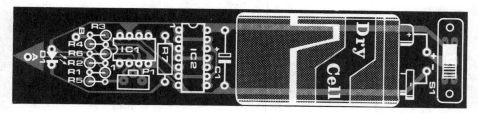

Parts list

Resistors:
R1,R3 = 22 k
R2 = 10 Ω
R4,R5 = 1 k
R6 = 470 k
R7 = 1k2

Capacitors:
C1 = 10 μ/10 V

Semiconductors:
IC1 = 741
IC2 = 4093
D1 = 3 mm LED red

Miscellaneous:
P1 = 10 k preset
S1 = single pole switch

156   voltage-controlled OTA

This application of the LM/XR 13600 deals with a voltage-controlled triangular-pulse oscillator. The operational transconductance amplifier (OTA) uses negative feedback derived from voltage divider R1-R2 and positive feedback derived via capacitor C. The current through C also flows through one of the diodes, and this establishes the trigger points at ± 0.6 V. The frequency, f, is calculated from
$f = [(U_c + 15)/2.4 \, R_c C]$ Hz
The output voltage, U_o, is computed from
$U_o = [1.2 \, (R1 + R2)/R2] \, V_{pp}$
It is assumed that the differential input voltage to the OTA is high enough for the current through C to equal
$I_c = [(U_c + 15)/R_c]$ A

National/Exar Application

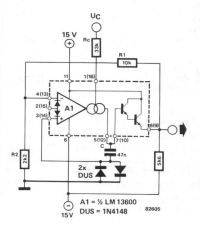

157   low cost temperature indicator

The novel use of components in this electronic temperature indicator make it very simple and economical to build. It uses only three ICs, an LM335 temperature sensor, a 723 voltage regulator and a TL489 five stage analogue level detector.
The temperature sensor (IC1) is supplied with a constant current from the reference output of the 723 (IC2). This provides a stable zero point setting enabling accurate

readings to be achieved. The circuit around the 723 is arranged to allow the output of the regulator to vary between zero volts and one volt.
It also acts as an amplifier with an effective gain of 26 dB. The output is fed to the input of the analogue level detector IC3. Depending on the voltage level at its input, this IC will light one or more of LEDs D1...D5. Since the sensitivity of the sensor

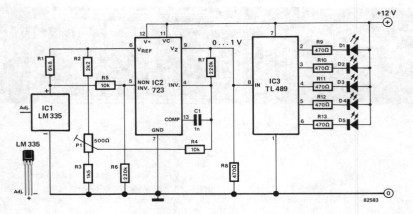

is 10 mV per degree Celsius (10 mV/°C), and the gain of the 723 is 20×, it follows that the TL489 requires an increase in voltage level of 200 mV at its input to light each successive LED. Therefore, one LED will light for every 1 degree rise in temperature registered.

Calibration is straightforward. The tem-perature measuring range (or temperature window) is set by P1; for example, 18...23°C (5°C). This range can be altered if desired by simply changing the values of resistors R6 and R7. For two degrees temperature change per LED, the resistor values must be 100 kΩ.

158   automatic switch for output amplifiers

People with a passion for hi-fi equipment and active speaker units are bound to have sought ways in which to switch on the output units via the pre amp. Funnily enough, many hi-fi manufacturers seem to regard automatic switches as an unnecessary luxury. They are, however, extremely useful and prevent the need of having to lay yards and yards of leads throughout the house. Instead, a single or several remote active units may be switched on by way of the original AF lead. As the switch is always listening in anyway, it is also able to detect the prolonged absence of a signal, in which

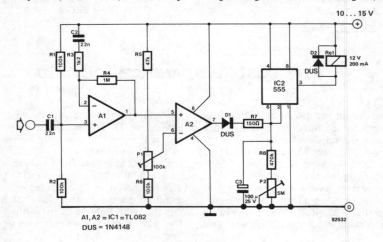

case it will simply switch off the output unit. Relatively few components are required for the circuit. Basically, it involves a double opamp, a timer IC, and a relay to switch the mains voltage. Opamp A1 is connected as a non-inverting amplifier. Note that its negative input is connected to the positive supply voltage by R3/C2. This prevents the relay from operating when the supply voltage is switched on. The gain of the opamp is high enough to prevent even low voltages from deenergizing the relay.

The second opamp, A2, is a comparator. P1 sets the switching threshold for AF signals at roughly 2.5 mV$_{rms}$.

Should the output voltage of A1 exceed the threshold value of the comparator due to the arrival of an AF signal, the comparator output will go high. As a result, capacitor C3 is charged via diode D1 and resistor R7.

When the charge level of the capacitor reaches about 2/3 of the operational voltage, the timer IC output will go low and the relay will be pulled up. The relay contacts connect the active unit to the mains. If no more AF signals are applied, C3 will discharge via R8/P2 within 1...5 minute(s). The relay will then drop out.

The supply voltage for the circuit is derived from the mains via a 12 V or 15 V voltage regulator and a small transformer together with a rectifier and smoothing capacitor.

Warning! The relay contacts are connected to the mains, so take care when servicing the circuit.

W. Wehl

159 voltage-controlled waveform generator

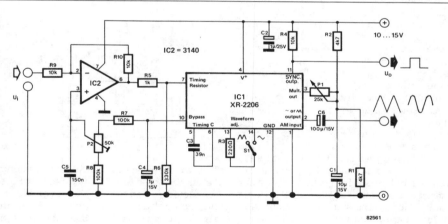

82561

The proposed circuit would be pretty familiar to many of you, were it not for the voltage control configuration around IC2. Basically, the frequency of this generator depends on the value of capacitor C3 and the current level at pin 7 of IC1.

According to Ohm's law, the current is dependent on the resistance in a circuit and the voltage across it. The voltage at pin 7 is stabilized at 3 V inside the IC. The current flowing through R5 depends on the voltage level at the output of IC2. Obvi-

ously, if this is 3 V there will be no current through R5! A maximum current of 3/1000 = 3 mA flows when the output of IC2 is 0 V. It is seen that the frequency is directly proportional to the output voltage level of IC2: the lower the voltage, the higher the current and the frequency.

The output voltage of IC2 increases with U$_i$ and the highest frequency is achieved with U$_{in}$ at 3 V. If U$_i$ rises above this value (up to the maximum supply voltage), the frequency remains the same. The IC will not be damaged, providing U_i does not become negative. The lowest possible frequency is determined by the lowest value of R6 which will still allow a little current into pin 7 when U_i is 0 V. This frequency is set by P2. This is carried out by turning P2 until the voltage across R5 is zero. It should also be possible to set the lowest output frequency by ear. This will be approximately 80 Hz with the values shown in the circuit diagram. The highest frequency is about 21 kHz and can be calculated from: $f = [U_iR6 + 3R5)/3R5R6C3]$ Hz where R5 and R6 are in ohms and C3 is in farads. The frequency will be 8.5 kHz when R5 = 1 k and C3 = 39 n. If C3 = 100 n the frequency range will be from 30 Hz to 10 kHz.

A range of 10 Hz to 3 kHz can be achieved when C3 = 330 n. The generator IC, is arranged in the normal manner. Switching between sine wave and triangular wave form outputs is carried out by switch S1. The output amplitude is set by P1: it is maximum 3 V_{pp} and 6 V_{pp} for sine and triangular wave respectively when $U_b = 12$ V. Any d.c. content in the output will be filtered out with C6. The output impedance is approximately 600 Ω. The other output of the IC is a square wave with an amplitude corresponding to the supply voltage.

160 stable amplitude low frequency oscillator

Thermistors and even light bulbs have often been used in oscillator circuits to stabilize the output signal. The resistance of such components is dependent on temperature and therefore on the effective voltage across it. Due to the fairly slow response of thermistors and light bulbs to rapid changes in voltage, the non-linear temperature/resistance characteristic means that there is virtually no distortion in the sinusoidal signal generated by the oscillator.

Things are different when the thermal inertia diminishes with respect to the time period of the signal. As far as oscillators are concerned, this normally happens at frequencies below 10 Hz, or thereabouts (for instance, the vibrato signal in electronic organs). This means that in this application a different approach will have to be taken. In the circuit described, a zener diode is used to limit the voltage. A bridge circuit (comprising resistors R1 and R2 and capacitors C1 and C2) determines the frequency of the oscillator. For the circuit to oscillate, the active devices (T1/T2) must give a gain of almost exactly X3. When the peak value of the output signal rises, the zener diode starts to conduct and reduces the gain of the amplifier stage, thereby damping the oscillation so that the sine wave tends to decay.

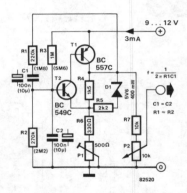

To prevent the zener diode from limiting the output signal too abruptly, resistor R5 is connected in series with the zener diode. This combination is in turn connected in parallel to resistor R4. Once the voltage threshold of the zener diode is reached, the impedance of the network gradually diminishes, allowing the sine wave to be stabilized in a gentle, low-distortion manner.

Even though only the positive half-cycle of the sine wave is limited, the negative half-cycle does not last long enough to allow the peak value to rise significantly.

Potentiometer P1 should be adjusted carefully to avoid severe clipping of the output signal. The negative half-cycle of the signal is linear, but the positive half-cycle is slightly distorted owing to the limiting. However, this will not be a problem where most applications (vibrato etc.) are concerned.

The oscillator output voltage can be adjusted by potentiometer P2 between $0 V \ldots 4 V_{pp}$. The frequency of the oscillator is determined from the formula:

$$f = \tfrac{1}{2} \pi \, R1 \, C1$$

(R1 $\approx$ R2; C1 = C2)

This gives a frequency of around 6 Hz with the values shown on the circuit diagram

(0.01 Hz with the values shown in parentheses).

Resistors R1 and R2 should have a value of at least a few hundred kilohms. Lower values may overload the amplifier stage, and with excessively high values the input impedance of the amplifier starts to play a role. At very low frequencies the negative half-cycle of the sine wave may start to clip, which will lead to considerable distortion. The DC component of the output signal may be filtered out by including a high value electrolytic capacitor in series with the output.

ITT application note

161   VCO

This voltage controlled oscillator (VCO) is capable of providing a triangular as well as a rectangular output signal. As with any other VCO, the frequency of the output signal depends on the level of the control voltage (U_c).

This design features a wide control voltage range; between 0 V and the positive supply voltage, U_b, which may be anywhere in the region of +3 V to +25 V. However, care should be taken when using low supply voltage that the maximum output level is at least 1.5 V below U_b.

The circuit is based on the integrator — comparator principle. Capacitor C1 is part of the integrator (constructed around opamp A1) and is charged by a constant current, the level of which is determined by the instantaneous level of the control

voltage. Consequently, the output of A1 falls linearly. The output of the comparator (constructed around A2) changes state and transistor T1 starts to conduct when the lower switching threshold of the comparator is reached. Capacitor C1 is now discharged causing the output of A1 to rise (again, the voltage rise will be linear). This process will be repeated when the output of A1 reaches the upper switching threshold of the comparator and T1 is turned off.

The duty factor of the output signal will be 50% when the values of R2 and R3 are the same and when the value of R1 is twice that of R4 (R2 = R3 and R1 = 2R4). The relation between the values of resistors R9 and R10 determines the DC level of the triangular output signal. With the values indicated in

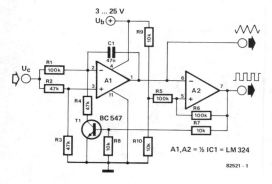

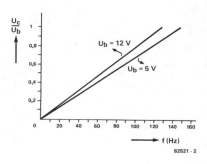

175

the circuit diagram, the DC level will be half the supply voltage. The peak-to-peak output level, U_{pp}, is

$$U_{pp} = [U_b R5/(R5 + R6)] \text{ V}.$$

The characteristics of the VCO with two (common) supply voltages are shown in figure 2. The maximum frequency (when $U_c = U_b$) generated by the circuit can be increased or decreased by selecting a lower or higher value, respectively, for capacitor C1. Owing to the slew rate of the opamp, the steepness of the rectangular signal will fall off at higher frequencies.

162 polystyrene cutter

Have you ever tried to cut polystyrene panels or blocks with a conventional saw? Messy is it not? Little bits of the stuff everywhere and you still have not achieved what you set out to do.

The only way to cut polystyrene efficiently is by the hot wire method. The wire has to be kept at just the right temperature otherwise it will either not cut or it will burn the material into horrible little black bits. A low voltage transformer delivering a current of approximately 2 A is sufficient for the circuit. By controlling the current flow through the wire the actual temperature can also be regulated. To reduce the consumption and power dissipation, the current is switched on and off intermittently by a triac.

One side of the hot wire (represented by R_L) is connected direct to the secondary winding of the transformer. N1 and N2 en-sure that the secondary voltage of the transformer is converted into a rectangular voltage. For this to happen, the values of R2 and R3 should be such that N2 switches on and off in phase with the AC supply. RC network R4/C2 differentiates the positive pulse; the internal clamping diode of N3 suppresses the negative pulse.

N3 and its surrounding components form a time switch which controls the triac. The switching periods are determined by C3. This capacitor is charged via P1, and discharged via R5 and D3. The charge and discharge levels of C3 are within the threshold levels of Schmitt trigger N3. It follows that the voltage across C3 will be logic 1 or 0. With a logic 1, N3 receives a positive pulse from N2 resulting in a short negative pulse at its output. This triggers N4 and in turn T1, which switches on the triac.

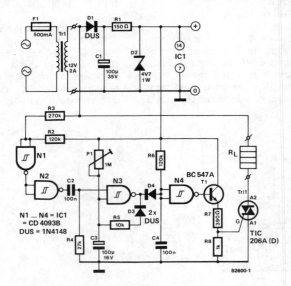

1

N1 ... N4 = IC1
= CD 4093B
DUS = 1N4148

82600-1

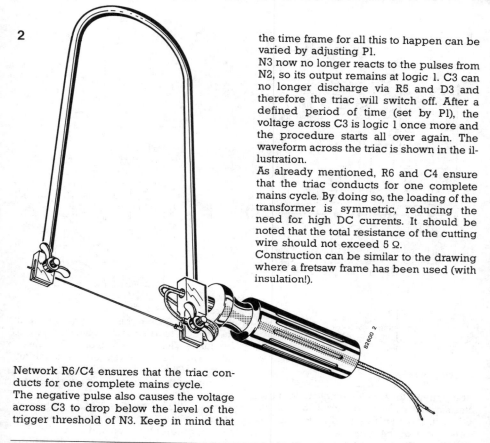

the time frame for all this to happen can be varied by adjusting P1.

N3 now no longer reacts to the pulses from N2, so its output remains at logic 1. C3 can no longer discharge via R5 and D3 and therefore the triac will switch off. After a defined period of time (set by P1), the voltage across C3 is logic 1 once more and the procedure starts all over again. The waveform across the triac is shown in the illustration.

As already mentioned, R6 and C4 ensure that the triac conducts for one complete mains cycle. By doing so, the loading of the transformer is symmetric, reducing the need for high DC currents. It should be noted that the total resistance of the cutting wire should not exceed 5 Ω.

Construction can be similar to the drawing where a fretsaw frame has been used (with insulation!).

Network R6/C4 ensures that the triac conducts for one complete mains cycle.
The negative pulse also causes the voltage across C3 to drop below the level of the trigger threshold of N3. Keep in mind that

163   stereo power amplifier

National Semiconductor's LM 2896 contains not one, but two high performance power amplifiers able to handle supply voltages up to 15 V. With a 12 V supply the IC can deliver 2.5 W per channel into 8 Ω. With the same supply and load, it is capable of delivering 9 W in bridge mode. These are certainly good figures, especially when you consider the small number of external components needed.

Figure 1 shows the circuit diagram of the complete amplifier. As you will note, the

specifications

	stereo		bridge mode
supply voltage		3...15 V	
quiescent current		max. 40 mA	
output		see figure 3	
distortion			
(1 kHz; 12 V; R_L = 8 Ω)		at 50 mW 0.09%	
		at 1 W 0.14%	
Gain	45 dB		51 dB
minimum input level		20 mV	
input impedance		100 kΩ	
frequency response (−3 dB)	30 Hz...30 kHz		30 Hz...20 kHz

1

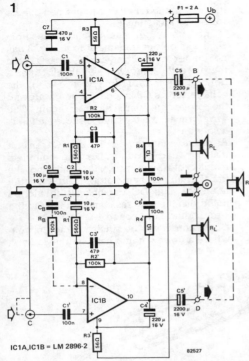

IC1A,IC1B = LM 2896-2

82527

2

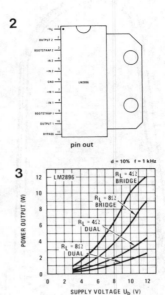

pin out

3

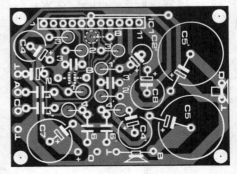

components for each channel are identical. Resistors R1 and R2 together with capacitor C2 form the negative feedback loop. The bandwidth of the amplifier is determined by R2 and C3. R3 and C4 ensure maximum gain, while R4 and C6 stabilize the output. Capacitor C8 smoothes the supply, eliminating any possible spikes.

In stereo mode operation, coupling capacitors (C5) are required at the output. Figure 4 shows the printed circuit for a stereo version using a single IC. A 10 k log potentiometer at the input controls the out-put volume. When the amplifier is used in the bridge mode, certain changes have to be made. These are denoted by dotted lines on the track pattern and circuit diagram. Obviously, to achieve high power in stereo, two complete circuits are required.

Figure 3 illustrates the power output vs supply voltage characteristics of the amplifier for different modes and loads.

When the circuit is operated in the bridge mode, RB and CB must be added, and coupling capacitors C5 replaced by wire links. Keep in mind that for high power applications the IC will require an adequate heat sink.

A simple power supply using a 7812 voltage regulator is adequate. For full output power into 4 Ω, a 1 amp supply is needed.

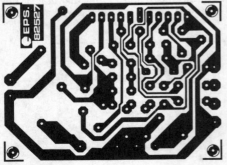

164   mini EPROMmer

With today's very reasonable prices of EPROMs, it is interesting to design logic functions with these devices instead of with conventional ICs.

The type 2716 EPROM contains 11 inputs (address lines A0...A10) and 8 data lines (D0...D7), which are connected as inputs during programming and as outputs for other functions. Therefore it is possible to program complex logic functions. A programmed EPROM can be used, for instance, as code converter. This leaves us with the problem of finding a suitable programming device. It is rather expensive to build or buy a programmer, if it is only to be used occasionally.

The circuit described in this article enables the associated data of logic functions to be stored in an EPROM quite easily. Sets of instructions can be programmed with it in a simple manner.

There is one crucial point which has to be considered when using EPROMs: the access time on which the operating speed of the complete circuit depends. The circuit must be constructed in the conventional manner, with gates, bistables, and so on, if an EPROM is too slow, owing to the access time, for a certain application.

The next question is: what is to be programmed? First, switch S21 must be set to position b. In this case, pin 21 of the EPROM is connected to the programming voltage and the data connections D0...D7 are connected as inputs. The corresponding data can now be set bit by bit by switches S1...S8. An open switch then stands for logic 1. After that, the corresponding addresses can be set with switches S9...S19.

Again, an open switch denotes a logic 1. Once the correct data and address bits have been selected, depressing S20 is suf-

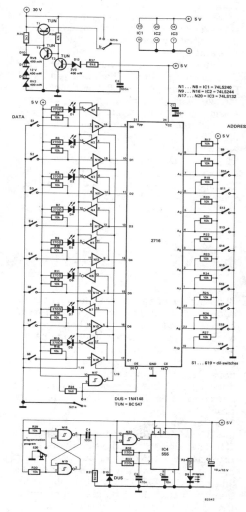

179

ficient to transfer them into EPROM. LED D9 lights to indicate the programming time. Obviously some form of check is necessary when the complete program is stored in EPROM, because if ever you have programmed by hand, you will agree that it is very easy to make an error. Set S21 in position a to check the program. LEDs D1...D9 will now indicate which data is stored in the address set with S9...S19. A stabilized voltage of 5 V at 400 mA will be enough to supply the circuit, and a 30 V at 30 mA supply is sufficient for the programming.

165   high performance video mixer

Terminals (the interfaces between computers and video screens) have to output two synchronization signals in addition to the actual video signal. The circuit presented here is a video mixer which combines these signals into a single video display control signal. The line (H) and field (V) sync signal control the horizontal and the vertical deflections of the electron beam respectively, while the video signal contains the picture information. All three signals are combined in the mixing stage around T1 and T2.
T2 mixes the sync signal; the transistor forms a NOR gate together with R2 and R3. Transistor T1 operates as an emitter follower. P1 sets the amplitude of the output signal, enabling the circuit to be

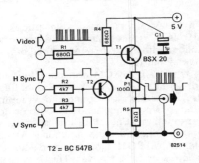

adapted to any type of monitor and/or TV set. A monitor will have to be used should your TV not have a video input socket. The video combiner is suitable for bandwidths up to 25 MHz.

166   fluid level detector

The number of applications for this circuit is enormous, ranging from a level control for hydro cultures to the-kitchen-is-under-water-because-of-the-washing-machine detector. It must be pointed out that the title is not quite correct as the LM 1830 from National Semiconductor will only detect conductive fluids, but, as most common liquids are conductive, this should not present a problem.
The frequency of the internal oscillator of the IC is 6 kHz (determined by capacitor C1). The oscillator output amplitude is approximately 2.4 V peak to peak and is fed to the probe via an internal resistor of 13 k and capacitor C2. When the probe is immersed in a conductive fluid, the output of the oscillator is effectively shorted to earth via the fluid. If the fluid level then falls

below the end of the probe, the detector input (pin 10) is presented with the 6 kHz output of the oscillator. Transistor T1 conducts and switches on one of the three indicator systems.
An a.c. signal was chosen for the probe because the **average** current through the probe is then zero, which obviates polarization of the probe. On-chip transistor T1 conducts only on the leading edge of the probe signal with the result that the loudspeaker (if used) will produce a 6 kHz tone. Increasing the value of C1 would lower the frequency. The LED also flashes at a frequency of 6 kHz but this is not visibly apparent. However, the relay would not take kindly to being switched on and off at this speed and therefore capacitor C3 is included to smooth the way. Personal

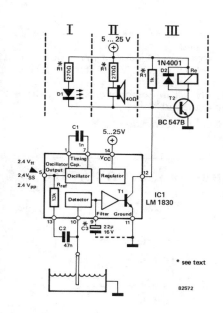

* see text

82572

preference and the application will dictate which of the three methods is used. Whatever choice is made, it should be remembered that the current passing through the internal transistor T1 must not be allowed to exceed 20 mA. The values shown in the circuit diagram for the series resistors (270 Ω) have been chosen for the minimum supply voltage of 5 V. These values must be increased for higher supply voltage levels.

If a 40 Ω loudspeaker proves to be difficult to find, it is possible to use one of a lower impedance. Unfortunately, this will mean a drop in volume but that may be acceptable.

(National Semiconductor)

167   electronic thermometer

The scale of a thermometer used for measuring the temperature of liquids is normally graduated from 40°C to 100°C. The circuit described here operates within this range and uses the KTY-10 temperature sensor from Siemens. The current produced (up to a maximum of 20 mA) is directly proportional to the temperature, allowing simple calibration without the need of complicated calculations. The circuit can be used to measure the temperature of, for instance, car oil, bath water, baby food, etc. (but not all at the same time!).

As can be seen from figure 1, the electronic thermometer is made up of a bridge circuit consisting of resistors R1...R3 and the sensor R_T. The voltage across the bridge is stabilized by zener diode D1. The bridge circuit is followed by an opamp, IC1. Any voltage difference at the input is amplified and fed to transistor T1. This determines the amount of current flowing through the load circuit R_L. This type of temperature to current conversion circuit is not affected by the overall resistance of R_L and therefore the length of the connecting leads to R_L is not critical.

The load circuit is in fact the display or indi-

1

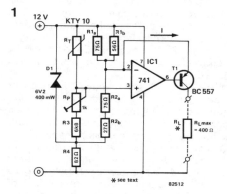

* see text   82512

2

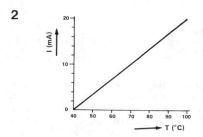

cator section. Either an analogue or a digital multimeter may be used. Preset potentiometer R_p should be adjusted so that the display section does not register temperature readings below 40°C.

The circuit can be used for other temperature ranges, if the values of resistor R1 and R2 are altered. If, for instance, the value of R1 is reduced and the value of R2 is increased, a lower temperature range will be obtained.

The value of R3 must, however, be reduced by 1 kΩ for each 25°C shift in the temperature range.

Lastly, all the components should have a tolerance of 1%.

Siemens application note.

168 positive triangular pulse generator

This circuit contains a small addition to the usual triangular pulse generator. This is the diode included in the feedback loop of IC2. The triangular pulse output is entirely positive in contrast to a conventional circuit. Without the diode the output would be a pulse that is symmetrical about the zero axis. All this is necessary because some equipment, such as curve tracers, are unable to process a negative pulse.

When the output of opamp IC2 goes negative, the diode will conduct so that pin 3 (non-inverting input) will also become negative. Since the inverting input, pin 2, is grounded the output will remain negative. This output is also fed to the inverting input of IC1 via R1. The output of this opamp then begins to rise at a linear rate (as C1 charges linearly).

When this voltage reaches the point at which pin 3 of IC2 becomes positive, the output of that opamp toggles and becomes positive. The inverting input of IC1 will follow suit, ending the charge cycle of C1. This capacitor will now discharge causing the output of IC1 to fall, again at a linear rate. The diode is now reverse biased so that when the non-inverting input (pin 3) of IC2 reaches zero, its output will again go negative, starting the whole process from

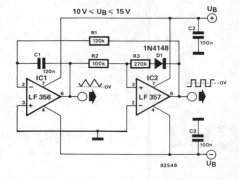

the beginning.

The oscillator now has two outputs: a square wave centred about the zero axis, and a triangular pulse above the zero line. The peak-to-peak triangular output voltage, U_t, is calulated from:

$$U_t = [R2(U_b-2)/R3]V$$

The pulse rate, f_t, of the output is determined by:

$$f_t = R3/2R1R2C1 \text{ Hz}$$

provided R3 > R2.

In these formulas, U_t and U_b are in volts, R1, R2, R3 are in ohms, and C1 is in farads.

R. Storn

169 frequency generator

One IC, a quartz crystal, three resistors, and two switches are all that is required to obtain sixteen different frequencies! Can it be more versatile than that? Motorola calls its IC MC1411 a bit rate generator which

can be used as a frequency source for numerous applications within the area of data transfer, such as teleprinters, video terminals, and microprocessor systems. A quartz controlled oscillator forms the

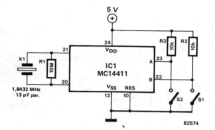

Rate	Select	Rate
B	A	
0	0	X1
0	1	X8
1	0	X16
1	1	X64

Pin No.	Output Number	Output Rates (Hz)			
		X64	X16	X8	X1
1	F1	614.4 k*	153.6 k	76.8 k	9600
17	F2	460.8 k*	115.2 k	57.6 k	7200
2	F3	307.2 k*	76.8 k	38.4 k	4800
16	F4	230.4 k	57.6 k	28.8 k	3600
3	F5	153.6 k	38.4 k	19.2 k	2400
15	F6	115.2 k	28.8 k	14.4 k	1800
4	F7	76.8 k	19.2 k	9600	1200
5	F8	38.4 k	9600	4800	600
7	F9	19.2 k	4800	2400	300
6	F10	12.8 k	3200	1600	200
8	F11	9600	2400	1200	150
14	F12	8613.2	2153.3	1076.6	134.5
13	F13	7035.5	1758.8	879.4	109.9
9	F14	4800	1200	600	75
18	F15	921.6 k	921.6 k	921.6 k	921.6 k
19	F16*	1.843 M*	1.843 M	1.843 M	1.843 M

*F16 is buffered oscillator output

master frequency source. The oscillator signal is buffered at pin 19. Moreover, the signal reaches a divider that produces five different output signals: The oscillator signal divided by two is always present at pin 18, the other four signals (:1, :4, :8, :64) can be fed to a 14 stage divider, as desired. So, with the two switches (S1, S2) in the open position it already supplies 4 different signals. In addition there are 14 + 2 signals simultaneously available. The table shows all the possible combinations. The output pins of the IC are not indicated in the circuit diagram, but are found in the table. One final remark: The IC can be 'fed' with an external clock signal via pin 21, so that the various division factors can be used to the full!

Source: Motorola

170   bio-electronic interface

ECG, EMG, and EEG are common expressions in bio-electronics, but they will probably be mumbo-jumbo to the general electronics enthusiasts. These abbreviations stand for: ECG = electrocardiogram, EMG = electromyogram, EEG = electroencephalogram.
All these deal with the measurement and display of electric voltages produced by the heart (ECG), muscles (EMG), and brain (EEG). The heart supplies the strongest signals and the brain the weakest (didn't we all know that?!)
Many microprocessor enthusiasts may have had some thoughts of performing physical tests with their computer. Unfortunately no suitable interface has been available...until now; this circuit solves

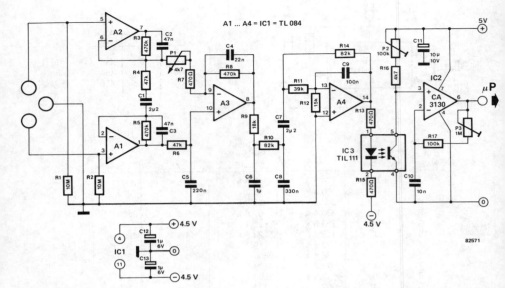

A1 ... A4 = IC1 = TL 084

82571

that particular problem.

Three copper plates are used as electrodes. They are connected via screened cable to the differential amplifier which forms the input of the circuit. The circuit consisting of A1...A3 can also be described as an instrumentation amplifier: a differential amplifier with opamps and *two* high impedance inputs. The output signal of this input stage is filtered by active low-pass filter A4 before being fed to the transmitter diode in the optocoupler.

It is advisable to derive the operational voltage for IC1 from two 4.5 V batteries. This is the only sure method of guaranteeing complete isolation of the measuring cir-

cuit from the power supply of the microcomputer system. For obvious safety reasons we strongly recommend that a mains derived power supply is *not* used for the circuit!

The receiver transistor in the optocoupler conducts the signal to IC2, where it is converted into a pulse-width modulated signal. The duty factor of the output signal (at the shorted input of the differential amplifier) is set to 50% by P2. The frequency of the output signal can be selected with the aid of P3. Last, but not least, the amplification factor of the input signal can be set with P1. Developing the software is up to the constructor.

171   CMOS switch Schmitt trigger

It is generally thought that a CMOS analogue switch can only be used as an electronic substitute for switching low power signals. However, this is not strictly true. It is possible to use a single CMOS switch as a Schmitt trigger, which can be very useful. If a Schmitt trigger is required and not all of the CMOS switches available in a single IC have been used, the circuit in figure 1 can avoid the expense of an extra IC. The resistor values required for the

1

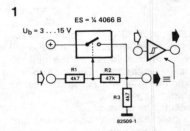

184

Schmitt trigger can be calculated as
follows:
0 to 1 transition:
threshold $= [U_b(1+R1/R2)]$ V
1 to 0 transition:
threshold $= [U_b(1-R1/R2)]$ V
An interesting variation of the circuit is
shown in figure 2. Here, the trigger section
is combined with the voltage divider in
such a way that the divider becomes
dependent on the trigger voltage level. Applications include limiters and auto-

2

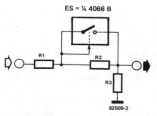

ES = ¼ 4066 B

ranging. It is advisable to ensure that the input voltage to the CMOS switch does not
drop below 3 V.

172 universal VCF

The term voltage controlled filter (VCF) frequently crops up in connection with synthesizers. As its name suggests, a VCF is a
filter that is controlled and adjusted by applying different voltages. This particular
circuit consists of a voltage controlled
audio band pass filter with a variable IF and
bandwidth. At the heart of the circuit there

is an active band pass filter around A2.
Capacitors C4 and C6 are connected in
parallel to frequency-determining
capacitors C5 and C7 by ES3 and ES4. The
electronic switches are controlled by a
high frequency signal with a variable duty
factor. When an electronic switch and a capacitor are connected in series, they have

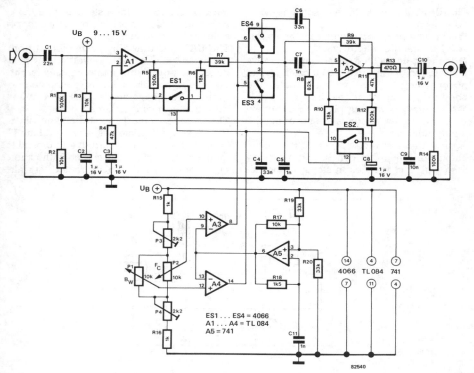

the same average duty factor as a variable capacitor. This enables the intermediate frequency (IF) range of the filter to be adjusted. Similarly, ES2 affects the gain of A2 and therefore the bandwidth, or rather the Q factor. Unfortunately, a reduction in bandwidth in this type of filter automatically leads to a rise in gain (A2), which would restrict the number of possible applications of the filter considerably. ES1, together with A1, compensates for this by providing a push-pull amplification control to the input.

A5 is connected as an astable multivibrator. But beware! Contrary to what you might expect, this AMV does not produce a rectangular pulse but a triangular voltage. The reason for this is simply that A5 is a 741 IC and much too slow to be able to produce a rectangular signal at such high frequencies. It therefore produces a triangular signal. The signal is applied to opamps A3 and A4 which act as comparators. They compare the triangular voltage to the signals adjusted by the potentiometers. The result is a rectangular voltage at the output with a constant frequency, but with a duty factor that can be adjusted by the voltage at the non-inverting inputs of the opamps. As neither the amplitude nor the frequency of the triangular voltage can be predicted with accuracy, the presets are used to interface the circuit to the signal generated by the 741 IC.

Due to its presettable 100 Hz...3 kHz IF range, the VCF illustrated here is particularly suited to audio applications. The filter bandwidth can be adjusted from around 0.5 kHz to 3 kHz.

---

173   single chip timer

The UAA3000 timer IC has some remarkable properties:
- it may be powered direct from the mains;
- it has on-chip triac drive;
- the triac connected to the chip is always switched on during a zero crossing point of the mains voltage, which obviates the need for additional decoupling;
- temporary power supply failures (not exceeding a few seconds) do not affect the timing function.

Against these advantages, there is a drawback: the times that can be set are fairly long — 1...15 minutes in steps of one minute, or 1...15 hours in steps of one hour. However, these times are perfectly acceptable for most applications.

The UAA3000 draws its power direct from the mains and operates internally with a negative supply: this is the reason why the positive terminal of C1 is connected to ground. This capacitor serves as a buffer during short mains failures.

The required time is set by making links J1...J5 as appropriate — see table 1. Link J5 is open if hours are required, and closed if minutes are wanted. The setting of the number of hours or minutes is effected by mak-

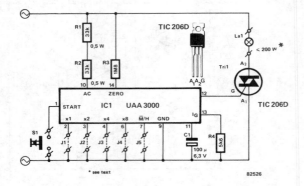

* see text

82526

Table 1

	minutes	hours
1	J1, J5	J1
2	J2, J5	J2
3	J1, J2, J5	J1, J2
4	J3, J5	J3
5	J1, J3, J5	J1, J3
6	J2, J3, J5	J2, J3
7	J1, J2, J3, J5	J1, J2, J3
8	J4, J5	J4
9	J1, J4, J5	J1, J4
10	J2, J4, J5	J2, J4
11	J1, J2, J4, J5	J1, J2, J4
12	J3, J4, J5,	J3, J4
13	J1, J3, J4, J5	J1, J3, J4
14	J2, J3, J4, J5	J2, J3, J4
15	J1, J2, J3, J4, J5	J1, J2, J3, J4

Parts list

Resistors:
R1,R2 = 33 k/0,5 W
R3 = 1M8
R4 = 5k6

Capacitors:
C1 = 100 μ/6V3

Semiconductors:
IC1 = UAA3000 (Philips)
Tri1 = TIC 206D

Miscellaneous:
S1 = push-button switch

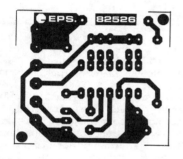
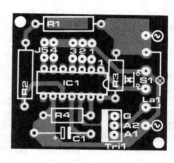

ing links as indicated in the table. The links may be replaced by switches so that the set time may be changed fairly easily.

Once the time has been set, the timer can be started by briefly pressing push-button switch S1. The IC then delivers gate pulses to the triac. The gate current is determined by the value of R4. When R4 = ∞, the gate current is 6.5 mA, and when R4 = 0, the gate current rises to 40 mA. With the value of R4 as shown, the current is 15 mA, which is sufficient to trigger a type TIC206D triac. The on-chip zero crossing detector gets its information from the mains via R3.

If the triac is not cooled, it can switch up to 200 W; with adequate cooling, this rises to 800 W.

Construction is facilitated by the printed circuit shown in figure 2. The dimensions of this board are small enough to make it possible for the pcb to be built into the housing of most wall-mounted light switches.

Typical applications are lights control in staircases; control of lights in bedrooms (switching off after a predetermined time); as timer in alarm installations to switch off the sirene or whatever after a predetermined time. No doubt, you will be able to think of some more.

174   VHF FM signal generator

This low power signal generator is an indispensable tool for calibrating and servicing VHF FM receiver, which will be appreciated by most RF hobbyists.

The circuit may be divided into a micro-phone amplifier with automatic gain control; an oscillator which is frequency-modulated by the output of the microphone amplifier; a MOSFET output stage that delivers 10...50 mW output; and an output

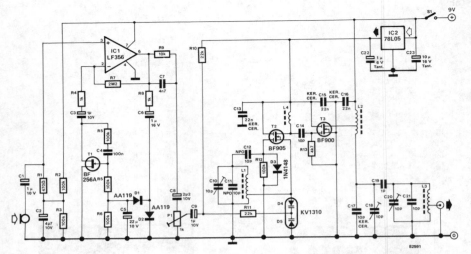

filter.

The microphone amplifier is formed by JFET opamp IC1. Part of the output of this amplifier is used as negative control voltage for T1. This FET forms a sort of variable resistance between the negative input of IC1 and earth. When this resistance diminishes, the gain of IC1 is reduced. The peak value of the amplified AF signal, and consequently the deviation ration, is adjustable with P1.

The AF signal is applied to the junction of varactors D4 and D5 via P1; the capacitance of these devices varies in rhythm with the AF voltages. As the varactors form part of the oscillator circuit, L1-C10-C11, their behaviour causes frequency modulation of the output of oscillator T2. Output amplifier T3 raises the level of the oscillator voltage,

which is then filtered in L2, L3, and C16...C21. Inductor L3 also ensures correct matching of the output stage to the aerial.

In the construction the usual rules for RF circuits should be observed: neat soldering; all connecting wires as short as possible; all decoupling capacitors as close to the correct position as possible. Inductor L4 consists of 4 turns of 0.8 mm enamelled copper wire through a ferrite bead. The other three inductors consist of 6 turn 0.8 mm enamelled copper wire on a T50-12 toroid. The tap is 2 turns from earth in L1; 3 turns from earth in L2; and 1 turn from earth in L3.

The connection between the signal generator and the receiver being tested must, of course, be via a coaxial cable.

175   0 to 60 V power supply

The novelty of this design is that it has a variable output from 0 V up without using a transformer with two secondary windings. The circuit can either be constructed with the well known 723 IC, or, for higher output voltages, the L 146, which, although less popular, is still easily available. The choice is left to the constructor. The output current limitation is also variable, but once set it is continuously effective. Table 1 shows all the different component values needed to

make three different versions (30, 40, and 60 V maximum output).

The circuit diagram illustrates the 40 V/0.8 A type. The L 146 IC was used because this can handle the higher output voltages far better than the 723. Normally speaking, 2 V is the minimum regulated voltage which either IC can provide. Resistor networks R3, R4 and R5, R6 get over this restriction so that the output can be adjusted right down to practically 0 V (with

Table 1

U_{out}	I_{out}	R1	R4,R5	R9	Tr1		C1/C5	IC1	T2	T3
0-25-30 V	1.3 A	0.47 Ω	33 k	2k7	24 V	2 A	40 V	723	BD 242	2N3055
0-40 V	0.8 A	0.82 Ω	47 k	5k6	33 V	1.5 A	63 V	L 146	BD242A	2N3055
0-60 V	0.6 A	1.2 Ω	68 k	10 k	48 V	1 A	80 V	L 146	BD 242B	2N3442

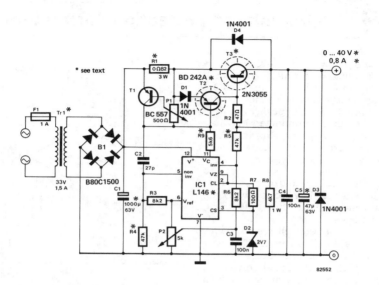

P2). These resistors ensure that sufficient voltage is present at pins 4 and 5 of the regulator (to keep it stable), even when voltages lower than their tolerated input level are required.

Another aspect of the design is the unusual way in which T3 is driven. When the required output voltage is below the tolerated minimum of the regulator, the potential at pin 4 is below that of pin 5. This results in the IC trying to compensate for this by attempting to increase the output voltage from pin 9. This, however, does not work because pin 9 is earthed via R7 and D2, which limits the voltage increase. Although the voltage cannot increase, the current certainly can, so R7 is also used to limit this to 6 mA. The current flowing through the IC (in at pin 11 and out at pin 9) causes a voltage drop across P1. This in turn drives T3 open (via T2), thereby increasing the voltage. As the wiper of P1 is connected to T1, it can be used to control the current limiting.

When the voltage drop across R1 exceeds 0.6 V, P1 is shorted by R1, and T3 is cut-off.

During normal operation (without current limiting), the voltage drop across P1 is a constant 1.2 V, made up of the forward voltage of D1 and the U_{BE} of T2.

A part of this voltage can be used to drive T1 before 0.6 V is reached across R1. This is possible because the base voltage of T1 is composed of the drop across T1 and the voltage at the wiper of P1. In the way just described, the output current can be controlled from 0 to the maximum available. Keep in mind that a 723 can only handle a maximum of 36 V. An L 146 should be used with any transformer supplying more than 24 V. As the L 146 can safely handle up to 80 V, the maximum size of transformer that can be used is one with secondary windings supplying 48 V. Whatever output requirements the constructor decides upon also determine the type of capacitors and semiconductors to be used. Remember that a 2N3055 is only rated to 60 V, therefore for 80 V a 40411 or 2N3442 should be used, and so on.

Table 1 indicates the component values needed to construct three different power

189

supplies dependent on the voltage range required. Bear in mind to limit the output current sufficiently to keep the power dissipation of T3 under 40 W. The maximum output current of a 40 V version is 0.8 A. It is possible to connect two 2N3055s in parallel (with emitter resistors) to double the output current, but then a 2 A transformer is necessary.

176 overvoltage protection for meters

Normally, the high impedance input of the front end amplifier in a digital voltmeter is protected against excessive voltages by two diodes. One diode is connected between the input and the positive supply rail, while the other is connected between the input and the negative supply rail. In principle, this form of overvoltage protection is perfectly satisfactory.

However, the diodes used would have to have a very low leakage current. The main problem here is that they are relatively difficult to obtain and also they tend to be rather expensive. Electronics enthusiasts prefer to utilize general purpose devices such as the 1N4148 silicon diode. This does mean that with an input impedance of 1 mΩ the leakage current of the diode gives rise to an offset voltage of a few millivolts. As it is quite common nowadays to wish to measure voltages below this level, the diodes are replaced by FETs. With a reverse bias voltage of 15 V, the diode has a leakage current of 5.2 nA, whereas the leakage current of the FET is a mere 12 pA! This means that the input impedance of the meter can be increased to 10 MΩ with no difficulty.

The circuit of the input section of a high impedance voltmeter based on the principle outlined above is shown in figure 1. Resistor R1 constitutes the 10 MΩ input impedance. FETs T1 and T2 can withstand a maximum current of 10 mA. The remainder

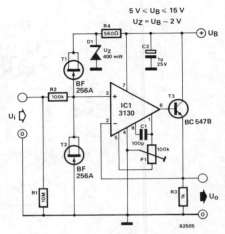

of the circuit, IC1 and T3 etc., comprises a voltage follower which provides a relatively low output impedance. The operating voltage (U_b) may be anywhere between 5 V and 15 V, and the rating of the zener diode should be two volts less than the supply.

Calibration of the unit is straightforward: preset P1 is adjusted until the voltage obtained at the output is the same as the voltage applied at the input.

In principle, the input can be protected against voltages up to 1000 V, but to achieve this the input resistors will have to be suitably high-voltage types.

177 analogue monostable

Monostables are automatically associated with digital circuits, but there is no reason why they should not be used for analogue purposes.

The opamp involved will not be used as an amplifier, but as a comparator. The 741 is used in both of the circuits shown here, although practically any type of amplifier will do.

Operation is quite straightforward. The in-

1

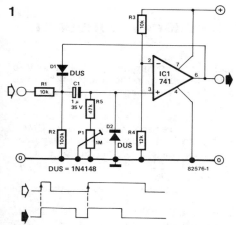

DUS = 1N4148   82576-1

2

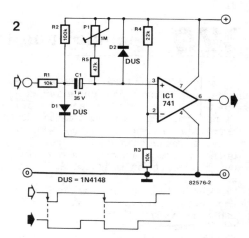

DUS = 1N4148   82576-2

verting input is set at a fixed level of slightly more than half the supply voltage via R3/R4. The non-inverting input is grounded by R5 and P1. The output is therefore also at ground potential and diode D1 does not conduct. A positive pulse at the input is fed to the non-inverting input by capacitor C1. For a short time this becomes higher than the inverting input. As a result, the output of the opamp will be connected to the positive supply voltage. Diode D1 will now conduct and make sure that point A remains positive even when the input signal is no longer applied. This situation will not change until capacitor C1 is charged via R5 and P1 and the voltage at pin 3 is lower again than that at pin 2. The opamp then toggles and its output is grounded once

more.

In principle, the same procedure applies to the negative response circuit. As can be seen in the pulse diagrams, the input signal should be either longer or shorter than the required output signal. The resultant pulse width is about

$[0.5C1(R5 + P1)]$ s. Potentiometer P1 sets the exact value, which is determined, to a certain extent, by the degree of saturation of the opamp output, and so can only be calculated approximately.

Just make sure that the input signal is always slightly smaller than the variation in amplitude at pin 6, because the signals might affect each other, especially if the input and output pulses have the same width.

178   inverter oscillator

This is an oscillator with a difference: unlike most of its counterparts its frequency is variable. The circuit consists of two inverters with same external components. Resistors R1 and R2 and the trimming capacitor C1 set the frequency. With the given component values, the oscillator frequency may be adjusted from 800 kHz to 12 MHz. The resistors set the frequency in just about the right region, while C1 provides the fine adjustment. The resistor values are not critical; just make sure that they are both the same. The circuit is also suitable as a stable crystal oscillator. All you have to do is replace C1 by a crystal of

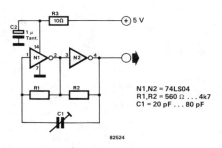

N1,N2 = 74LS04
R1,R2 = 560 Ω ... 4k7
C1 = 20 pF ... 80 pF

82524

appropriate frequency. If, for instance, the oscillator frequency is to be 1 MHz, the crystal will have to be a 1 MHz type.

Although a temperature to voltage converter may be more common, a temperature to frequency converter is much more useful when digital circuits are used for temperature measurement. This type of converter can be connected to either a frequency counter or a microprocessor, without the need of an additional A/D converter.

The circuit described here is remarkably accurate. A 10 Hz/°C conversion factor is maintained within 3 Hz throughout the 5°C to 100°C range.

An LM 335 is used as the temperature sensor. The IC comes in a plastic transistor package. The ADJ pin is not used in this application. The voltage, U_2, across this IC is 1 mV for each degree centigrade above −273°C.

Therefore, at 0°C the voltage is exactly 2.73 V. So that the voltage to frequency converter can be calibrated in degrees centigrade, this voltage is negated by an equal and opposite (negative) voltage. Instead of using a negative supply voltage for this, a little trick is employed. A +5 V regulator, IC3, boosts the GND connection of IC1 to +5 V with respect to supply common. The input offset can now be taken from preset P1. At the other end, the LM 335 is fed by the current source around T1.

The output of the LM 331 (IC1) is a pulse whose level varies from +5 V (GND for this IC!) to positive supply. It is not difficult to relate this signal to the actual 0 V rail: two switching transistors, T2 and T3, take care of this level conversion.

T3 has an open collector output, so that it can easily be used to drive TTL or CMOS logic circuitry. Alternatively, frequency counters with an AC input can be connected direct to pin 3 of IC1 while T2 and T3 can be omitted.

To calibrate the circuit, a mixture of crushed ice and water gives a good 0°C reference. With the sensor in this slush, the voltage between the positive end of IC2 and pin 4 of IC1 (GND) can be set to 0 V by P1. A further reference is now required at approximately mid-scale — warm water at 50°C, as measured with a good thermometer. The output frequency is then set with P2 to give 500 Hz at 50°C. For good temperature stability of the circuit, metal film resistors should be used for R5...R7, and a polycarbonate capacitor for C4. Preferably, P1 and P2 should be cermet multi-turn potentiometers.

One final point. If the circuit is used to measure air temperature, this will invariably imply that the circuit itself will also be warmed up. In this case, the output may drift up to +0.5°C off mark. The solution is to...recalibrate the thermometer! Alternatively, try and keep the circuit as cool as possible, using plenty of heat sinks.

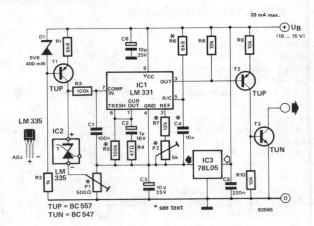

TUP = BC 557
TUN = BC 547

* see text

180 voltage controlled TTL oscillator

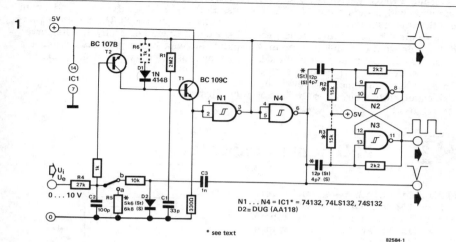

N1 ... N4 = IC1* = 74132, 74LS132, 74S132
D2 = DUG (AA118)

* see text

82584-1

Not having the right IC to hand is an well known stumblingblock for constructors. When a VCO (voltage controlled oscillator) is required, the ideal IC is invariably not available and those that are will probably not suit the purpose. Whenever an oscillator with an adjustable frequency is required, it is desirable to use one that is voltage controlled, because this is as versatile as it is possible to get. Whereas a potentiometer is fine for manual setting, a control voltage is far more useful for automatic frequency control purposes. The circuit must have a wide frequency and supply range for it to be suitable for the majority of applications. This particular circuit has a frequency range of more than 1 : 1000 and can be used from AF up to 50 MHz.

The basis of the circuit is the wellknown TTL Schmitt-trigger oscillator. The emitter follower T1, connected in front of N1, increases the input resistance and allows high values for the feedback resistor R1. The following section around T2 is the frequency control stage, which is connected in parallel to R1. Diode D1 ensures that the capacitor charges very quickly. However, its discharge via T2 is controlled by the input voltage U_i. Therefore, the output of the gate consists of a train of narrow pulses of variable frequency. Strictly speaking, R1 is superfluous, but it guarantees that the oscillator will start to operate, even in the ab-

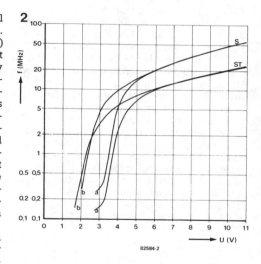

82584-2

sence of an input voltage.

The pulse duration mainly depends on the propagation delay of the Schmitt-trigger used (N1). Standard and LS TTL need about 30 ns and S TTL about 15 ns. A divide-by-two circuit (N2 and N3) follows the actual oscillator. This supplies a rectangular output signal of half the oscillator frequency. The top end frequency limit is 15 and 30 MHz for the LS and S-type respectively. With the very small coupling capacitors in mind, care must be taken with wiring.

193

Further, a ceramic capacitor of 10...1000 nF must be fitted between pins 7 and 14 of the TTL IC. Resistors R2 and R3 must be used with standard and LS TTL, to prevent the divider from oscillating. Negative feedback via C3 and D2 is provided to linearize the non-linear control stage of T2. A frequency-proportional, negative voltage level is provided across C2. Resistor R4 determines the level and was calculated in this circuit for a control voltage range of 0...10 V. The higher the control voltage, the bigger R4 can be, and the better the linearity. Figure 2 shows the control characteristic of the oscillator with standard LS TTL (curves St) and with Schottky TTL (curves S). The negative feedback can be switched off by S1. The curves indicated with b are produced when the negative feedback switch is in position b.

N. Rohde

181   LED tuning indicator

This LED field strength meter can be connected to FM receivers in which the CA 3189E IC is used in the IF stage. It consists of a bar display constructed with a UAA 180 and twelve LEDs.
Preset P1 sets the sensitivity of the circuit. The voltage across P1 is stabilized to 5...6 V by R1 and D13. The input to the UAA 180 is connected to pin 13 of the CA 3189E. The relation between the operational voltage U_o, and the input voltage, U_i, is shown in figure 2. Preset P1 is adjusted so that at the strongest transmitted signal all the LEDs are just lighting.
The circuit can also be used with other IF stages, but then there may be a problem in calibration. Luckily, many commercially made FM receivers already have a field-strength indicator of some kind, which will show not only where to connect the input, but will also give some calibration parameters. The consumption of the circuit is only about 40 mA. If desired, diodes D1

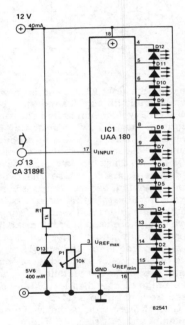

and D2 can be removed and substituted by wire links. The reason for this is that the first two LEDs will always flicker as a result of the ever present IF noise of the IF stage, and eliminating them will allow more effective use of the remaining LEDs.

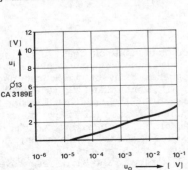

182 keyless lock

Out of the enormous variety of ICs produced today, the ones that are designed for use in one specific application represent a relatively small part. The proposed circuit contains an IC that is from this category. It is the LSI 7220 from LSI Computer Systems and meets all the requirements of an automatic keyless lock system. However, it is possible to use it for domestic purposes, as an electronic safe lock, for instance. When it is fitted to a car, the ignition circuit is immobilized until the correct code combination is entered via a keyboard consisting of ten or more keys. Other facilities are also available from the IC. A LED displays the condition of the lock (locked/unlocked). A very cunning feature is that the lock combination is set by the constructor. It is possible to allow another person to drive the car without disclosing the code or even the existence of the system.

With so many facilities available, the circuit could be expected to be a rather fearsome affair and this would be true if it were not for the IC. While this could be said of virtually any IC, the specialized nature of the one used here reduces the discrete components greatly. In fact, so little of an actual circuit exists that, having stated that a logic

1 from pin 13 of the IC will switch on the relay via T1, we have said it all! Not quite true of course, but the relay is the operative element — it switches the ignition system on.

What else are we left with? The object of the exercise is to enter a code into the system and this is carried out via **four** of the keys shown in the diagram, S7...S10. These keys must be pressed in precisely that order to operate the relay. The remaining six switches to the left (S1...S6) may, at first sight, appear to be a waste of time until it is realized that they are dummies. That is, we (and now you) know that if any of these switches is pressed, the lock will remain locked, regardless of the combination entered on the other keys (S7...S10). The trick is to physically place all the switches in any order (not as shown here!) and number them in that order. This means that only you know the position of the dummies! For instance, S7 here (a code switch) could end up as number four (for argument's sake) and S1 (a reset switch) could end up as number 5 and so on. It should be noted at this point that as many reset (or dummy) keys as desired can be used.

There are still two switches left to deal with

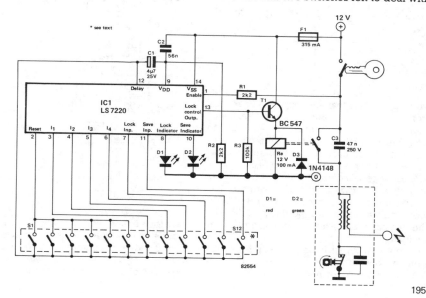

82554

and the first of these, in logical sequence, is S12, termed the save key. In short, depressing this key before the ignition is switched off will allow the car to be started straight away next time without the need to enter the combination to the lock. This is used when the car is placed in a garage for servicing, for instance. This (effectively out of service) state of the lock will be indicated by LED D2 being lit. To return the lock to normal, brings us to the last switch, S11. This must be pressed just before turning the ignition off to return the lock to its normal operational status, as indicated by LED D1!

So, now what is left? Sharp-eyed readers will have noted that there is some sort of delay noted at pin 12 of the IC and this is easily explained. Visualize the situation when the car engine stalls on a busy roundabout! With the rest of the world encased in motor cars attempting to go round, under or through you, you are frantically trying to enter the correct combination into the keyboard! No, it does not happen this way,

because C1 provides enough time (about 10 seconds) for the ignition to be switched off and on again without the need to enter the code.

Only one further point of note: The enable input to the IC (pin 1) is taken direct from the ignition switch as shown. Capacitor C3 is used to disable the ignition circuit and is about as good a method as any. It is best fitted (and disguised) as close as possible to the distributor.

The usual points apply about hiding or disguising the protection wiring and (perhaps most important) the relay. The latter should be of the best quality and may be fitted together with the circuit inside a diecast aluminium box mounted directly onto the bulkhead. If the wiring is then fed through the back of the box, straight through the bulkhead, it will be even more difficult to trace, especially if all the visible wiring looks similar to the existing wiring in the car.

183 dissipation limiter 2

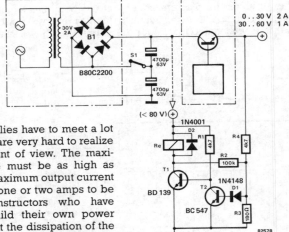

Variable power supplies have to meet a lot of requirements that are very hard to realize from a technical point of view. The maximum output voltage must be as high as possible while the maximum output current needs to be at least one or two amps to be of some use. Constructors who have already tried to build their own power supply will know that the dissipation of the power transistors can become pretty high. Here is a way to get around this problem for the majority of cases — and quite economically!

Maximum dissipation occurs with high currents at low output voltage levels. For this reason switched primary windings on the

transformer are used in many cases as an effective way to limit the losses. However, the circuit shown here might present a solution to many of you who do not want the added expense of a transformer of this type. It is possible to realize double the voltage and half the current with the aid of a single switch contact, which can be operated manually or automatically. The two electrolytic capacitors are the most expensive components in the circuit.

The existing power supply is inside the dotted lines shown on the circuit diagram. Either normal full wave rectification or voltage doubling can be selected by switch S1. In the first case S1 will be open. The transformer voltages shown in the circuit diagram are intended as an example. The circuit will function just as well with other voltages, of course, on the condition that the electrolytic capacitors and transistors are able to cope with these values.

Automatic switching can be achieved by the circuitry constructed around T1, T2 and a relay. As soon as the output voltage of the stabilization circuit exceeds 30 V (this value can be set by varying R3), T2 will conduct and the relay will drop out. S1, which is a normally open contact of the relay will now close, so that voltage doubling ensues.

The auxiliary circuit with T1 and T2 can be fed from a separate supply, preferably with a voltage that has the same value as that of the relay coil. However, it is also possible to derive this supply from the voltage across the smoothing capacitors. In this case, particular attention has to be paid to the fact that T1 and the relay must be able to cope with the maximum voltage and T2 should be able to deal with at least half of this value.

H. Burke

184   reciprocal amplifier

The normal circuit design for a reciprocal amplifier uses four ICs. Two opamps, ICs 2 and 4, serve as input buffer and output driver respectively. Half of a dual timer (IC3a) forms a clock oscillator for a modulator (IC3b). Gates N1 and N2 convert the output signal of IC3b into a rectangular pulse. This circuit is based on the PPM (pulse pause modulation) principle and the variable pulse width of the rectangular pulse is dependent on the DC voltage level fed to the modulator. Note that the frequency remains unchanged! For example, if the input to the circuit is a high voltage level, the pulse width of the rectangular pulse will be small.

The output of IC3 is cleaned up by gates N1 and N2 and then converted into a DC voltage level by the filter network consisting of R6/C6 and R7/C7.

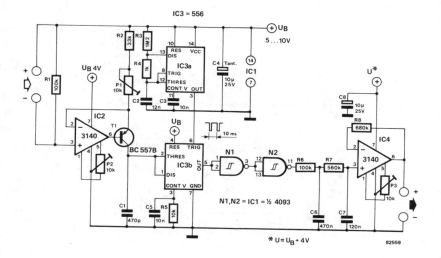

We may have a reciprocal amplifier now but this does not imply that a voltage of 10 mV at the input becomes 100 V (1/10 mV) at the output.

Firstly, the amplifier is limited by the supply voltage of maximum 10 V.

Secondly, 1/10 mV = 100 V is not quite correct. Therefore a correction factor C is introduced. This is about 0.02 V² when P1 is set to minimum. Now the output voltage level will range from 2 V to 20 mV with an input voltage of 10 mV...1 V. The calibration procedure is quite simple. Feed a voltage level of 20 mV to the input and set P2 so that exactly 20 mV can be measured between the emitter of T1 and U_b. As already mentioned, P1 determines the correction factor C and last but not least, P3 takes care of the offset (if necessary). One final point, the supply voltage must be fully stabilized.

185 high-voltage converter

Given a 30 V power supply the circuit described can deliver a high voltage ranging from 0 to 3 kV (type 1), or from 0...10 kV (type 2). Gates N1...N3 are connected as an astable multivibrator (AMV), and drive the darlington configuration T1/T2 with a 20 kHz rectangular pulse. Due to the low current flow (determined by R4) through the transistors, they cannot be saturated, resulting in a fast cut off. The extremely fast switching of the transistors produces a pulse of approximately 300 V in the primary winding of Tr1. This voltage is stepped up in proportion to the number of secondary turns. The first version (type 1) of the circuit uses half-wave rectification. Type 2 is simply a cascade rectifier out of an old TV set. Version 2 delivers a voltage three times higher than version 1 because the cascade rectifier acts as a voltage multiplier (3X).

Opamp IC2 regulates the output voltage by comparing the voltage across P1 with that at

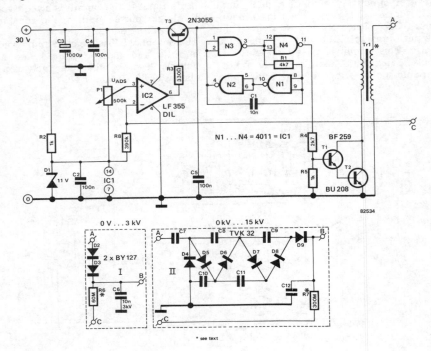

the junction of the voltage dividers R6/R8 or R7/R8. If the output exceeds the preset voltage level, IC2 will reduce the supply voltage to the output via T3. The most important part of the circuit is the transformer. Even though it is essential, its construction is not that critical.

A variety of E, El or ferrite cores with a diameter of 30 mm can be used. The core should not have any air gap; an A_L value of 2000 nH is about right. The primary winding consists of 25 turns of 0.7 mm...1 mm enamelled copper wire and the secondary is 500 turns of 0.2...0.3 mm wire. The primary and secondary windings must be properly insulated from each other!

With respect to the high voltages, the constructor should pay special attention to the following points:

■ Capacitor C6 must be able to cope with at least 3 kV.

■ R6 in version 1 consists of six 10 MΩ resistors in series. R7 is made up by using 10 MΩ resistors, also in series. This is done to avoid spikes at the output.

Either circuit consumes approximately 50 mA without a load and 350 mA when delivering 2...3 W into a load. Transistors T2 and T3 will require heat sinks.

E. Stöhr

186 super low noise preamp

Technical data

input sensitivity (200 mV output):		2.5 mV/1 kHz
input impedance:	—	49 k/280 pF
maximum input voltage (at 1 kHz):		110 mV
distortion factors (200 mV) output):		
	100 Hz:	< 0.001%
	1 kHz:	< 0.001%
	20 kHz:	< 0.001%
overload distortion factors at +32 dB		
(8.4 V output):	100 Hz:	<0.016%
	1 kHz:	<0.01%
	20 kHz:	<0.01%
deviation from the IEC characteristic:		
C4...C7 with 5% tolerance:		< ± 0.55 dB
with 2% tolerance:		< ± 0.25 dB
frequency response		
(C4...C7 at 5% tolerance):		0 Hz...40 kHz and ± 0.55 dB
signal-to-noise ratio		>86 dB

Preamplifiers for magnetic pick-ups suffer from one major problem: their own noise. This noise is produced mainly by the irregular current flow in the PN junction of the input transistor. The cause of this irregularity is manufacturing tolerances. Some manufacturers, especially Japanese, have designed extremely low noise transistors, but unfortunately these components are very hard to find and rather expensive. For these reasons, this circuit is based on the physical law that voltages of noncorrelating noise sources that are connected in parallel add geometrically, thus reducing the over-all noise of the parallel circuit. This preamp contains 8 transistors that are connected in parallel thus lowering the noise by $\sqrt{8}$, which is 9 dB.

The completely symmetrical circuit and the class A mode output transistor stage, formed by T17 and T18, allows low distortion factors that cannot be achieved by any integrated circuit. Another remarkable feature is the differential amplifier circuit. Besides other advantages, this circuit is able to suppress spurious signals produced by the supply voltage (for example hum and noise) by at least 50 dB. Together with the transistors T19 and T20 (connected as gyrators) and voltage regulators IC1 and IC2 a noise suppression of more than 150 dB is obtained. This is essential since the measures to screen the interference on the supply voltage are as important as the construc-

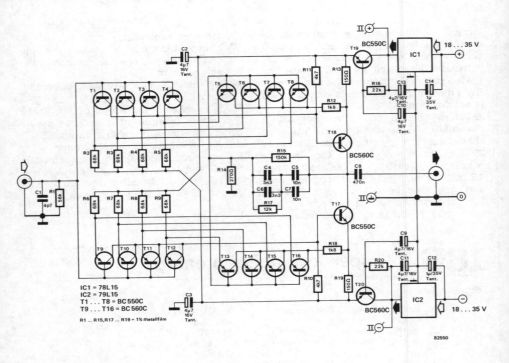

IC1 = 78L15
IC2 = 79L15
T1 ... T8 = BC 550C
T9 ... T16 = BC 560C

R1 ... R15, R17 ... R19 = 1% metallfilm

82550

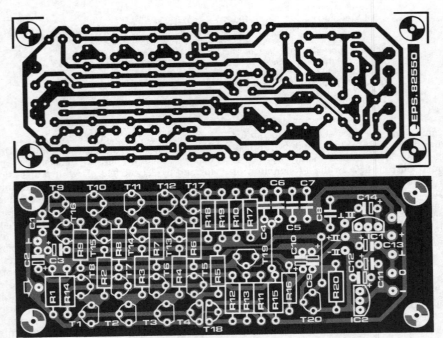

Parts list

Resistors:
R1 = 56 k/1%
R2...R9 = 68 k/1%
R10,R11 = 4k7/1%
R12,R18 = 1k8/1%
R13,R19 = 150 Ω/1%
R14 = 270 Ω/1%
R15 = 150 k/1%
R16,R20 = 22 k/5%
R17 = 12 k/1%

All 1% resistors metal film

Capacitors:
C1 = 4p7 (see text)
C2,C3,C9...C11,C13 = 4μ7/16 V, tantalum
C4,C6 = 3n3/2% (see technical data)
C5,C7 = 10 n/2% (see technical data)
C8 = 470 n, folio
C12,C14 = 1 μ/35 V, tantalum

Semiconductors:
T1...T8,T17,T19 = BC 550C, BC 414C
T9...T16,T18,T20 = BC 560C, BC 416C
IC1 = 78L15
IC2 = 79L15

tional tricks to reduce the inherent noise of the amplifier stage, to obtain a high signal-to-noise ratio.

The preamp does **not** contain a coupling capacitor at its input, as this would produce additional noise. Therefore the transmission range starts at the DC voltage level. At first sight you may be worried about the large number of transistors, but you will soon find out that it is not difficult to mount all components on the printed circuit board. This design does not suffer from oscillation tendencies or other related problems.

The cost of the components is quite reasonable. The voltage regulator ICs are only required once and the components

C11...C14 and IC1, IC2 can be omitted when constructing a second (stereo) channel. The connections II⊕, II⊥ and II⊖ on both boards must be connected together. A small 2 × 15 V...24 V/50 mA transformer will suffice for the power supply. The value of the smoothing capacitors must at least be 470 μF.

The input impedance of the preamp can be adjusted to any cartridges by simply changing the values of R1 and C1. The amplification factor is determined by R14. With a 100 Ω resistor for R1 and a 27 Ω resistor for R14, the preamp will be suitable for moving coil cartridge. In contrast to other preamps, the output connects direct to the auxiliary socket of the amplifier.

---

187 digital timer

The analogue brother of this IC is our old friend, the 555. The digital version here, the LS 7210, is less well-known. It can be used to set delay times between approximately 11 μs and 42 minutes. The IC contains an oscillator of which the frequency determining elements are connected externally (R1 and C1). This provides the frequencies as shown in table 1. The IC is programmed for internal oscillator operation by connecting pin 4 to 0 V. The delay time τ is derived from the formula:

$$\tau = [f(1 + 1.023N)]\ s$$

where f is the frequency according to table 1, and N is the multiplication factor as determined by pins 8...12. These pins have the following values: pin 12 = 1, pin 11 = 2, pin 10 = 4, pin 9 = 8, and pin 8 = 16. For example, if N is to be 25 then pins 8, 9 and 12 must be logic 0 (0 V). In this

case, with the oscillator frequency set to 0.013 Hz, the total delay time will be 34 minutes.

As shown in the circuit diagram, the IC is used as a retriggerable monostable. The output becomes logic 1 at the same time

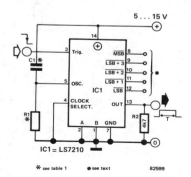

82599

R (kΩ)	C (pF)	+Ub (V)		
		5	10	15
47	100	128 kHz	139 kHz	185 kHz
	200	79 kHz	83 kHz	85 kHz
	500	37 kHz	37 kHz	36 kHz
	1000	22 kHz	21 kHz	20 kHz
	50000	610 Hz	500 Hz	475 Hz
470	100	15 kHz	16 kHz	16.5 kHz
	200	9 kHz	9.5 kHz	9.5 kHz
	500	4 kHz	4 kHz	4 kHz
	1000	2.4 kHz	2 kHz	2 kHz
	50000	63 Hz	51 Hz	47 Hz
2000	100	4.2 kHz	4.7 kHz	5 kHz
	200	2.5 kHz	2.7 kHz	2.8 kHz
	500	1.1 kHz	1.1 kHz	1.1 kHz
	1000	670 Hz	617 Hz	610 Hz
	50000	17 Hz	14 Hz	14 Hz
10000	10 μF	.02 Hz	.015 Hz	.013 Hz

Table 1. Oscillator frequencies for various values of R1, C1 and +U$_b$.

that a leading (negative going) edge arrives at the trigger input, pin 3. The output level reverts to logic 0 at the end of the preset delay time period, provided no further trigger pulses arrive at the input. Should this happen, the preset delay period will be initiated again, but the output will remain high. A leading (positive) input edge has no effect on the timing. The result of this is that, in principle, any length of time delay can be realized by cascading 2 or more ICs in series.

The output of the IC consists of a FET with open drain connection. Therefore, to obtain current switching between 0 and 1, a pull-down resistor, R2, is necessary. However, if the output is to be used as a current source, this resistor can be omitted.

LSI application

188 mixing console

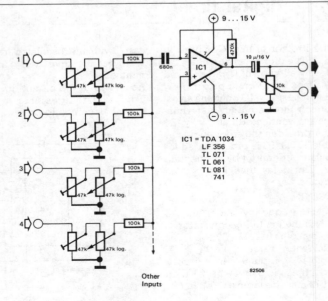

IC1 = TDA 1034
LF 356
TL 071
TL 061
TL 081
741

Other Inputs

82506

The majority of audio mixer circuits require a relatively large number of components. However, a simple system could also prove effective, especially when only a few signals are to be mixed together.

The circuit described here uses a single opamp as the summing amplifier. The individual input signals are connected to the 100 kΩ adder resistors at the inverting input of the opamp via mixing potentiometers. Normally, there will be no need for any series capacitors to be connected to the inputs, as the majority of today's signal sources do not produce a DC voltage. Nevertheless, if it is considered necessary, 330n capacitors could be included.

You may add as many inputs as you like. The overall quality depends entirely on the type of opamp used. Recommended types are TL071 or TL081, but a 741 will also perform satisfactorily. The summed signal is amplified by a factor of 4.7 and the output level can be adjusted as required. The output is short-circuit proof and has a very low impedance. The input impedance (which can be adjusted by the 47kΩ potentiometers) is approximately 40kΩ. This means that most commonly available signal sources, such as tuners, cassette decks, tape recorders, etc., can be mixed together without any difficulty. Dynamic microphones and turntables with magnetic cartridges do, however, require a small preamplifier.

For a stereo system the circuit is simply constructed twice and tandem potentiometers are used. The circuit can be powered by 9 V (PP3) batteries as the current consumption of the opamp amounts to fractions of milliamps.

189   stable start stop oscillator

Start/stop oscillators are indispensible in video interface circuits. Such oscillators have to be synchronized with differentiated character clock pulses and produce 7...12 pulses between character clocks. There are two aspects which are important to note here:

■ the oscillator must start producing pulses after a delay of about 15 ns. This prevents the first pulse (the output signal) from coinciding with the positive-going edge of the trigger signal;

■ the oscillator must stop as soon as the control signal goes low again. The oscillator shown in the circuit diagram meets both of the above requirements. It starts

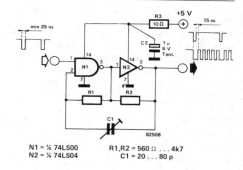

N1 = ¼ 74LS00   R1,R2 = 560 Ω ... 4k7
N2 = ¼ 74LS04   C1 = 20 ... 80 p

after a slight delay whenever the input signal goes high and stops immediately the input signal reverts to logic zero.

190   logic probe

The circuit diagram shows that T1, R3, R4, D5, and D6 constitute a current source for LEDs D3 and D4. As a result, the current to the LEDs will be approximately 12 mA, irrespective of the supply voltage. The LED cathodes are grounded by either N1 or N2 enabling.

The LEDs are switched on and supplied by a constant current. The circuit's other task depends on the voltage applied to the disconnected end of R1. If, for instance, a relatively high voltage with respect to ground is applied, N1 will invert the high level, and ground the cathode of D3. D3 lights to indicate a logic 1, but D4 remains out, as its cathode is high. It does not light

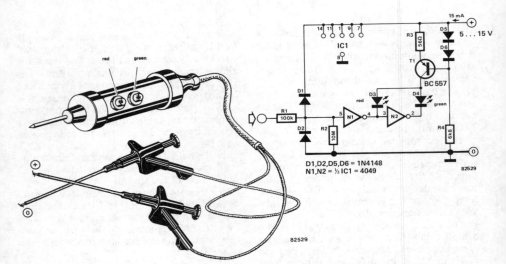

R3 560
R1 100k
R2 10M
R4 6k8
IC1
T1 BC 557
5...15 V
15 mA
N1 N2

D1,D2,D5,D6 = 1N4148
N1,N2 = ⅓ IC1 = 4049

82529

until a very low voltage (less than ⅓ of the supply voltage) is applied to R1, in which case the low level will be inverted twice before reaching the cathode of D4. Resistor R1, and diodes D1 and D2 protect the circuit against an input overload.

The high-impedance input resistor (R2) limits the load to the circuit under test. It also cuts off the input of the first inverter N1 when the test input is disconnected. This prevents the circuit from going hay-wire, should there be any interference at the input.

All the components combine to form a very effective, straightforward logic probe for TTL and CMOS signals. In TTL circuits, the logic levels displayed by the tester do not quite match their exact definition, but it should be adequate for a rough estimate. Incidentally, when pulse sequences are applied at the input of the circuit, both LEDs

will light irrespective of the corresponding frequency. In other words, they will be lit continuously in most cases. The logic tester does not require its own power supply, as it operates on an automatic level matching basis. This means that the supply voltage is derived from the circuit being tested. As a result, the logic probe will always respond correctly to the level in force at any particular moment.

The entire circuit can be housed in a plastic tube or even in the plastic holder of a ball-point pen. The test pen is provided with a probe at one end and two connecting wires including clamps at the other. Once the two clamps are connected to the power supply of the circuit-under-test, the probe merely has to touch a test point for the LEDs to instantly indicate the correct logic level at that point.

191   5 V super power supply

The subject of power supplies seems to be of little interest since the introduction of the 3 pin voltage regulator ICs. However, these are usually restricted to the versions that can deliver up to a maximum output of 1 A. Anything above this requires some form of heavy duty regulator stage. Regulator ICs capable of 5 A and 10 A do exist, but it usually works out more economic for most

people to go straight into some form of discrete regulator.

The idea of adding a power output stage consisting of one or more transistors in parallel is not bad at all! For this reason it is applied, with one or two modifications, to the circuit described here. Power supplies that are insensitive to interference and can deliver high current levels to large

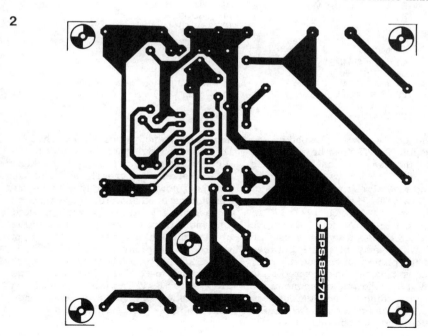

1

TIP 142   BD 139

BCE   ECB

D1 ... D3 = *D3
1N4001

IC1
7812

2 x
TIP 142

* 2.5 ... 6 V
6 ... 8 A

IC2
723

B1
40 V/10 A

* see text

82570

microprocessor systems would certainly benefit from such an approach. The ideal IC for this job remains the good old 723. This IC may well have been overshadowed by the new 3 pin regulators, but its versatility cannot be questioned and its technical specifications are in many respects superior. It is used here in a standard circuit, intended to deliver output voltages between 2 and 7 V.

The necessary supply for the IC is obtained after voltage doubling of the smoothed and rectified secondary voltage of the transformer via a voltage regulator, which in this case is of the three pin variety. This method was chosen for the very good reason that the secondary voltage of the transformer must be kept as low as possible to hold the power drop across the series transistors T1...T3 to within reasonable limits. While

2

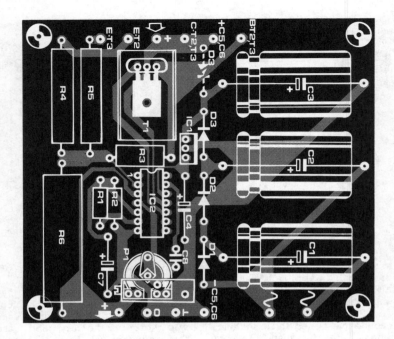

Parts list:

Resistors:
R1,R2 = 3k3
R3 = 100 Ω/1 W
R4,R5 = 0.15 Ω/5 W*
R6 = 0.1 Ω/10 W*
P1 = 5 k preset

Capacitors:
C1,C2 = 470 μ/50 V
C3 = 220 μ/50 V
C4 = 1 μ/16 V
C5,C6 = 1000 V μ/25 V
C7 = 10 μ/16 V
C8 = 470 p

Semiconductors:
B = 10 A/40 V bridge rectifier (not pcb mounting)
D1...D3 = 1N4001
T1 = BD 139
T2,T3 = TIP 142 (Darlington)
IC1 = 7812
IC2 = 723

Miscellaneous:
Tr = 10 V/10 A toroidal transformer
S1 = double pole mains switch

* see text

on the subject of power dissipation, the heat sinks for T2...T3 must be sufficiently large. For the same reasons, the values shown for R4...R6 are best obtained by connecting several resistors in parallel: for R4 and R5 twice 0.33 Ω 5 W; for R6 and an output current of 6 A twice 0.22 Ω 5 W or three times 0.33 Ω 5 W for 8 A output. Furthermore, these resistors must be mounted with plenty of space between them and the printed circuit board.
The output voltage can be increased up to about 14 V if the following components are modified accordingly: the transformers, resistors R1, R2, and capacitors C5 and C6. Voltage doubling components C1, C2, D1,

and D2 are then unnecessary. The anode of D3 must then be connected direct to the rectified and smoothed supply. It should be noted that although the TIP142's look like any other power transistor, they are in fact darlingtons. In other words, they cannot be replaced by any ordinary power transistors. One more point to give some idea of the good regulation of this supply. The output voltage of the prototype was set at 5.5 V. When loaded by a 0.68 Ω resistor (which corresponds to a current of 8 A), the voltage dropped to 5.32 V! This is a drop of 3.3% at 7.8 A. Furthermore, under the same conditions the ripple was less than 25 mV$_{rms}$.

192 mini high performance voltage regulator

The input level to most voltage regulators must be several volts higher than the wanted output. If for some reason there are very few volts at the input to start with, then there is a limitation in the output voltage range (fewer volts to throw away!). In this case, it is not possible to use a normal IC voltage regulator and we have to resort to a discrete design. The circuit shown here will operate with 6 V input and provide a regulated 5 V output, which is ideal for battery powered equipment.

With a little study the trick in the circuit will be apparent. The load is connected to the collector of the series transistor. This means that this transistor can be switched hard on into saturation, so that the drop across the emitter-collector junction is just the small saturation voltage. The level of this depends, of course, on the current and the type of transistor. In this case at a maximum current of 0.5 A the voltage loss will be only 0.2 V, to which must be added the voltage drop across R6, required for current limiting.

At approximately 0.5 V across R6, T3 starts to conduct and limits the output current. LED D1 has two purposes in life; as an indicator and as a voltage reference diode which sets a level of 1.5 V...1.6 V at the

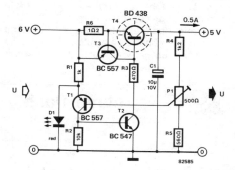

emitter of T1. The base drive current for this transistor is derived from the voltage divider consisting of R4, P1 and R5. Depending on the difference between the reference and output voltage levels, T1 is more or less conducting. The same then applies to T2 which will supply more or less base drive to T4. Capacitor C1 is included to filter the output stage.

Instead of the BD 438, other wellknown types can be used like the BD 136, BD 138, and BD 140, for instance. However, these transistors do have a slightly higher saturation voltage.

It must be noted that since D1 acts as a reference source, it must be a red LED. Other colours have different parameters.

193 symmetrical opamp supply

A simple and well-known circuit: a symmetrical supply constructed **with** an opamp **for** opamps and of course other small circuits that require a positive as well as a negative supply voltage. Both voltages are derived from one battery. Resistors R1 and R2 form a high impedance, and therefore energy saving, voltage divider. The opamp takes care that the artificial ground potential remains the same as that at the junction of R1 and R2. The relation between R1 and R2 determines the relation between the two output voltages; if R1 and R2 have the same value, the same will hold good for

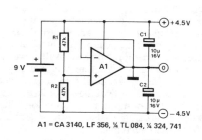

A1 = CA 3140, LF 356, ¼ TL 084, ¼ 324, 741

82522

both output voltages (symmetrical). This brings us to the most pleasant characteristic of the circuit: the relation does not depend on the battery voltage! Another advantage of this active voltage divider is that (in contrast to a simple resistor divider chain) it adapts itself well to changing load currents passing to and from the earth potential, particularly in the case of unsymmetrical load current conditions.

There are various types of opamps that can be used for this circuit. The 3140 and 324 are excellent, even with a battery voltage of 4.5 V. Bear in mind that the maximum tolerated load of the artificial ground depends on the opamp being used (normally about 20 mA)

J. Wallaert

194   slave flash

1

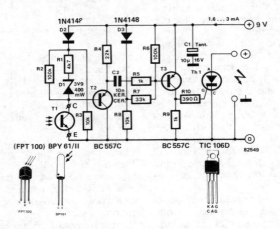

Electronics have been making significant inroads into photography for some time now and it appears that many people want to push the frontiers even further. The super fast, super sensitive (and super insensitive) circuit here can be used for flash photography indoors as well as outdoors. The apparent confusion between super sensitive and at the same time super insensitive is easily explained. The slave unit is super sensitive to the master flash gun, but super insensitive to the ambient light conditions. It will react within about 10 μs depending on the light power of the master flash gun. This means that when using a computer controlled flash gun with a flash duration of 1 ms, 99% of the slave flash is included in the computer's calculation. This makes it ideal for use with automatic flash/camera systems.

The total range of the slave is set by T1, R1, R2, and D1. The setting is to achieve maxi-

mum sensitivity in low and average light levels. A special shield for difficult light conditions is not normally required. However, if the slave is to be used for daylight fill-in flash photography, a certain amount of protection from sunlight will be advantageous. On the other hand, switching a normal incandescent lamp on and off in the same room will not trigger the slave. There is very little to be said about the circuit itself and photographers with sufficient electronic know-how will be satisfied with the following information. A brief flash from the master reaches photo transistor T1 and causes a pulse at the base of T2. This pulse is boosted and passed via T3 to the gate of the thyristor. When the thyristor fires, it effectively shorts the contacts of the flash gun which is connected at this point. For the electronics enthusiast with an interest in photography we can say a little more. The slave flash gun is connected in parallel with

208

2

 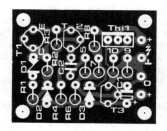

EPS. 82549A

Parts list

Resistors:
R1 = 4k7
R2,R6 = 100 k
R3,R8 = 10 k
R4 = 22 k
R5,R9 = 1 k
R7 = 33 k
R10 = 390 Ω

Capacitors:
C1 = 10 μ/16 V tantalum
C2 = 10 n ceramic

Semiconductors:
D1 = Z-Diode 3V9/0,4 W
D2,D3 = 1N4148
T1 = BPY 61/II, FPT 100
T2,T3 = BC 557C
Th1 = TIC 106D

Miscellaneous:
9 V compact battery
Flash extension lead
PCB 82549

the thyristor. Apart from this a 9 V compact battery is required and should last for quite a long time. The resistors are mounted vertically on the printed circuit board to keep the board as small as possible. One further tip, for the connection to the slave flash gun use...a flash gun extension cable!

G. König

---

195   X(N)OR opamp

Nowadays, digital techniques are finding their way into more and more analogue circuits. Fortunately, this does not always call for the use of special integrated circuits, as it is quite common to see opamps being used to provide the logic functions NOT, AND, NAND, OR, and NOR. However, this does not (normally) apply to the logic functions XOR and XNOR. Nevertheless, the latter can be obtained by using LM 324 or LM 358 type opamps. These opamps have the advantage that their outputs can be driven to 0 volts without the need for a negative supply voltage.

As can be seen from the circuit diagram, when both inputs A and B are grounded (= logic zero) point a will be low. As a result, resistor R5 will have no effect on the state of the inverting input of the opamp. Resistor R6, however, does affect the non-inverting input via diode D2. This causes the voltage at the non-inverting input of the opamp to be lower than that at the inverting input, leading to a low level at the ouput. If

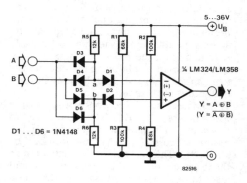

$Y = A \oplus B$
$(Y = \overline{A \oplus B})$

D1...D6 = 1N4148

82516

the two inputs A and B are taken high (= supply voltage), point b will also go high via diodes D5 and D6. Thus, resistor R5 now affects the state of the opamp instead of R6. This causes the voltage at the inverting input to be greater than that at the non-inverting input, and therefore the output of the opamp is once again low. If one of the inputs is held high and the other low, point a will go low and point b will go high.

This means that now the voltage level at the non-inverting input will be greater than that at the inverting input, resulting in a high level at the output of the opamp. In other words, a genuine XOR gate!

The XNOR function can be obtained very easily indeed. Simply swap around the inverting and the non-inverting input connec-

tions. Now the output of the opamp will go low whenever the two input levels are different and will go high when the input levels are the same.

A. Rochat

196   car PDM amplifier

This power amplifier, designed for use in a car, delivers 10 W into 4 Ω and, because it uses the principles of PDM (pulse duration modulation), its efficiency is nearly 100%. The block diagram is shown in figure 1. An

1

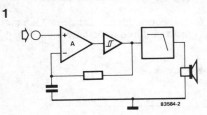

83584-2

opamp drives a Schmitt trigger, the output of which is integrated and fed back to the inverting input of the opamp. The system regulates itself so that the voltage is the same at both inputs of the opamp. That can only happen if the pulse width (pulse duration) is variable, otherwise the circuit tries to change the oscillating frequency as a method of regulation.

The heart of the PDM system (figure 2) is made up of IC2, N1...N6, T1, and T3. To build this up into a power amplifier, an out-of-phase control signal is formed by N7...N12. This is not the ideal situation as these are not part of the feedback loop and also there is some cross-over distortion because switching takes a finite time. However, the quality is improved somewhat by using a symmetrical feedback loop consisting of the components around IC1. This digital amplifier operates much the same as an analogue equivalent, which would have to be much bigger. The BD 131/132 transistors give an output of 10 W with a total harmonic distortion of 0.3%. The maximum power without clipping (10% distortion) is

about 12 W. If BD 241/242 transistors are used, these figures are not quite so good because the cut-off frequency (actually the −3 dB frequency) is much lower. With a total harmonic distortion of 0.3% the output is only 8 W and the maximum power available without clipping is 10 W. The minimum input signal to the circuit is 800 mV and current consumption is about 1.5 A.

Because of all the noise on car voltage lines, the supply must be filtered. Generally this only requires a simple LC filter with a 2200 μ/25 V capacitor and a 1 mH inductor with a low coil resistance. In principle,

Parts list

Resistors:
R1,R2 = 47 k
R3,R4 = 22 k
R5,R6 = 100 k
R7,R8 = 270 k
P1 = 5 k log potentiometer

Capacitors:
C1,C2,C8,C9 = 100 n
C3,C4 = 1 μ/16 V
C5 = 470 p
C6 = 680 n
C7 = 220 μ/25 V
C10 = 220 n
C11 = 100 p

Semiconductors:
T1,T2 = BD 131, BD 241A
T3,T4 = BD 132, BD 242A
IC1 = CA 3140
IC2 = CA 3130
IC3,IC4 = 4049B

Miscellaneous:
L1,L2 = 40 μH, 3 A inductors
4 heatsinks for the power transistors
PCB 83584

210

2

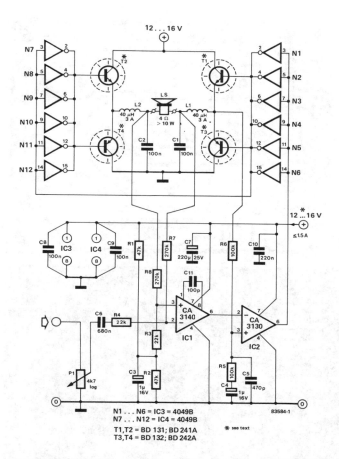

N1 . . . N6 = IC3 = 4049B
N7 . . . N12 = IC4 = 4049B
T1,T2 = BD 131; BD 241A
T3,T4 = BD 132; BD 242A

* see text

83584-1

3

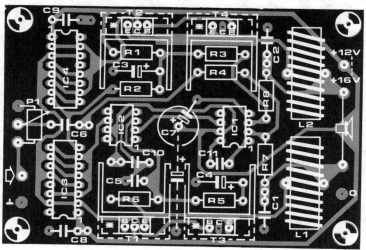

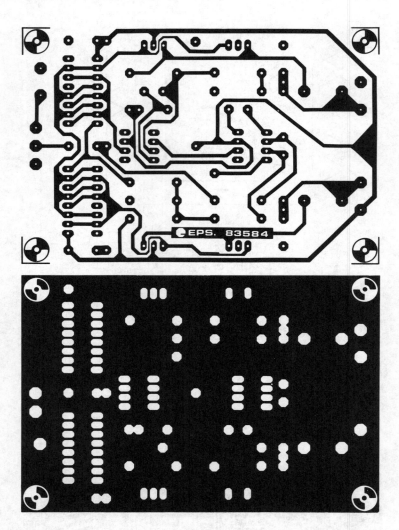

EPS. 83584

more than one amplifier can be used and fed from a single low-pass filter. Because it has to be mounted in a car, this amplifier should be put in a sturdy case. There is a difference in size between the BD 131/132 and BD 241/242 transistors and this must be taken into account during construction. The photo shows the method of mounting heat sinks and clearly the end result is a very compact amplifier.

197   distance meter for thunderstorms

The clouds in the sky are dark, giving an ominous warning of the thunderstorm that is on its way. Sure enough, the first flash of lightning is seen; it would be interesting to know how far away the thunderstorm is. The circuit described here is intended to provide the answer to that question.

Light (including lightning) travels at a

speed of 300 000 m/s. Sound, in this case thunder, travels in air at an average speed of 333 m/s, depending on the ambient temperature. This is the reason why the thunder is usually heard a few seconds after the lightning flash is seen. The thunder needs about three seconds longer to travel one kilometre than does the lightning; this is the same as 0.3 seconds per 100 metres.

The circuit puts this theoretical knowledge into practice. The 555 timer IC operates as an astable multivibrator with a frequency of 3.33 Hz; the period is 0.3 s. This is exactly the time differential between the propagation speeds of the lightning flash and the thunder. As soon as the flash is seen, the distance meter is started by briefly pressing pushbutton S2. Counters IC2 and IC3, which are connected in series, are given a reset signal which resets them to zero. The output signal of IC1 is applied to the clock input of the first counter (IC2) and is then processed by the latter. LED D1 lights after 0.3 s. Each subsequent clock pulse actuates the next higher output after 0.3 s. The counting operation is interrupted by pressing pushbutton S1 as soon as the thunder is heard.

The distance of the thunderstorm from the user's location is indicated by one or two of LEDs D1...D18. Counter IC2 counts the distance from 100 m to 900 m. If the thunderstorm is further that that, counter IC3 handles the kilometres. If, for example, only LED D5 lights, the thunderstorm is at a distance of 500 m; if LEDs D16 and D3 light, the distance is 7300 m (maximum distance = 10 km).

The maximum current drawn by the circuit does not exceed 30 mA; a 9 V battery is therefore sufficient to power the circuit.

A digital watch with chronograph function is used to align the circuit. P1 is adjusted so that the last LED D18 lights up 27 seconds after S2 has been released (the stopwatch must be started simultaneously!).

Further refinements could include an LDR that will allow the lightning to automatically start the counter, and a microphone to stop it. However, the LDR would be useful only at night and the problems associated with catching distant thunder with a microphone...

Perhaps it would be better after all to do what we do... put your head under the pillow and forget the whole thing!

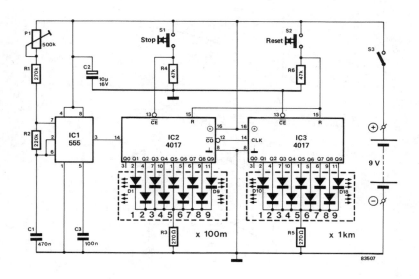

83507

198   reproducible delay

There are many occasions when a switching delay is required. One way of achieving this is to use an RC network and an inverter (see figure 1). This is quite practical and obvious as there are nearly always some gates left over in a circuit. Unfortunately, every electronic component has a definite tolerance and so it is virtually impossible to determine the delay precisely in advance. However, a considerable improvement can be achieved by connecting two inverter/RC networks in series as shown in figure 3.

The nominal threshold voltage of the inverter in figure 1 is half the supply voltage and has a tolerance of $\pm$ 30%. Figure 2 shows the signal input to the gate. If this input is between $U_c = 0.35 U_b$ and $U_c = 0.65 U_b$ the inverter may consider it either logic 0 or 1! These voltages occur when a capacitor is charged through a resistor after a period of 0.43 τ and 1.05 τ respectively (τ is the time constant of the circuit and is equal to RC). The nominal threshold voltage $U_c = 0.5 U_b$ is reached after a time of t = 0.69 τ.

If the two inverters and RC networks of figure 3 are used, each RC network must produce the same delay, equal to half the total value of figure 1. The total delay will then be $\frac{1}{2} \times 0.43 \tau + \frac{1}{2} \times 1.05 \tau = 0.74 \tau$ at its worst case! This is a lot closer to the nominal value of 0.69 τ.

The foregoing should make it clear why the circuit of figure 4 gives such consistently reproducible results. However, for really satisfactory operation, CMOS inverters must be used. The reason is that these gates have a threshold value of about half the supply voltage. Further, their output will always be either zero or the supply voltage. Schmitt triggers should not be used!

If the delay times using 4000 series CMOS are found to be too long the new 74HCXX series can be used. These are pin and function compatible to the 74LSXX series and just as fast!

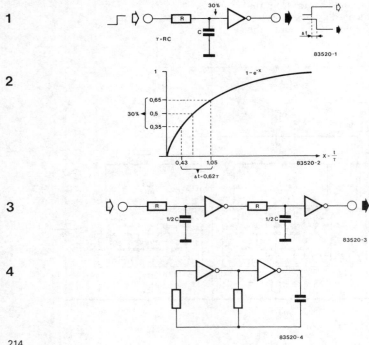

1

2

3

4

83520-1

83520-2

83520-3

83520-4

199   simple baud rate generator

The generator described is a good-value-for-money alternative to the commercially available types; it uses only one CMOS-IC and provides up to seven different baud rates.

Each serial data interface requires a baud rate generator: terminal, printer, tape interface... It is often not possible to use the same generator for input and output, so it would be useful to add one to, for instance, the UART (universal asynchronous receiver/transmitter) in the computer or the UART in the terminal. To keep the costs of such an addition down, we have developed a generator which uses just one IC, two resistors, one preset potentiometer, and a capacitor. The CMOS 4060 is a 14-stage binary counter with an internal oscillator which only requires the frequency determining RC components. As the reset is connected to earth, the counter begins to count upwards when the supply is switched on.

A clock frequency then becomes available at the outputs: the higher the number of the output, the lower the frequency available as it. In the circuit shown the frequencies available at the various outputs are:

Q4 = 9600 baud   Q8 = 600 baud
Q5 = 4800 baud   Q9 = 300 baud
Q6 = 2400 baud   Q10 = 150 baud
Q7 = 1200 baud

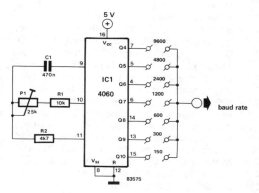

If the outputs are wired as shown in the circuit diagram, the required baud rate can then be selected with a wire link.

The oscillator frequency can be set precisely with P1, and measured either at pin 9 of the 4060 or at one of the outputs Q4...Q10. With the values shown, the frequency at pin 9 should be 38.4 kHz; at the outputs Q4...Q10 the relevant baud rate. It is often required that the clock frequency is 16 times the baud rate (for instance, with asynchronous operation of the 6850, 8251, Z80-SIO...). In that case, C1 must be replaced by a 27 nF capacitor and the oscillator frequency must be set to 614.4 kHz.

200   darkroom light

Working in a darkroom is always fraught with problems. You surely know Murphys Law of..., but let's not go into that here. Suffice it to say that normal lights cannot be used in a darkroom when photographs are being developed — not even if you drop your glasses! The circuit here is a simple, inexpensive design for a darkroom torch (or light) that can be mounted in a case small enough to fit into your pocket even with a 9 V battery included. It gives enough light for note-taking or finding this or that in a darkroom, but the light is emitted by three special

yellow LEDs which can safely be used near black/white or colour paper. Red LEDs are used for orthochromatic material. An energy saving circuit is included that automatically switches the lamp off when the ambient light is above a certain level.

The circuit diagram makes it look like a mini power supply. When the circuit is switched on with S1, T2 conducts and provides, in turn, a base drive current to transistor T1. This transistor then supplies the base current for T2 via R5 and P1. Switching S1 off, causes C1 to deliver a negative pulse to the base of T2 and this transistor then stops conducting. T1 also stops conducting and the LEDs go out.

The energy saving circuitry requires the addition of just one component, the LDR. When enough light falls on it, the LDR's resistance causes T2 to switch off and extinguish the LEDs. The light level at which this happens is set with preset P1. LEDs D3...D5 must be high efficiency types and either red or yellow depending on what sort of photographic paper is used. There are various high intensity LEDs available, although the light intensity level can also be changed by varying the current flow through T1 (by substituting another value of resistor for R1). With the values stated, about 20 mA flows through the LEDs and, as the current consumption when the LEDs are off is only a few nA, the 9 V battery should last quite a while.

Finally, it is important to remember that

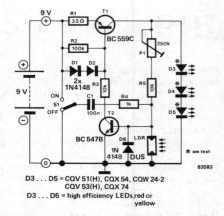

D3 ... D5 = CQV 51(H), CQX 54, CQW 24-2
CQV 53(H), CQX 74
D3 ... D5 = high efficiency LEDs, red or yellow

some types of photographic paper are sensitive to all colours, including red and yellow, so check this before using the lamp.

201 noise and vibration detector

Whether it is the hi-fi next door, the cat purring quietly, or a knock at the door, the detector described here does not miss a thing. Whenever it picks up a sound or vibration, it emits an ear-piercing tone.

The circuit is based on the use of an 8 Ω loudspeaker as microphone/loudspeaker. As the signals from this microphone are very small, they are amplified in A1 and rectified. The resulting DC signal is then compared with a reference voltage in A2. When a noise or vibration is picked up by the microphone, the voltage at the inverting input of A2 (pin 6), rises suddenly to about 4 V and then slowly decays to 0 V. The decay time depends on the time constant R6C3.

The voltage at the non-inverting input of A2 (pin 5) is held constant at 0.7 V by R3/R4. When the input at pin 6 rises above 0.7 V,

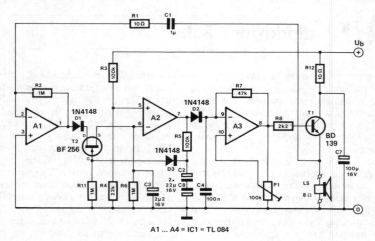

A1 ... A4 = IC1 = TL 084

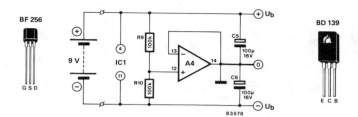

the output of A2 (pin 7) instantly switches to −4 V, which causes oscillator A3 to start. The frequency (tone) of the oscillator can be adjusted by preset potentiometer P1. The oscillator output (pin 8) is fed to amplifier stage T1 which drives the loudspeaker. The oscillator will continue to run, however, so C3 charges steadily and will keep the output at pin 7 of A2 negative.

As this is not the purpose of the circuit, the incoming signal must be interrupted somewhere in the chain. To do this, an FET, T2, is used as a switch. As soon as the output of the comparator becomes negative, D3 conducts, T2 is cut off and the incoming signal is interrupted. When C3 has discharged to the extent that the voltage across it drops to below 0.7 V, the output of A2 (pin 7) becomes positive, D3 is cut off and T2 conducts. This should, however, not happen too rapidly, otherwise there is the risk that a false alarm may be given.

Therefore, the gate (drive input) of T2 is connected to earth via capacitors C2 and C8. The consequent delay ensures that the circuit is not reactuated before half a second after the loudspeaker has gone quiet. The earth potential is fixed by voltage divider R9/R10 and impedance converter A4, which derive a symmetrical supply of ± 4.5 V from the 9 V battery.

When T1 conducts, the supply voltage will drop a little because a battery cannot deliver energy as well as a mains power supply. It can therefore happen that the output signal of A3 is superimposed on the supply voltage. This undesired feedback should be prevented by C5 and C6.

If in spite of these capacitors difficulties are encountered, it may be beneficial to increase the values of R5, C2, and C8 by trial and error. If that fails to improve matters, increase the value of capacitors C5 and C6.

202 thermal indicator for heat sinks

The temperature of a heatsink can be measured with a wet finger: if it sizzles, the temperature is too high. The circuit in figure 1 is an alternative method of checking that does not cause blisters: a thermal traffic light. A green LED lights as long as the temperature of the heatsink does not exceed 50 degrees Celsius, an orange LED for temperatures of 50...75 degrees Celsius and a red LED for temperatures above 75° Celsius.

The circuit is simplicity itself, two special zener diodes, D1 and D2, are connected in series to ensure an accurate zener voltage of 5.96 V at 25 degrees Celsius. The zener voltage will rise by 20 mV for each degree Celsius rise in temperature. The voltage level corresponding to the temperature of

the heatsink is compared with two reference voltages by IC1 and IC2. When the temperature reaches 50 °C, the output of IC2 goes high so T3 conducts and causes D4 to light and at the same time D5 is extinguished by T4. At or above 75 °C, the output of IC1 is high and T2 and T3 then conduct to make D3 light and D4 extinguish.

Under normal conditions, that is, considering a heatsink of sufficient cooling area, a temperature of 75 degrees Celsius will never be reached. Figure 2 shows the $P_d/P_{o_{max}}$ vs $P_o/P_{o_{max}}$ characteristic of a class B amplifier operating with a sine wave input. The effect of the quiescent current on the dissipation has been ignored. It is seen that the maximum temperature does

1

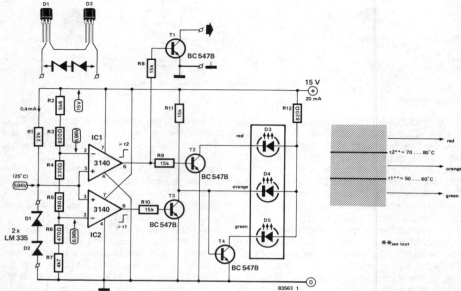

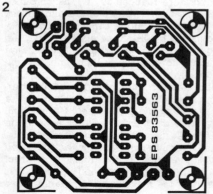

not occur at maximum but at 40 per cent output. By comparison, the dissipation in a class A amplifier is highest in its quiescent mode and lowest at full output.

Under abnormal conditions, the heatsink can get very hot. If the output is shorted, for instance, P_O is nil, but the alternating output current is far from zero and the totally internally dissipated power is converted into heat.

Assuming that the extremely high temperature of the heatsink is caused by a very low load resistance, T1, which conducts at a temperature of 75 degrees Celsius and

higher, is used to remove the low load from the amplifier output. If it is required to monitor both channels of a stereo amplifier such as the Crescendo, the thermal indicator circuit can be duplicated or expanded. To expand the circuit, diodes D3, D4, D5 and resistor R12 remain as shown, while the LEDs are controlled by parallel connected transistors T4 and T4', T3 and T3', and T2 and T2'. In that case, the higher of the two heatsink temperatures determines which LED will light.

It is fairly simple to vary the temperatures corresponding to the orange and red, if so

2

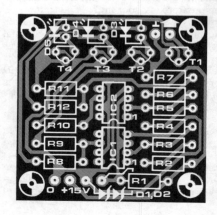

Parts list

Resistors:
R1 = 22 k
R2 = 5k6
R3,R12 = 820 Ω
R4 = 220 Ω
R5 = 180 Ω
R6 = 470 Ω
R7 = 4k7
R8,R9,R10,R11 = 15 k

Semiconductors:
D1,D2 = LM335 (National Semiconductor)
D3 = LED red 5 mm
D4 = LED orange 5 mm
D5 = LED green 5 mm
T1,T2,T3,T4 = BC 547B
IC1,IC2 = 3140
PCB 83563

required. The reference voltage, U_r, of a comparator can be derived from the temperature, t, according to the following formula

$$U_r = [5 \cdot 96 + 0.02 \, (t - 25)] \, V$$

It is possible to set the two reference voltages very accurately by means of voltage divider R2...R7.

203 very narrow crystal filter

Good filters are expensive; good crystal filters are very expensive. A CW filter with a 6 dB bandwidth of 500 Hz can set you back £30 or more. Good enough reasons to construct your own narrow-band filter at a much lower cost.

The proposed filter is constructed from standard components and yet has a super narrow bandwidth, which makes it ideal for CW applications. As the circuit diagram shows, the filter is a simple ladder type with standard 1 MHz crystals. These crystals are very easy to obtain at reasonable retail prices (around £3.00). The photograph, taken from a spectrum analyser, clearly indicates how narrow the filter is: 6 dB bandwidth is 120 Hz, while the bandwidth at −60 dB is only 400 Hz! Note that the scale of the y-axis is 10 dB per division and that of the x-axis is 200 Hz per division. The insertion loss in the pass band is not greater than 4 dB. As the tolerance of the 1 MHz crystals is small, the reproducibility of the filter is excellent.

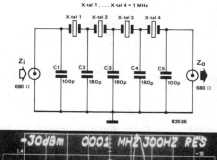

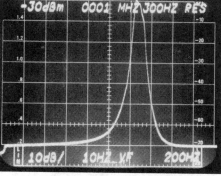

204 5 V logic tester

The full title for the description of this circuit should be three-state 5 V logic tester, which hints at the fact that this logic tester is something out of the ordinary. And indeed it is, for not only does it differentiate between the two normal logic levels (high and low), but also it indicates when the signal under test is neither of these, be it a negative voltage, more than 5 V, or even an alternating voltage. Similarly, it recognizes unpolarized TTL or LS circuit inputs. And that is not all..., this circuit also

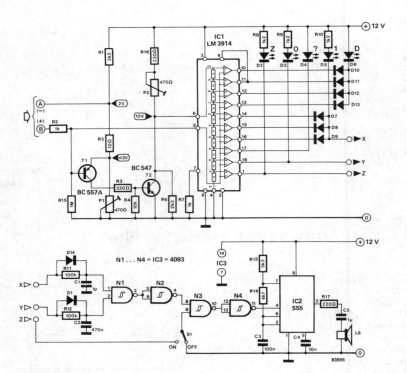

enables the logic level indication to be made audible, so there is no need to concentrate on anything other than the circuit under test.

To do all this, the circuit uses an LM 3914, which is an IC that can sense analogue voltage levels and can directly drive ten LEDs to provide a linear ten-step display.

The IC, among other things, has its own adjustable reference source that controls the internal ten-step divider chain. The reference level (at pin 6) is set to 10 V, providing 1 V between each step in the dividing chain. The upper half of the drawing contains the circuit for the ten-step divider and display. The reference level is adjusted by P2. The circuit illustrated in the lower half is that of the audio indicator, a useful accessory to the logic tester. The various uses of the tester will be understood by the indications given by the display.

D2 lights: in this case the Z output is active low (set to ground), to indicate high impedance; there is no voltage at the B input and the input (pin 5) of the LM 3914 is held at slightly less than 2 V by R5, P1, and T1.

D3 lights: point A acts as a reference point

and is tied to the ground of the circuit under test, (which may be different from that of the tester), and point B is taken to the same potential as point A; pin 18 goes logic low and output 0 is active, indicating low logic level. This particular arrangement of A as a reference point also prevents the power supply of the tester from being affected by the logic levels of the circuit under test.

D4 lights: when the potential difference between A and B is between 1 and 2 V, to signify a logic not sure.

D5 lights: if the voltage at point B is between 2 and 5 V to indicate that there is a high logic level present.

D6 lights: if there is a negative voltage between A and B, T1 conducts, as does T2, which short-circuits R6. Immediately the voltage at pin 6 drops D6 lights to signal a defect. Similarly this LED lights if the potential between A and B is more than 5 V.

The audible indication circuit consists of the four NAND gates of a 4093 and a 555 timer, and these are all that is needed for a simple but usable device. The acoustic signals are as follows:

- D2 lights (high impedance): silence.
- D3 lights (low logic level): short tones.
- D4 or D6 light (fault): continuous tone.
- D5 lights (high logic level): long tones.

Current consumption is about 37 mA without the audible indication circuit, or about 50 mA with. One point to note is that precision resistors and a good quality voltage regulator must be used because of the accuracy required for the 2 V and 10 V references.

C. Bajeux

205 universal a.f.c.

This a.f.c. (automatic frequency control) circuit is suitable for frequencies up to 100 MHz for use in frequency generators, waveform generators, and all sorts of receiver.

The signal to be controlled is first amplified in two transistor stages, T1 and T2, and then applied to the D input of bistable FF1. The clock input of this multivibrator is connected to the Q8 output of IC1 which is a 14-step counter and crystal-controlled oscillator. The frequency of this oscillator is 32.768 kHz, so that a rectangular wave of frequency 64 Hz becomes available at output Q8 (pin 13). This is used to clock FF1 and the input signal is therefore sampled 64 times per second. Bistable FF2 is fed from output Q9 (pin 15) of IC1 to provide an output of 16 Hz at its Q output. The trailing edges of the sampled signal and the

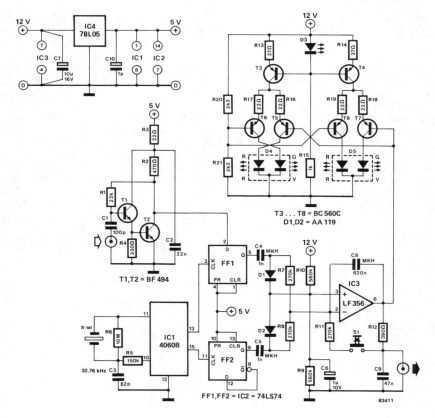

T3 . . . T8 = BC 560C
D1,D2 = AA 119

T1,T2 = BF 494

FF1,FF2 = IC2 = 74LS74

83411

leading edges of the 16 Hz signal are summed by C4, C5, D1, R7, and R8 and applied to the inverting input of opamp IC3. The non-inverting input of the opamp (and the junction of D1 and D2) is held at half the supply voltage via R9, R10, and C6. IC3 integrates the difference between the output signals of FF1 and FF2. The output signal of IC3 is taken through a low-pass filter (R12, C9) and may be used for fine adjustment of the oscillator frequency (for instance, with a varicap).

With the sampling and reference frequencies used, the fine adjustment is variable over a range of ± 16 Hz. The separation between the two ranges is always 64 Hz. The a.f.c. adjusts the oscillator frequency, therefore, always to the nearest multiple of 64 Hz. Once the oscillator is adjusted, its frequency stability is better than 1 Hz.

An indicator, formed by T3...T8, is also connected to the output of IC3. T3 and T4 are connected as a current source, while D3 provides the reference voltage. The outputs of the current sources are applied to two comparators, T5/T6 and T7/T8. One two-colour LED is connected to each of the comparators. The output voltage of IC3 is compared with half the supply voltage (to which T6 and T8 are connected) by T5 and T7. If the output voltage of IC3 is lower than half the supply voltage (that is, the oscillator frequency is too high), the red section of D4 and the green section of D5 will light; when the oscillator frequency is too low, the green section of D4 and the red section of D5 will light. When the output voltage of IC3 is exactly equal to half the supply voltage, and therefore the oscillator frequency is right, both LEDs will glow orange/yellow. If the colours of the LEDs are the same tint, the a.f.c. is at dead centre. This is a very precise method of indication.

206 d.c. voltage doubler using a 4049

This simple circuit can produce a d.c. voltage which is approximately twice the supply voltage in the no-load condition. The 4049 IC contains a total of six inverters. Two of them, N1 and N2, together with R1 and C3, form an oscillator, of which the frequency is about 10 kHz. The remaining inverters, N3...N6, are connected in parallel and operate as a buffer stage to reduce the load-dependence of the circuit.

Depending on the clock signal of the oscillator, point A in figure la is connected to the earth rail for part of the time per period and to the supply voltage for the rest of the time. When point A is connected to earth, capacitors C1 and C2 charge to the supply voltage via diodes D1 and D2. The oscillator then switches point A to the positive supply rail, which causes capacitor C1 to transfer a part of its charge to capacitor C2. This causes the voltage across capacitor C2 to rise to almost twice the supply voltage.

When D1 is connected to earth and the polarities of diodes D1, D2 and capacitors C1, C2 (figure 1b) are reversed, the output at A will be a negative voltage which, in the no-load condition, will be at the same level as the supply voltage.

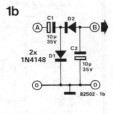

In both cases, unfortunately, the output voltage is dependent upon the load. As the load increases, the output voltage drops; in contrast, the superimposed a.c. level rises. The table shows the values measured in the circuit for load currents of 5 mA, 10 mA, and 15 mA.

G. Ramm.

Table

Supply voltage (V)	I_{out} (mA)	U_{out} (V) 1a	U_{out} (V) 1b	U_{ac} (mV$_{pp}$)	η (%) 1a	η (%) 1b
10	5	17	− 7.5	30	68	49
	10	16	− 6.5	60	70	52
	15	14.5	− 5	90	68	44
15	5	27.5	−12.5	40		
	10	26.5	−11.5	75		
	15	25.5	−10.5	115		

207 pulse/pulse train generator

This circuit has two modes of operation. If the push button is pressed once, a single noise-free pulse appears at the output; the pulse is positive at A and negative at B. If the push button is pressed and held, after a short delay a pulse train is produced which continues until the button is released. This dual-function operation makes this a very handy circuit which can be used, for example, where a counter must be driven either step-by-step or at a fixed frequency. The circuit consists of an anti-noise network (R2/C1), a pulse shaper (N1), an oscillator (N2), and two Schmitt triggers (N3 and N4), which enable it to produce both positive and negative pulses. When S1 is pressed once, R2/C1 eliminate any interference which might be present (switching noise for example), and Schmitt trigger N1 then delivers a clean pulse, which is further cleaned up by N3 (and ultimately N4), and

finally appears at the outputs. If S1 is held longer, there follows a certain time delay (which can be varied by P1) during which C2 is charged via R4 and P1 to such a level that oscillator N2 starts. This gate produces a pulse train whose frequency is adjustable with P2. This pulse train travels via N3 and N4 to the outputs.

R3 and D1 ensure that C2 discharges quickly so that if S1 is quickly pressed and released repeatedly the oscillator will not

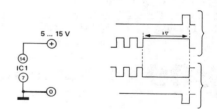

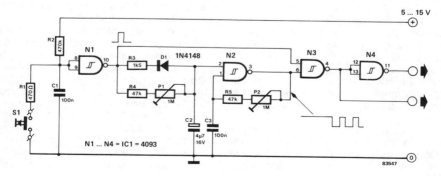

start. If the range of P1 is found to be too small, C2 can be changed for another value, and the same applies for P2 and C3. The approximate oscillator frequency is given by the formula 1/C3 (R5 + P2). The actual frequency also depends on the triggering threshold of the IC used, and this can vary from manufacturer to manufacturer. Total current consumption of the circuit is only a few mA.

208 synchronous, constant-amplitude sawtooth generator

This circuit provides a constant-amplitude sawtooth pulse train that can be synchronized with an input pulse. It can, therefore, be considered as a control system comparable with an analogue subroutine. The average output signal level of opamp A1 is compared with a reference voltage by comparator A2. If necessary, the two levels are equalized by T1 and T2.

The time constant of the control system is formed by resistor R4 and capacitor C3. If it is made too small, the leading edge of the sawtooth will tend to become sinusoidal and the linearity of the signal will suffer. With the values shown, the frequency range lies between 100 Hz and 5 kHz, which can be extended upwards by the use of an opamp with a higher gain. The value of capacitor C1 will then have to be modified accordingly.

The output signal can be calculated from the formula: $U_o = R6/U_b(R5 + R6)$. The circuit has been designed for a supply voltage, U_b, of 12 V: the current consumption is not greater than 10 mA.

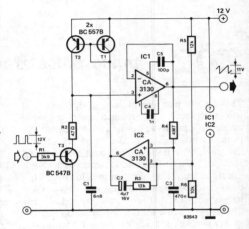

209 DC-DC converter

When using a digital measuring instrument with another electronic circuit, it is often necessary or desirable to completely separate the supply for the meter from that for the rest of the electronics. The problem can be solved by using two separate supplies, but it can also be done with a single supply and a DC-DC converter. The type of converter described here is quite compact and can deliver a current of about 50 mA.

The circuit consists of an astable multivibrator (IC1), which switches the voltage supply for a transformer (Tr1) on and off via a transistor (T1). The transformer

secondary voltage is half-wave rectified and smoothed. The output voltage is then limited by zener diode D5.

The transformer used should have a turns ratio of 1:1. The firing transformer used for silicon-controlled rectifiers (SCRs) is ideal for the job, but a small audio transformer (from a pocket radio) is also suitable. The frequency and pulse width of the circuit can be adapted to the type of transformer used by P1 and P2. Firing transformers give the best results at frequencies of about 100 kHz, while audio transformers usually work best between 0.5 and 40 kHz. The transformer must, of course, be connected

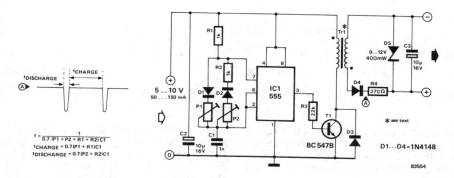

with correct polarity.
The frequency is found as follows:
$f = 1/[0.7C1(P1 + P2 + R1 + R2)]$ Hz
$t_{charge} = 0.7C1(P1 + R1)$ s
$t_{discharge} = 0.7C1(P2 + R2)$ s

A. Bovee

210 video pattern generator

The focusing control of a black-and-white TV receiver can just about be set by eye, but this haphazard method of tuning is totally out of the question with a colour TV set for which a pattern generator is essential. Ferranti produce a complete video pattern generator on a single chip. When combined in a circuit with a few external components, this IC delivers an excellent synchronization signal (CCIR standard) and five possible patterns.

These patterns are (with switch positions of S2 shown in parentheses): vertical lines (B), dots (C), crosshatch (D), horizontal lines (E), and degrees of grey (F). The breadth of the vertical lines and the intensity of the shades of grey can be set with P2 and P1 respectively.
Mixing the video and synchronization signals is done by T1. Both the video signal and blanking signal (via D5) are supplied to the base of this transistor. The synchroniz-

1a

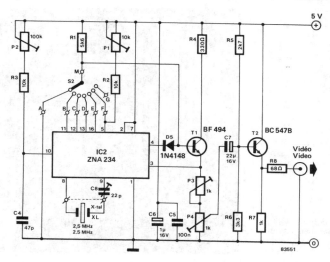

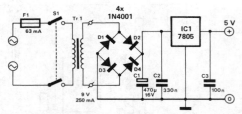

ation signal is set with P3 and P4 during the blanking signal (with T1 not conducting). The relation between video and synchronization is set with P3, output level is set with P4.

The signal output from this preset is again buffered by T2, so that with a load of about 75 Ω, a signal of 1 V_{pp} is obtained. The current consumption of the whole circuit is about 150 mA. The simple stabilized supply

2

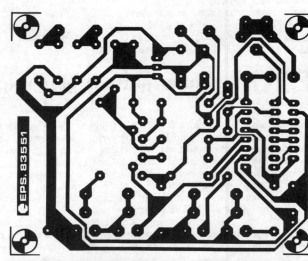

Parts list

Resistors:
R1 = 5k6
R2,R3 = 10 k
R4 = 330 Ω
R5 = 2k7
R6 = 3k3
R7 = 1 k
R8 = 68 Ω
P1 = 10 k preset
P2 = 100 k preset
P3,P4 = 1 k preset

Capacitors:
C1 = 470 μ/16 V
C2 = 330 n
C3,C5 = 100 n
C4 = 47 p
C6 = 1 μ/16 V
C7 = 22 μ/16 V
C8 = 22 p trimmer

Semiconductors:
T1 = BF 494
T2 = BC 547B
D1...D4 = 1N4001
D5 = 1N4148
IC1 = 7805
IC2 = ZNA 234

Miscellaneous:
X1 = 2.5 MHz crystal
F1 = 63 mA slow blow fuse
Tr1 = 9 V 0.25 A transformer
S1 = double pole mains switch
S2 = single pole 12 way rotary switch

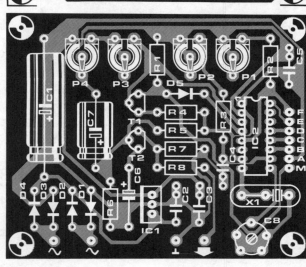

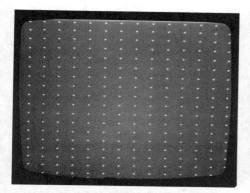

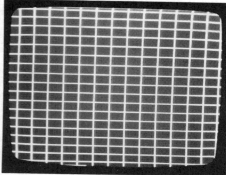

consisting of IC1 and the associated components can easily deliver this without the need for a heat sink.

Construction of the video pattern generator is simplified by the use of the pcb in figure 2. The power supply is also included on this board and only the transformer and switch S2 are mounted off the board.

211   VHF/UHF-TV-modulator

This easy-to-build circuit will modulate a video signal onto an RF carrier to give a signal that may be fed direct to the aerial socket of a VHF or UHF television receiver. It provides the link between the video interface and the TV set.

To illustrate the principle of the TV modulator it is useful to look at a typical video waveform and the corresponding modulated RF signal, both of which are illustrated in figure 1.

Figure 1a shows one line of a video waveform. The maximum positive excursion of the signal is known as white level, since it is the signal obtained from white areas of the picture. Line sync pulses are, of course, present at the beginning of each line, and are distinguished from picture information by the fact that they are negative-going pulses from 33% of white level down to zero (sync level). Picture information, on the other hand, extends from 33% (black level) up to 100% (white level). This description of a video signal is necessarily rather brief, and the various levels, etc. for broadcast video signals are, of course, defined much more rigorously.

An RF signal amplitude-modulated with this video signal is shown in figure 1b. It will be noted that the type of modulation employed is *negative modulation*, i.e. minimum video signal level (sync level) corresponds to peak RF signal level and vice versa. This type of modulation is used in the practical modulator circuit, which

must be used with UHF 625-line sets designed for negative modulation. The VHF output capability of the modulator is intended principally for use in countries outside the UK which use VHF systems employing negative video modulation.

In a broadcast TV transmitter great care is taken to ensure that the carrier is a pure sinewave, otherwise spurious signals could occur around harmonics of the carrier frequency. Steps are also taken to reduce wastage of transmitter power by partial suppression of the carrier, and one of the sidebands of the signal is also partially suppressed to minimize the bandwidth of the transmitted signal.

In a TV modulator for domestic use none of these criteria apply, since the signal is not going to be broadcast (and care must be taken to ensure that is it *not* broadcast). There is no need to suppress the carrier or one of the sidebands, and the presence of harmonics of the carrier frequency is a positive advantage since (if the carrier fundamental is in the VHF band) it allows TV sets to be tuned to these harmonics right through from the VHF band to the UHF band. This means that a single modulator can supply signals to both VHF and UHF sets and makes tuning easier, since the set can be tuned to a signal at one of several frequencies throughout its tuning range.

The fundamental carrier frequency is derived from a 27 MHz crystal in an oscillator circuit based on T1 in figure 2. For

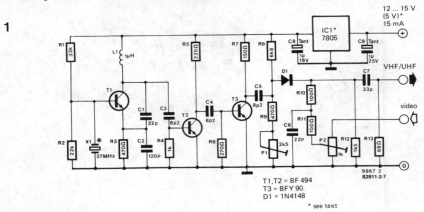

1

T1,T2 = BF 494
T3 = BFY 90
D1 = 1N4148

* see text

228

2

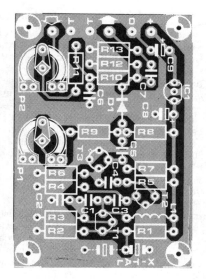 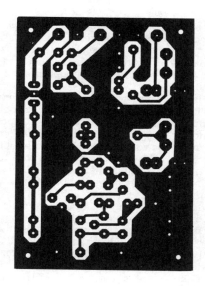

domestic use, crystal stability is not always required. In that case the crystal, X1, can be replaced by a 10 n capacitor. The output signal of this oscillator is amplified by T2 and T3 and differentiated by the three RC networks C3/R4, C4/R6 and C5/(R9 + P1). The resulting waveform at the junction of R8 and R9 is a sequence of short spikes containing harmonic multiples of 27 MHz up to around 1 GHz.

The video signal is fed in via P2 and modulates the carrier by varying the forward bias on D1 and thus changing its impedance. This causes the level of the RF signal appearing across R10 to vary in sympathy with the video input signal, i.e., the carrier signal is amplitude modulated. The signal is coupled out via C7 to a coaxial output socket. R13 matches the output impedance of the modulator to that of the coaxial cable.

Potentiometer P1 can be used to set the carrier level by varying the static forward bias on D1, while P2 adjusts the video input level and hence the modulation depth.

A printed circuit board track pattern and component layout are given in figure 4. Two alternative mounting positions are provided for the crystal, allowing for two different pin spacings.

Because of the high frequencies involved, the board is designed with a generous earth plane for stability. In addition, a

Parts list to figure 2

Resistors:
R1 = 33 k
R2 = 22 k
R3,R9 = 470 Ω
R4 = 1 k
R5 = 220 Ω
R6 = 270 Ω
R7 = 150 Ω
R8 = 6k8
R10,R11 = 100 Ω
R12 = 1k5
R13 = 68
P1 = 2k5 (2k2) preset potentiometer
P2 = 1 k preset potentiometer

Capacitors:
C1,C7 = 33 p
C2 = 120 p
C3,C4,C5 = 8p2
C6 = 22 p
C8,C9 = 1 μ/16 V tantalum

Semiconductors:
T1,T2 = BF 194, BF 195, BF 254, BF 255,
 BF 494, BF 495
T3 = BFY 90
D1 = 1N4148
IC1 = 7805 (see text)

Miscellaneous:
L1 = 1 μH
X1 = crystal, 27 MHz approximately (or X1 =
 10 nF, see text)

screening plate, made of tinplate or a piece of copper laminate board, is connected between the oscillator and modulator. The completed board *must* be mounted in a metal box to avoid the possibility of stray radiation.

The modulator may be powered from a +12 V to +15 V unstabilized DC supply, which is stabilized at +5 V by the IC regulator on the board. Alternatively, the unit may be powered direct from an existing stabilized +5 V supply, in which case IC1 should be omitted and the holes in the board for its two outer pins should be bridged by a wire link.

Setting up the modulator is very simple. Connect the modulator to the aerial input of the TV set using 75 Ω coaxial cable, then switch on the modulator and the TV set. Set P1 to its midposition and tune the TV set to one of the harmonics of the carrier. This will be around channel 7 (189 MHz) in the VHF band and at a number of frequencies in the UHF band. When the carrier is picked up, the screen of the TV set will darken and noise (snowstorm effect) will disappear.

A video signal may now be fed in, and P2 should be adjusted so that the video signal level does not exceed 3 V peak-to-peak at its wiper.

The TV set may now be tuned to the sideband which gives the best picture. If tuned to the wrong sideband the picture will tend to appear negative. If the picture lacks vertical synchronization (i.e. rolls) it will be necessary to adjust P1 until it stabilizes. P2 is used to adjust the contrast by varying the video input level, but should not be turned up too much or the modulator will overload, causing the picture to appear negative on highlights.

Finally it should be noted that, when using the modulator, the output should always be connected direct to the TV set via a length of coaxial cable and must never be connected to any unscreened wire or other conducting object that could act as an aerial.

212 symmetrical voltages from a doorbell transformer

This circuit is of interest not only because it uses a bell transformer with a single secondary winding to provide symmetrical voltages for low-current applications, but also because the final output voltages are greater than the secondary transformer voltage. This increase is achieved by the use of two voltage doublers each consisting of two diodes and two capacitors, connected head to tail. Each diode/capacitor couple operates during alternate half cycles of the 8 V_{rms} voltage so that the output voltage U_0 is (theoretically) equal to 1.414 U_{rms}, where U_{rms} is the root-mean-square value of the output voltage of the transformer.

A current of 150...200 mA and 1 V of ripple can be expected with the capacitor values shown here. To increase this current without a similar increase in ripple, the values of the capacitors may be made greater, but C1 must be approximately the

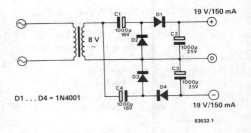

same as C2, and C3 about the same as C4. To get a stable symmetrical output of ± 15 V, two voltage regulators, a 7815 and a 7915, should be used. This will allow a bell transformer to be used for any small circuits that require a symmetrical supply of 14 or 15 V and a current of 0.1...0.2 A.

R. Storn

230

213 resistance comparator

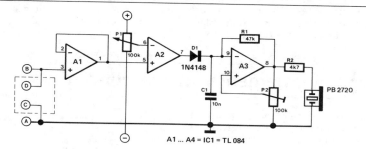

A1 ... A4 = IC1 = TL 084

The circuit indicates by a bleep whether a resistance being measured with the multimeter is smaller than a predetermined value; it can also be made to do so when the measured resistance is larger than the reference value.

The device compares the voltage drop across the resistance under test with a reference voltage. Required components are a quad opamp, a diode, a crystal buzzer, a capacitor, two electrolytics, two trimmers and four resistors. Power is provided by a 9 V battery.

In the circuit diagram shown in figure 1 the voltage drop across R_x, which is in parallel with the multimeter, is taken from sockets A/C and B/D. The high internal resistance of the multimeter is hardly affected by the parallel connection of the comparator because A1 is connected as an impedance converter. Stage A2 compares the voltage at the output of A1 with a level preset by potentiometer P1. If the voltage at the + input of A2 is larger than the value set by P1, the output level of A2 is nearly equal to the positive supply voltage. Diode D1 conducts and capacitor C1 cannot discharge. Opamp A3, in conjunction with C1, R1 and preset potentiometer P2, forms a squarewave oscillator of which the trigger level is set by P2. The squarewave voltage at the output of A3 is applied to the crystal buzzer via R2.

The earth potential of the circuit is determined by the output of A4. The voltage divider R3/R4 at the input of A4 is symmetrical, so that the 9 V of the battery is converted in a simple manner to 2 × 4.5 V.

The simplest method of calibration is to connect a resistor of, say, 1 k between the two test probes and adjust P1 such that the bleeping tone just disappears. If a smaller

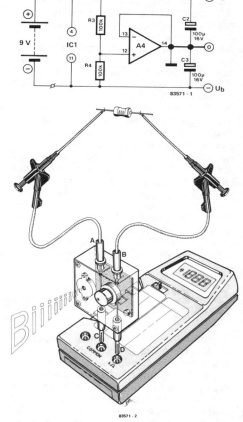

resistance is now connected between the probes, the bleep will be heard again. It must of course be borne in mind that the comparator, as well as the resistance under test, have a tolerance.

If it is required that the circuit indicates larger resistances than that of the reference, the inputs of A2 must be interchanged.

Figure 2 illustrates how the comparator can be built into a small case which plugs directly into the sockets of the multimeter.

The test leads are then plugged into sockets fitted at the top of the case.

The frequency and volume of the bleep tone can be set with P2; they are, of course, to some extent interrelated.

214   emergency mains cut-out

If the voltage of the mains supply to a computer rises too high, components on the printed circuit boards can easily be damaged or even destroyed. This emergency cut-out placed between the mains supply and the load interrupts the supply when the voltage level exceeds a predetermined value.

For many reasons it is possible for the output voltage of a power supply to rise to a dangerous level. The emergency cut-out described here has been set to the maximum supply voltage of 5.25 V that is stated by the manufacturers of TTL ICs.

Zener diode D1 starts conducting just before the stated zener voltage is reached. A small current flows in the anode-gate circuit of silicon-controlled rectifier (SCR) Th1; the level of this current can be set with preset potentiometer P1 connected in parallel with the gate-cathode circuit of Th1. When the mains supply rises, the current through the zener diode becomes large enough to cause the SCR to fire. The firing level lies between 5.2...6 V.

As soon as the SCR fires, the mains supply voltage drops substantially because the

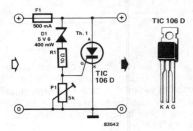

SCR virtually short-circuits the mains supply. In the case of a supply without current limiting, fuse F1 prevents the current attaining too high value. The rating of the fuse depends, of course, on the load requirement.

During testing and adjusting of the circuit, it is important that the SCR continues to conduct after it has been fired until its current has dropped to zero. The firing voltage level can be set with a mains supply with a current limiter before it is put into use. If it proves impossible, for instance, because of the tolerances of the zener diode, to set the firing voltage to the required value, try using a 5.1 V zener diode.

215   event counter

An event counter, as could be expected, counts events, or, to be more precise, it counts the occurrences of a particular event. The counter here may seem a bit limited, as it can only go to 99, but in fact it can be expanded almost infinitely. The read-out consists of two lines of LEDs, one for units and the other for tens. Only one LED per line (at most) will light at a time so the current consumption is quite low, certainly when compared to a set-up with 7-segment displays.

The actual counter consists of two 4017 decade counters. When the reset button is pressed, both Q0 outputs go high. Every clock pulse arriving at pin 14 of IC1 makes the next output of the IC go high. At every tenth clock pulse the CO output goes high and clocks IC2 and at the same time IC1 is reset to 0. After 99 pulses, both IC1 and IC2 reset to zero and the sequence starts again. In principle, the carry output of IC2 can be used to extend the circuit infinitely.

The outputs of a 4017 cannot drive LEDs

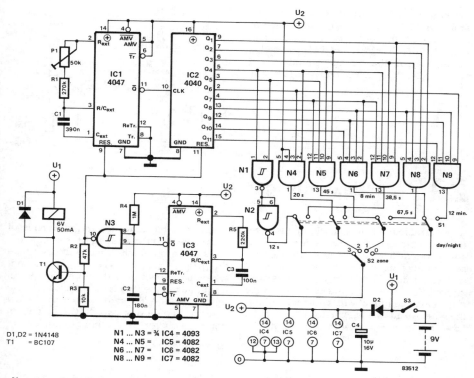

D1,D2 = 1N4148
T1 = BC107

N1 ... N3 = ¾ IC4 = 4093
N4 ... N5 = IC5 = 4082
N6 ... N7 = IC6 = 4082
N8 ... N9 = IC7 = 4082

direct so it is necessary to add a simple buffer stage, consisting of a transistor and a resistor, to each output. A single common resistor (820 Ω at 15 V supply) per line is all that is needed as each IC drives only one LED at a time.

All that remains now is to consider the clock or counter pulses. Sometimes these can be taken direct from another circuit

and if this is the case, check that the power supply is suitable and, if necessary, change the values of R20 and R21. In other situations the circuit based on N1 ... N4 can be used. A clock pulse is generated every time S1 is closed, or S2 is opened, and, to alleviate any problems, the effects of contact bounce are suppressed by N2, N3, C3, and R25.

216   LED current source

If an LED is used in a circuit, the current for that LED is normally set with a limiting resistor. The LED can then be switched on and off by a transistor. However, the method shown in figure 1 does not take into account any variations in the supply voltage. A small variation in the LED current can be very conspicuous, especially when high efficiency LEDs are used.

The addition of just one transistor can

transform the circuit of figure 1 to a current source which can be switched on and off (for instance, with TTL levels). The circuit of figure 2 shows that resistor R1 has been moved to the emitter of T1. When a drive voltage is applied to the input of T1, this transistor conducts which causes a current through R1. Transistor T2 controls the base current of T1 such that the voltage drop across R1 remains at 0.6 V. The current, I,

233

through the LEDs and R1 is calculated by $I = 0.6/R1$. If, for instance, R1 is 12 Ω, the current through the LEDs is 50 mA. Bear in mind that the dissipation of T1 is somewhat higher than in the circuit of figure 1, but against that, the dissipation in R1 is not as high.

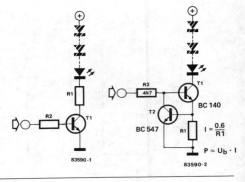

217   dexterity game

In electronics, as in everything else, we must be able to laugh, to have fun now and again, and games circuits are always particularly well received. The principle of electronic manual-dexterity games is well known: the player attempts to pass a metal ring along a length of wire without touching the wire. An alternative version uses a metal tube which is open along its length (il-lustrated in the drawing). In this version of the game, the tube is divided into four sections, each of which is more difficult than the preceding one. The sound emitted, when the ring touches the tube, changes in frequency as the ring is moved closer to the end of the tube. The circuit consists of a few resistors and diodes, two CMOS ICs and, of course, a buzzer. The sound generation cir-

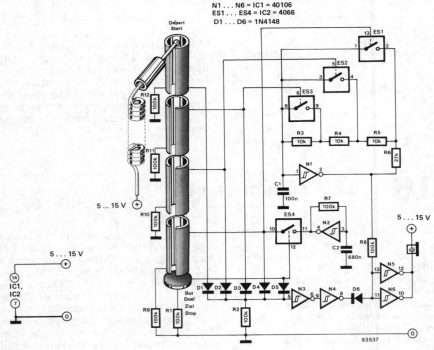

cuit is based on N1, a Schmitt trigger inverter, and the oscillating frequency is dependent upon the number of resistors R3...R5 short-circuited or left in series by the analogue switches ES1...ES3. If only R6 (and capacitor C1) is in the feedback loop from the output of N1 to its input, the frequency of the signal is maximum. This will occur if the ring touches the final section of the tube.

At the end of the tube the ring touches the finishing line and actuates ES4 which sends the signal produced by the oscillator at N2 to ES1, thus switching from highest to lowest frequency. Every time the ring touches the

tube, the D1...D5 diode network connected to inverters N3 and N4 drives N5 and N6 through D6. Gates N5 and N6 are connected as a power stage that drives a buzzer while the ring touches the tube.

The current consumption of such a simple circuit is quite small ($\approx$ 5 mA) so it should be considered as a pocket game powered by a battery. The values of resistors R3...R5 are a matter of experimentation as the tone for each stage is a something for each user to decide. The same is true of the switching tone between two stages and at the end of a run.

218 variable zener

One of the problems encountered in the design of circuits lies in the selection of correct values for various components. Often trial-and-error is used to find the most suitable value for a particular circuit. There is, however, one major problem with this method: most people who build electronic circuits as a hobby do not possess vast quantities of components to cover all the various values which might be needed. And, of course, there is always Murphys law to consider: you always have every value of component possible — except the one that you need. So, having been bitten (not literally) once again by Murphy, we came up with a design for a zener diode with variable zener voltage. Compared to normal zener diodes, the input impedance is somewhat higher (20...50 Ω), the maximum load lower, and the temperature coefficient only about —2 mV/°C. The circuit is, however, quite straightforward and U_z can be varied over the range 3...25 V. As soon as the voltage at the base of T1 is greater than 0.6 V, this transistor conducts. Conse-

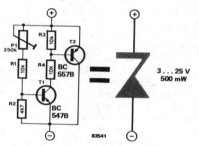

quently, T2 conducts and the voltage cannot rise any more, just as in a zener diode. The ratio between P1/R1 and R2 defines the zener voltage of the circuit. To set the zener voltage, the circuit must be connected via a 10 k resistor to a supply, and potentiometer P1 should be adjusted until the desired zener voltage is reached. If the circuit is used to replace a zener in an existing setup, the extra 10 k resistor is not needed, of course. The maximum permitted current through this variable zener is 100 mA. Transistor T2 can dissipate a maximum of 100 mW.

219 180 watt DC/AC converter

This is a portable converter intended for use with a 12 V lead-acid battery. Whether it's in the car, boat, caravan, or mobile home, this converter provides a mobile

250 V a.c. supply suitable for powering small electrical appliances, such as lights, soldering irons, or electrial tools. The circuit requires only six transistors, a mains

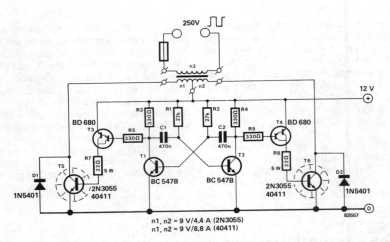

n1, n2 = 9 V/4,4 A (2N3055)
n1, n2 = 9 V/8,8 A (40411)

transformer, and some capacitors and resistors. An astable multivibrator (AMV), consisting of transistors T1 and T2, provides a square wave at a frequency of about 50 Hz. As T1 and T2 conduct alternately, the output stages also operate in push-pull. When T1 conducts, a current also flows through T3; this switches on T5 and this transistor connects one half of the secondary winding of mains transformer Tr across the 12-volt battery. When T2 conducts, transistor T6 switches the other half of the mains transformer across the battery. If RCA 40411 transistors are used in the output stages, the current through the secondary winding can be as high as 10 A, giving a possible power output of 180 watts. If 2N3055 transistors are used, the power output will be about 90 watts. As the output transistors are driven into saturation, they should be mounted on very large (100 mm high fins) heat sinks. If a toroidal mains transformer is used, the converter can be constructed as a very compact unit.

The advantages of a simple construction and high efficiency are offset by the disadvantage of a square wave output voltage which, in the absence of a regulator, is load-dependent: at low loads the output voltage may be well over 250 VAC. This presents no problems for small electrical appliances, but drills with electronic speed control or light dimmers may not work effectively as they are designed for sine-wave-operation only. It is definitely not advisable to try to operate colour television sets, video recorders, or hi-fi equipment from this converter.

220   simple D/A converter

Special ICs are available to achieve an analogue output from a computer. A digital to analogue converter using these devices can be simple but expensive. However, a simple circuit can also be constructed from standard components. The circuit described is simple in conception; no special components (not even high stability resistors) are used and it provides two outputs: one pulsewidth and one analogue. The operation of the converter can be seen from the block schematic diagram in figure 1. An 8-bit data word from the computer determines the level of the analogue output voltage, and this data (0...255) is stored in a latch. An 8-bit counter continuously counts from 0 to 2^8 (256). The output data from the latch and those from the counter are compared by a comparator. The A > B output of the comparator will be logic 1 during the time it takes for the counter to run from 0 to the number in the latch. From that point on (that is from the number in the latch to 2^8), it will be logic 0. This output

236

1

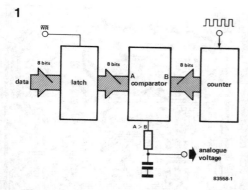

therefore delivers a pulsewidth modulated signal, of which the pulsewidth is determined by the data the computer supplies to the latch. The available signal can be converted to an analogue voltage by integration and for this only a resistor and capacitor are required.

The circuit of the D/A converter is given in figure 2 in which the latch (IC1), comparator (IC2 and IC3), and the counter (IC4) are immediately evident. Other stages are a clock oscillator (N1, N2 and N3) and a buffer for the analogue output (IC5). The integrator (R3 and C2) is preceded by two CMOS gates, the supply of which can be derived from a reference voltage.

To start reading of the data, an enable pulse must be given at pin 11 of IC1. The oscillator is switched on and off by an open input at f. It is possible to connect a second, external oscillator to this input, in which case the clock frequency will be that of the external oscillator. With the component values shown, the clock oscillator frequency will be about 300 kHz. This results in a pulsewidth modulated signal at output P with a frequency of 1/256 of the clock frequency, i.e., a little higher than 1 kHz. The clock can go up to 10 MHz. If lower frequencies are desired, the value of integrator capacitor C2 must be increased.

2

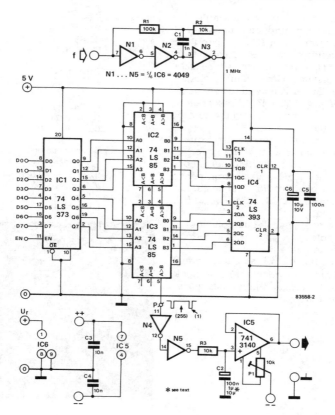

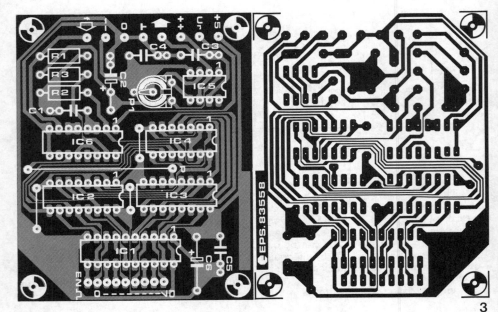

IC1...IC4 are supplied from a single 5 V line at a current consumption of the order of 50 mA. The inverters in IC6 are supplied from a reference voltage U_r. This voltage must be about 5 V and determines the stability and the maximum level of the analogue output signal. Buffer IC5 needs a symmetrical supply of $\pm$ 12 V...$\pm$ 15 V. Preset potentiometer P1 is included for adjustment of the off-set of the opamp.

The pulsewidth signal can be used direct or via an amplifier to control the speed of d.c. motors (which react well to pulse control). This signal can be taken from either pin 11 of N4 or pin 15 of N5. If the analogue output is not used, R3, C2...C4, P1, and IC5 can be omitted.

The simple digital to analogue converter is best constructed on the printed circuit board shown in figure 3.

The photograph is that of the output signal of the comparator (lower trace) at a clock frequency of 100 kHz and input data corresponding to number 15.

Parts list

Resistors:
R1 = 100 k
R2,R3 = 10 k
P1 = 10 k preset potentiometer

Capacitors:
C1 = 1 n
C2 = see text
C3,C4 = 10 n
C5 = 100 n
C6 = 10 μ/10 V

Semiconductors:
IC1 = 74LS373
IC2,IC3 = 74LS85
IC4 = 74LS393
IC5 = 741, 3140
IC6 = 4049

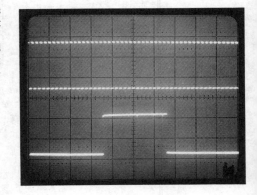

221 portable egg timer

Packing a rucksack to go camping always poses problems. Either you pack everything exept the kitchen sink and stagger under the weight, or you keep the weight down but find yourself without something essential. An egg timer is not absolutely essential, of course, but it is often very handy. This circuit is intended for people who want a small, battery-powered timer, which could also be used at home. One half of the 556 timer is used to sound the buzzer. It is connected as an astable multivibrator and oscillates at about 2 kHz. The actual timing is controlled by the other half of the timer. The sequence starts when S3 connects the trigger input of the IC to

ground. The length of the timing pulse is determined by the P1/R3/C network. For the prototype, C consisted of seven 47 μF/6 V capacitors in parallel. The total capacitance, about 300 μF, gives a time of 6½ minutes with P1 in mid-position. S1 is the power switch for the circuit. Assuming this is 'on', pressing S2 resets the timer. Then the duration to be timed can be set with P1 and started by pressing S3. In case of a false start, S2 will reset the circuit. Current consumption is about 23 mA. A scale can easily be calibrated in minutes and mounted behind the dial of P1, otherwise timing will still be a hit-or-miss affair!

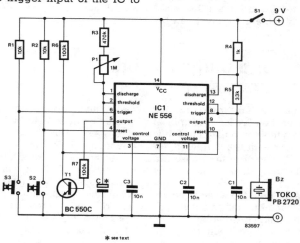

✳ see text

222 auto trigger

This circuit gives an output voltage when the input voltage rises above a given reference level which is derived from the positive and negative peak values of the input signal. Therefore the trigger circuit is fairly independent of the amplitude of the signal and could be used, for example, as a trigger for an oscilloscope.
Opamp IC1 is connected as a buffer stage and its non-inverting input is set to half the supply voltage by R1...R3 and C2. The ref-

erence voltages are derived from the (buffered) input signal via D1, D2, C3, and C4. Capacitor C4 charges through D1 to half the supply voltage plus the positive peak voltage of the input signal. C3 is charged through D1 and P1, but in this case diode D2 ensures that the voltage across C3 is not more than half the supply voltage minus the peak negative voltage. The values chosen in this part of the circuit are such that the reference voltages across the

239

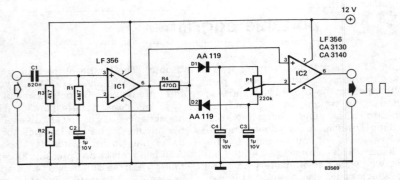

capacitors stay constant when the input signal has a frequency of more than about 10 Hz. The signal output from IC1 travels direct to the non-inverting input of comparator IC2. The inverting input of this comparator is connected to the wiper of P1, and this potentiometer is used to set the reference voltage. This reference level can be anywhere between the positive and negative peaks of the input signal. As long as the level of the input signal is now above the reference value, IC2 will deliver an output voltage (which is in practice equal to the supply voltage). If the level of the input signal falls below the reference level, the output of the opamp falls back to zero.

223 anti-burglar lights

Burglars are often grateful for the fact that someone goes on holiday for a couple of weeks and leaves the home untended. It is often made very easy for the burglar: if, for instance, no light is seen in the house for, say, a week, it is pretty certain that nobody is at home.

This circuit was designed to mislead potential burglars: the anti-burglar light switches on one or more of the house lights when it gets dark and leaves them on for 1...5 hours. During that time the lights are switched on and off at random.

When darkness sets in, the resistance of the light dependent resistor (LDR) R1 increases causing the output of gate N6 to go to logic 0. The point at which this occurs can be preset with P1. The reset input (pin 12) of counter IC1 is then also logic 0 and IC1 begins to count. The counter contains an internal clock oscillator the frequency of which is determined by capacitor C2, potentiometer P2 and resistor R4. P2 enables the adjustment of the frequency between 0.9 Hz and 4.5 Hz. From the time that IC1 starts to count, the output of N5 will be logic 1 but the output of N7, and therefore transistor T1, will remain unaffected until a

logic 1 also appears from N8. This will obviously be generated by IC2 and its associated gates. During the time that IC1 is counting, it is feeding clock pulses to IC2. These are taken from the Q9, Q10 or Q12 outputs (pins 13, 15 or 1) of IC1. The outputs of IC2, together with gates N1...N4, N8 and N9, form a quasi random generator that, via gate N7, controls transistor T1 and switches the house lights on and off. This hopefully puts off our burglar by giving the appearance that the house may not be as empty as he would have liked!

After a certain period of time (1 to 5 hours), output 14 of IC1 eventually returns to logic 1. This causes a number of things to happen. Via diode D1 it stops the internal clock oscillator. This then holds Q14 at logic 1. Now gate N7 is inhibited, thus switching off the house lighting. All will remain at peace with the house (our phantom occupants are in bed) until the following evening when the process begins again. By now, our less than happy burglar has gone off to less active residences!

Calibration of the random generator is fairly simple. The sensitivity of R1, that is the light level at which N6 desides to switch, is set by P1. The total operation time (of IC1) is set by P2 while the random pattern is determined by which of the Q outputs of IC1 is used to clock IC2.

If the random generator is not required, IC2 and its collection of gates can be omitted. However, do not forget to connect pin 6 of N7 to the positive supply line.

The house lights can be switched on and off by a relay connected to T1. Take care that the maximum current drawn by the relay does not exceed 50 mA. In the event that more current is required at this point, T1 and the mains transformer must be uprated.

One final note. The LDR should not be mounted in a situation where street lights or car headlamps could cause false triggering of the circuit. If this should happen the house lights could go on and off all night. Our insistent burglar could come to the conclusion that there is an all night party going on and decide to join after all . . .

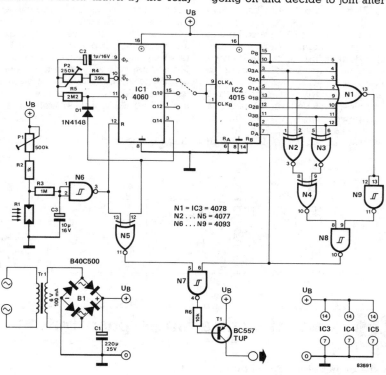

224 thermometer

A common or garden diode like the 1N4148 is in principle an excellent sensor for a reasonably accurate electronic thermometer because the voltage drop across the diode decreases by 2 mV for every degree Celsius rise in temperature.

As can be seen in figure 1, a constant reference voltage is applied to the non-inverting input of the opamp. The current flowing through the resistor, and therefore through the diode, is also held at a constant level. Variations in the output voltage of the opamp can occur only as a result of a change in the voltage drop across the diode and this in turn can only be caused by temperature variations. The output voltage is therefore directly proportional to the temperature of the diode. In the complete

1

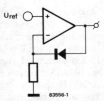

circuit diagram shown in figure 2, the opamp is A2 and the diode is D1. The reference voltage is derived from IC1 via voltage divider R3/P1/R4. The output voltage of A2 is amplified by opamp A3.

The non-inverting input of A3 is also held at a constant level (again derived from R3/P1/R4) and the values of R6 and R8 have been chosen so that 0 V corresponds to 0°C ambient.

To enable the measuring of temperatures above and below zero without the use of a symmetrical power supply, a rather uncommon solution was arrived at. The first requirement was a regulator, IC1, which

provides a reasonably constant reference voltage for A2 and A3. An additional amplifier, A1, together with R1 and R2, generates a voltage of +2.5 V line relative to the negative supply line. This 2.5 V is then used as the earth for the rest of the circuit.

Pin 11 of IC2 is therefore at −2.5 V and pin 4 at +6.5 V with respect to this earth. The supply to the opamps is therefore symmetrical.

The current consumption of the circuit is about 5 mA so that for incidental temperature measurements a 9 V battery will be adequate. If continuous use is required, a simple mains supply will have to be used; this need not be stabilized in view of IC1. Most voltmeters will be suitable as an indicator. The circuit is calibrated be setting P1 to obtain 0 V at 0° Centigrade and then P2 to obtain 0.999 V at 99.9° Celsius.

A. van Olderen

2

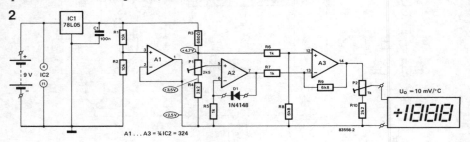

225 on/off with a single push button

Basically the output of the Schmitt trigger N1 changes (toggles) when the switch is closed momentarily. This toggle function is achieved in such a simple circuit by the fact that the inputs of the trigger are held between the switching threshold levels. If we assume that the output logic level (Q) of the trigger is at logic 1, capacitor C1 will charge via R1. When switch S1 is closed the input of the trigger will be taken to logic 1 (because the capacitor is fully charged) and the Q output will of course become logic 0. The capacitor will now discharge but not completely because the closed switch will hold the level to that existing at the wiper of P1. However, this drop in voltage at the input of

1

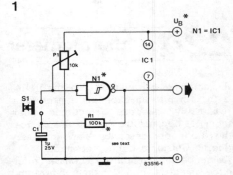

the gate will not cause its output to change state again because the input level will still be above the lower switching threshold of the Schmitt trigger.

This intermediate voltage level will remain while the switch is closed. When the switch is eventually released, C1 will discharge completely. The 0 V across the capacitor will not affect the trigger since it is no longer connected to the capacitor (the switch is open). Now, when the switch is closed, the 0 V will reach the input of the gate and its output will once again change state. It is essential that P1 is set correctly for

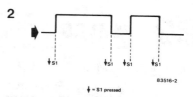

the circuit to function, but it will be found in practice that this presents no problem.

Various types of Schmitt trigger are suitable for this circuit: 4093, 40106, 74LS14, 74LS132. If TTL ICs are used, the supply voltage must be 5 V ± 0.25 V; for CMOS ICs it should lie between 5 V and 15 V.

226   preset the hard(ware) way

Since the inspired eureka of one R. Moog while pondering the concept of voltage-controlled sound synthesis modules, electronic music making has virtually stood still. Peremptory though it may seem, this statement is none the less true and the same can be said of other up to date electronic musical instruments.

In fact, there is only one novelty of note and that is the advent of musical microprocessors, and these are already commonplace in modern synthesizers. Their task is not really to supply music, rather to make up for the deficiencies suffered by many musicians who play from memory and cling blindly to programming. Programming and memorizing certainly give undeniable benefits which simply were not possible before. But not everybody is willing to pay the (high) price and many may prefer a completely different solution, so it is worthwhile considering a wired, discrete, inexpensive alternative. What we propose here is the basis of a system which can be expanded at will.

A main switch allows a selection to be made between ordinary manual mode (with the original potentiometers acting as usual), and programming mode. In this latter case the normal potentiometers are disabled; a multi-way switch (S2) switches, in turn, batteries of programming presets, each delivering the exact voltage needed to obtain a specific sound.

All the control lines are connected by a system of diodes which prevent any interac-

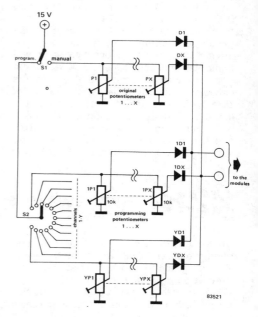

tion between the control signals which are inactive and those which are active.

In order for this circuit to operate, the original wiring must be modified and, of course, care must be taken in rewiring, but this is a small price to pay for what could be the ultimate solution!

227 S.P.T.S.

single pole toggle switch

As can be seen in circuit 225, a press on/press off function (toggle) from a single pole push button can be achieved quite easily. In this case, the circuit is slightly more sophisticated and uses an opamp to provide the toggle function. Switch bounce (where the contacts quite literally bounce and provide a number of pulses instead of one), the ever present problem with all mechanical switches, is removed in this circuit. Even though an opamp is involved, the circuit is still very simple. The gain (amplification) of the opamp is very high which means that its output can easily be high ($+U_b$ or logic 1) or low ($-U_b$ or logic 0). A small portion of the output voltage level (about 1/23) is fed back to the non-inverting input of the opamp.

Pressing push button S1 will connect capacitor C1 to the inverting input of the opamp. If the output is low, the opamp will immediately change state and C1 will begin to charge via R1. However, if S1 is held, the capacitor will only charge to a value of $U_b \times R_2(R_1 + R_2)$ which works out to about 0.01 U_b. When S1 is released, the capacitor will continue to charge right up to U_b. Now that S1 is open, C1 is no longer connected to the opamp and its output information is

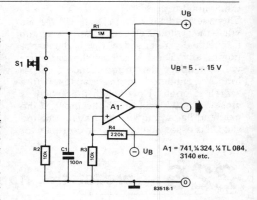

$U_B = 5 \ldots 15$ V

A1 = 741, ¼ 324, ¼ TL 084, 3140 etc.

retained. If S1 is then closed once more, the logic 1 across the fully charged capacitor will appear at the inverting input of the opamp. The opamp will again change state to provide a logic 0 at its output and the capacitor will discharge. Back where we started!

It must be remembered that when an opamp is used with an asymmetrical supply, the junction of R2/R3 must not be connected to earth but to a point midway between the positive and negative supply level ($\frac{1}{2}U_b$). A potential divider consisting of a pair of resistors will be sufficient for this purpose.

228 stay awake alarm

Do you turn over in the morning and then often oversleep? This circuit could prevent you being late for work, but it can also be used as an egg-timer (soft-boiled only).

When you first wake up, switch on this alarm: nothing happens at first, but after a time lampse of between 20 seconds and 4 minutes, adjustable by potentiometer P1, a soft warning tone sounds. If you're still awake, press the reset button. If you do not, because you fell asleep again, the alarm tone, which is a lot louder than the warning tone, will really tear you away from those dreams. You can press the reset button again and doze off for another alarm cycle, or if you're really awake you can switch the

alarm off!

Operation of the circuit is as follows: N5 functions as a clock generator for the seven-stage binary counter IC1. After every 16 clock pulses, output Q4 of IC1 changes state from '1' to '0' or vice versa. After 128 pulses output Q7 is logic 1, but as Q4 is then logic 0, the output of gate N1 remains '1'.

Now the inputs to N3 are '1', so the output of N4 is also '1' and this drives the audio oscillator consisting of N7, R5, and C4, which in turn drives transistor T2 and sounds the warning tone.

Sixteen clock pulses later, Q4 again becomes logic 1, and the output of N4 becomes logic 0. Audio oscillator N7 is cut

1

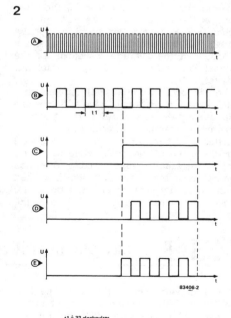

83406-1

off and the warning tone stops. At the same time, however, the output of N2 becomes '1' and actuates alarm tone oscillator N6. This drives T1 and the alarm tone sounds.

After yet another 16 clock pulses, output Q4 is '0' again, and the output of N1 is logic 1. Again, the warning tone is sounded. And so on . . .

If the reset button is not pressed, output Q7 is again logic 0 after 256 clock pulses. The outputs of N1 and N3 both become logic 1 and N2 and N4, '0': both oscillators are now cut off and the situation is as it was on switch on.

As the logic 1 level for the reset signal is taken from output Q7, the counter can only be reset via S1 when Q7 is 1. If you want to cheat, you can, of course, unsolder R3 from the IC and connect it directly to the 9 . . . 15 V supply.

Neither T1 nor T2 conducts when the oscillators are off so this reduces the quiescent current to only about 0.2 mA. As shown, the current drawn is about 4.3 mA during the warning tone and 120 mA while the alarm tone sounds. The loudness of both tones can be adjusted to meet individual requirements by changing the values of R6 and R7, but neither should be less than 10 Ω.

The oscillator frequencies can also be varied by C3/R4 and C4/R5 respectively. Instead of output Q4, it is also possible to

2

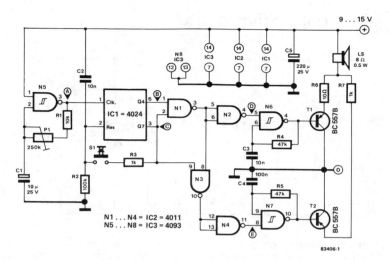

83406-2

t1 ≙ 32 clockpulses

use outputs Q3 or Q5. When Q5 is used, the change-over between warning and alarm tones takes twice as long as when Q4 is used, whereas Q3 gives half the time lapse of Q4.

229 capacitive switch

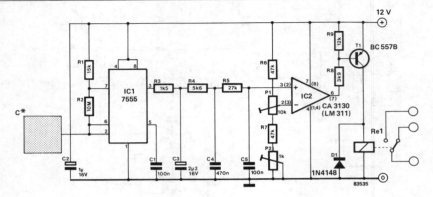

Take a square wave signal with a given frequency and integrate it. This gives a stable continuous average voltage. By changing the existing frequency of the signal the average integrated value remains the same but, at the instant when the frequency is changed, a positive or negative voltage peak will appear due to the momentary change in the average waveform of the signal. This is the principle upon which our switch is based.

The 555 or 7555 timers will oscillate in a stable manner. However, if we add an external capacitive sensor, it becomes possible to vary the oscillation frequency.

In this circuit, the square wave is integrated by the triple RC network, while IC2, used as a comparator (with a variable reference value), uses the changes in the integrated voltage to alternately make and break the relay. Thus when you move close to C the relay makes; if you remain stationary the relay breaks. It may seem a bit basic but it is a valid idea and it is worth looking at it in greater detail. To obtain better results, you could take the signal after integration and differentiate between negative pulses (the frequency decreases as the value of C increases: when the sensor is approached) and positive pulses (the frequency increases again if the sensor is no longer affected) and compare them. Without this refinement, the size of the sensitive plate must be such that the frequency of oscillation be at least several kHz. Failing this, the operation of the circuit would often be disrupted by false detections. Coarse and fine adjustment is provided, by P1 and P2, to reduce the risk of incorrect switching.

Note: The numbers in parentheses are the pins if an LM311 is used in place of the CA3130.

230 simple stabilizer

This is a very simple but none the less reliable stabilizer circuit which can be used in place of a 78XX series IC regulator.

The heart of the circuit is based on a type CA3130 operational amplifier, A1, and one transistor. The reference voltage, U_r, is derived from the output by R1 and zener diode D1 and is therefore very stable. Operation is simple: if the output voltage, U_o, shows a tendency to rise, the potential difference at junction R2/R3 will increase. The voltage at the non-inverting input of A1 will then become higher than that at the inverting input, because the latter is held at U_r by zener D1. The output of A1 therefore increases, resulting in T1 being cut off and in a reduction in the output voltage of the stabilizer. If U_o drops below the nominal value, the above operation is reversed. The advantage of this circuit is the low voltage drop between input and output, which is dependent solely on the saturation voltage of Tl. The unstabilized input voltage does not therefore need to be more than 0.5 V higher than the required output voltage.

The calculation of the various parameters is simple: assuming a current of 1 mA through R2/R3 and a zener current of 5 mA, we arrive at the following formulas which everyone can compute without a pocket calculator.

$$R1 = (0.2R2) \text{ k}\Omega$$
$$R2 = (U_o - U_r) \text{ k}\Omega$$
$$R3 = (U_r) \text{ k}\Omega$$

in which U_o is the required stabilized output voltage and $U_r = U_{D1}$ which is slightly lower than U_o. If, for instance, a stabilized

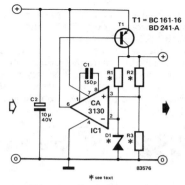

output voltage of 8 V is required, the following values are obtained: $U_r = 6.8$ V; R1 = 220 Ω; R2 = 1k2; R3 = 6k8.

231 low cost CMOS lock

A decimal keyboard, a CMOS IC, three transistors and an opto-coupler...that is about all that is needed to make this electronic lock with a three digit combination. Locking is achieved by a cascade of analogue switches, each of which is connected, through a programming matrix, to one of the keys on the keypad. Suppose line A is connected to key 2, line B to key 9, and line C to key 5. If key 2 is now pressed, ES1 closes and stays closed because of the current delivered to it through R7. If key 9 is then pressed, ES2 closes and remains closed (because ES1 is already closed). Now all that is needed is to press key 5, whereupon ES3 closes thereby actuating the opto-coupler, whose transistor then conducts.

The keys not used in the ABC code must all be connected to the D line. When one of these keys is pressed, in error or in ignorance, line D sets ES4 to an active high logic level (which it keeps because of R6) and T1 conducts and thus disables the circuit completely; in fact, even if ES1 is again actuated, by the relevant key, it will not auto-hold as long as T1 is conducting. To start again, push button S1 must first be pressed, thus opening ES4 and cutting off T1. It is also useful to be able to reset the lock externally and this is achieved by T2, which is connected parallel to the reset circuit and controlled by the # key. Key * could be

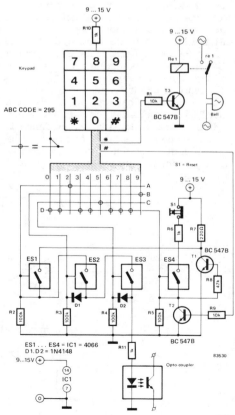

used as an ordinary bell push, actuating relay Re through transistor T3 and thereby driving the bell transformer.

One further word about the operation of the lock: consider again our combination of 295, and assume that the first key pressed was not 2 but 9, which is not wrong, merely misplaced. The B-9 connection causes ES2 to close but it cannot remain closed when key 9 is released because ES1 is open.

An opto-coupler is used here in preference to other alternatives which might be chosen in other applications, and proves to be simple, inexpensive and effective in this circuit.

232   simple PA system

A very nice power amplifier delivering 10 W into 2 Ω (two 4 Ω loudspeakers in parallel) can be built from the TDA2003 IC and a few passive components.

The circuit diagram shows that a fully operational circuit need not be big and complicated. The signal input is via capacitor C1 to pin 1 of the IC. There is a feedback loop between pin 4 (the output) and pin 2 (the feedback input). The gain factor is defined by the relation between resistors R1 and R2; in this case, the amplification is about 100 times. Resistor R4 and capacitor C7 ensure that the amplifier remains stable at higher frequencies.

The loudspeaker is connected to the output via electrolytic capacitor C4. Network R3/C5 acts as a part of the output load and compensates for the rising impedance of the loudspeaker at high frequency. The power supply is connected to pins 3 and 5 and maximum supply voltage is 18 V.

Higher supply voltages will not necessarily damage the IC but will mean that the output d.c. voltage drops to such a level that the IC is no longer driven. The IC also includes short-circuit, overload, and thermal protection.

To maintain stability, it is recommended that separate wires are used to connect the earth connection of the printed circuit board and that of the loudspeaker independently to the main earthing point on the chassis.

After construction is completed, the current consumption of the circuit should be checked. It should be about 50 mA, and the value of the d.c. voltage at the output should be about half the value of the supply voltage. The output power is 10 W into 2 Ω, 6 W into 4 Ω, and 3 W into 8 Ω.

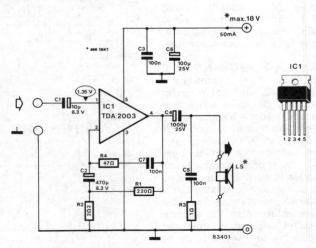

83401

233 electronic switch for audio signals

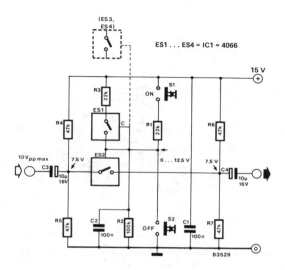

ES1 . . . ES4 = IC1 = 4066

83529

The complexity of the problems associated with switching audio signals is proportional to the sophistication of the playback system. In this field all roads lead to the mixing desk where the bundles of cables start or finish. The same signal must be sent, for example, to the control amplifier (monitor), the tone correction stages, the special effects stages, an output amplifier, a tape recorder. . .and so on. In other words there are cables everywhere! So either the cables must frequently be moved from one place to another or some form of switching mechanism is needed. Mixing desks often have mechanical switches for this but these are far from ideal simply because they are not of high enough quality.

Electronic switches, on the other hand, provide a very satisfactory solution and are devoid of clicks and other such undesirables.

The circuit consists basically of two integrated circuit analogue switches controlled by two push buttons. In the rest state, the voltage at point C (the control input of switch ES1) is low. When the on button is pushed, the voltage rises and reaches the switching threshold of ES1, which then closes. When the push button is released, the control input of ES1 remains at almost the same voltage as before because, in closing, the switch completes the circuit which ties its control input to +15 V via R3. The switch is then latched and stays closed. Pressing the off button causes the control voltage to decrease and ES1 to open. The circuit is then at rest again.

The output of ES1 controls switch ES2, through which the signal to be switched passes, so switching is simply a matter of pressing the right button.

The control signal provided by ES1 could be used to simultaneously open or close several analogue switches, either carrying the same signal in different directions, or different signals in the same direction. Two of these parallel switches (ES3 and ES4) are shown dotted.

This simple circuit makes no pretentions to being perfect; the problems posed by switching a sinusoidal audio signal during its cycle (rather than when it crosses zero) are not soluble by such a simple circuit but, by the same token, it is far better than what is often hidden under the shiny surface of many a hi-fi mixing desk!

234 zero-crossing detector

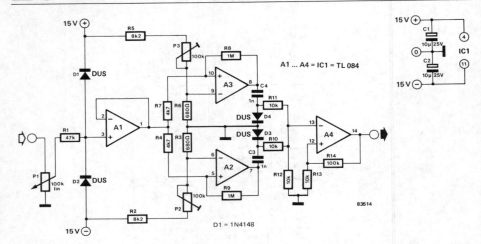

A1 ... A4 = IC1 = TL 084

D1 = 1N4148

There is nothing very special about a zero-crossing detector. However, this particular circuit has an unusual feature. A certain signal level must be present at the input of the circuit before the signal at the detector results in an output signal. This therefore makes it possible for the circuit to ignore interfering signals at the input (such as noise and low-amplitude mains pickup).

Potentiometer P1 is used to set the sensitivity of the detector. The trigger threshold of the circuit is 300 mV$_{pp}$ when P1 is fully rotated. Opamp A1 is connected as a voltage follower. The signal is then applied to two Schmitt triggers whose hysteresis is determined by the ratios R9:R4 and R8:R7. Opamp A2 detects the zero-crossing of the

rising input voltage. Preset potentiometer P2 is adjusted so that the output of A2 switches from logic 0 (—15 V) to logic 1 (+15 V) precisely at the instant of zero-crossing of the rising input signal. Opamp A3 has a different response. At the zero-crossing of the negative-going signal, the output switches from logic 1 (+15 V) to logic 0 (—15 V). The signals obtained in this way trigger the Schmitt trigger (A4) which operates as a storage bistable. The result is an output signal which is synchronized with the zero-crossing of the input signal, without being affected by low-amplitude interfering signals.

O.M. Kellogg

235 high and low tester

The present circuit offers something new: a seven-segment display that shows H or L and a small loudspeaker that emits a corresponding tone. And all that at very reasonable cost.

When the supply is switched on, the decimal point of the display lights and indicates that the unit is ready for use. If this is not the case, or an undefined signal is applied to the input, the display, apart from

the decimal point, remains dark and the loudspeaker remains silent. If the input signal is logic 0, the display shows L and the loudspeaker emits a low note. When the input signal is logic 1, the display shows H and the loudspeaker emits a note which is an octave higher than the low tone.

Operation of the circuit can be seen from the circuit diagram in figure 1 and the truth table in figure 2.

250

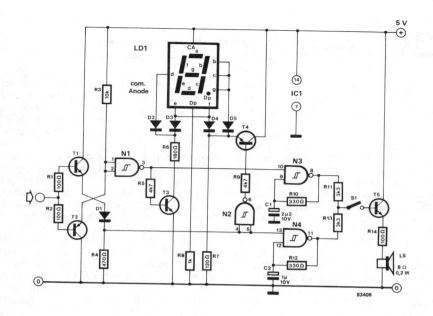

Input & Display	U_{in} (N1)	U_{in} (N2)	N1 out	N2 out
non-defined	$> U_t$	$< U_t$	0	1
H	$> U_t$	$> U_t$	0	0
L	$< U_t$	$< U_t$	1	1

U_t = trigger-level

When the input signal is 1, transistor T1 conducts taking the input of gate N2 above the trigger threshold and the trigger output goes to logic 0. Transistor T2 (PNP!) is cut off, the input of gate N1 is also above the trigger threshold and this trigger output is therefore also logic 0. Both switching transistors T3 and T4 are off and a current flows through the corresponding segments (b, c, e, f, g), diodes D4 and D5 and R7.
When the input signal is logic 0, T1 is cut off and T2 conducts. The voltages at the inputs of gates N1 and N2 are below the trigger threshold and both outputs are logic 1, switching on transistors T3 and T4; the emitter voltage of T4 rises and cuts off diodes D4 and D5. This causes a current to flow through segments d, e, and f, diodes D2 and D3, resistor R6 and transistor T3.

With non-defined inputs (between 0.8...2.15 V) and an open circuit input, both input transistors are cut off. The output of N1 is then logic 0 and that of N2 is logic 1: no current can therefore flow through any of the segments.
As regards the drive for the two oscillators, during low inputs N3 is driven by the output of N1 and during high inputs N4 is driven direct by T1. If required, the loudspeaker can be switched on by S1. The switch can, of course, be omitted if the audio tone is always required. If you have an ear for music, R10 and R12 may be replaced by a 220 Ω resistor and a 250 Ω preset potentiometer so that the tone can be adjusted to your particular liking.

R. Storn

251

236   code-lock with door opener

Anyone who has ever locked him or herself out with the front door key inside will appreciate the electronic door-opener described here. If you can memorize four digits in a row and do not mind an investment in an electric door-opener and a small electronic circuit, you will never need a front door key again. The door can be opened by pressing the keys on a keyboard fitted beside the frontdoor. If you don't know the four-digit code, you cannot open the door. Of course, this doorlock cannot prevent the door being broken open, just as a normal lock cannot do so.
The electronics for this codelock is based on an integrated circuit specially manufactured for this purpose: the LS 7220.
The keyboard has ten keys for the digits 0...9, four of which are used to key in the code; they are connected to pins 3...6 of the IC. The remaining keys are connected to reset input pin 2. The circuit diagram shows the connections for code number

4179 (pins 3...6 determine the sequence of the code: in the sample, pin 3 is connected to key 4, pin 4 to key 1, and so on). When the correct code is keyed in, output pin 13 of the IC connects the positive supply line to T1 and T2. These transistors then conduct and operate the door-opener. Resistor R2 and capacitor C3 determine the time during which the door-opener remains active. If the door is not opened during that time, the code must be keyed in afresh. If required, this time can be lengthened by giving C3 a higher value.
The supply voltage for the circuit and door-opener can be provided by a commercial 8 V bell transformer in conjuction with a simple smoothing and stabilizing circuit as shown in figure 2. The electrical door-openers that are commercially available are normally operated by the AC output of a bell transformer, but will, of course, work perfectly well from the DC voltage provided by the supply shown.

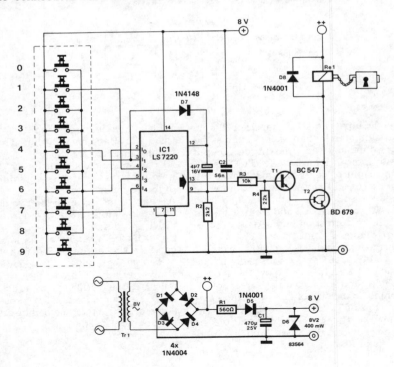

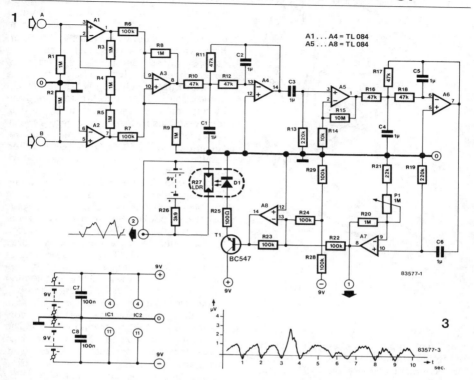

That trees and plants have a soul has been known to plant lovers and gardeners for a long time. For all those who have never given this a thought and who have never done more to plants than water them, here is a circuit which will make it possible to get into closer contact with those oft-forgotten members of this or her 'family'. Many will dismiss this experiment as belonging to the realms of parapsychology, but it has already been possible to measure a non-periodic signal between 1 and 40 Hz with an amplitude which varied between 0 and a few microvolts. These signals can without any doubt be traced back to plant activities.

The oscilloscope traces are often not directly connected with manipulation of plants. Particularly at the beginning of a series of experiments, a violent reaction could be observed in the plant before the traces shown in figure 3 could be made.

Whatever caused the traces, it is certain that in order to understand plant behaviour and make further measurements, an amplifier with a high degree of amplification and noise suppression is necessary.

The input circuits (see figure 1) are therefore high-input-impedance amplifiers, A1 and A2; the input impedance is 1 M (R1 and R2). The signal is subsequently applied to a differential amplifier, A3, which has an amplification factor of about 10. The amplification of the input amplifiers has therefore been kept low, so that A3 can not be driven to saturation. Mains hum and high frequencies are filtered from the output of A3 and this is done by active low-pass filter A4, the cut-off frequency of which is about 50 Hz. A passive high-pass filter (C3, R13) then removes any DC components which have not been filtered by A4; the cut-off frequency of this filter is about 1 Hz. Subsequently, the signal is fed to a

253

83577-2

non-inverting amplifier, A5, of which the amplification factor is about 1000. Because of the high input impedance of A5, it does not have much effect on the high-pass filter. As each amplifier stage reintroduces noise and mains hum onto the signal, these must again be filtered in a low-pass and a high-pass filter. It would be possible, with a suitable oscilloscope, to make measurements across R19, were it not for the fact that we want to connect a recorder or VCO or something similar and the signal will therefore have to undergo further amplification. This is effected by A7. The total amplification of the circuit can be adjusted by potentiometer P1 between 85 dB and 120 dB. At maximum amplification, the '1 V per scale division' range of the oscilloscope will measure 1 microvolt.

To prevent mains interference in this highly sensitive amplifier, the supply is provided by two batteries. And to really be able to make full use of the sensitivity, mains interference should also be filtered from the oscilloscope or recorder or VCO mains supply. This could be done with an optocoupler but an LED (light-emitting diode)

254

and LDR (light-dependent resistor) in a light-proof box will do nicely. The absorption circuit of the LDR could be supplied from a mains power unit, but here again a battery would be preferable to prevent interference finding its way to the amplifier. If you want to obtain measurements which can be used as proof, a series of measurements will have to be made over a period of time (including when you're not home). This cannot, unfortunately, be done by just an oscilloscope, but by a data recorder. This is, however, a very expensive piece of equipment and can be substituted by a VCO (voltage-controlled oscillator) of which the signals are recorded on tape.

And now for the method of measurement. The first that's needed is a signal detector and the simplest is a set of gold-plated pins from an IC socket. Better are small sensor plates which have been lightly covered with conductive paste before they are attached to the plant. Three pins or sensors are required: the central one must be connected to the screen of the connecting cable; the other two go to inputs A and B. It is important that both these conductors are separately screened, the screen being connected to earth at the amplifier end. The detectors should be attached to branch or plant stem not more than 2...3 cm from one another (figure 2). The recording equipment must be earthed at the mains input. It is also advisable to build the amplifier into the smallest possible case; an earthed metal one is not absolutely necessary, but it cannot do any harm.

With properly functioning equipment, the output signal should resemble the traces shown in figure 3: these give the required information as to the voltage variations occurring in plants and trees. The resolution in case of a data recorder should, of course, be such that a readable trace is produced: paper feed speeds of 0.5...1 cm per second are ideal, but to keep paper costs down, it is advisable to use lower speeds. Finally, we would be most interested in hearing from readers about their researches into plant physiology.

238 common base mixer

Mixing of audio signals is normally effected by a so-called virtual-earth mixer, in which the various input signals are applied to the virtual earth, that is, the inverting input of an opamp, via a series of resistors. The mixer described here uses a different approach.

The circuit is designed on the common base principle in which the input voltages are transformed into alternating currents which, when added together, constitute the collector a.c. component. The emitter of a common base configuration is low impedance and acts as virtual earth, so that crosstalk between the various input signals is virtually impossible. The output signal is taken from the collector of T1. The amplification of the circuit is equal to $R6 \div R_i$ where R_i is the input resistance (= one of the resistors R1...R5). A current source, consisting of T2 and T3, has been provided in the emitter circuit of T1. This current source is high impedance for alternating

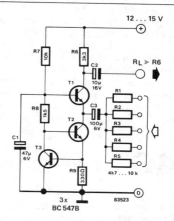

voltages so that it does not affect the signals at the emitter of T1. The base voltage of T1 is set by resistors R7 and R8. Capacitor C1 ensures that the base of T1 is decoupled effectively. The number of inputs can be extended as required.

239 glitch suppressor

A glitch is a pulse of very short duration usually caused by the differences in path times of various signals in a digital circuit. They can be the very devil to find (if at all) and create havoc in complex digital circuits. The circuit described here was designed to suppress glitches in the output

signal of a word recognizer, where it is essential that the logic analyser is not triggered by the spurious signals.

The circuit consists of a monostable multivibrator (MMV) and six inverters. If pin B of the MMV is connected to +5 V (wire bridge in position 2), glitches will not

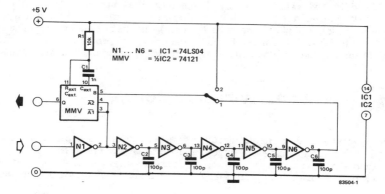

be detected. A signal at the input of N1 is inverted and applied to inputs $\overline{A1}$ and $\overline{A2}$ of the MMV. The multivibrator is triggered by the leading edge of the input signal and emits a pulse of about 7 μs (duration determined by the values of R1 and C1).

With the wire bridge in position 1 as shown, the circuit will suppress glitches of 80 ns and shorter, a time based on the delay line in inverters N1...N6. The output of N6, and consequently the input at pin B of the MMV, is logic 0. As long as this situation persists, the MMV will not react to signals at its inputs $\overline{A1}$ and $\overline{A2}$. If a pulse appears at the input of the circuit, it will arrive at inputs $\overline{A1}$ and $\overline{A2}$ after about 10 ns (that is, the delay of N1).

After about 90 ns the pulse will arrive at the output of N6, so that this output, and therefore input B, becomes logic 1 and inputs $\overline{A1}$ and $\overline{A2}$ are 'open'. If the input pulse is shorter than about 80 ns, it is no longer available at $\overline{A1}$ and $\overline{A2}$ by the time the delayed pulse arrives at input B. In this way the MMV will only pass signals which are longer than 80 ns.

240   mini compressor

This is a circuit for a feed-forward dynamic compressor which, unlike a feedback system, does not use the output signal as a feedback into the control system. So, rather than use a control loop, this circuit uses parallel control.

The diagram shows most of a feed-forward set-up. The design criteria were for a simple dynamic compressor using only one active component (T1). The audio signal received at the input normally travels via C1, R1, D1, C2, and R2 to the output. However, a part of the audio signal also feeds the detector of D3/D4 and sets up a control voltage for T1. The higher the value of the input audio signal, the more T1 conducts and the more current will flow from its emitter through diode D1. This diode in turn conducts more and more and shorts to ground an ever greater amount of the audio signal received via R1. That, basically, is how the circuit works.

Diodes D3 and D4 are forward biased by T2 and R4 so that the detector can work with even very small input signals. The decay time of the control system is defined by the values of C4 and R5. There is no timing con-

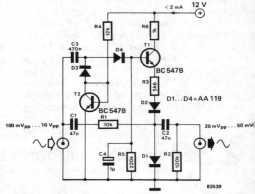

trol (unlike a similar feedback system), as such a timing signal can easily cause over-driving.

Because of its very simplicity, this compressor is most effective. With an input varying by about 50 dB the output stays constant to within ± 3 dB. The asymmetric set-up does not actively keep distortion down to a particular level (it is a few percent), but that does not matter in most applications. One obvious use of this compressor is in an amateur radio transmitter.

241   mains wiring tester

Here we have yet another simple circuit, consisting of two neon lamps (with built-in series resistors) a push-button, and an optional 100 k resistor. Can this circuit really be considered as a piece of 'test equipment'? Of course it can. In fact, simple ideas are the ones that are used over and over again until they become indispens-

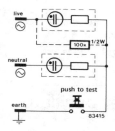

checked by simply pressing a button. When the circuit is connected to the mains, both neons will light dimly. If the push button is now pressed, one lamp will go out completely and the other will light properly. This in fact tells us three things: there is a phase present, the live line is the one with the lit neon, and all three lines (live, neutral, and earth) are working.

In correctly wired domestic systems, the live and neutral connections are known in advance. In this case a further 100 k resistor can be added as shown. The lower neon should then light initially; operating the push button should cause the upper neon to light. Any other result indicates a fault!

A. Scragg

able. Consider how simple a phase tester is! However, those devices can only show whether the live mains connection is good or not, which leaves the user guessing about the neutral and earth lines. . .But not any more! The mains wiring tester shown here will enable all three lines to be

---

242 optical voltage indicator

This circuit indicates, by a flashing LED (light-emitting diode), when a voltage being monitored or measured falls below a predetermined value. The only active component is an opamp which functions as comparator and as oscillator.

The voltage to be monitored is applied to terminal A and the reference voltage to terminal B. As long as the voltage at the non-inverting input of the opamp is larger than that at the inverting input, the output of the opamp is 12 V and the LED does not light. If the voltage at terminal A, and therefore U^+, drops below the reference voltage, U^-, the opamp inverts and the LED lights. A feedback loop, R2/R1, causes U^+ to be reduced somewhat. Capacitor C1 charges via R3 and the output of the opamp. Diode D1 cuts off, so that the voltage at terminal B no longer affects U^-. When U^- has dropped till it is just below the level of U^+, the opamp changes state again, the LED' extinguishes and, because of feedback via R2, U^+ is increased a little. C1 discharges until U^- becomes just larger than U^+; the output of the opamp becomes logic 0 and the LED lights again. In this way the LED will flash on and off as long as the voltage to be monitored or measured lies below a predetermined value.

The circuit can be used, for instance, as a coolant temperature indicator in a car: if

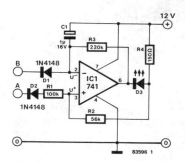

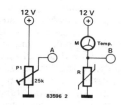

the temperature becomes too high, the LED will start to flash. For this purpose, the network shown in figure 2 is connected to the circuit in figure 1. The temperature indicator (sometimes thermometer) and temperature sensor are already fitted in the car. Calibration is carried out as follows. Switch on the car electrics (but not the

257

engine) at the ignition switch. Connect across the temperature sensor a resistor with a value which causes the needle to just get into the red sector of the meter. Then adjust P1 so that the LED just starts to flash.

Do not forget to remove the resistor from across the temperature sensor once calibration is completed.

Siemens applications

243 programmable crystal oscillator

Programmable crystal oscillators (PXOs) are not new. They normally consist of a discrete stabilized oscillator, quartz crystal, and one or more dividers which are controlled by logic levels. What is new about the range of PXOs from Statek Corporation, one of the largest oscillator manufacturers in the USA, is that the oscillator, dividers, and selector circuits are constructed as a CMOS-IC which is housed together with the quartz crystal in a standard 16-pin DIL package. Statek has already brought eight of these PXO units onto the market: the only difference between them is the fundamental quartz frequency. This frequency is indicated by the number in the type-coding on the unit: for instance, in a PXO-600 it is 600 kHz. Standard crystal frequencies at this moment are: 192 kHz, 327.68 kHz, 600 kHz, 768 kHz, 983 kHz, 1 MHz, 1.3 MHz, 1.6 MHz, and 1.97 MHz. Statek can meet individual customer's requirements for non-standard frequencies.
The internal construction and pinout are

shown in figure 1. The direct output of the internal oscillator (OSC) is amplified and then available at pin 11 (F_{out}). The oscillator is also connected to the selection logic (SEL) which is controlled from pin 13 (CSEL). When this pin is logic high (TTL-level), the selector connects an external clock (EXC-pin 12) instead of the internal oscillator to the first divider.
The divide ratios of the two dividers are determined by three inputs each (PROG 1...3 and 4...6 respectively): table 1 correlates the inputs and the ratios. A little arithmetic will show that 57 different frequencies are available from a single crystal.

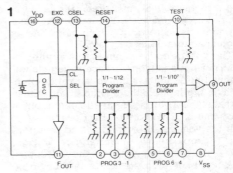

84015-1

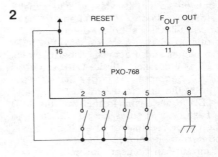

84015-2

258

Table 1

Prog 1	Prog 2	Prog 3	Divide ratio	Prog 4	Prog 5	Prog 6	Divide ratio
0	0	0	1/1	0	0	0	1/1
0	0	1	1/10	0	0	1	1/10
0	1	0	1/2	0	1	0	$1/10^2$
0	1	1	1/3	0	1	1	$1/10^3$
1	0	0	1/4	1	0	0	$1/10^4$
1	0	1	1/5	1	0	1	$1/10^5$
1	1	0	1/6	1	1	0	$1/10^6$
1	1	1	1/12	1	1	1	$1/10^7$

Table 1. The divide ratios of the two dividers can be set independent of one another — note that the program numbers do NOT coincide with the pin numbers!

Table 2

Program pin levels			P4	0	0	0	0
			P5	0	0	1	1
			P6	0	1	0	1
P1	P2	P3					
0	0	0		768k	76.8k	7.68k	768
0	0	1		76.8k	7.68k	768	76.8
0	1	0		384k	38.4k	3.84k	384
0	1	1		256k*	25.6k	2.56k	256
1	0	0		192k	19.2k	1.92k	192
1	0	1		153.6k**	15.36k	1.536k	153.6
1	1	0		128k	12.8k	1.28k	128
1	1	1		64k	6.4k	640	64

Program pin levels			P4	1	1	1	1
			P5	0	0	1	1
			P6	0	1	0	1
P1	P2	P3					
0	0	0		76.8	7.68	0.768	0.0768
0	0	1		7.68	0.687	0.0768	0.00768
0	1	0		38.4	3.84	0.384	0.0384
0	1	1		25.6	2.56	0.256	0.0256
1	0	0		19.2	1.92	0.192	0.0192
1	0	1		15.36	1.536	0.1536	0.01536
1	1	0		12.8	1.28	0.128	0.0128
1	1	1		6.4	0.64	0.064	0.0064

*33% duty factor   **40% duty factor

Table 2. Output frequencies of the PXO-768 model for various logic levels at the PROGram pins (Unit shown: Hz.)

Table 3

Output freq. kHz	19.2	38.4	76.8	153.6	768
Baud rate	1200	2400	4800	9600	48000
Pin 2	0	0	1	1	0
Pin 3	0	1	0	0	0
Pin 4	1	0	0	1	0
Pin 5	1	1	0	0	0

Table 3. Some baud rates — in baud second — available from the generator in figure 2.

The output of the second divider is amplified and then available at pin 9 (OUT). A logic 0 at the RESET input (pin 14) sets the dividers to 1/1 and the OUTput (pin 9) to logic low.

A somewhat unfortunate designation has been given to pin 10: TEST. When this pin is logic high, the output frequency is multiplied by 1000, provided the overall divide ratio is not lower than 1/1000. Internal pull-down resistors in the dividers, and a pull-up resistor in the reset circuit, ensure a non-ambiguous logic level, even if the relevant pins are not connected. Pins 1 and 15 are not used.

Other important technical parameters are:
■ high calibration tolerance — standard ± 100 ppm
■ low ageing — maximum 10 ppm in first 12 months
■ high frequency stability — maximum drift ± 0.015% over the temperature range −10°C...+75°C (not including the calibration tolerance)
■ low current consumption (CMOS), yet fully TTL compatible

■ very short rise and decay times (in the PXO-600, for instance, typically 70 ns and 30 ns respectively)

A typical application is shown in figure 2 where a PXO-768 is connected as a baud rate generator. Table 2 shows typical rates available from this unit. The baud rate is obtained by dividing the output frequency by 16: the extreme values of 0.0004 and 48000 baud/sec are, of course, hardly ever used. It is, unforunately, not possible to obtain all baud rates encountered in practice from each PXO unit: a rate of 75, for instance, cannot be derived from a PXO-768 (although it can from a PXO-600). The PXOs can also be used for a variety of other applications, such as a square-wave generator, a rectangular-wave generator with variable duty-cycle, or a monostable multivibrator.

Further information from:
I.Q.D. Limited
29 Market Street
Crewkerne
Somerset
TA18 7JU
Telephone: (0460) 74433

244 microprocessor aid

Faultfinding in microprocessor systems is an arduous and time-consuming task. It would be a great help if it were possible to display the information on the data and address bus of the processor. And that is exactly what the circuit described here does: the conversion of data and address into hexadecimal code onto six displays.

The displays are controlled by an IC which combines all the necessary functions: the 9368. This IC accepts a four-bit binary code, converts it into the corresponding hexadecimal number, and makes it visible on a seven-segment LED display. A latch memory is also provided and the LED display is controlled directly by the IC.

1

LD1 ... LD6 = 7760 (common cathode)

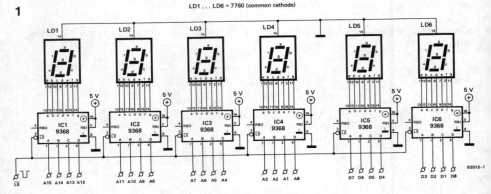

5 V
750 mA

C1 — 10μ 10V
C2 — 100n
C3 — 100n

Parts list

Capacitors:
C1 = 10 μ, 10 V
C2,C3 = 100 n

Semiconductors:
IC1...IC6 = 9368
LD1...LD6 = 7760 (CC) LED display

From figure 1 it will be seen that, apart from the six ICs and six displays, nothing further is required. The power requirement is 5 V at 750 mA.

The printed circuit board for the aid is shown in figure 2. After all components have been mounted, the circuit is connected to the microprocessor. This is made easier by the use of an additional 40-pin socket with wire-wrap pins as shown in figure 3. The circuit is then connected to the 40-pin socket by a suitable length of ribbon cable. The various connections are made so that the first four displays show the ad-

2

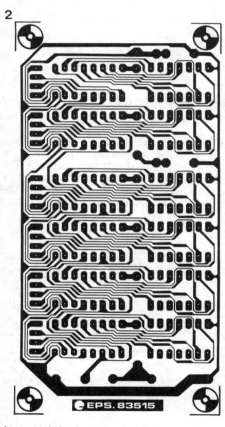

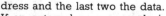

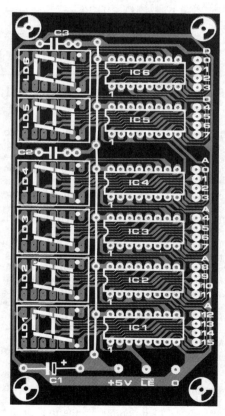

dress and the last two the data.

If an external power supply is used, the earth of the supply must be connected to the 0 V of the microprocessor board.

There are two methods of using the circuit. The first is single step mode in which case the LE (latch enable) must be taken to 0 V

and the display will read the data and address of each step. In the second method, the LE is controlled by the computer itself to enable a specific (and maybe momentary) data and address to be retained. The fact that it is not necessary for the computer to stop is an added advantage.

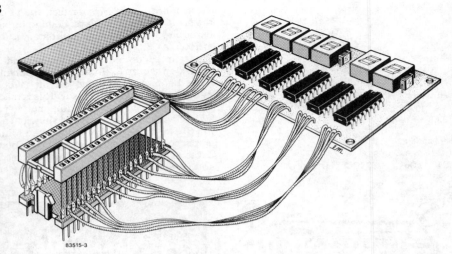

83515-3

245 stepped-voltage generator

This circuit converts an input signal into one that is composed of a number of discrete steps but which remains otherwise identical to the input signal. Because the steps are of equal height, the harmonic content of the output signal will be dependent upon the amplitude of the input signal. This characteristic is extremely useful in the making of electronic music.

The circuit uses quantized pulse-width modulation for the adding of the step-shaped input signal. Pulse-width modulation is obtained by comparing a triangular voltage with the analogue input signal by a comparator; the quantizing, that is, the adding of the steps, takes place by replacing the triangular voltage with a stepped voltage.

The stepped-voltage generator consists of three gates, N1...N3, and transistor T1. Gate N1 operates as an astable multivibrator that oscillates at a frequency depending on the value of C1 and R1. Transistor T1 functions as charger circuit: each time the output of N1 is logic 1, the transistor transfers the charge on C2 to capacitor C4. During the next half cycle C2 is recharged via D1. In this way the voltage across C4 increases in discrete steps, the height of the steps being determined by the ratio C2:C4.

When the voltage across C4 rises above a certain value, N2 switches transistor T2 on via gate N3 and discharges capacitor C4. When the capacitor is completely discharged, N2 switches off T2 and C4 continues to charge again in discrete steps.

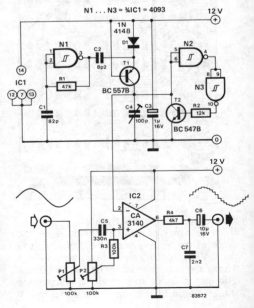

The stepped voltage is set to the inverting input of IC2 which is connected as a comparator. Low-pass filter R4/C7 in the output of IC2 converts the pulse-width modulated signal back to an analogue one. The d.c. voltage level at the non-inverting input is set by potentiometer P2 to half the magnitude of the stepped voltage. The setting of P1 is dependent upon the input signal which must be attenuated such that the maximum value at the slider of P1 is always smaller than the maximum value of the stepped voltage. The number of steps can be selected by varying the value of C4. It is possible to use a varactor in place of C4 with the varactor voltage being controlled by the music program or the input signal. Interesting and individual effects can be obtained in this way.

246 microprocessor stethoscope

It is often necessary to see exactly what logic activity is occurring on the address, data or, control buses of a microprocessor system. This is easily done by displaying it on an oscilloscope but not everybody can lay their hands on an oscilloscope at short notice. The stethoscope here enables a microprocessor system to be tested without the need for an oscilloscope. Of course, it is not intended as the be-all and end-all of test equipment, but then even a doctor's stethoscope has limitations. The actual circuit is fairly simple. The stethoscope probe is connected to the clock input of a divider. The frequency of the input signal is divided by a certain factor. This factor depends on what output of IC1 is selected with S1 and can be between 488.3 Hz/MHz (with S1 in position 1) and 15625 Hz/MHz (S1 in position 6). By changing the position of this switch we can ensure that there will always be an audible output equal to the divided input frequency.

For example: assume we want to trace a clock signal of 1 MHz to see if it is present at various test points. If S1 is in position 1 then a tone of about 488 Hz will be heard. The clock signal is an example of a periodic signal which is always present. If periodic signals are to be present on the three buses, the microprocessor must be working on a program(loop). This could be part of the monitor program, for example, a routine to test whether any key has been pressed. Special test programs can also be used and there are thousands of possibles, depending on what is to be tested. For instance, the 6502 programs shown below

CLC
LOOP BCC LOOP
(18 90 FE)
CLC
LOOP BCC LOOP
(18 90 FD)

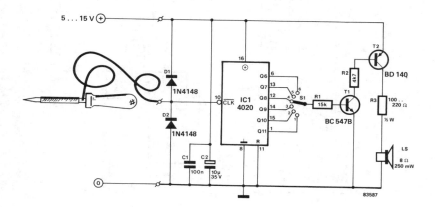

S1	divide factor	frequency
1	2^{11} (2048)	488.3 Hz/MHz
2	2^{10} (1024)	976.6 Hz/MHz
3	2^{9} (512)	1953.1 Hz/MHz
4	2^{8} (256)	2906.3 Hz/MHz
5	2^{7} (128)	7812.6 Hz/MHz
6	2^{6} (64)	15625.2 Hz/MHz

can be used to test data lines and address lines. Test programs can be placed direct (without modifications) in virtually any location of memory. Because the processor reads periodic opcodes and operands, the R/W signal will appear periodically. As there are a certain number of clock periods needed for a number of periodic instructions, we can expect this to be reflected in a number of outputs whose dividing factor is reduced.

This stethoscope is powered by the circuit it tests. The probe itself is not very expensive as it can be made from a small screwdriver.

247 signal purifier for SSB telegraphy receiver

It is a well-known fact that the readability of radio telegraphy signals is often affected by interference. The circuit proposed here will remove most of the interference. The (compressed) AF output of the receiver is fed to two tone decoders, IC1 and IC2, which are connected in parallel to increase the bandwidth. The pass bands of the tone decoders overlap to give a resulting pass band of 100 Hz centred around 800 Hz. The

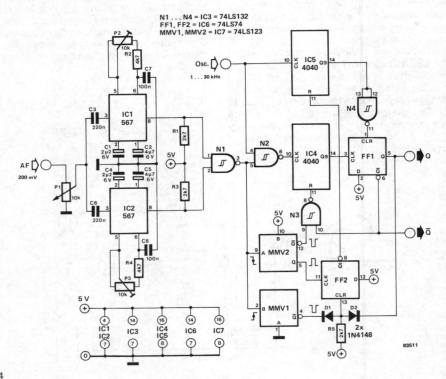

exact position of the pass bands can be set with potentiometers P2 and P3.

Ideally, the receiver used should have its optimum AF sensitivity at 800 Hz.

The output of N1 will be logic 1 if a signal between 750...850 Hz is applied to the inputs of the tone decoders. As long as this situation continues, N2 will pass the output of an external oscillator to the clock input of counter IC4. This counter moves one step for each pulse. After 256 clock pulses its output Q9 will become logic 1, causing bistable FF1 to change state: output Q of this bistable will then become 1. Consequently, output $\overline{Q}$ of FF1 becomes 0, gate N3 is blocked and the counter resets. The counter does not react to pulses at its input as long as the reset input is held at a logic 1. The fact that outputs Q9 of IC4 and Q of FF1 are logic 1 indicates that an AF signal was applied to the inputs of the two tone decoders 256 pulses before. As soon as the AF signal ceases, the output of N1 (0) triggers MMV2. Output Q of this monostable then becomes 1 and causes bistable FF2 to change state. The consequent logic 0 at output $\overline{Q}$ of FF2 then allows IC5 to start counting. After 256 clock pulses its Q9 output becomes 1, thus clearing FF1 via N4. The Q output of FF1 going to logic 0 indicates the end of the AF input signal plus a delay of 256 clock pulses.

When FF1 is cleared, its output $\overline{Q}$ becomes 1, so that NAND gate N3 opens counter IC4. The cycle can now start afresh.

The frequency of the external oscillator lies between 1 kHz and 30 kHz: because of the likelihood of morse signals being received, this frequency should be set so that the period of time taken by 256 clock pulses is shorter than the time taken by one morse dot.

If it happens that the output of N1 becomes logic 1 (due to an interference signal), it will become 0 again, to trigger monostable multivibrator MMV2, before IC4 has counted 256 pulses. This will clear MMV2 and via the output of N3 (logic 1) IC4 will stop counting. Bistable FF2 is not affected by the Q output of MMV2 becoming 1 because it is blocked by the Q output of FF1 via gate D1/D2. The blocking of IC4 thus causes the interference signal to be eliminated.

When counter IC4 causes FF1 to change state after 256 clock pulses, FF2 is no longer blocked. If MMV2 is triggered by a negative interference voltage, FF1 changes state and causes IC5 to start counting. This counter then clears FF1 after 256 clock pulses. However, before the count has reached 256, the negative interference signal has ceased, which causes MMV1 to be triggered. Output Q of MMV1 becomes 0, output $\overline{Q}$ of FF2 becomes 1 and this blocks counter IC5. And that eliminates the negative interference...

P. von Berg

248 simple sawtooth generator

Sawtooth generators are frequently required in most branches of electronics. Here is a new design for a circuit which makes use of components which can be found in almost every box of used components.

The basic version of the circuit as shown in figure 1 uses a 9 V PP3 battery as supply. The circuit itself can be readily understood: capacitor C1 is linearly charged by constant current source T1, R1, P1. Transistors T2 and T3 are used as substitute for a silicon controlled rectifier (SCR) and if you bear this in mind, the circuit is somewhat easier to understand.

The SCR is not, as usual, fired by a pulse. Instead, the gate is biased by voltage divider R3/D2 and once the anode to cathode voltage exceeds this bias, the SCR conducts. C1 then discharges rapidly through the SCR and current limiting resistor R2. When the voltage across the capacitor has dropped to about 1.4 V, the current through the SCR has become low enough for it to cut off. C1 again charges and the cycle repeats. The resulting sawtooth output voltage is shown in figure 1. The frequency of the output voltage can be adjusted over a range of about 10^2; with the values shown the frequency range is 5...500 Hz. The

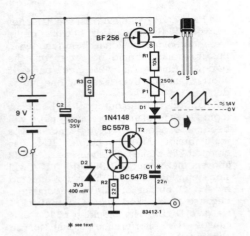

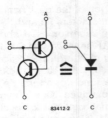

therefore be modified by changing this diode. It should, however, be borne in mind that the zener voltage must not be more than half the supply voltage to ensure correct operation of the generator.

If an exponential ramp is required instead of a linear one, T1 can simply be omitted and R1 connected direct to the supply voltage. C1 will then charge directly from the supply and automatically provide an exponential waveform.

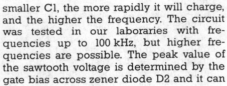

smaller C1, the more rapidly it will charge, and the higher the frequency. The circuit was tested in our laboraries with frequencies up to 100 kHz, but higher frequencies are possible. The peak value of the sawtooth voltage is determined by the gate bias across zener diode D2 and it can

R. Oppelt

249 faultfinder for ASCII keyboard

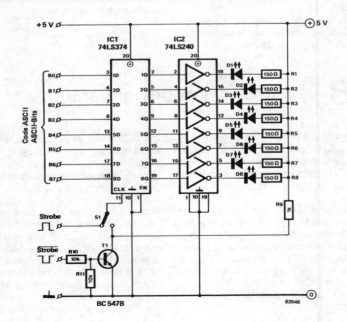

To be able to check the connections to an unknown ASCII keyboard, you want to know first of all where the supply voltage is connected. This can quite simply be done by removing the cover and tracing a pair of the wider tracks to the ICs. Next, the strobe connection has to be found. After the supply voltage has been connected, pressing one of the keys must produce a short (strobe) pulse at one of the output pins. If an oscilloscope is used to find this pulse, it will be seen at once whether it is positive or negative. Once these preliminary checks have been carried out, the faultfinder can be used. Connect the outputs of the keyboard to the faultfinder. Set the strobe input to positive or negative with switch S1. A positive strobe is connected directly to S1; a negative strobe is first inverted by transistor T1 as shown in the circuit.

When one of the keys is pressed, a strobe pulse is produced which triggers the eight-stage bistable IC1. The signals present on the data lines are stored by the bistables and the resulting outputs are applied to IC2, which comprises eight inverting driver stages. If one of the bistable outputs is logic 1, the output of the corresponding driver is 0. Consequently, the corresponding LED lights.

If the input to one of the driver stages is logic 0, its output is 1 and therefore virtually of the same level as that at the anode of the respective LED which thus remains off.

Now all that's needed is an ASCII table and the various connections are soon sorted out (see table 1).

A final important note: in the case of

keyboards which have not only a parallel but also a serial output, it is possible that on pressing one of the keys a series of pulses is produced of which the level lies at ± 12 V. If you are therefore not sure whether the keyboard under test has only a parallel output, check this before connecting the faultfinder to it.

Table 1

Display-Data	ASCII-Character	Display-Data	ASCII-Character
01000000	@	00100000	
01000001	A	00100001	!
01000010	B	00100010	"
01000011	C	00100011	#
01000100	D	00100100	$
01000101	E	00100101	%
01000110	F	00100110	&
01000111	G	00100111	'
01001000	H	00101000	(
01001001	I	00101001	)
01001010	J	00101010	*
01001011	K	00101011	+
01001100	L	00101100	,
01001101	M	00101101	—
01001110	N	00101110	.
01001111	O	00101111	/
01010000	P	00110000	0
01010001	Q	00110001	1
01010010	R	00110010	2
01010011	S	00110011	3
01010100	T	00110100	4
01010101	U	00110101	5
01010110	V	00110110	6
01010111	W	00110111	7
01011000	X	00111000	8
01011001	Y	00111001	9
01011010	Z	00111010	:
01011011	[	00111011	;
01011100	\	00111100	<
01011101	]	00111101	=
01011110	∧	00111110	>
01011111	—	00111111	?

↑ Control-Bit   ↑ Control-Bit

250 negative printhead supply

Thermal and metal foil printers are equipped with a printhead that usually requires a rather high driving voltage. For example, a metal foil printer needs a voltage of approximately 30 V. Some thermal printers require as high as 50 V! The maximum current demanded from printhead power supplies is vital but good stabilization is less important. The printhead of metal foil printers heats the surface of the foil paper, so that the metal parts of the foil evaporate, leaving print that is

wanted. The current required for this process is about 1 A.

Basically, the circuit is an ordinary stabilized power supply. Resistor R1 ensures that the circuit can start. The output voltage can be set with preset P2 via a feedback circuit, consisting of D1, P2, R7, and T2. The range mainly depends on the value of zener diode D1 and the level of the input voltage. In our case, the level can be set to between −22 V and −33 V. The complete control range can be shifted by choosing another

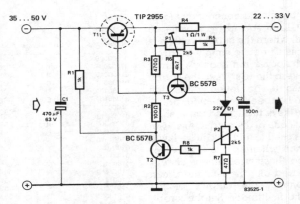

value for D1, say, 40 V. A rule of thumb is that the zener voltage must be identical to, or just below, the minimum output voltage. The circuitry around T3 takes care of the current limitation of the power supply. The maximum output current can be set between 1 and 2 A, with P1. Obviously, the circuit requires only minor changes to obtain a positive output voltage. The recipe for a positive output voltage is that T1 becomes 2N 3055, T2 and T3 both become BC 547B, and D1 and C1 must be turned upside down to maintain the correct polarity.

251   action flash

Very fast acoustic electronic-flash releases as used by professional photographers and in fast-motion film cameras for action filming are beyond the means of most amateur photographers. Simpler acoustic releases are normally not fast enough: a picture of a **burst** balloon is not very interesting; one of a **bursting** balloon is!

If you want to film events which happen in a split second and which make a sound at the same time, the circuit described is just right for you. To make possible the filming of events which are over before the sound reaches the camera, we have designed a simple light barrier through which, for instance, a drop of water can be made to fall (see below). The level at which the electronic flash fires is then preset by either P1 (acoustical) or P2 (light barrier). The output is connected to the timing input of the electronic flash unit. The power supply is no problem: as the current consumption of the circuit is only about 30 mA, a 9 V battery will last quite a time. First a few words

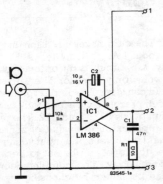

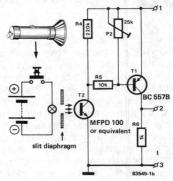

slit diaphragm

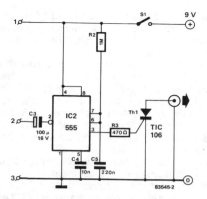

about the circuit. IC1, an audio amplifier IC, is used as microphone amplifier with a maximum gain of 200. IC2 is used as a monostable multivibrator (MMV). If a pulse caused by a noise input arrives at pin 2 of

IC2, it triggers the multivibrator. The output of the multivibrator (at pin 3) triggers silicon-controlled rectifier (SCR) Th1 which in turn triggers the SCR in the electronic flash unit. Where the light barrier is used, the part of the circuit to the left of terminals 1...3 in figure 1 is replaced by the light barrier circuit shown in figure 2.

And finally a few hints on the use of the circuit. When you are photographing (naturally, in a darkened room) a falling drop of water at the moment of impact, try out various colour filters. A (dim) coloured light source can produce interesting effects. Try also to let the drop fall onto a mirror; if the photograph comes out well, if should be one of the more remarkable ones in your collection. If unwanted reflections from the mirror spoil the photograph, try out various filters and also change the angle between the axis of the camera and the mirror.

252 capacitance meter

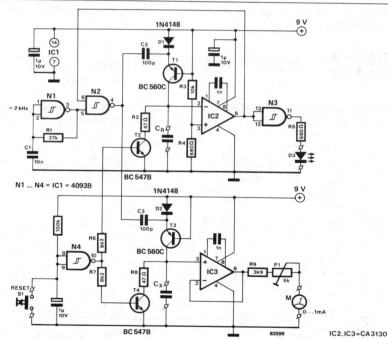

In this circuit, the value of a capacitor is determined by giving it the same charge as a reference capacitance and then comparing the voltages across them. This relies on the formula $C = Q/V$ where C is the capacitance in farads, Q is the charge in

269

coulombs and V is the voltage in volts. If, therefore, two capacitances have equal charges, their values can be calculated when the voltages across them are known. Two circuits ensure that reference capacitor C_r and the capacitor to be measured, C_x, are charged equally. The circuit for C_r consists of C2, D1, and T1 and that for C_x of C3, D2, and T3. Each time the output of gate N2 rises, the charges of capacitors C2 and C3 are transferred to C_r and C_x by transistors T1 and T3 respectively. When the output of N2 drops, C2 and C3 recharge via diodes D1 and D2. Gate N2 is controlled by astable multivibrator N1 which operates at a frequency of about 2 kHz: C_r and C_x are therefore charged at that frequency.

The voltage across C_r is compared by IC2 with a reference voltage derived from the power supply via R3/R4. When the voltage across C_r exceeds the reference voltage, comparator IC2 inverts which inhibits N2 and causes N3 to light D3. The charges on C_r and C_x are now equal and the meter indicates by how much the voltage across C_x differs from that across C_r. Buffer IC3 presents a very high load impedance to C_x. Pressing reset button S1 causes both C_r

and C_x to discharge via T2 and T4 respectively, after which the charging process restarts and the circuit is ready for the next measurement.

The meter is calibrated by using two identical 10 nF capacitors for C_r and C_x. Press the reset button and, when the LED lights, adjust preset P1 to give a meter reading of exactly one tenth of full scale deflection (fsd). That reading corresponds to $1 \times C_r$. If, therefore, $C_r = 100$ nF and $C_x = 470$ nF, the meter will read 0.47 of fsd.

To ensure a sufficient number of charging cycles during a measurement, C_r and C_x should not be smaller than 4.7 nF. To measure smaller values, capacitors C2 and C3 will have to be reduced. For instance, to enable a capacitor of 470 pF to be measured, C2 and C3 have to be 10...20 pF. The circuit is reasonably accurate for values of C_x up to 100 μF. Above that value the measurement will be affected by leakage currents. To measure capacitors of up to 100 μF, the values of C2 and C3 should be increased to 1 μF. Current consumption is minimal so that a 9 V battery is an adequate power supply.

253 solar tracking system

There are some hopes that the sun will become a main source of energy in the 21st century. By then, sources of oil will be almost exhausted and will only play a minor

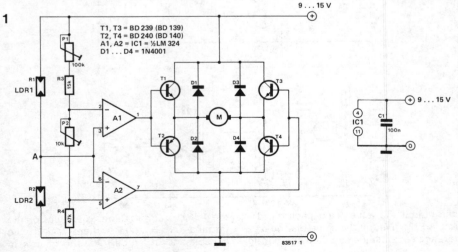

1

9...15 V

T1, T3 = BD 239 (BD 139)
T2, T4 = BD 240 (BD 140)
A1, A2 = IC1 = ½LM 324
D1...D4 = 1N4001

83517 1

part in the supplying of energy. The present interest in solar energy is therefore not surprising. Some work has already been done with solar cells and solar panels. However, these only operate with optimum performance when positioned exactly at right-angles to the sun. Unfortunately, this situation is not usual in our latitudes unless the solar panels are rotated with respect to the sun. The efficiency of a solar panel system can be improved if the panels track the sun, and remain as long as possible at the most favourable angle of incidence.

The circuitry required is relatively simple. It uses a window comparator which keeps the drive motor idle, as long as the two LDRs (light-dependent resistors) are subjected to the same illumination. Half the operating voltage is then applied to the non-inverting input of A1 and to the inverting input of A2. When the position of the sun changes, the illumination affecting LDRs R1 and R2 is different, if they are at an angle to each other as shown in figure 2. In this case, the input voltage for the window comparator deviates from half the supply voltage, so that the output of the comparator provides information to the motor for clockwise or anticlockwise rotation. Transistors T1...T4 in a bridge circuit cater for reversing of the motor. Diodes D1...D4 serve to suppress voltage peaks which can be produced when the motor is switched. Preset potentiometers P1 and P2 are used for alignment. They are adjusted so that the motor is idle when the LDRs are subjected to the same illumination. If less light reaches R2 than R1, the voltage at point A rises to more than half the supply voltage. The result is that the output of A1 goes high and transistors T1 and T4 conduct. The motor then runs. If the illumination of the LDRs is changed so that the voltage at point A drops to less than half the supply voltage, output A2 goes high and transistors T3 and T2 conduct. The motor then rotates in the opposite direction. Small

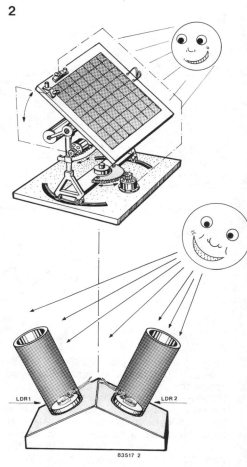

2

geared motors of the type used for models, with a suitable voltage and maximum operating current of 300 mA, are suitable for driving the solar panels. The use of this control circuit makes it possible to control the solar panel in one plane. Of course, to track the sun from sunrise to sundown, two control circuits will be required: one for horizontal and one for vertical tracking.

254 economic LED

The usual method of operating an LED (light-emitting diode) from a voltage which is higher than its forward voltage is well known. A limiting resistor is used to limit the LED current to its rated value. Calculating the value of the resistor is simple enough: supply voltage minus LED forward voltage divided by the maximum

1

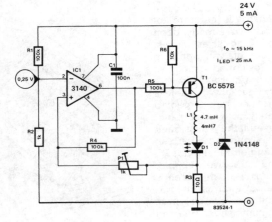

2

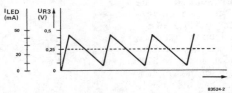

current rating of the LED:

$$R = [(U_b - U_L)/I_L] \; \Omega$$

Thus, the difference between supply voltage and forward voltage is dropped across the limiting resistor.

However, the disadvantage is that the power dissipated by the limiting resistor is fairly high if the supply voltage is relatively high. Thus, for example, with a supply voltage of 24 V and a current of 25 mA the power dissipated is greater than 0.5 W.

There is an alternative: the circuit shown here, which only requires 0.1 W. It is effectively a switched current source.

The current source is based on transistor T1 and the oscillator uses a 3140 operational amplifier. When transistor T1 conducts, a current flows via coil L1, D1, and resistor R3 to earth. The current curve is shown in figure 2. As soon as T1 turns on and a current flows, the current rises together with the voltage at R3 from zero. The voltage across R3 is applied to the non-inverting input of the operational amplifier. A reference voltage of approximately 0.25 V is applied via voltage divider R1/R2 to the inverting input. If the rising voltage at the non-inverting input reaches the level of the reference voltage, the output of the operational amplifier goes high. Transistor T1

272

turns off and the current through the LED flows via diode D2. As shown in figure 2, the current drops; the voltage at R3 therefore drops also. Once the current and voltage are sufficiently low, the operational amplifier goes low again and the transistor turns on. This operation is repeated periodically.

The switching point is adjusted with preset potentiometer P1. This governs the changeover voltage at pin 3 of the operational amplifier which, in turn, governs the maximum LED current. It should not exceed 50 mA.

The frequency of the oscillator (which is also the switching frequency for the transistor) is determined by coil L1 and by the switching hysteresis adjusted with P1. With the specified value of 4.7 mH the switching frequency is about 15 kHz with a period of approximately 65 μs. Two other switching frequencies for different inductances are given in the following table:

L	T	f
2.2 mH	35 μs	30 kHz
10 mH	150 μs	6 kHz

P1 should be adjusted to obtain the lowest frequency at which the circuit still starts to oscillate.

255 heat sink thermometer

The thermometer does not only display the temperature of the heat sink on two displays, but it also provides a switched output which, for instance, can be used to switch on a fan if the temperature rises above a pre-determined value.

The circuit consists of four parts: a reference voltage source, IC1; the sensor, IC4; the display section, IC2 and IC3; and the switch section, IC5. IC1, a 723, provides a stable supply voltage for the sensor and switch section. This voltage is about 8 V. The temperature sensor provides a temperature dependent voltage of 10 mV/K. At 0 °C, for instance, the voltage across IC4 amounts to 273 × 0.01 = 2.73 V (0 °C = 273 K). The display section is constructed around two ols faithfuls: ICs CA 3161E and CA 3162E. IC2 contains the A/D converter and the multiplexing circuit for the displays. IC3 is a BCD seven-segment decoder driver. Only two displays are used, so that the temperature can be read in degrees. IC2 measures the difference be-

tween the voltage provided by the sensor and the reference voltage set by pot P1. This is necessary to eliminate the '273 degrees below 0', that is, the voltage of 2.73 V. To make this possible, the read-out section and the measuring/switching section are powered separately. The earth of IC2 and IC3 is connected to the wiper of P1 which is at a potential of 2.73 V, while the input of 'meter' IC2 is connected to sensor IC4. In this way, the 2.73 V is compensated so that the voltage measured by IC2 rises at 10 mV per degree Celsius from 0 °C and the displays read degrees Celsius.

The last, but not least, part of the circuit is the comparator and switching output (IC5 and T3). The voltgae provided by the sensor is compared by IC5 with a voltage derived by R9 and R10 from the reference voltage of IC1. When the sensor voltages rises above this secondary reference voltage, the output of IC5 changes state and the transistor conducts. T3 can, for instance, by means of a relay switch on a fan to provide additional

1

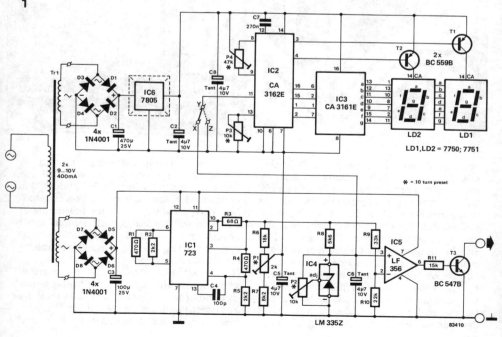

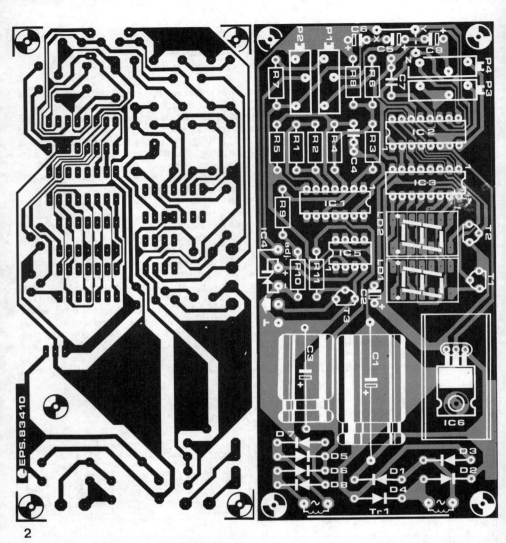

2

cooling of the power transistor. It is also possible to switch off the loudspeakers by means of the protection relays in the amplifier, so that the dissipation in the power transistors is greatly reduced, assuming, of course, that the loudspeaker drive was the cause of the overheating! With values of R9 and R10 as shown, the comparator changes state at about 80 °C. This depends also, of course, on the reference voltage provided by IC1 which has quite a tolerance. The temperature at which IC5 changes state can be altered by changing the value of R9. If the thermometer is built on the printed circuit board shown, nothing much can go wrong. It is important, however, that the earth of the supply for IC1, IC4, and IC5 is connected to the earth of the power amplifier. The power supply for the thermometer must be self-containes with a transformer having two isolated secondaries. The sensor must be fitted as close as possible to the power transistors on the heat sink.

If you want to built the circuit on a board of your own design, bear the following points in mind. The two power supplies must be kept isolated from one another. The only two connections between the meter and

Parts list

Resistors:
R1,R4 = 470 Ω
R2,R5 = 2k2
R3 = 68 Ω
R6 = 18 k
R7 = 8k2
R8 = 5k6
R9 = 33 k
R10 = 22 k
R11 = 15 k
P1 = 2 k, 10 turn preset
P2,P3 = 10 k, 10 turn preset
P4 = 50 k, 10 turn preset

Capacitors:
C1 = 470 μ/25 V
C2,C5,C6,C8 = 4μ7/10 V tantalum
C3 = 100 μ/25 V
C4 = 100 p
C7 = 270 n

Semiconductors:
D1...D8 = 1N4001
LD1,LD2 = 7750, 7751 (CA)
T1,T2 = BC 559B
T3 = BC 547B
IC1 = 723
IC2 = CA 3162E
IC3 = CA 3161E
IC4 = LM 335Z
IC5 = LF 356
IC6 = 7805

Miscellaneous:
Tr1 = mains transformer 2 × 9 V/0.5 A (isolated secondaries), heat sink for IC6

the measuring section are clearly indicated on the circuit diagram. IC2 and IC3 have a separate supply line from the output of the 5 V regulator, while the emitters of T1 and T2 must have a separate supply line from the output of IC6. IC3 must have its own 0 V line from the regulator. These precautions are necessary to prevent IC2 being affected by interference caused by high peak currents occurring during the multiplexing of the two displays.

An accurate, preferably digital, meter is required for adjustment of the thermometer. First, link Y and Z together and adjust pot P4 to obtain a reading of 00 on the displays. Then, remove the link and apply a d.c. voltage of about 0.9 V to Y. Next, adjust P3 to obtain a display of the same value as that at Y (measured with the accurate meter!). Bear in mind that the last digit is not displayed! For instance, if the voltage at Y is 883 mV, the display will read 88. Then link Y and X together. Measure the voltage across C5: if necessary, this should be adjusted to 2.73 V with pot P1.

As regards the temperature sensor, if you are happy with an accuracy of about 3 °C, pot P2 can be omitted. If you want a more precise thermometer, the sensor should be immersed in melting ice and P2 adjusted to give a display of 00. It is also possible to immerse the sensor in water at about 37 °C, and measure the temperature of the water with a clinical thermometer. P2 is then adjusted to give a display equal to the reading of the clinical thermometer.

256   drill speed controller

This simple circuit enables drill speed to be controlled irrespective of the load on the drill. The design makes use of the fact that as the load increases the back EMF of the drill falls and the current increases.

It is clear, looking at the circuit diagram, that this circuit is not all complicated, and the same is true of its operation. During the positive half cycles of the mains, C2 is charged through R1 and D1, until the voltage across this capacitor is equal to the zener voltage of the circuit at T1. The circuit based on T1 is an adjustable zener in which the zener voltage is determined by

the setting of P1. In fact, the voltage between collector and emitter is dependent on the ratio between resistors R3 and R2 + P1. The voltage drop across R3 is always equal to the base-emitter voltage of T1 (0.6 V) so that the zener voltage is [0.6 (P1 + R2 + R3)/R3] V. The motor is not connected in the usual place at the beginning of the circuit, but immediately after silicon-controlled rectifier (SCR) Th1. The firing time of the SCR is thus defined by the difference between the zener voltage and the back EMF of the motor. If the motor becomes more heavily loaded, the SCR will fire sooner.

Because an SCR is used, the circuit can only control 180° of the supply cycle; so with this circuit is not possible to vary the drill speed from 0 to 100%, but such a controller is usually only used in low speed applications. A disadvantage of this circuit is that the motor stutters a bit when it is not under any load but this effect disappears when there is a load on the drill.

Inductor L1 and capacitor C1 are used to filter out high frequency effects caused by phase-chopping. The SCR must be mounted on a heat sink to ensure effective colling.

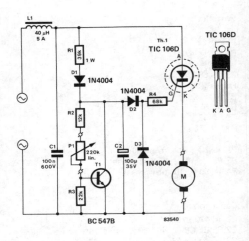

257 frequency comparator

In the circuit described here, a reference voltage level is derived from the comparison of the frequencies of two signals. Basically, the comparator has two input signals, one of which causes a capacitor to partly discharge while the other causes it to charge. The average charge on the capacitor (the desired reference level) will therefore be a function of the frequencies of the two inputs. The reference capacitor is C1 in the circuit diagram. In the quiescent state, the capacitor will be charged to half the supply voltage by the voltage divider consisting of R3 and R4.

One input signal is fed to the base of T1

which switches on and off at the frequency of the input. There then follows what is commonly referred to as a diode pump. The action of this aptly named circuit is to produce a series of pulses that correspond to the frequency of the input signal. The pulses are used to control transistor T2 which proceeds to switch on and off thereby discharging C1 in pulses, again at the frequency of input 1. Eventually, of course, C1 would be completely discharged but this is prevented by the activities of the other side of the circuit. Here, the input at T4 drives another diode pump, consisting of T3, C3, and D2, that is at-

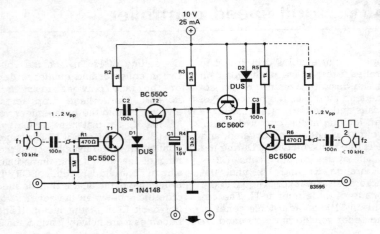

tempting to charge C1, again in short pulses that correspond to the frequency at input 2. The end result is that the charge level on C1 averages out to provide a reference level that is a comparison of the two input frequencies!
It will be obvious that if the two input frequencies are the same, the charge and discharge cycles of C1 will be identical and therefore the voltage level across C1 will be equal to half the supply voltage. If the frequency of input 1 is lower than that of input 2, the reference voltage will be lower than 5 V. If input 1 has a higher frequency the reference voltage will be higher than 5 V.

258 universal active filter

The full title of the Reticon R5620 is 'a second order switched capacitor filter network'. It is able to implement the five basic filter modes: low pass, bad pass, high pass, all pass, and notch. One further, very useful, function of this IC is that of a programmable sine-wave oscillator.
One could be forgiven for expecting to find all this in a large IC of the LSI variety. In fact, it is all contained in an 18-pin package thanks to one further feature of the R5620: all functions of the IC are fully programmable. This includes the filter centre frequency and the Q factor both of which are independently programmable by means of two five-bit binary codes. For example, to program the filter for a given Q factor, table 1 provides the binary code required — no potentiometers, no coils and, best of all, no calculations! The same is of course true for the filter centre frequency. As can be seen from the table, clock frequency to centre frequency ratio (f_c/f_o) can be varied over two octaves, from 50 to 200, in 32 logarithmically spaced increments. The Q factor range is also in 32 steps from 0.57 to 150 with approximately logarithmic spacing.
The filter mode selection is determined by routing the AF input to the tree inputs of the IC (see table 2) by means of switches. All this is illustrated in the circuit diagram of figure 1.
To make practical use of the R5620, we have featured the IC in a circuit for a universal filter suitable for use as test equipment in the workshop.
The AF input signal is fed to the appropriate inputs of IC1 by wafer switches S3A...S3D. The switches also ensure that unused inputs are taken to earth.
The five-bit codes for programming the Q factor and centre frequency are presented

Table 1

binary code at pins 6...2	Q factor	binary code at pins 13...17	f_c/f_o
00000	.57	00000	200.0
00001	.65	00001	191.3
00010	.71	00010	182.9
00011	.79	00011	174.9
00100	.87	00100	167.2
00101	.95	00101	159.9
00110	1.05	00110	152.9
00111	1.2	00111	146.2
01000	1.35	01000	139.8
01001	1.65	01001	133.7
01010	1.95	01010	127.9
01011	2.2	01011	122.3
01100	2.5	01100	116.9
01101	3.0	01101	111.8
01110	3.5	01110	106.9
01111	4.25	01111	102.3
10000	5.0	10000	97.8
10001	5.8	10001	93.5
10010	7.2	10010	89.4
10011	8.7	10011	85.5
10100	10.0	10100	81.8
10101	11.5	10101	78.2
10110	13.0	10110	74.8
10111	15.0	10111	71.5
11000	17.5	11000	68.4
11011	19.0	11001	65.4
11010	23.0	11010	62.5
11011	28.0	11011	59.8
11100	35.0	11100	57.2
11101	40.0	11101	54.8
11110	80.0	11110	52.3
11111	150.0	11111	50.0

to IC1 at pins 2...6 (Q) and 13...17 (f_o) respectively. As a glance at table 1 will show, all that we require to generate the two five-bit codes is a pair of 5-pole 32-way switches!
Both IC2 and IC3 are 7-stage (we only use 5 here) binary ripple counters that will count up (and only up) when presented with a clock input at pin 1. This is provided by the oscillator formed by a 555 (IC4) and its

277

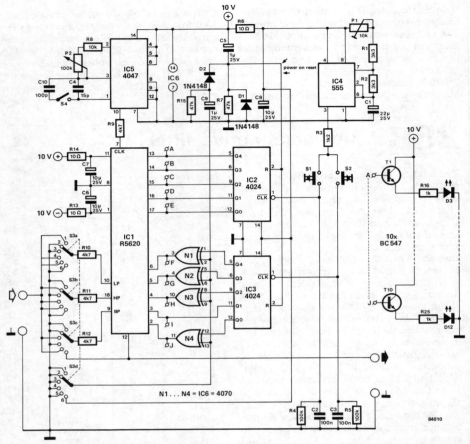

Table 2

S3 in position	filter mode
1	low pass (LP)
2	high pass (HP)
3	band pass (BP)
4	notch
5	all pass
6	oscillator (see text)

associates. With the component values given the frequency is fairly low and it is possible to step the binary counters along by means of the pushbutton switches S1 and S2. The RC networks consisting of R4/C2 and R5/C3 are included to debounce the switches. When the required binary number is arrived at, the switches are released and the R5620 will then be programmed according to table 1.

As stated, ICs 2 and 3 are up counters only and, therefore, to return to the starting code of 00000, the entire binary code must be run through to the end. This method of operation was chosen simply for the sake of economy (it's a shade cheaper than 32-way switches anyway!) but the circuit can be modified at will.

It is a simple matter for the codes to be made visible by means of driver transistirs

and LEDs. In the circuit diagram these are T1...T10 and D3...D12. The bases of the transistors are connected to the terminal points at the inputs to IC1 marked A...J. The connections to pin 2 of ICs 2 and 3 (the 'reset' inputs) enable the two counters to be automatically set to zero when the power supply is first switched on. They also serve a second, slightly more subtle, function. In the beginning, it was said that the R5620 was also able to operate as a sine-wave oscillator. This is entirely true and for this function the output is switched back (via S3c) to the band-pass (BP) input while the LP and HP inputs are taken to earth. No problem here but there is a strange quirk in the R5620 to be taken care of. To function in the oscillator mode, the Q factor inputs (pins 6...2) must be programmed to 11101. This is carried out by the four EXclusive OR gates, N1...N4, between IC3 and IC1. When the common inputs to these gates are taken low, (by switch S3d in positions 1...5), the binary outputs of IC3 are unaffected and pass straight through to IC1. When the oscillator mode is selected (S3 in position 6), the commoned inputs to the gates are taken high by wafer S3d. At the same time, a reset pulse is fed to the reset input of IC3 with the result that all its outputs revert to logic zero. However, the gates now function as inverters and therefore the binary number presented to IC1 will be 11101. The R5620 will now operate as a sine-wave oscillator providing pushbutton S2 is not touched! If this should happen inadvertently, simply switch S3 to another position and then back to 6.

All that we have left to discuss in the circuit is IC5 and its surrounding components. This is the clock oscillator for IC1 and its frequency is variable by means of potentiometer P2. We can now clarify the relationship between the clock frequency and the binary number that appears on pins 13...17 of IC1. When the code is 00000, the centre frequency of the filter is 1/200th of the clock frequency as can be seen in table 1. It will now be apparent that the code sets the centre frequency to a ratio of the clock frequency. This gices a very wide filter response range.

Some final points worthy of note! It is of course possible to do away with the switches and counters and simply 'hard wire' the R5620 inputs to whatever function and parameters that are required. Bear in mind that 10 V can be considered as a maximum for the power supply voltage and some protection from turn-on transients must be included. The clock frequency range is fairly wide and can be anywhere between 10 Hz and 1.25 MHz.

In conclusion, the R5620 uses NMOS technology ans its chances of instant death due to mishandling are inversely proportional to the quantity you have of them at that time!

The R5620 is available from:
EG and G Reticon,
34/35 Market Place,
Wokingham,
Berkshire.

259   flashing running light

Roadworks are usually marked during the hours of darkness by yellow flashing lights. These may often be linked together to form a running flashing light. Road diversions and the like are then clearly visible. The circuit described here provides a similar effect but for use in model roadways, for instance.

The speed of the running row of LEDs is determined by the frequency of clock generator N1.

Depending on the type of IC used, this frequency will be of the order of 6 Hz ± 30% when potentiometer P1 is in mid position. The output of the clock generator is fed to Johnson counter IC1. The outputs of this counter become logic 1 in sequence. The counter is reset to the start when Q4 goes to logic 1. This explains the link between pins 15 and 10 of IC1. Outputs Q0...Q3 are connected to four monostable multivibrator circuits consisting of N2...N5. The multivibrators are triggered by the negative going edge of the pulse outputs of Q0...Q3. The pulse period can be preset with potentiometers P2...P5 which of course determine how long each group of LEDs will light. These periods need to be more or less equal to ensure smooth running of the lights.

The circuit uses four groups of four LEDs each. The LEDs in each group will light simultaneously. Figure 2 shows how the LEDs should be connected for road markings in a bend: LEDs D16, D15, D14, and D13 light first, followed by D12, D11, D10,

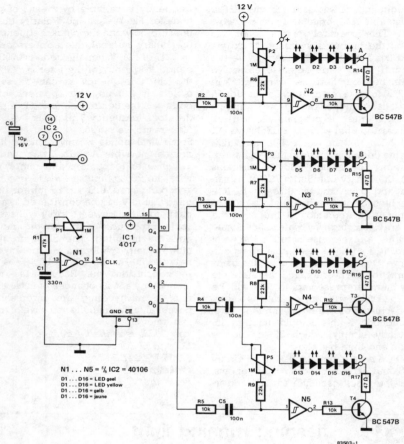

1

N1 . . . N5 = ⁵⁄₆ IC2 = 40106

D1 . . . D16 = LED geel
D1 . . . D16 = LED yellow
D1 . . . D16 = gelb
D1 . . . D16 = jaune

83503-1

2

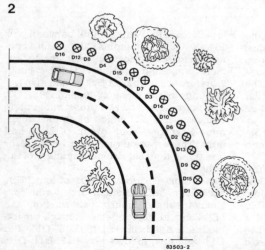

83503-2

Parts list

Resistors:
R1 = 47 k
R2...R5,R10...R13 = 10 k
R6...R9 = 22 k
R14...R17 = 47 Ω
P1...P5 = 1 M preset potentiometer

Capacitors:
C1 = 330 n
C2...C5 = 100 n
C6 = 10 μ/16 V

Semi-conductors:
T1...T4 = BC 547B
D1...D16 = LED yellow
IC1 = 4017
IC2 = 40106

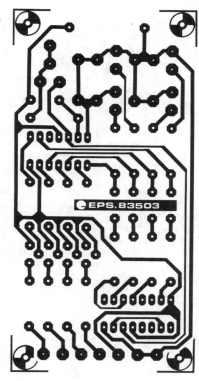

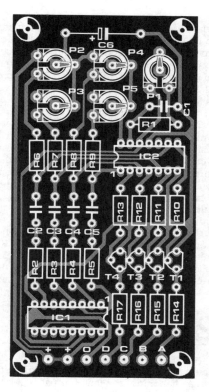

and D9, and so on.

Schmitt triggers N2...N5 are not capable of supplying sufficient current for the LEDs and therefore the buffers T1...T4 are included. The current through the LEDs is about 30 mA during each flash; the average current taken by the circuit operating at the highest frequency is of the order of 30 mA. When, however, the flash period is longer than the running period, the current con-

sumption may rise to a maximum of 100 mA.

The printed circuit board (see figure 3) is fairly compact. The preset potentiometers are neatly grouped together and all terminals are located at one edge. The four groups of LEDs are connected to pins A...D which are clearly marked on the circuit diagram and the board.

260   stable zener

As everybody knows, the voltage drop across a zener diode is dependent on the current passing through the diode. Therefore, depending on the type and power of the device, there can be very noticeable deviations from the nominal zener voltage. This can be a problem, especially in circuits where a stable d.c. voltage is essential. The most logical way of

solving the problem is to keep the current through the diode constant so that the zener voltage can not change. In order that the load connected to the zener diode draws a constant current, the zener can be supplied by a current source. Then the current through the current source is made dependent on the zener voltage.

In our circuit we use a zener diode with a

zener voltage of 6 V. Other zener values could be used if resistors R1...R4 are changed to suit another value. The maximum input voltage is mainly limited by the power which can be dissipated by T1 and T2. The d.c. input voltage must be at least as high as the sum of the zener voltages of D1 and D2. The current source consisting of T1, R1, and D1 ensures that the current through D2 remains constant. Transistor T2, resistor R2, and zener diode D2 in turn form a current source for zener D1 so that the current through this diode also stays constant. Diode D3 and the voltage divider, consisting of R3 and R4, ensure that this circuit can start.

As soon as the voltage is switched on, a current flows through D3 causing T2 (and therefore T1) to conduct. The value of R3 must be selected such that diode D3 blocks as soon as the voltage across the zener diode has stabilized. So care must be taken

that the voltage at the anode of D3 is less than the zener voltage of D2 plus the diode's own voltage drop of 0.6 V. This is defined by the formule:

$[U_i R4(R3+R4)] < [U_{D2}+0.6]$. Also, the voltage at the junction of R3 and R4 must be at least 1.2 V, otherwise T2 will never conduct.

---

261   useful tip . . .

There is often a need for a transistor with somewhat higher than normal specifications for the collector voltage and current, maximum dissipation, and current gain. This can successfully be achieved by using a combination of complementary transistors connected to work as a single n-p-n or p-n-p transistor.

In the circuits shown here four transistors are used. By carefully choosing the values of R1, R3, and R4, the overall current gain will be of the order of one and a half million! The circuit characteristics are virtually the same as those of a 2N3055, so that a maximum of 115 W can be dissipated at 25 °C, while the maximum collector voltage and current are 60 V and 15 A respectively. The saturation voltage of the n-p-n combination is about 2 V, that of the p-n-p combination around 3 V.

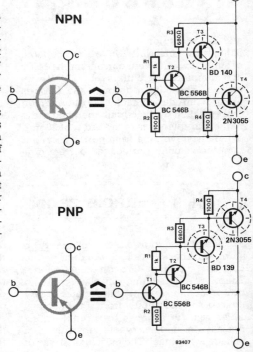

262 voltage booster regulator

There are various ways and means of drawing more current from a voltage regulator IC than it was originally intended to supply, but most methods have their disadvantages. If, for instance, a power transistor is connected in parallel with the IC, the supply will no longer be protected against short-circuits. That can, of course, be remedied by adding a current sensor in the shape of an extra transistor which, during overload conditions, cuts off the base current to the power transistor. But this solution suffers from a heavy power loss during short-circuit conditions, which is not really acceptable either. The circuit given here shows that a simple solution is possible: the power transistor, T1, is provided with an emitter resistor! This effectively solves the problem, because the current through T1 is then proportional to the current supplied by the voltage regulator. If the 78XX regulator and T1 are mounted

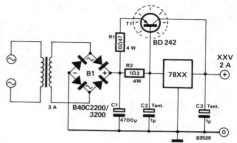

onto the same heat sink, the transistor is also thermally protected! The output voltage is dependent only on the type of voltage regulator used and, as drawn here, the circuit is suitable for currents up to 2 A. If higher values are required, some components need to be changed according to the table. For currents above 7 A, transistor T1 must be replaced by two parallel-connected transistors each of which has an emitter resistor, R1 and R1' respectively.

Output Current (A)	Tr current (A)	B1 (Type)	C1 in μF	R1 in Ω/4 W	R1' in Ω/4 W	R2 in Ω/4 W	T1	T1'	Heatsink in K/W
2	3	B40 C2200/3200	4700 (2 × 2200)	0,47	–	1,2	BD 242	–	5
3	4,5	B40 C3200/5000	6800 (3 × 2200)	0,39	–	2,2	MJ 2500	–	3
4	6	B40 C5000/7000	10.000 (2 × 4700;) (4 × 2200)	0,27	–	2,2	MJ 2500	–	2
5	7	B40 C5000/7000	10.000	0,22	–	2,2	MJ 2500	–	1,5
7	10	B40 C10.000	15.000 (3 × 4700)	0,27	2,7	2,2	MJ 2500	MJ 2500	2 × 2
10	14	B40 C10.000	22.000 (2 × 10.000) (4 × 4700)	0,18	0,18	2,2	MJ 2500	MJ 2500	2 × 1,5

263 joystick interface 2

It happens from time to time that it would be nice to read the position of a potentiometer with a micro-processor. For those many computer enthusiasts we have designed a simple circuit to do this. Only one 555 and one input line to the processor are needed. Care must be taken in the construction to prevent hum. The interface should also be of interest to other computer enthusiasts who just want to experiment with their equipment.

Integrated circuit IC1 oscillates continu-

37E8		00170	INPUT	EQU	37E8H
A000	010000		START	LD	BC,000
A003	1E80	00190		LD	E,80H
A005	21E837	00200		LD	HL, INPUT
A008	7E	00210	LOOP0	LD	A, (HL)
A009	A3	00220		AND	E
A00A	28FC	00230		JR	Z, LOOP0
A00C	7E	00240	LOOP1	LD	A, (HL)
A00D	A3	00250		AND	E
A00E	20FC	00260		JR	NZ, LOOP1
A010	03	00270	ZERO	INC	BC
A011	7E	00275		LD	A, (HL)
A012	A3	00280		AND	E
A013	28FB	00300		JR	Z, ZERO
A015	C9	00310	STOP	RET	
0000		00320		END	
00000	TOTAL	ERRORS			

ously: capacitor C1 is charged via resistor R1 and potentiometer P1 and then discharged through P1. This means that the discharge time is dependent on the setting of P1 and this, in turn, means that the time during which the output of IC1 (pin 3) is logic 0 is directly proportional to the resistance of P1. If the resistance of P1 becomes less than 10 kΩ, there is a likelihood that oscillations will cease.

When the mircoprocessor measures the time that the output of IC1 is low, it produces a number which is directly proportional to the resistance of P1. This can be done easily by incrementing a register until the output of IC1 becomes logic 1 again. A large value of P1 gives a high count.

The program is a sub-routine which can be placed on any free address in a Z80, 8080, or 8085. Instructions LD A, (HL), and AND E read the level at pin 3 of IC1 which in this case was connected to the seventh data bit (E contains 80_{16}). During loop 0 there is a delay until the output of IC1 becomes 1; this is necessary because it may happen

that the routine is started during a '0'. Subsequently, during loop 1 there is a delay until the output of IC1 is low. Thus the real count-loop zero continues as long as pin 3 of IC1 is logic 0. Counting takes place in a double register (BC) but can equally well be done in a single register. In the latter case, the run is slightly faster, that is, 27 instead of 29 clock pulses.

Input is the address to which the output of IC1 is connected. In line 190 the input mask in register E is set: only bit 7 is read.

Finally, the calculation of C1. If P1 has a value of 100 kΩ, BC must contain for instance, 100_{10}, for which $100 \times 29 = 2900$ clock pulses are required (for a 4 MHz clock this would be 725 µs). The time, t_o, during which the output of IC1 is 0 is given by $t_o = 0.69 P1 C1$. In the case being considered, C1 would be 10.5 nF; in practice, the next standard value of 12 nF would be used and P2 adjusted until the register has the correct value.

If you have to buy IC1, choose the 7555 CMOS version which causes far less interference to the power supply!

264 VFO with variable inductor

An LC oscillator as shown in figure 1 is not exactly something new: transistor T1 is connected in a common base configuration and its emitter functions as virtual earth. Transistor T3 is a voltage follower buffer; its emitter voltage, in conjunction with the impedance of the series LC circuit, determines the collector current of T1. If

therefore the resistive losses of the LC circuit at resonance are smaller than the collector resistor R4, the LC circuit will oscillate. The level of the oscillator voltage across R9 is determined by the value of R9, the collector current of T1, and the current through R8.

An LC oscillator with variable capacitor

1

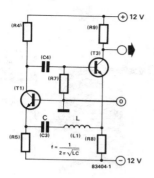

$$f = \frac{1}{2\pi\sqrt{LC}}$$

83404-1

The reduction in magnetic field-strength is effected by replacing T1 in figure 1 by a long-tailed pair, T1 and T2, in figure 2. As you probably know, the collector currents in a long-tailed pair are in anti-phase; their ratio is determined by the dc voltage applied to the base of T1. This voltage is set by resistors R1 and R2, diodes D1...D3, and potentiometer P1. When the wiper of P1 is set for maximum resistance, T2 is cut off, L2 does not oppose L1 and the total self inductance of the circuit is maximum: the oscillator frequency is then minimum. When the base voltage of T1 is reduced, T2 begins to conduct, L2 starts to oppose L1 and the oscillator frequency rises. When T1 and T2 are balanced as far as dc supply is concerned, the self inductance of the circuit is theoretically zero: the consequent, infinitely high oscillator frequency is, however, unattainable because the oscillator has stopped long before this frequency is reached. In a practical circuit, with C3 = 500 pF and L1 = L2 = 365 μH, the oscillator can be tuned between 370 and 520 kHz; if C3 = 56 pF and L1 = L2 = 5.5 μH, the frequency range is 9...12 MHz. In view of the stringent requirements as to the magnetic coupling between L1 and L2, these coils must be bifilar wound as indicated in figure 3. For instance, a value of 365 μH is obtained when the number of turns, N = 191, wound on a former of diameter, d = 2 cm,

tuning has been around for some time as well: change C (C3) in figure 1 to a variable type and you'll be able to adjust the oscillator frequency over a certain range. An LC oscillator with variable inductor tuning as shown in figure 2 is not so usual. Two coils, L1 and L2, are mutually coupled (coupling factor, k = 1). If the currents through the coils are in anti-phase, the magnetic field of L2 will oppose that of L1: the self inductance of L1 appears to become smaller. Therefore, the larger the magnetic field of L2, the higher the oscillator frequency. As the current through L2 is kept to a fraction of that through L1, the magnetic field of L2 cannot exceed that of L1.

2

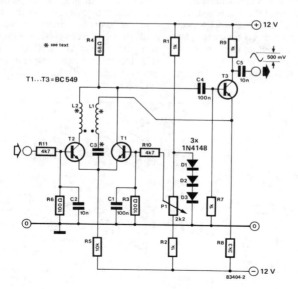

83404-2

285

and a coil length, $l = 4$ cm.

The variable inductance oscillator instead of the familiar variable capacitance version is not just 'nice to know', but has sound practical applications. After all, it makes it possible to control frequency by means of voltage control of the base potential of T2: you can now tune the IF stages of an FM receiver visually, for instance, and in general you can sweep or wobbulate to your heart's delight!

The inductance of the coil may be calculated from:

$$L = [4\pi A N^2 / 10^7 l)]H$$

or,

$$L = [d^2 N^2 / l]\mu H$$

where

L = inductance
A = cross-sectional area of coil former in m²
N = number of turns
l = length of wound coil in m
d = diameter of coil former in m

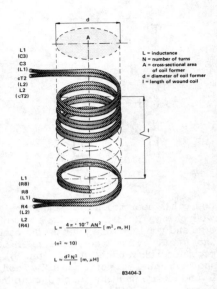

L1 (C3)
C3 (L1)
cT2 (L2)
L2 (cT2)

L = inductance
N = number of turns
A = cross-sectional area of coil former
d = diameter of coil former
l = length of wound coil

L1 (R8)
R8 (L1)
R4 (L2)
L2 (R4)

$$L = \frac{4\pi \cdot 10^{-7} AN^2}{l} \ [m^2, m, H]$$

$(\pi^2 \approx 10)$

$$L \approx \frac{d^2 N^2}{l} \ [m, \mu H]$$

83404-3

A.B. Bradshaw

265 electronic tuning fork

A standard tuning fork produces a tone of 440 Hz, that is, the international A (orchestral pitch). It is not very difficult to make an electronic alternative. An oscillator, a divider, a loudspeaker, and a battery are all that is required. To be useful, an electronic tuning fork must, of course, be a compact unit.

As the use of special, and therefore costly,

crystals was precluded, a little research showed that it would be possible to use relatively simple and standard components. It appeared that the required frequency can be derived from a readily available 1 MHz crystal which, by means of a trimmer, can be pulled to 1 000 120 Hz which is the nearest frequency containing a whole number times 440 Hz.

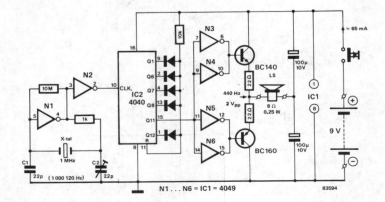

The oscillator is constructed around gates N1, N2 and tuned to 1 000 120 Hz (with a frequency counter if possible), by trimmer C2. The oscillator output is fed to IC2 which divides by 2273 ($2^0 + 2^5 + 2^6 + 2^7 + 2^{11}$). A practically symmetrical signal of 440 Hz is then available at output Q11 of IC2.

This signal is then buffered by gates N3...N6 and the balanced output stage gives a level sufficient to drive a small loud-speaker.

In spite of the current consumption of 65 mA, a standard 9 V (PP3) battery (preferably alkaline-manganese) will suffice, because tuning forks are by their nature used for short periods only. If the fork is used for longer periods, it might be advisable to consider a rechargeable battery.

266   key bleep

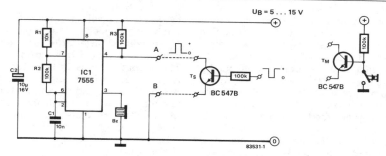

$U_B = 5 ... 15$ V

83531-1

There are many situations where an audible indication for a button pressed would be very useful. Two particular cases are: a morse key, where it is otherwise impossible to know that the key has been operated, and an ASCII keyboard.

This circuit is based on a 7555 timer IC (the CMOS version of the well known 555) which is connected as an astable multivibrator (AMV). Its output is a rectangular pulse at a frequency of about 700 Hz which is used to drive a small buzzer. The circuit will be prevented from oscillating if pin 4 of the IC is taken to 0 V, in other words, a short between points A and B in the circuit diagram. As mentioned, the key bleep is ideal for use as a key push indicator with the ASCII keyboard. In this case a tone will be produced each time the key is pressed making it unnecessary to continually look at the screen to verify correct operation. Don't worry, only one key bleep circuit is needed, not one for each key of the keyboard! The circuit can be controlled by the strobe pulse which can, of course, be either a logic 1 or a logic 0. If it is a 1 the strobe can be connected directly to point A. If on the other hand, it is a 0, transistor stage TS will have to be connected between points A and B. The strobe output is then fed direct to the base of transistor TS.

If the circuit is to be used with a morse key, transistor stage TM is required. The emitter and collector of the transistor are connected to points A and B and the key is placed between its base and 0 V.

267   window comparator

This window comparator uses only three CMOS inverters, two resistors, two preset potentiometers, and one diode. Of course, the simplicity of the circuit means that some concessions must be made with regard to quality. High-frequency input signals with short rise and decay times cannot be properly processed. Nevertheless,

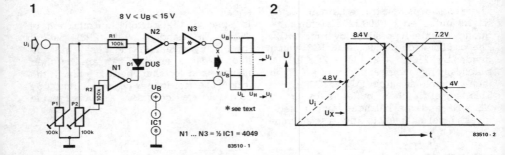

N1 ... N3 = ½ IC1 = 4049

83510 - 1

83510 - 2

the circuit provides an inexpensive and simple alternative to the usual window comparators.

The circuit itself (figure 1) does not require much of a description. The switching thresholds are adjusted with preset potentiometers P1 and P2. The adjustment of P1 governs the lower switching threshold U_L, whilst that of P2 governs the upper switching threshold U_H and thus establishes the window width $U_H - U_L$.

Figure 2 clarifies the function of the circuit. The values indicated apply to a supply voltage of 10 V. A triangular voltage is shown at the input of the window compara-

tor, as well as the output voltage at point X. If the input voltage exceeds the lower value U_L set with P1, the voltage at output X goes to logic 1 via inverters N2 and N3. If the input voltage reaches the upper threshold U_H set with P2, inverter N1 ensures that the voltage at output X goes to logic 0 again. The output remains in this state until the trailing edge of the input voltage drops below U_H again and the output goes back to logic 1. It reverts to logic 0 as soon as the input voltage reaches the lower threshold U_L.

R. de Boer

---

268 power backup for CMOS ICs during mains power failures

Even very brief mains power failures cause problems for electronic circuits. Stored data are lost and the operating statuses are no longer what they were before the power failure. Mains power failures cannot be prevented, but methods can be employed to provide a voltage backup for the duration of the fault. For this reason, mains-powered equipment is often fitted with backup batteries (NiCd or lithium cells) to maintain operation during a mains power failure. In view of the low currents (microamperes) required for data storage with modern RAMs, there is an alternative backup method which is well worth considering: power backup with an electrolytic capacitor for energy storage!

The circuit diagram shows just such an application. The power stand-by capacitor C1 is 4700 μF, so that with a maximum load current of 10 μA, the discharge time at an output voltage of 5 V is approximately 53 minutes. The operating voltage of the circuit itself is 15 V, 10 V higher than the output voltage. As long as the 15 V supply voltage is applied, capacitor C1 charges to the value of the operating voltage via diode D1. Simultaneously, a bias voltage of approximately 2.3 V is applied to the gate of field effect transistor T1 via voltage divider R1/R2. This ensures that T1 is turned on and capacitor C2 is charged. The output voltage at the source terminal of the second field effect transistor remains a constant 5 V. The two FETs can be thought of as a voltage divider.

If the supply voltage fails, electrolytic capacitor C1 will become the temporary power supply. Since the gate voltage is removed from T1, this turns off. Capacitor

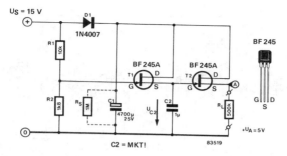

US = 15 V

1N4007

BF 245

BF 245A   BF 245A

C2 = MKT!

83519

+UA = 5V

C2 is no longer being charged. However, it can only discharge very slowly because T2 has a very high input resistance. The voltage across C2 remains almost constant. Capacitor Cl supplies the operating voltage required for T2 so that it conducts and maintains the output voltage at 5 V. Capacitor Cl discharges very slowly, as a function of its insulation resistance ($R_{INS} \approx$ 1 M) and the load current. The output voltage at the source lead of T2 remains a constant 5 V, until the voltage across Cl has also dropped to 5 V. If this voltage drops even further, T2 remains turned on but the output voltage decreases proportionally.

For correct functioning of the circuit, it is very important to select an MKT type of foil capacitor for C2. (M stands for metallised and KT is the standard designation for polyester foil.)

(Siemens Application)

269   telephone indicator

The typewriters are rattling away in the open-plan office. Several people sit down at a table for a discussion. Suddenly a telephone starts ringing somewhere. But which phone is ringing? With the noise level in an open-plan office, it is not always easy to know. Some people leave the discussion and go to their telephones, only to notice that it wasn't their phone after all. This telephone indicator picks up the normal ringing of the phone and generates an auxiliary signal with adjustable pitch and intervals. It is then a simple matter to know which phone is ringing.

The circuit diagram of figure 1 is straightforward. Coil Ll picks up the ringing and the signal is amplified by IC1 and rectified by diode D1. If the signal level is higher than the trigger threshold set with P1, comparator IC2 switches over and applies a logic 1 to pin 12 of gate N4. The latter is thus switched on, allowing the individual ringing tone to be applied to the piezo-buzzer. Diode D2 serves as an additional, visual ringing indicator.

The auxiliary ringing tone is generated by gates N1 and N2. Both operate as astable multivibrators. Gate N1 is responsible for the pitch, which is adjusted with preset potentiometer P2. The intervals between ringing signals are controlled by gate N2, depending on the frequency set with P3. The piezo-buzzer (Toko) is loudest at a resonant frequency of approximately 4.6 kHz; this depends on the setting of preset P2. The case serves as a console for the telephone and should therefore be big enough for the telephone to be situated on it firmly. Coil Ll is mounted in the top of the case. Figure 2 shows the shape and method of winding the coil. The coil former can be made of a strong piece of cardboard, shaped into a square with 10 cm sides. The gauge of the enamelled copper wire is not critical.

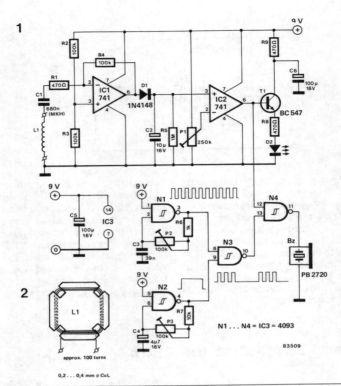

270 LED amplifier

The light emission of an LED (light-emitting diode) is normally pretty low. If more brightness is required, the following circuit will help. The LED to be amplified is replaced by an LED in an opto-coupler which switches a lamp (for instance, a signal lamp) connected to the mains supply.

When the LED in the opto-coupler lights, the photo transistor conducts. This causes a gate current to flow to the triac* via R1: the triac fires and the lamp lights. Resistor R1 is connected to 30 VDC which is derived

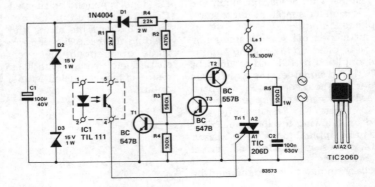

from the mains supply via D1 and R4. Two zener diodes, D2 and D3, limit the voltage across buffer capacitor C1 to 30 V. The three transistors T1...T3 ensure that the triac can only be fired at the moment the mains supply changes from positive to negative, thus reducing interference problems. When the voltage in the positive half-cycle of the mains supply rises above 7 V, the voltage at the junction R3/R4 becomes high enough to cause T1 to conduct. The current through R1 is then fed to T1 so that

the opto-coupler can no longer feed a gate current to the triac. The same thing happens during the negative half-cycle but then T2 and T3 conduct when the voltage across R2, R3, and R4 goes more negative than −7 V. This is a form of zero voltage switch which ensures that firing of the triac can only take place when the mains supply is about 0 V.

*A triac is a special version of a silicon-controlled rectifier (SCR).

271 current source for photodiodes

There are many circuits available today which use modulated light signals to transmit information. Generally, the actual receiver consists of one or more photodiodes. In such applications it is important that the dynamic range of the photodiode is sufficient. However, increasing the dynamic range can cause the sensitivity of the diode to decrease. Another disadvantage is that photodiodes are sensitive to changes in ambient light conditions. The circuit described here increases the dynamic range of the photodiode without affecting its amplification. It also filters out the effects of slow variations in light intensity so that the problems with ambient light are greatly reduced.

As the diagram shows, the circuit is very simple. When light falls on D1, this diode produces a photocurrent, proportional to the intensity of the light. If the current is small, transistor T1 just conducts. When the light intensity (and thus the photocurrent) increases, the current through T1 also increases and this shorts excess current to ground. With rapid fluctuations in the light intensity falling on D1, T1 presents a high impedance (because C1 does not have time to charge). The input signal is then output

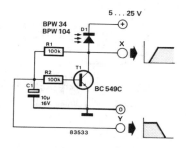

directly at X. This means in effect that the dynamic range of the diode has been increased without reducing the amplification. The signal at point Y, even though it is not directly proportional to the light intensity, can be used to examine the changes in the average light intensity falling on D1.

In virtually all applications it is important that when the light is frequency modulated at 50 Hz (such as house lights) this must not be seen as a modulated signal. To ensure this, C1 must be at least 1.5 μF. With this value of capacitor, the change-over point from high-pass to low-pass is about 50 Hz. If, as shown in our diagram, C1 has a value of 10 μF the change-over point is about 7 Hz.

272 horse paces simulator

In horse riding it is very important to know exactly what the horse is doing with its legs at all times. A simple electronic circuit can be used to demonstrate, with LEDs (light-

emitting-diodes), an idealized order of footfalls to indicate when each foot comes to the ground. The only problem is how do you explain to your horse that he has been

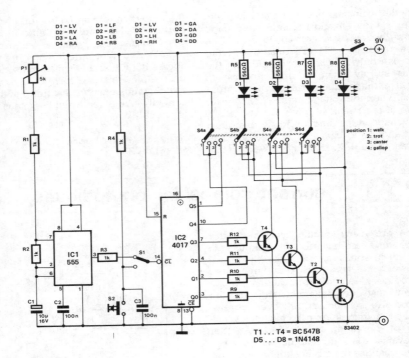

D1 = LV
D2 = RV
D3 = LA
D4 = RA

D1 = LF
D2 = RF
D3 = LB
D4 = RB

D1 = LV
D2 = RV
D3 = LH
D4 = RH

D1 = GA
D2 = DA
D3 = GD
D4 = DD

position 1: walk
2: trot
3: canter
4: gallop

T1 . . . T4 = BC 547B
D5 . . . D8 = 1N4148

83402

replaced by an electronic circuit?

The circuit diagram for this device is given in figure 1, and it is obvious that no complicated electronics is involved. Despite this simplicity, the circuit does have a few nice features. Obviously, every horse moves in a slightly different manner, and this also depends on the age and level of training of the horse (and its rider), so what we have here is an idealized version of how a horse moves.

One LED is used for each foot; when the LED lights the foot is on the ground. There are basically four different ways of moving catered for: walking trotting, cantering, and galloping, and each lights the LEDs in a different sequence. The speeds at which the LEDs are lit is also controllable and there is even a 'one step at a time' mode.

The circuit contains a counter (IC2) driven by a 555 timer (IC1). The latter provides a clock signal, the frequency of which can be changed by varying P1, thus determining how fast the sequence of lighting LEDs is. The actual sequence is realized by the counter. The outputs of IC2 (pins 2, 3, 4 and 7) are connected to driver transistors

T1...T4, the open collectors of which are connected to an encoding module. It is the design of this encoding module which determines which LEDs are illuminated at any particular time. Because there are four different sequences (walk, trot, canter, and gallop) there are also four different encoding modules. These can either be designed as separate entities to be plugged into the control board, or all four can be incorporated into the control unit printed circuit board and switched using a 4 pole 4 way switch as shown. Each of these modules simply consists of wiring, with a different layout used for each.

Each of the counter outputs goes high (logic 1) in turn and this causes the appropriate transistors to conduct. This then drives the LEDs, D1...D4. Switch S1 is used to select either clock-controlled or step-by-step operation, and in this latter case S2 is used to advance to the next step.

D1 = right fore leg, D2 = left fore, D3 = left rear and D4 = right rear leg.

B. Darnton

292

273 amplified triac drive

A well-known shortcoming of virtually all electronic components is their sensitivity to temperature changes. It is true that triacs are not too bad in this respect, but they do not like low temperatures: they just stop working! This is because triacs require a higher gate current at low temperature. Triacs are often triggered by opto-couplers which are not capable of supplying these higher currents. The circuit described, in contrast to normal triac triggers, contains an amplifier which ensures sufficient gate current under all temperature conditions.

The amplifier is formed by transistor T1, which raises the signal from the opto-coupler to more than adequate level. The use of capacitor C2 as a dropping reactance ensures that the dissipation in the drive circuit is virtually nil; it also prevents the circuit presenting a DC load to the mains supply. The switch-on current surge is limited to a safe value by resistor R3. As the drive circuit is supplied directly from the mains, the mains voltage must, of course, be reduced to an acceptable level. This voltage is therefore rectified by D1 and smoothed by C1. Zener diode D2 stabilizes the supply to the circuit to 15 V. As soon as

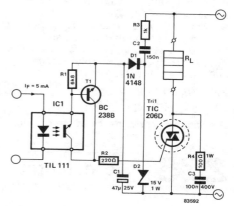

transistor T1 conducts, capacitor C1 discharges via T1 and the triac gate provides a gate current of about 40 mA. The discharge time, and consequently the trigger pulse, is not greater than 1 millisecond. Network R4/C3 protects the triac against high voltage peaks.

Siemens application.

Note. A triac is a special version of silicon-controlled rectifier, SCR. The SCR was formerly known as a thyristor.

---

274 temperature indicator

A simple, inexpensive temperature indicator to show the temperature of a heat sink in high power circuits can be very useful; accuracy is not an important factor.

In the design for the temperature indicator, the voltage drop across a diode at ambient temperature is used as a reference level. The temperature is measured by a transistor mounted on the heat sink or close to the power transistor in question. In the circuit diagram the temperature sensor is transistor T1 and its base emitter voltage is compared to the reference level at the junction of D1 and R1 via preset P1. The transistor will remain switched off as long as its temperature remains below a certain level, which is effectively set by P1. The base emitter voltage of the transistor will drop by

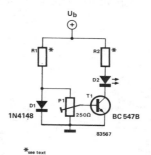

about 2 mV for a rise in temperature of about 1 degree Celsius. When the base emitter voltage of the transistor drops below the voltage level at the wiper of P1, the transistor will conduct and light D2. This will happen gradually and thus provide an indication over a fairly wide range.

The values of R1 and R2 are, of course, dependent upon the supply voltage, U_b, and can be calculated from:

$$R1 = [(U_b-0.6)/5] \text{ k}\Omega$$
$$R2 = [(U_b-1.5)/15] \text{ k}\Omega$$

For optimum performance of the circuit, it is important that the reference diode is situated in the free air at room temperature — definitely not above the heat sink! The transistor should be mounted on (or even in, if drilling the heat sink is acceptable) the heat sink as near the heat dissipating element as is practical. It must be remembered, however, that the maximum expected temperature should not exceed 125 °C if you value your transistor.

The current consumption of the temperature indicator will be little more than the LED current, about 20 mA, and then only when things are starting to cook!

275 lie detector

The principle of a lie detector may be considered well-known: emotional states are not only betrayed by a faster heartbeat and trembling hands, but also by an increase in skin surface moisture. Because the skin becomes moist, its resistance will be lower, and it is this that makes the lie detector react. The lie detector described here actually gives two readings: one for when a guinea pig is asked difficult questions and one to indicate the general emotional condition of a person.

Two bare, flexible wires wound round the fingers or the wrist can be used as receivers. That means, of course, direct contact with the circuit and this must therefore be fed from two 9 V batteries or the emotional state of the guinea pig may be upset by mains voltages!

Each change in resistance, and therefore voltage, at the input of the circuit will be amplified by opamp A1, which also acts as a buffer; its consequent output signal will cause a current through R3 and the meter, which will give a reading. The most suitable meter for this purpose is the type used in FM receivers as tuning indicator: that is, with a centre zero. Capacitor C1 ensures the suppression of any hum present. The general emotional condition of a person can be ascertained by measuring the average resistance of the skin over a period of time. This indication is provided by a meter connected to point B in the circuit. Opamp A2 is connected as an integrator and enables the circuit to adjust automatically to the average skin resistance. The period of time during which the skin resist-

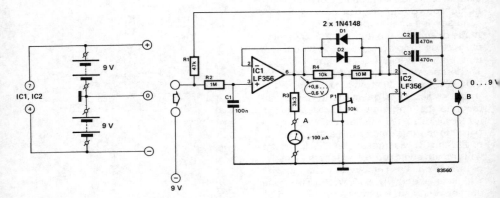

ance must be measured is determined mainly by R5, C2 and C3. Until this time has lapsed, a meter (a universal meter is suitable) connected across output B will not give any reading, although diodes D1 and D2 ensure that the circuit reacts as quickly as possible.

Potentiometer P1 enables setting of the delay time of the circuit.

Because the skin resistance varies from person to person, it may be necessary to alter the value of resistor R1. As a further refinement, this resistor can be replaced by a potentiometer if desired. Too high a reading on the meter at output B indicates that the skin resistance of the 'guinea pig' is low (which is characteristic of people with clammy hands) and it would be advisable to reduce the value of R1.

276 machinegun-soundgenerator

Computer games are even more fun when they are accompanied by sound effects. As most such games have a more or less destructive character, a machinegun-sound generator will often come in very handy. The circuit consists of three nearly identical generators of which the output signals are added in a particular ratio. This gives the impression that there are three machinegun posts. Each sound generator consists of three astable multivibrators (AMVs) which are connected in series by diodes. Each AMV can only oscillate if the output of the preceding AMV is logic 0. Two of the generators have a preset potentiometer associated with the final pair of AMVs to enable control of the frequencies. These frequencies determine the 'speed' of the gun fire. The output level can be set with potentiometer P3. The current consumption of the circuit is not greater than 2 mA for a supply voltage of 5 V. The simulated gun fire sounds best if the final amplifier is adjusted for maximum bass and minimum treble. The volume should be set so that the amplifier does not clip, as this will produce unnatural sounds.

If you don't like the sound of machinegun fire, the circuit can be used to imitate the sound of a woodpecker. This is rather more peace loving, but it will be difficult to find an exiting computer game heavily involved with woodpeckers!

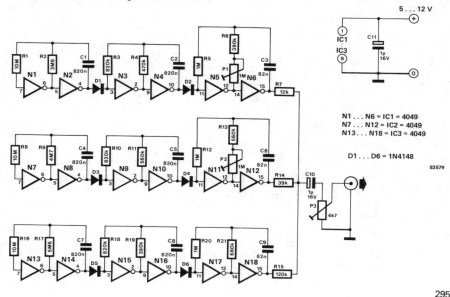

295

277 constant light source

In many occupations it is important that the light incidence at a certain location remains as nearly constant as possible. When the sun appears from behind the clouds (it happens sometimes!), it causes an increase in light in a room or onto an object. Such varying ambient light is tiring on the eyes for many people when painting, reading, and so on. If ambient light does not vary too wildly, the light source described here may offer a solution. The circuit controls a light bulb so that the brightness of the bulb is matched with the incidence of ambient light. The bulb will therefore light more brightly if the sun disappears behind the clouds again. The circuit can, of course, be connected to the lighting of a living room or study: if it gets darker outside, the lights in the room will then compensate. This circuit is a real solution if you don't like working or sitting in semi-darkness.

The principle is fairly simple: a sensor measures the incidence of the artificial light and the ambient light. As soon as the ambient light changes, the brightness of the bulb is changed accordingly so that the total light level remains the same.

The heart of the circuit is a rather unusual IC, the OPL 100 from TRW-Optron. It is housed in an 8-pin DIL package with a transparent top and includes control electronics together with a light sensitive diode. A constant current produced by T2 and T3 and preset by P1 serves as a reference to IC1. The integrated circuit will control the pulse width of its output (and therefore the brightness of lamp La) such that the current supplied by pin 1, which is directly proportional to the quantity of light falling onto the sensor, is equal to the current flowing through T3 and preset by P1. If the ambient light decreases, the current supplied via pin 1 will drop. As the adjusted current through T3 is then larger than the current supplied through pin 1, the voltage at pin 1 drops and this causes the pulse width of the output signal to change. Triac Tri 1 conducts for a longer period for each cycle of the mains frequency and the lamp will glow more brightly until the ambient light returns to its original level. Capacitor C3 ensures that the control of the circuit is smooth. The value of this capacitor also determines the speed at which the circuit reacts to light

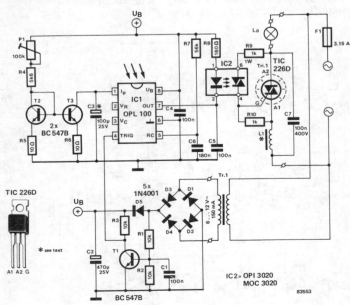

1

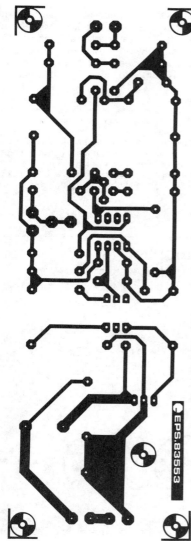

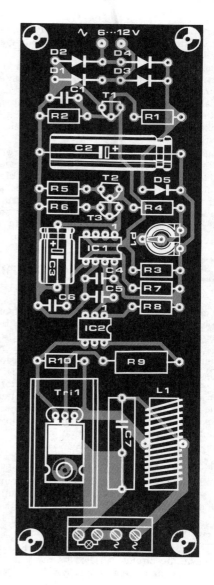

2

© EPS.83553

Parts list

Resistors:
R1,R2,R3 = 10 k
R4 = 5k6
R5,R6 = 10 Ω
R7 = 56 k
R8 = 180 Ω
R9 = 1 k (1 W)
R10 = 1 k
P1 = 100 k preset potentiometer

Capacitors:
C1,C4,C5 = 100 n
C2 = 470 μF/25 V
C3 = 100 μF/25 V
C6 = 180 n
C7 = 100 nF/400 V

Semiconductors:
D1...D5 = 1N4001
T1...T3 = BC 547B

Tri1 = TIC 226D
IC1 = OPL 100
IC2 = OPI 3020 (MOC 3020) (IC1, IC2 from Norbain Opto-electronics)

Miscellaneous:
F1 = 3.15 A
L1 = choke 50...100 μH

Heat sink for IC2 (35 × 20 × 15 mm)
Tr 1 = mains transformer 6...12 V/150 mA

297

variations. The smaller the value of C3, the faster the reaction of the circuit, but the value should be kept above 1 μF.

The mains supply frequency is used to switch T1 and this transistor then ensures synchronization of the control pulses for the triac provided by IC1 with the mains supply. The opto-coupler, IC2, ensures that the circuit is electrically isolated from the mains supply.

Take care with the choice of transformer! During the testing of our prototype we found that a small, inexpensive (printed circuit board) transformer caused quite a phase shift. Even during full sunlight incidence on the sensor, the lamp continued to light, albeit dimly. The phase shift in a good quality transformer is minimal; the lamp can then be controlled over the full range of 180° (in each half period). The maximum power drawn from the circuit should not exceed 500 W (resistive load) which is ample for most applications.

Footnote
Light flux, measured in lumens, is the rate at which light is passing to, from, or through a surface or other geometrical entity.
Light incidence, measured in lux (lumens per square meter), is the flux per unit area, normally perpendicularly incident upon a surface.
Light intensity, measured in candela, is the flux per unit solid angle raditing (or diverging) from a source of finite area.

---

278 four quadrant multiplier

This four quadrant multiplier can be built with just one opamp, whose gain can be preset with a potentiometer.

The input signal, U_1, is applied to the inverting input of the (741) opamp via resistor R1. As R1 = R2, the signal is amplified by 1. However, U_1, is also applied to the non-inverting input of the opamp via potentiometer P1 and dutyresistor R3; the signal level at the non-inverting input is therefore determined by the position of P1. The resulting total output voltage is given by $U_2 = (2x-1)U_1$ where x represents the position of P1. For example, with the wiper of P1 fully clockwise (up in the circuit diagram) x = 1, in the mid position x = 0.5, and fully anticlockwise x = 0. It should be noted that U_1 may be a d.c. or an a.c. signal (f_{max} = 5 kHz).

By adding an extra potentiometer, P2, as shown, the circuit can also be used as an analogue hand-held multiplier. The input

level can then be preset with P2 and the gain with P1. Both potentiometers can be provided with a scale as shown.

---

279 cricket simulator

This simulator gives a faithful reproduction of the chirping of a cricket. The circuit comprises four oscillators of which the first, N1, produces the basic high note. The frequency of this note is set by potentiometer P1 such that it lies within the resonant range of the crystal buzzer: the tone is then loudest.

To obtain the typical chirping noise, the 4 kHz rectangular output of N1 is amplitude

298

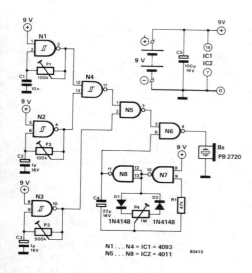

ously but with suitable pauses. This is effected by oscillator N7/N8 and frequency changer N6. The oscillator output has a duty factor which is directly proportional to the ratio of the two sections of potentiometer P4, and can therefore be changed as desired. The duration of the total oscillator cycle is about 30 seconds, but because of tolerances this can vary appreciably. If the pauses can not be set long enough, C4 should be replaced by a larger value.

The initial adjustment to the circuit is that of P1 to achieve the basic tone. For this the buzzer must be connected directly to the output of gate N1 (pin 3 of IC1). The buzzer is then connected to pin 11 of IC1 and P2 is adjusted to obtain the typical chirping tone of a cricket. Next, connect the buzzer to pin 3 of IC1 and adjust P3 so that the chirping noise is heard three to six times per second, according to taste.

Finally, connect the buzzer to the output of the simulator and the (artificial) cricket is ready for use. Depending upon the value of C4 and the setting of P4, it may take a little while before the cricket emits its first chirp. As the current consumption of the circuit is only about 1 mA, the cricket can chirp away quite happily for a long while on a 9 V battery.

modulated by a frequency of 10...20 Hz. This frequency is produced by oscillator N2 and the modulation takes place in digital frequency changer N4.

To make the end-result realistic, the 'cricket' must, of course, not chirp continu-

280   logarithmic amplifier

The performance of the logarithmic amplifier, the circuit diagram of which is shown in figure 1, is best seen from its input/output characteristic shown in figure 2. For small input voltages, the amplification is high; when the input voltage rises, the gain levels off and finally remains almost static for further increases in input voltage.

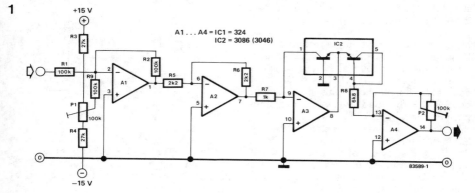

1

2

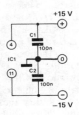

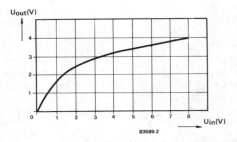

83589-2

Some applications of a logarithmic amplifier are: driving a graphic recorder in weather stations, and in remote control systems (for instance, to avoid a too sudden and strong deflection of a servo arm). When used in conjunction with other equipment, the logarithmic amplifier is very flexible: analogue instruments as well as a row of LEDs can be connected to its output.

Operational amplifiers A1 and A2 form a non-inverting pre-amplifier. As the input signal of A3 should not under any circumstances become negative, the input level of the circuit can be shifted with potentiometer P1 as required. At the same time, this stage works as a high-impedance input buffer for A3.

As shown, the amplifier accepts inputs up to 8 V. If a higher value is required, the gain factors of A1 and A2 can be suitably modified.

The logarithmic part of the circuit consists of A3 and transistor array IC2: the voltage at pins 4 and 5 of the array is related logarithmically to the output signal of A2. The output stage of the circuit consists of amplifier A4 which amplifies the inverted signal from A3. As the gain of this stage can be altered by preset potentiometer P2, the output of the circuit can be matched to the load. To preset P2, connect a multimeter to the output of the circuit and a signal at maximum level to the input: adjust P2 to the required output voltage.

---

281 voltage monitor

The 555 (or 7555) timer IC is connected as a monostable multivibrator and monitors a voltage. This can be, for example, the +5 V supply line of a microprocessor system. The voltage being monitored is applied to trigger input pin 2 via preset potentiometer P1. The timer is in the quiescent state when the input voltage is higher than the trigger threshold set with P1. Output pin 3 is then logic 0. The green LED lights, indicating that everything is in order.

If the input voltage drops below the set trigger threshold, the level at the output of the timer changes to logic 1. Diode D2 goes out, but D3 lights. This means that the input voltage has dropped below the minimum permissible value.

Brief voltage failures are extended by the 555 so that the red LED can clearly indicate them. In the event of a longer voltage failure, the monostable restarts continually. The on-time of the timer (in seconds) is equal to 1.1R1C1 (R in ohms; C in farads): it

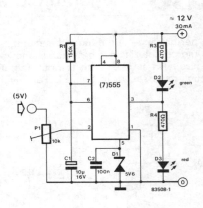

is approximately 1.65 s with the values specified. When the voltage monitor is switched on, the red LED lights until capacitor C1 has charged to more than 2/3 of the supply voltage.

282 microprocessor faultfinder

During faultfinding in a microprocessor system, it is not always possible to work in single-step mode, as the processor would then have to stop completely. Not all processors have a wait-input; the Z80 (which is the system we used to evaluate this circuit) has such an input, but with this there is the problem that the refresh of any dynamic bined with the Memory Request ($\overline{MREQ}$), Read ($\overline{RD}$), and Write ($\overline{WR}$) signals of the computer system so that a latch enable ($\overline{LE}$) pulse is present at the output of N3 after the MMV time of IClb has elapsed. This $\overline{LE}$ pulse is sent to the microprocessor aid which then reads and holds the data and address present at that moment. The pulse

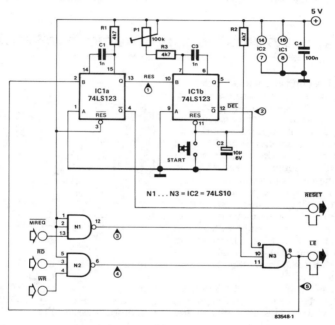

1

N1 . . . N3 = IC2 = 74LS10

83548-1

RAMs used is lost if the processor is stopped. With the faultfinder described here, and the microprocessor aid in circuit 244, both addresses and data can be looked at without the processor having to be stopped for any length of time.

Operation is as follows. After the circuit sends a short reset pulse to the processor, the program is executed. This $\overline{RESET}$ pulse is supplied by monostable multivibrator (MMV) ICla; pulse duration is about 2 μs (the pulse has to be short or the data in the dynamic RAMs might be corrupted). At the same time, the second MMV, consisting of IClb, is triggered. The duration of the pulse supplied by IClb can be adjusted with ten-turn potentiometer Pl. This pulse is com-

2

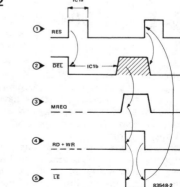

83548-2

also goes to the input of IC1a so that when this LE stops, another RESET pulse is automatically sent to the processor.

In this way it is possible, simply by turning P1, to look at all the memory cycles one after another. This system gives a reliable read-out of programs that are not more than some tens of bytes long. However, the time delay is not stable enough for the system to be usable with longer programs.

This circuit uses the RD, WR, and MREQ signals, so that during a read or write operation the information content is read into the microprocessor aid. If only RD and MREQ were used, only read instructions could be saved for examination. Using WR and MREQ only, write instructions are latched into the microprocessor aid, and using RD and MI only, opcode fetches; other combinations are also possible, of course. RD and/or WR must still be used as addresses and data are only valid when these signals are active.

If processors other then the Z80 are used, this circuit will have to be adapted to use the available signals.

283   symmetrical harmonic oscillator

The remarkable thing about this oscillator is not that it operates on the third overtone of a crystal, nor that it is symmetrical, but that it does not use a tuned circuit. Oscillators without tuned circuits normally operate on the fundamental crystal frequency: as soon as it is required to work on harmonics, a tuned circuit becomes necessary to resonate at the desired overtone.

The oscillator is reminiscent of an astable multivibrator, but it uses a novel way of connecting the crystal: between the emitters of the two transistors and in series with a small trimmer (C5 = 40 pF). It is the trimmer that enables the tuning of the oscillator to the fundamental as well as to the third harmonic of the crystal.

The circuit has been designed for crystals with a fundamental frequency of 6...20 MHz, which gives an oscillator fre-

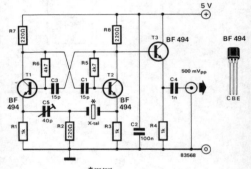

quency between 18...60 MHz: a pretty good range. Moreover, the oscillator can be built around most normal RF transistors. Finally, the output voltage of 500 mV$_{pp}$ is sufficient for most applications.

284   1 MHz time base without crystal

Clock generators, for instance, those used in microprocessor systems, are normally crystal controlled. Although crystals have become cheaper over the years, they are still expensive items. A ceramic filter offers an inexpensive alternative.

The sixth significant digit is not often of great importance in a 1 MHz time base, but high frequency stability is. And that is guaranteed by a ceramic filter. The circuit

shown produces a clock frequency of precisely 1.07 MHz and is eminently suitable as clock generator for a microprocessor system.

There is not much to say about the circuit which consists of two ICs, a resistor, a trimmer, and the ceramic filter. The oscillator proper consists of N1, N2, P1, R1, and the ceramic filter: its output is applied to inverter N3 which improves the slopes of the

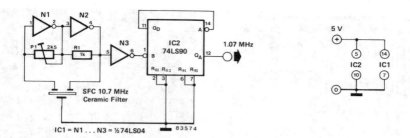

signal. The signal is then fed to input B of decimal counter IC2. As output Q_D is fed back to input A, the frequency of the output available at Q_A is exactly one tenth of the oscillator frequency.

IC2 can also be connected as a 5:1 divider to give a clock frequency of 2.14 MHz, which may be of interest to Z80 enthusiasts. The circuit also works very well with a

455 kHz ceramic filter. To ensure correct operation of the oscillator at this low frequency, preset potentiometer P1 has been included. The clock frequency is, in this case, 45.5 kHz (or 90.1 kHz if a 5:1 division was decided upon).

A final note about the 74LS90. Contrary to usual practice, the power supply pins are: pin 5 (+) and pin 10 (−).

285 RC generator

This tone generator uses two RC networks connected in series to achieve the necessary phase shift. The frequency range is 20 Hz to 20 kHz and distortion is kept to a

minimum by the extensive use of amplitude stabilisation.

Opamps A1 and A2 are the bases for two phase shifting networks in the circuit

1

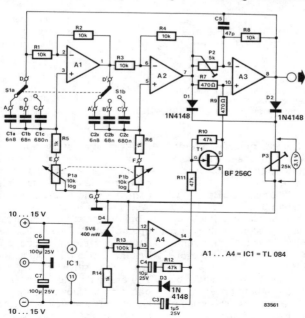

2

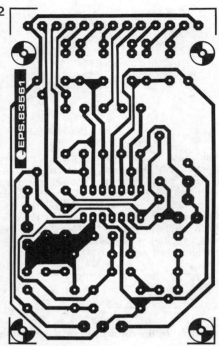

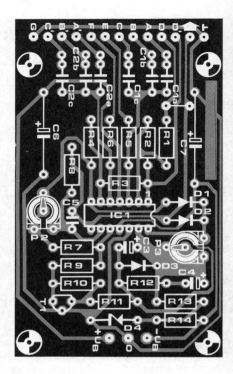

Parts list

Resistors:
R1...R4,R8 = 10 k
R5,R6,R14 = 1 k
R7,R9 = 470 Ω
R10...R12 = 47 k
R13 = 100 k
P1 = 10 k log stereo
  potentiometer
P2 = 5 k preset potentiometer
P3 = 25 k preset potentiometer

Capacitors:
C1a,C2a = 6n8
C1b,C2b = 68 n
C1c,C2c = 680 n
C3 = 1µ5/25 V
C4 = 10 µ/25 V
C5 = 47 p
C6,C7 = 100 µ/25 V

Semiconductors:
D1,D2,D3 = 1N4148
D4 = zenerdiode 5.6 V/
  400 mW
T1 = BF 256C
IC1 = TL 084

Miscellaneous:
S1 = 2 pole, 3 way rotary switch

diagram of figure 1. Stereo potentiometer P1 sets the frequency so that each network shifts the phase of the signal by 90°. Switch S1 selects the required range; 20 Hz...200 Hz, 200 Hz...2 kHz, or 2 kHz...20 kHz. Opamp A3 provides a further 180° phase shift and amplifies the signal so that the system will keep oscillating. Capacitor C5 is included in the feedback loop of A3 to suppress HF oscillation above 100 kHz.

The output of A2 and A3 is rectified by diodes D1 and D2 before being passed, via P3, to the inverting input of A4. This opamp compares the feedback signal to a refer-

ence voltage set by zener diode D4. The output op opamp A4 causes T1 (which acts as a variable resistor) to conduct to a greater or lesser extent. This controls the gain of A3 and maintains its output at a constant level. Capacitor C3 in the feedback loop of A4 integrates the input signal to this opamp, while C4 and R12 are included to suppress rapid fluctuations in the control system. Diode D3 protects the FET against any high positive voltages.

The printed circuit board layout for the RC generator is shown in figure 2. C3 and C4 are mounted vertically. The circuit requires a symmetrical supply of between 10 and

304

15 V. Current consumption is about 8 mA (positive supply) and 12 mA (negative supply).

The circuit is adjusted as follows. Set P3 to its mid position and adjust P2 so that the d.c. voltage at the output of A4 is between −1 and −2 V. Then adjust P3 to provide an output voltage from A3 of 1.5 V_{rms}. The distortion measured in the prototype was extremely low; at 1 kHz it was about 0.01%, rising to 0.03% at 20 kHz. At 20 Hz the distortion was 0.1%. Amplitude stability within any range was about 0.1 dB.

W. Meislinger

286 reaction tester

Not only do reaction testers provide a lot of fun for all ages, they can also be used for more serious applications (testing a driver's reactions, say, or an athlete's reflexes).

The unit is simple to operate: once the start button has been pressed, there is a delay until a LED (light-emitting diode) lights. The challenge is to press a button as quickly as possible. The elapsed time (between the LED lighting and the button being hit) is measured, and indicated as reaction time in milliseconds on a 4-digit display.

It is also possible for two people to compare their reaction times. In this mode, each person must press his own button when the LED lights. The difference in elapsed time between the pressing of both buttons is then indicated on the display. Two further LEDs indicate who of the two contestants pressed his button first. Since only one LED can light at any one time, home quizzes can be arranged on the principle of the TV version: the first one to press a button may reply first and gains a point.

The circuit of the reaction tester contains well-known ICs. Timer IC4 is used as a monostable multivibrator with a period that can be adjusted from 2 to 15 seconds by potentiometer P2. This provides a variable delay between the pressing of the start button and the lighting of the LED. The monostable is triggered by start button S4. Gates N1...N4 form two R-S bistables whose set inputs are connected to the reaction buttons S1 and S2 of the two players; the reset inputs are connected to the start button (S4). The output signal of IC4 causes transistor T5 to turn on and actuate D3, the reaction LED.

When S4 is pressed, the monostable multivibrator starts and the bistables are reset. The outputs N1 and N3 are at logic 0.

Additionally, IC5 (counter and display driver) is reset via N7 so that the display indicates '000.0'. During the delay time of the monostable, the output of IC4 (pin 3) is at logic 1 so that D3 remains dark and a logic 1 is present at S1 and S2. Pressing S1 and/or S2 during this delay therefore has no effect. At the end of this period the output of IC4 goes to logic 0, causing D3 to light and buttons S1 and S2 are enabled. The circuit is now ready for the players' reactions!

The outputs of N1 and N3 are connected to the inputs of XOR gate N9. This controls an astable multivibrator consisting of N8 and N10, which in turn provides rectangular pulses for the clock input of IC5. During the delay time of monostable IC4, the outputs of N1 and N3 were at logic 0 so that the square-wave generator was inhibited via N9. Now, as soon as one of the players presses his button and the corresponding bistable toggles, the output of N9 goes to logic 1 and the pulse generator is enabled. The number of pulses generated between the pressing of S1 and S2 is registered by IC5, evaluated, and indicated on the display. Since the frequency of the pulse generator is set to 10 kHz and the decimal point lights in LD3, the reaction time (difference) can be read off in milliseconds up to a maximum of 999.9 ms.

N5, N6, T6, T7, D1, D2, and R5 evaluate who of the two players pressed his button first. D1 lights if S1 was pressed first, and D2 lights if S2 was pressed first. N5 and N6 form an interlock circuit ensuring that only one of the two LEDs can light at any one time. IC5 contains a counter and a complete display control circuit with drivers and multiplexers for a 4-digit display. The display segment currents are limited by resistors R9...R15.

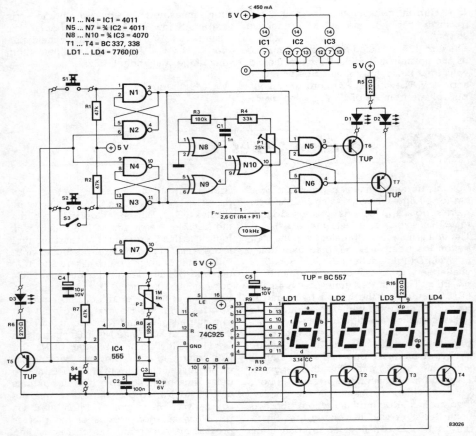

N1 ... N4 = IC1 = 4011
N5 ... N7 = ¾ IC2 = 4011
N8 ... N10 = ¾ IC3 = 4070
T1 ... T4 = BC 337, 338
LD1 ... LD4 = 7760 (D)

$$F \approx \frac{1}{2{,}6 \; C1 \; (R4 + P1)}$$

TUP = BC 557

83026

The circuit described so far is for a reaction time **difference** tester. It can be converted to a reaction tester for one person simply by adding a single switch. This switch (S3) is connected in parallel with S2. When it is closed, the multivibrator is started immediately after D3 lights. If S1 is pressed, the time elapsing between the LED lighting and S1 being pressed appears on the display.

The power supply for the circuit must be capable of supplying at least 450 mA at 5 V. The wiring is not critical. However, capacitor C4 should be as close to pin 8 of IC4 as possible and C5 should be close to pin 16 of IC5.

A frequency counter is required for accurate calibration of the astable multivibrator. Adjust P1 so that the frequency is precisely 10000 Hz. If no frequency counter is available, P1 can remain

set to its midpoint. In this case, the displayed time will not be so precise, but in most applications this is not so important. The power supply consists of an appropriate mains transformer with bridge rectifier, smoothing capacitor, and 5 V voltage regulator IC (with heat sink).

The front panel of the housing contains D1 and D2 and, immediately below them, the corresponding buttons S1 and S2. The start LED (D3) should be situated between the two buttons so that it can be clearly recognized by both players. Start button S4, potentiometer P2 (delay time adjustment), and mode switch S3 should also be positioned on the front panel.

based on an idea by L. van Boven

306

287 main beam dimmer

1 U_L (v)

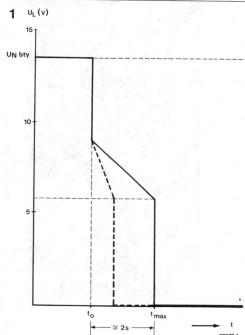

is approximately 0 V. A low current flows via the emitter-base junctions of T2 and T3, and via D3. Stage T1/T2/T3 performs like a zener power diode so that a voltage of about 4.2 V is present across transistor T1. At this instant, therefore, the bulb voltage is approximately 9 V (at a battery voltage of 13.2 V).

On account of the relatively constant voltage across the emitter-base junctions of T2 and T3 and over zener diode D3, a constant charging current for electrolytic capacitor C1 now flows via P1. With P1 set to its midpoint, the current is approximately 190 µA. The voltage across C1 rises at a rate of 4 V/s. Once it reaches 7.5 V (voltage across the emitter-base junction of T4 and across zener diode D4), T4 conducts and capacitor C1 charges very rapidly to the maximum voltage. Transistor T1 then turns off completely so that the current for the main beam bulbs ceases to flow. A minimum voltage rise, i.e. a dimming time, of 2 V/s can be set with P1.

Diodes D1 and D2 ensure that capacitors C1

How does this main beam dimmer operate? Figure 1 clarifies the situation. Until the instant of dipping (t_0) the full battery voltage is applied to the two headlight bulbs. When the dipswitch is actuated, the bulb voltage drops by about 4 V, clearly indicating that the main beam has been removed. The bulb voltage then continues to drop, so that headlight brightness decreases. Finally, t_{max} is reached — the instant at which the main beam is fully switched off — and only the dipped headlights are active.

Fortunately, the apparently complicated response illustrated in figure 1 can be duplicated with fairly simple electronics. Figure 2 shows the circuit of the main beam dimmer. This dimmer/dipper can be compared to a power supply with series-pass stabilization. However, the regulation between t_0 and t_{max} takes place considerably more slowly.

At time t_0, the relay contact for the main beam is opened. At this instant, capacitor C1 is discharged. Thus the voltage across it

2

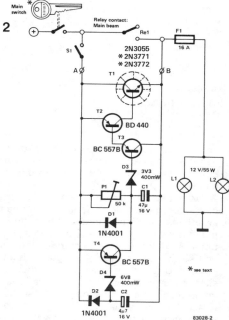

3

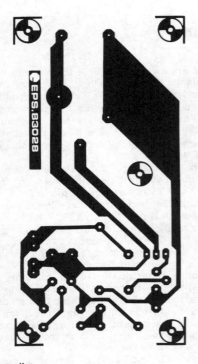

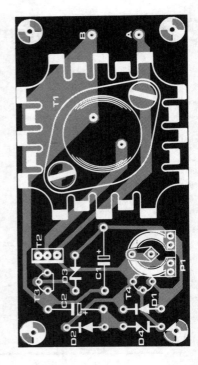

Parts list

Resistor:
P1 = 50 k preset

Capacitors:
C1 = 47 μ/16 V
C2 = 4μ7/16 V

Semiconductors:
D1,D2 = 1N4001
D3 = zener diode
  3V3/0.4 W

D4 = zener diode
  6V8/0.4 W
T1 = 2N3055
T2 = BD 440
T3,T4 = BC 557B

Miscellaneous:
Finger-type heat sink for T1
  (45 mm × 45 mm × 25 mm),
  (e.g. FK 201)

and C2 can discharge immediately after the headlight flasher is actuated or the main beam is switched on, thus making the circuit operational again.

An important point to note is that on some cars the ignition lock is also the main switch, as shown in figure 2. When the ignition is switched off, there is no voltage at point A. If the engine is started, then of course the effect shown in figure 1 is encountered. But we just have to live with this situation! The current flowing at this instant could result in a much more unpleasant effect. In laboratory trials the 2N3055 survived all attempts to destroy it. However, those

308

readers with any doubts should substitute a 2N3771 or 2N3772 for the 2N3055.

Construction is made simple by the printed circuit board of figure 3. Transistor T1 is fitted to the pcb together with the fingertype heat sink. Use serrated washers between the nuts and the copper surface to ensure good electrical contact.

The two leads are made from vehicle-type wiring and appropriate lugs or spade terminals are fitted to their ends. The other two ends are soldered directly to the pcb. Grommets are fitted to the through-holes for the two leads and it may be necessary to seal them. The assembly is then installed in a case (whether waterproof or not will depend on the mounting location) and fitted at a suitable point — preferably near the fusebox.

The relay contact for the main beam must now be located and the two leads A and B connected according to figure 2 (do not reverse them!). The main beam dimmer can be disabled with switch S1.

All that remains is a functional check. The unit should operate in accordance with figure 1. A functional check with the headlight flasher should also be made.

288   servo-tester

One possible cause of failure in radio-controlled models is a malfunctioning servo. The problem is: how can this be checked when the model is being operated in the field? Certainly during contests when you are forbidden to use the transmitter for testing. What we need is a battery-operated test circuit which supplies a PWM (pulse-width modulation) signal. The signal transmitted to the servo from the remote control receiver has a pulse width of 1.5 ms for the neutral position of the servo, and the pulse widths for the two end positions are 1 ms and 2 ms respectively. Obviously, our servo-tester must generate the same signals.

As shown in figure 1, the total component count is one IC, three resistors, one potentiometer and two capacitors: a NiCd 4.8 V battery is also needed to power the circuit. The IC is a 4001 CMOS type which contains four NOR gates. Gates N1/N2 are connected as an astable multivibrator which oscillates at a frequency of 50 Hz; the output pulse width is approximately 10 ms. The total period is 20 ms, which is one of the requirements the servo-tester must meet. The next step is to make the output pulse of the tester adjustable from 1 ms to 2 ms. This task is performed by the monostable multivibrator N3/N4. Each positive-going edge from the astable multivibrator triggers the monostable; the latter, in turn, produces an output pulse that can be varied from 1 ms to 2 ms by means of P1.

The output pulse is positive, so that the circuit described so far is only suitable for servos which respond to a positive input pulse. For servos requiring a negative input pulse, some modifications must be made to the circuit. First the IC is replaced by a pin-compatible quad NAND gate 4011. Pin 6 of gate N1 (point A) must be connected to the positive supply and the lower end of R3 (point B) must be grounded.

1

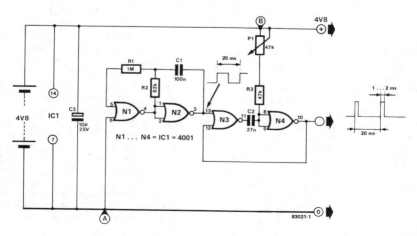

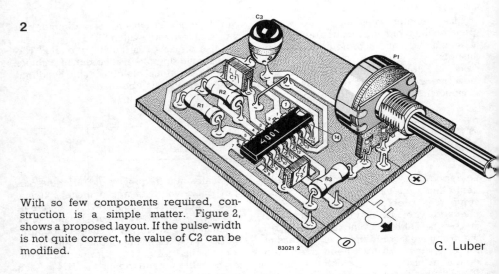

With so few components required, construction is a simple matter. Figure 2, shows a proposed layout. If the pulse-width is not quite correct, the value of C2 can be modified.

83021 2

G. Luber

289 kitchen timer

The two most critical parameters in cooking are expertise and timing. We have to admit that our knowledge of the first (and foremost) requirement could be written on the outside of a 2716. However, the second point is a different kettle of fish. If electronics is good at anything at all it surely must be period timing. The circuit here allows four independent periods to be pre-programmed and selected when required. A further asset of the circuit is the absence of any display that requires watching. The end of the period is given by an audible gong.

The circuit diagram shown in figure 1 can be broken down into four main parts: the counter (IC1); a comparator (IC2); a memory (IC3); and the sound generator (IC4). The presetting of periods is carried out by the 16 switches at the right of the diagram. The use of quad DIL switches would be ideal for this purpose.

The function of the circuit is fairly straightforward. With the circuit in the quiescent state, the $\overline{Q2}$ output of FF2 will be at logic 1 and counter IC1, will be inhibited via the reset input. Its outputs will be held low. The A=B output of the comparator (IC2) will also be low and the memory (IC3) will receive a reset pulse via gate N2. The comparator is now ready to

accept data relative to the required preset time period. This is preset in BCD format on one set of four switches: S1...S16. Once selected, the time code is entered into the memory by pressing the relative switch S17...S20.

There is now data in the memory and this is presented to the comparator causing the A<B output to change to logic 1. Bistable FF2 will toggle which will allow the counter to begin to do its job. This is a very useful IC in that it also includes an oscillator which is used to provide the clock frequency for the timer. The frequency is determined by the network consisting of C1, R1, R2, and preset P1. The latter is included to allow for fine tuning of the oscillator frequency if required.

When the reset level is removed from pin 12 of IC1, the counter is enabled and its outputs will count up from 0 at the clock frequency. The Q4 output of the counter is used to switch the LED on via transistor T1 as a reminder that the timer is in operation. The counter will continue doing just that until the A=B output of IC2 goes high which will occur when the counter output equals the memory. A number of events will now happen. A logic 0 reset pulse will reach IC3 (via N2) and the memory will be cleared. The output of the memory, and

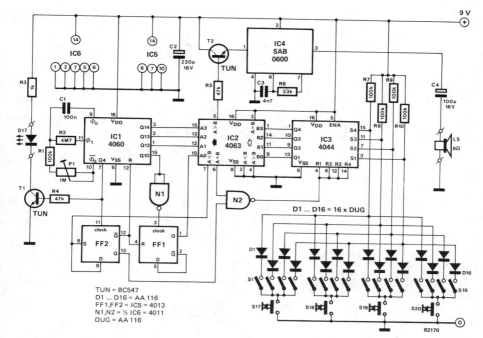

TUN = BC547
D1 ... D16 = AA 116
FF1,FF2 = IC5 = 4013
N1,N2 = ½ IC6 = 4011
DUG = AA 116

therefore the B inputs of the comparator, will all be at logic 0 and, because the count still exists on the A inputs of the comparator, the A>B output will revert to logic 1. This will provide a pulse via T2 to the sound generator, IC4, and the gong will sound to signal the end of the time period.

By this time the A<B output of IC3 will have returned to zero (the A inputs of the comparator are no longer less than the B inputs), allowing FF2 to change state on the next incoming clock pulse from the counter. When this arrives, the counter will be reset to zero (the Q̄ will go to logic 1) and we are back where we started, waiting for the next period to be entered via one of the switches S17 to S20.

Although the circuit is rather more com-

plex than the usual 555-based timer circuits, it does provide the very useful possibility of a number of preset periods. The circuit diagram shows four but more are possible if needed. Simply add another switch (S21 for instance) and four more diodes.

The power consumption of the circuit is about 3 mA and the 9 volt battery will last for a good many eggs.

It will be obvious that the applications for this particular timer do not necessarily have to end in the kitchen. It is versatile enough to find a great many uses wherever accurate timing is needed.

M.R. Brett

290   multitester

The multitester is a very simple circuit with many useful points — not the least of which is its extremely low cost. Basically, the circuit consists of little more than three ICs and a small loudspeaker. Its simplicity

does not prevent it from being able to check four different parameters at any point in a circuit under test.
1. A voltage below 0.8 V, interpreted as a logic 0.

1

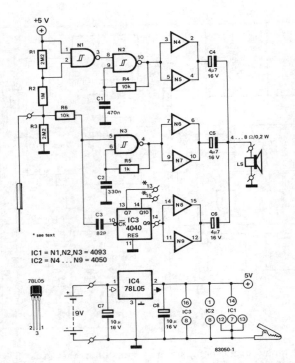

IC1 = N1,N2,N3 = 4093
IC2 = N4 . . . N9 = 4050

83050-1

2. A voltage between 1.8 V and 5 V, indicated as a logic 1.
3. A test point that has an undefined level (a three-state output) or is open circuit.
4. The existence of a clock signal or pulse train.

All these conditions are indicated by a different acoustic signal. The existence of a logic 0 is announced by a low tone while a logic 1 is a high tone. With an undefined level, or open circuit, the speaker will remain silent. If a pulsed signal is detected, such as a clock signal, the multitester will produce an audio output that oscillates between the high and low tones at the frequency of the detected signal. These four clear acoustic indications provide a quick and easy method of simple fault tracing.

The simplicity of the multitester is clearly illustrated in the circuit diagram of figure 1. Two oscillators, gates N2 and N3, and counter IC3 form the basis of the circuit. The detector probe is connected to the junction of R2 and R3. If the probe touches a point in the circuit under test that is at 0 V, resistor R3 will be short-circuited. This will cause the voltage at the junction of resistors R1 and R2 to fall. The output of gate N1 will

rise to logic 1 to actuate the oscillator formed by gate N2. If the probe is taken to +5 V, the oscillator formed by N3 will be switched on.

The existence of high frequency pulse signals at the probe will not affect either of the two oscillators but they will reach the counter (IC3) via C3. By frequency-dividing the pulse train, the counter will convert the high frequencies into audible tones. The divisor of IC3 can be selected by deriving the output from pin 13 (divide by 128), pin 14 (divide by 512), or pin 15 (divide by 1024). Although it is not shown in figure 1, it is, of course, possible to select these outputs by a rotary switch. The frequency of the oscillators N2 and N3 are determined by the time constants C1R4 and C2R5. Obviously, changing the value of any of these components will alter the frequency of the oscillator. Bear in mind that to make it easier to distinguish between the high and low tones it is advisable to keep the frequencies as far apart as possible.

The outputs of buffers N4...N9 are connected in parallel and fed to the miniature loudspeaker. The three electrolytic capacitors C4, C5, and C6 are included to

312

protect against d.c. voltage levels appearing across the speaker (it would not appreciate this at all!). Do not forget to tie down the inputs to the unused gate N10. If necessary, the multitester can derive its power supply direct from the circuit being tested. However, this is far from ideal and it would be better to make it fully independent and provide it with its own power source. Since the supply required must be +5 V, a voltage regulator will be needed even if batteries are used. The 78L05 voltage regulator IC will be adequate for the purpose. There is a slight disadvantage with the use of the regulator. Without it, the circuit has a current consumption of only 0.3 mA, but this rises to 2.4 mA when a regulator is used.

The completed circuit together with a miniature speaker can be mounted in any convenient case — with the accent on small. The easier it is to handle, the more useful it will be!

2

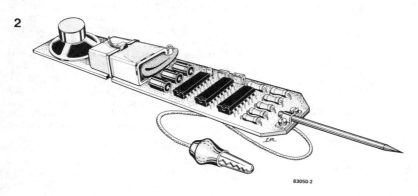

83050-2

291 electronic aerial switch

Many radio- and TV-amateurs have often wished they had a simple means of switching from one aerial to another. The normal solution is to do this by plug and socket arrangements, because a loss-free switch for changing aerials is not as simple as it sounds. The problem revolves around the losses caused by a mechanical switch.

1

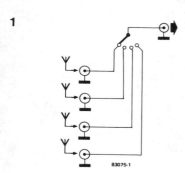

83075-1

2

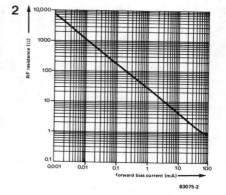

83075-2

At relatively low frequencies (medium- and short-wave) such losses are not serious, but in the VHF and UHF bands they become a nasty problem. Even so, the most obvious and by far easiest way of selecting one of a number of aerials is by a mechanical switch as shown in figure 1.

There is, however, a means of obviating the disadvantages of a mechanical switch at high frequencies and that is by using PIN diodes which are ideal for this purpose.

What are PIN diodes? Briefly, they are special switching diodes of which the most important property is a very low self-capacitance while at high frequencies they are virtually purely resistive. The resistance can be varied between 1 and 10000 Ω by means of a direct current, the so-called forward bias current, as shown in figure 2. It is clear from this figure that the resistance of such a diode changes linearly over a wide range of values of current. This characteristic is ideal for a number of applications: by varying the forward bias current, the PIN diode can be used for the attenuation, equalization or even amplitude modulation of high frequency signals; by switching the forward bias current, pulse modulation and phase-shifting of high frequency signals becomes feasible.

In the aerial switch described here, the PIN diodes are used in a simple way: as a high frequency switch. The forward bias current is set relatively high and, apart from this current, the only requirement is a switch. Figure 3 shows how this works: when the switch is closed, the diode conducts; when the switch is open, the diode is cut off.

With PIN diodes, the switching between four aerials does not, therefore, present a real problem. All that is required is a current supply, a 4-position switch, and four PIN diodes (see figure 4).

3

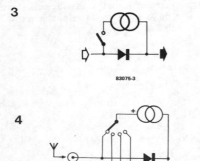

83075-3

4

83075-4

5

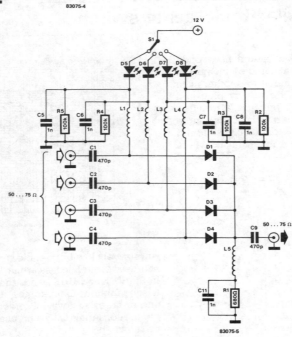

83075-5

Parts list

Resistors:
R1 = 680 Ω
R2...R5 = 100 k

Capacitors:
C1...C4,C9 = 470 p ceramic
C5...C8,C11 = 1 n ceramic

Semiconductors:
D1...D4 = PIN diode BA 244
D5...D8 = LED, red, 5 mm

Chokes:
L1...L5 = see text

Miscellaneous:
S1 = switch, 1-pole, 4-way
aerial input and output connectors

In practice, there is, of course, a little more to it, but not much, as can be seen from the complete circuit diagram in figure 5. The required forward bias current can be obtained from a normal +12 V supply (mains transformer, bridge rectifier, and regulator IC, for instance). LEDs D5...D8 are connected in series with the supply to give a ready indication which aerial has been switched in.

Depending upon the position of switch S1, the forward bias current first passes through one of the LEDs, subsequently through one of the chokes L1...L4, then through the relevant PIN diode (D1...D4), and finally to earth via choke L5 and resistor

R1. This latter resistor determines the value of the current; at 680 Ω, as in figure 5, the current is 15 mA which is sufficient to ensure reliable switching of the diodes and satisfactory lighting of the LEDs.

Capacitors C1...C4 and C9 are necessary to prevent DC appearing at the input and output of the circuit. Chokes L1...L5 prevent the HF signal leaking to earth via the power supply line. Capacitors C5...C8 decouple the power supply line for HF. Resistors R2...R5 ensure that the anodes of the diodes not in use are earthed so that mixing of the various aerial signals is impossible.

In view of the small number of parts, the construction of the electronic aerial switch is a fairly simple matter. The only point which needs watching is that all wiring must be kept as short as possible to ensure satisfactory operation.

Chokes L1...L5 can be wound on a ferrite bead: using enamelled copper wire of 0.3 mm diameter, two turns will suffice for UHF and five for VHF inputs. It is, of course, possible to buy them ready-made: 1 μH is required for UHF and about 5 μH for VHF. The circuit has been designed for aerial input impedances of 50...75 ohms. Isolation between the various inputs is not less than 30 dB. Although the loss caused by switch S1 is minimal, the PIN diodes will deteriorate the noise factor of the receiver a little, but this will not be more than 1 dB.

from an idea by C. Abegg

292 precision voltage divider

In the construction of measuring equipment, you normally require a number of precision components. Particularly voltage and current dividers need resistors of 1% tolerance. The simple four-way voltage divider shown in figure 1 has a total resistance of 1 MΩ and requires four resistors: 900 kΩ, 90 kΩ, 9 kΩ, and 1 kΩ. And that's where your troubles are likely to start. If you're not lucky enough to find a complete divider somewhere, forget about buying the individual resistors. It's extremely unlikely that you'll find the above four values in the

high-stab range in one shop.

Fortunately, it is possible to make a precision voltage divider with an input impedance of 1 MΩ from standard value resistors. The solution lies in connecting two high-stab resistors in parallel to obtain the required value as shown in figure 2. If a shop stocks high-stab resistors, it's pretty certain that it has standard values of 1 MΩ, 100 kΩ, and so on. And that's what the divider of figure 2 depends on! The resulting resistances are 909.09 kΩ, 90.909 kΩ, 9.09 kΩ, and 1.01 kΩ. The deviation from

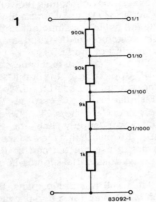

1

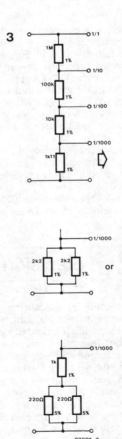

2

3

the ideally required divisors is smaller than 0.01% so that in practice the variations are entirely dependent upon the tolerances of the resistors used.

In parallel connections as used in figure 2, not all resistors need be 1% types. Because each combination consists of two resistors of which one has ten times the value of the other, the larger one has a much smaller effect on the result than the smaller one. As a consequence, the tolerance of the larger resistor is of much less importance than that of the smaller one. Even if 5% types are used for the larger resistors in the parallel branches, the overall stability will be sufficient. The same is true of R7 because this is pretty small compared with R8.

As an example of the above: if R2 deviates exactly 5% from its nominal value, the variation of the resultant value of R1/R2 is only 0.4%. You might say that the tolerance of the larger resistor improves roughly by a factor equal to the ratio of the two resistors. Parallel connections have a further advantage: statistically there is only a very small probability that two resistors in a parallel branch both deviate in the same direction. In other words: there is a good chance that the network of figure 2 is more precise than the one constructed from 1% resistors as shown in figure 1.

All in all, the above gives enough reasons to use parallel-connected resistors. Figure 3 gives an alternative which uses fewer resistors. However, its theoretical stability is rather worse than that of figure 2: 0.01% instead of 0.001%.

293   transistor selector

This transistor selector will enable you to determine the class — A, B, or C — into which a transistor falls. The class is defined by the d.c. current gain, h_{FE}, as follows:

class A: h_{FE} up to 200
class B: h_{FE} 200...400
class C: h_{FE} above 400

This is roughly the same classification as used by manufacturers on low-power transistors.

The classification A, B, or C, given by manufacturers in their data books does not always indicate exact values. Normally, the three classes are given minimum, maximum, and typical values, and therefore they overlap to some extent. It may sometimes be necessary to check the class printed on the transistor. Or it may be that you want to find a replacement in the 2N...-series for a BC...type with an equivalent d.c. current gain. In such cases you will find this selector a very useful tool. The selector can, of course, be used for both n-p-n and p-n-p transistors. For clarity, we have split the complete circuit diagram shown in figure 3 into two parts: figure 1 for n-p-n transistors and figure 2 for p-n-p types.

If a PP3 (9 V) battery is used as power supply, the base current in the transistor under test amounts to about 10 μA. The collector voltage is then given by

$$U_C = U_b - U_{R2} = U_b - I_C R2 = U_b - h_{FE} I_B R2$$

where U_C = d.c. collector voltage
U_b = supply voltage = 9 V
U_{R2} = voltage drop across resistor R2
I_C = d.c. collector current
I_B = d.c. base current = 10 μA
h_{FE} = d.c. current gain

Substituting the known values into this formula, we obtain:

$$U_C = 9 - 0.015 \, h_{FE} \text{ volts}$$

If we now substitute the turn over values of h_{FE}, we obtain values for U_C of 6 V when h_{FE} = 200 and 3 V when h_{FE} = 400. In other words, the greater the d.c. current gain, the smaller the collector voltage. A moment's reflection will show why: the greater the d.c. current gain, the greater the collector current and resulting voltage drop across R2, and the smaller the voltage across the collector-emitter junction of the transistor being checked.

The collector voltage is applied to the non-inverting inputs of three comparators: opamps IC1...IC3. The inverting inputs of these opamps are derived from a voltage divider, R4...R6, across the supply voltage (R3 is, of course, short-circuited by diode D1). When U_C is smaller than 3 V ($h_{FE} > 400$), the output of IC3 is low and

1

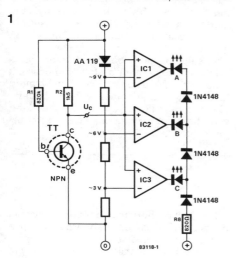

83118-1

2

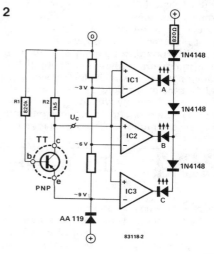

83118-2

317

3

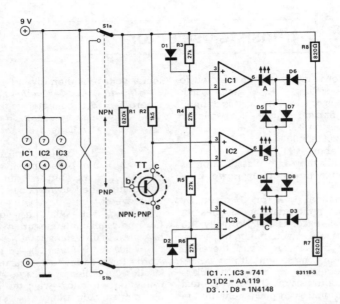

IC1 . . . IC3 = 741
D1,D2 = AA 119
D3 . . . D8 = 1N4148

83118-3

LED C lights. The ouput of the other two opamps are also low, but the anode voltage of LEDs A and B is too low for the LEDs to light. When U_C is greater than 3 V, the voltage at the output of IC3 is nearly 9 V. No current then flows through LED C and LED B lights. When U_C is greater than 6 V ($h_{FE}<200$), the output of IC2 is nearly equal to U_b and only the output of IC1 remains low so that LED A lights. The above reasoning depends upon a voltage drop across R8 which ensures just sufficient anode voltage for the lighted LED. It may be that owing to circuit tolerances in your particular case this is not entirely possible: the solution is then to increase R8 to, say, 1 kΩ.

The corresponding diagram for selecting p-n-p transistors is shown in figure 2. The arrangement of the LEDs for classes A, B, and C, remains as before. Now, however, because the supply voltage polarity has been reversed, a higher d.c. current gain will cause a higher collector voltage. The

voltage applied to the comparators is, therefore, in this case not that across the collector-emitter junction, but that across R2. Otherwise the operation of the circuit is identical to that for n-p-n transistors.

The complete circuit is not so difficult to follow now. The sections for n-p-n and p-n-p transistors have been combined. The polarity of the supply voltage is reversed by means of a double-pole switch, S1. Diodes D1 . . . D3 and D6 ensure that the circuit operates satisfactorily whatever the position of S1. We have used germanium diodes in the D1 and D2 positions, as these have a smaller voltage drop than silicon types.

The selector may be constructed on a piece of vero or other prototyping board: it is not critical. This board may then be fitted in a small case, together with the battery. The case should, of course, be provided with three connecting clips for the transistor to be checked.

294   trick battery

Everybody enjoys a good joke... except maybe the victim. The question is whether the victims of this circuit will see anything to laugh about, but that is your problem.

What we have here is an apparently normal battery which is quite abnormal when a meter is connected across it. This battery is so unusual, in fact, that the victim is likely to

1

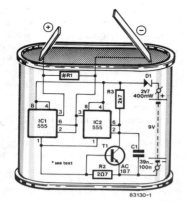

83130-1

dismantle his multimeter to see what is burned out.

It all revolves about the fact that anybody metering a battery will attribute any unusual results to the multimeter — after all, who would suspect something like that of an ordinary battery?

The idea is to hand this trick battery to a friend or acquaintance and ask him to check it with his multimeter. Chances are he will begin by measuring the voltage. This will be a steady 4.5 volts. Now the short circuit current, and...wait a minute...shouldn't the needle of the meter go the other way? How can it do that? Try the voltage again: yes, that is still correct and the plus and minus are connected where they should be. Now the current again: and the needle still goes the wrong way! The only possible conclusion seems to be that there is something seriously amiss with the meter. So the instrument is swiftly taken apart to have a look for the damage.

This is probably the best time to reveal the joke, before your victim does some real damage by trying to repair some imaginary fault.

What we have here is no ordinary battery, that is obvious even from the title of this article. We started with a normal flat (in more than one sense) 4.5 V battery which is first hollowed out and then 'refilled' with a 9 V battery and a small 'trick circuit'.

This circuit operates as a sort of current controlled switch. As long as there is very little current passing through the circuit, there is a voltage of 4.5 V at the connections of the battery — and it even has the correct polarity. So when the voltage is

measured, everything seems to be right. When the current from the trick battery is measured, a much greater current flows and this causes the polarity of the connections to be reversed.

The trick circuit is shown in figure 1. The switch is made up of two 555s which are connected here as inverting schmitt triggers, whose input is the junction of pins 2 and 6. The amperemeter consists of resistor R2 and transistor T1.

The operation is straightforward. At rest or when the voltage between the positive and negative connections is being measured, very little current flows, and hardly any voltage is dropped across R2 so T1 does not conduct. The voltage at the input of IC2 is therefore far greater than the upper triggering level and pin 3 will be low. As a result, the output voltage of IC1 is high and the voltage at the connections is just the same as for a normal battery.

When measuring current, the voltage drop across resistor R2 causes T1 to conduct. The output of IC2 therefore changes around, while IC1 inverts this signal and will then have a low level at its output. The positive and negative of the trick battery are now interchanged and the current

2

flows in exactly the opposite direction as previously. During switch over there is, of course, a moment when the voltages at the outputs of IC1 and IC2 are the same. The current then drops and the circuit tends to return to its initial state. The current immediately increases again and, to prevent the circuit from continually switching from one state to the other, C1 is needed. This keeps the input of IC2 low during the switching, and T1 is also prevented from conducting. To make everything look as real as possible, the output voltage must be exactly 4.5 V. The voltage is already about this value but it is not precisely 4.5 V. This can be improved by loading the output with R1. Admittedly, this is not a very elegant solution, but it works. Some experimentation is needed to find the right value of resistor. We found 330 Ω suitable for our prototype.

This circuit is so simple that it can be easily and quickly constructed on a piece of veroboard. The majority of the work involves preparing the battery. First the cap on the top is removed. With a sharp knife the black material is separated from the walls of the battery and then it should be possible to remove the innards with a pair of pliers. Then the 9 V battery is put inside along with some packing material to make the battery about the right weight. The circuit is then placed on the top. If the circuit is fitted with a battery clip, the trick battery can be disconnected after use.
The photo of figure 2 shows the prototype and gives an indication of how everything fits together.

L. van Boven

295 ZN 415 — a complete AM radio tuner

Ferranti's ZN415, an extended version of the well-known ZN414, has a claim to be 'the smallest radio in the world'. Because of its really small size and the few external components required to make up a complete radio receiver, this new IC has become very popular.
Although ICs should normally be treated as black boxes, we felt you might be in-

terested in knowing 'what goes on inside' Basically, the ZN415 consists of a ZN414 — itself a ten-transistor radio frequency tuner — and a two-stage a.f. amplifier (see figure 1). The tuner covers the frequency range 150 kHz...3 MHz which includes the medium and long wave broadcast bands. A.F. output is 1.0...1.5 mW into 64 Ω. Because of its high input resistance (of the

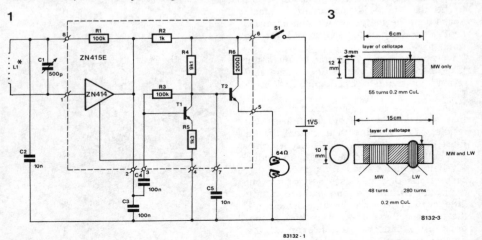

83132 - 1

*see text

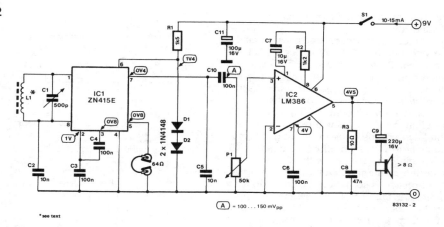

(A) = 100 ... 150 mV_pp   83132 - 2

* see text

order of 4 MΩ), selectivity is good: 8 kHz bandwidth at —6 dB points. The a.g.c. characteristic shows an increase of less than 7 dB in a.f. output for more than 30 dB r.f. input. The circuit is packaged in 8-pin DIL.

Although the IC is capable of driving good-quality headphones satisfactorily, we felt it would be interesting to add a tuned aerial circuit, an a.f. amplifier to drive an 8 Ω loud-speaker, and a volume control which is lacking on the basic IC (see figure 2). This made it necessary to increase the required supply voltage to 9 V (the IC itself operates from 1.5 V) so that a PP3 would do nicely. Power dissipation is of the order of 120 mW. Note that reception via 64 Ω headphones is still possible.

If reception on medium wave only is re-quired, the aerial can be constructed from a single layer of 55 turns close wound onto a 60x12x3 mm ferrite rod using enamelled copper wire SWG36. If both medium and long wave are wanted, a 150x12x3 mm fer-rite rod is needed. The aerial for the medium wave is then a single layer of 48 turns and that for the long wave a multi-layer of 280 turns close wound enamelled copper wire 36 SWG. Details of these win-dings are shown in figure 3. If both medium and long wave are used, a 10 p capacitor should be connected across the LW winding. A switch to select between the two bands must then also be incorporated.

Literature:
Ferranti Semiconductors — Advance Product Information: ZN415E an AM Radio Receiver

---

296   doorbell memory

On occasion, it may be useful to know when a visitor has called in your absence. This is especially true in the case of an en-forced absence when a visitor is expected. Confusion reigns supreme on these oc-casions. The circuit here helps to rectify the situation by providing a memory for the doorbell. On your return, a LED will advise you whether or not a visitor called. The cir-cuit is powered by the bell transformer via diode D1 and capacitor C1. This provides a d.c. voltage sufficient for the memory. Under normal conditions (with no one ring-ing the doorbell), transistor T1 is switched off and T2 conducts to provide a form of latch for T1. Obviously, D3 will never light under these conditions!

Now our visitor arrives! With a joyful cry of 'Avon calling' they press the doorbell — only to lapse into total embarrasment when there is no answer! However, our circuit now leaps into action. Via D2 and R1, the doorbell switch S1 provides a base drive current to T1 which switches off T2 and, in passing, D3 on. Now the transistor latch (T2) swings the other way, and T1 is held on by the current through S2 (normally closed), R5, and R6.

The unfortunate visitor goes away totally deflated but the LED will indicate his past presence! On your return, the LED will be noted and the circuit reset. This is carried out by simply pressing S2 which breaks the base currents holding T1 on, causing this transistor to switch off. In doing so, the LED is switched off and T2 will be switched on. The latch will be back in the original position where T1 is held off by the fact that R5 is effectively in parallel with R2.

A further refinement would be to provide an automatic reset when the front door is opened. In this case, S2 is a switch operated by the opening door. However, the LED must then be mounted outside the door (possibly in the doorbell switch housing) or the LED will be off by the time you get into the house to look!

On the other hand, a second circuit could be built as a 'memory' for the 'automatic' memory and then it would be no problem to open the door! This second circuit will of course require a reset switch!

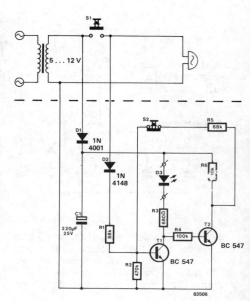

297   simple power supply regulator

The cost of high grade, regulated power supplies has dropped with the advent of modern ICs. For many applications te requirements are not that stringent, and a simple, discretely constructed regulator as described here will suffice.

With values as shown, the output voltage is 12 V and the output current is limited to 0.5 A. For applications not requiring current limiting, the circuit van supply up to 1 A. The current limiting components can then be left out.

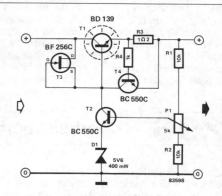

Table 1

U_i (V)	R_L (Ω)	U_o (V)
15	∞	12.00
	100	11.95
	22	11.72
17	∞	12.02
	100	11.97
	22	11.78
20	∞	12.06
	100	11.66
	22	11.50

Correlation between input and output voltage and load resistance

The relation between input voltage, load resistance, and regulated output voltage is shown in table 1. This table can therefore be used to determine whether the regulation for a particular application is sufficient. The 'geart' of the regulator, high-power low-frequency transistor T1, must be fitted onto an adequate heat sink. FET T3 operates as a current source with an output maximum of 11...18 mA: this limits the base current of T1, of course, but the alternative would have been a very low value resistor; this would have resulted in large power losses under low load conditions. To ensure correct operation of T3, the input voltage must be at least 3 V higher than the output voltage; for optimum regulation, 1 5 V difference is recommended. The base circuit of T2 is driven by voltage divider R1, P1, and R2. Potentiometer P2 is set such that T2 taps some of the current of T3; the smaller this current, the higher the base current of T1 and therefore the output voltage. This raises the voltage across the

voltage divider, and consequently the base voltage of T2; T2 then takes some more current from T3: this reduces the base current of T1 and again the output voltage. In practice, an equilibrium is soon reached.

Transistor T4, in conjunction with resistors R3 and R4, forms a simple current limiter with the limit being determined by the values of R3 and R4. This stage also taps some of the current from T3. If current limiting is not required, T4, R3, and R4 can be omitted. The emitter of T1 is then connected directly to the positive output terminal.

298   car lights warning device

Anyone who has ever forgotten to switch the car lights off after having driven in poor weather conditions, and returned later in the day to find the car battery flat, will appreciate this circuit.

The circuit sounds a buzzer when you turn off the engine and have forgotten to switch off the head-lights. When required, the circuit can be reset with push button S1. This may be necessary, for instance, when you have your headlights on, get stuck in a traffic jam and turn the engine off to keep the carbon monoxide level down.

When you turn the ignition key and start the engine, the dynamo or alternator runs, relays are operating, the electric fan comes on, the automatic radio aerial extends...

All these produce large voltage spikes on the car's electrical system and any electronic circuit must be protected against these.

The circuit is connected to contact breaker S3 and lighting switch S2. At first sight, the use of the contact breaker as an indicator for 'engine running' may seem surprising but, during the testing of the circuit, it became apparent that if the ignition switch is used instead, the circuit will not work properly. The cause for this was found to be variations in the battery voltage.

The pulses from the contact breaker charge capacitor C1 via resistor R1. Once C1 is fully charged, there is a stable DC voltage at the collector of transistor T2: the

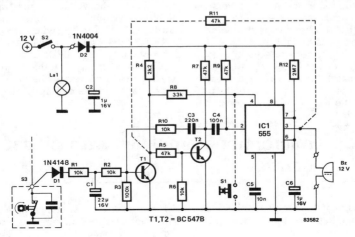

T1,T2 = BC 547B

trigger input (terminal 2) of the timer IC (555) is then not driven.

When the engine is turned off, C1 discharges, T1 is cut off, and the base-emitter voltage of T2 rises. This causes the collector voltage of T2 to drop to 0. This voltage change is converted into a trigger pulse for the timer IC by differentiating network R9/C4.

The IC is then operative and causes the buzzer to sound; with values as shown, the warning tone will last for three seconds. The time can be lengthened by increasing the value of C6.

The circuit does, of course, not operate with the car lights switched off as it is powered from the car lights switch!

J. Glauser

299 h$_{FE}$ tester

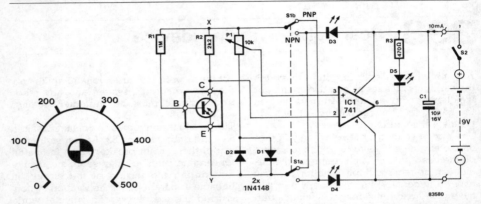

This h$_{FE}$ tester is interesting because of its simplicity and because it enables the β of both PNP and NPN transistors to be measured. Furthermore, the measurement is independent of the supply voltage of the tester. As the diagram shows, the base current of the transistor under test travels via R1. This base current I_B is equal to $[(U_{XY}-U_{BE})/R1]$ A. The voltage drop across the collector resistor is h$_{FE}$ × I_B × R2. Preset P1 is used to set a reference voltage derived from voltage $U_{XY} - U_{D1}$ (or D2 for a PNP transistor). This means that the setting of the potentiometer is directly proportional to the h$_{FE}$ of the transistor under

test and is independent of supply voltage. The voltage across R2 and the voltage set with P1 are compared by IC1 which is connected as a comparator. Potentiometer P1 is now set so that the LED at the output of the opamp just lights or is just dimmed. At this setting, the voltage across the potentiometer is equal to the voltage across R2. Switch S1 is used to switch from NPN to PNP (or vice versa) by reversing the polarity of voltage U_{XY}. LEDs D3 and D4 in the supply lines ensure that the input voltages to be measured are within the common mode range of the opamp used.

300 microphone amplifier with preset tone control

The active parts of the circuit (amplifiers A1 and A2) shown in figure 1 are contained in IC1.

A1 operates as a non-inverting amplifier and the microphone input is applied to pin 1 via coupling capacitor C1. The gain of

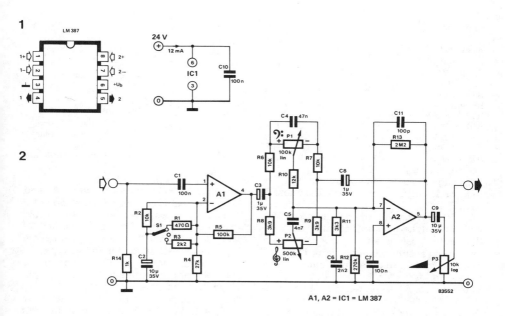

1

LM 387

2

A1, A2 = IC1 = LM 387

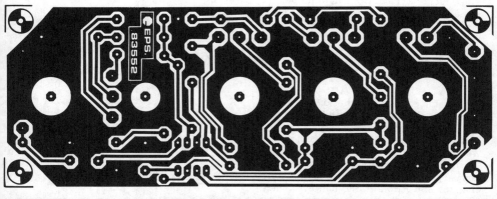

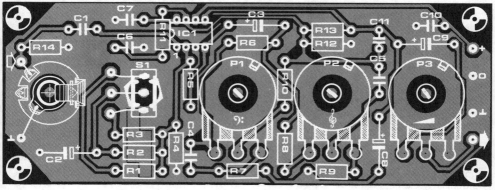

Parts list

Resistors:
R1 = 470 Ω
R2,R6,R7 = 10 k
R3 = 2k2
R4 = 27 k
R5 = 100 k
R8,R9 = 3k9
R10 = 12 k
R11 = 3k3
R12 = 270 k
R13 = 2M2
R14 = 1 k
P1 = 100 k lin. preset
P2 = 500 k lin. preset
P3 = 10 k log. preset

Capacitors:
C1,C7,C10 = 100 n
C2,C9 = 10 μ/35 V
C3 = 1 μ/35 V
C4 = 47 n
C5 = 4n7
C6 = 2n2
C8 = 1 μ/35 V
C11 = 100 p

Semiconductors:
IC1 = LM 387

Miscellaneous:
1 switch, miniature, single pole change-over, centre off
1 microphone socket (mono)

this stage is determined by the ratio of resistor R5 to the parallel combination of R1...R4.

With R1 switched in, the gain is about 225, with R3 switched in about 60, and with S1 in the centre position about 14. As the effective input sensitivity can be altered by S1, it can be matched to different input levels or microphones.

The output of A1 is applied to a tone control stage, A2. The ratio R13/R12 determines the amplification (about 18 dB) of this stage. The effect of R11 and C6 is, in principle, the same as that of R2 and C2: a smaller value of C6 increases the lower cut-off frequency. The RC network between A1 and A2 is the real tone control. Potentiometer P1 sets the bass level and P2 the treble level. Use is made of the characteristic of capacitors behaving as frequency-dependent resistances for AC voltages.

The output signal of the amplifier is available for connection to the main amplifier via C9 and potentiometer P3.

This microphone amplifier has not only been tested in the Elektor laboratories but also by the designer during searching on-stage tests.

---

301 offset-less rectifier

In an active rectifier, the offset of the opamp can cause the rectified output voltage to be incorrect.

This is especially bad in applications where precise measurement is essential. The offset can, of course, be set to zero but this very correction can cause temperature changes and ripple in the supply voltage which can cause even more problems.

The rectifier circuit shown here is not affected by offset, because the input and output of the opamp are isolated from d.c. voltages by two capacitors (C1 and C3). If the circuit is imagined without these two capacitors, it appears as a normal active rectifier.

The feedback for the positive half cycle is via D1 and R2, and feedback for the negative half cycle is via D2 and R3. Resistor R4 controls the d.c. setting of the opamp. At the output we get the rectified a.c. voltage component of the input voltage. Between output 1 and output 2 the full rectified signal is available; the rectified positive half

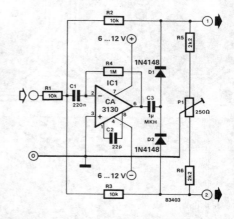

cycle is between output 1 and ground and the rectified negative half cycle is between output 2 and ground. In measuring these values, the supply for the meter must be totally isolated from the supply for the opamp.

Note that IC1 reverses the phase of the in-

326

put signal so that the negative half cycle becomes positive (output 1) and the positive half cycle becomes negative (output 2). Potentiometer P1 is used to set the symmetry of the positive and negative regulated signals. For precision applications, the whole circuit should be built using 1% tolerance resistors and the diodes should be compared to see that they have the same voltage drops. The maximum input voltage is 4 V_{pp}, frequency range is up to 20 kHz. The opamp is powered by a symmetrical supply of between 6 and 12 V. Current consumption is very small (a few mA) so a battery could be used to power the circuit.

302 inexpensive 45 MHz crystal filter

A receiver with an intermediate frequency, IF, which is higher than the highest received frequency, f_c, has the great advantage that the separation between the received frequency and the image frequencies, $f_c \pm 2IF$, is large. A filter with a high centre frequency and narrow pass-band which is eminently suitable for SSB reception can be built from relatively few components.

Oscillator crystals often have one or more spurious resonances and this makes their application in filters undesirable because of the risk of unwanted pass-bands. The broader the filter response, the greater this

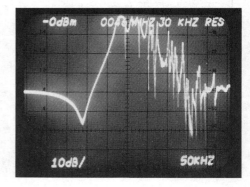

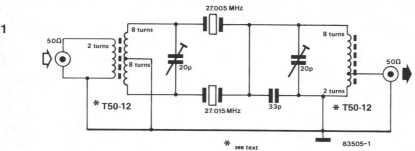

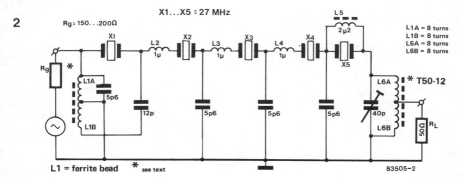

risk becomes. It is possible to use 27 MHz third-overtone crystals (standard in most CB equipment) in their fifth overtone mode. Figure 1 shows the circuit of a coarse 45 MHz filter using two 27 MHz crystals. The photo shows that the attenuation outside the pass-band is far from satisfactory: there is hardly any difference between the required and the unwanted pass-bands. With the use of more crystals, the pass-band of the filter becomes narrower and the likelihood of spurious frequencies coinciding becomes smaller.

Figure 2 shows the circuit of a ladder filter using five crystals, which reduces the likelihood of spurious pass-bands greatly.

The 6 dB bandwidth of the filter of figure 2 is about 3 kHz, while that at the 40 dB points is only 5 kHz. The input impedance, Rg, lies between 150 Ω and 200 Ω and the output impedance is 50 Ω. Its insertion loss is 7 dB.

Coil L1 is a bifilar winding of 2×8 turns of enamelled copper wire of 0.2 mm diameter. As this coil is not critical, it may be wound on a ferrite bead. Moulded RF chokes may be used for L2...L5. Coil L6 is again a bifilar winding, 2×8 turns, enamelled copper wire of 0.2...0.5 mm diameter on a T50-12 former. The filter can be built on a small piece of vero board. The coils must be screened from one another by earthed screens. The crystal housings must also be earthed.

Further signal processing is best done at a much lower second IF of, say, 10 kHz, obtained by mixing the 45 MHz IF with the output of a crystal oscillator operating at 45 MHz $\pm$ IF2. The oscillator can also use a CB type third overtone crystal operating in its fifth overtone mode.

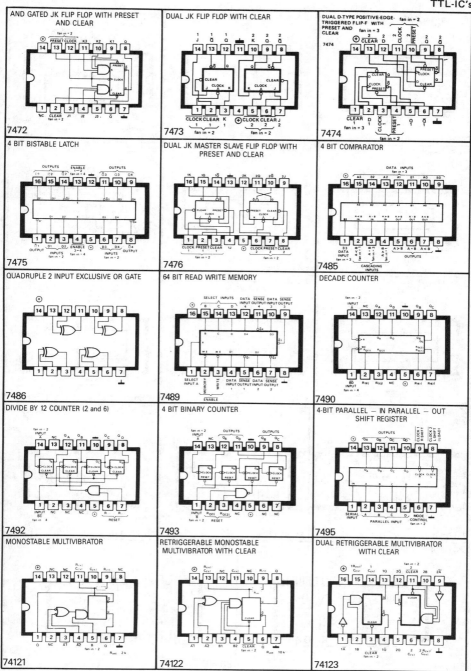

AND GATED JK FLIP FLOP WITH PRESET AND CLEAR — 7472

DUAL JK FLIP FLOP WITH CLEAR — 7473

DUAL D-TYPE POSITIVE-EDGE-TRIGGERED FLIP-F WITH PRESET AND CLEAR — 7474

4 BIT BISTABLE LATCH — 7475

DUAL JK MASTER SLAVE FLIP FLOP WITH PRESET AND CLEAR — 7476

4 BIT COMPARATOR — 7485

QUADRUPLE 2 INPUT EXCLUSIVE OR GATE — 7486

64 BIT READ WRITE MEMORY — 7489

DECADE COUNTER — 7490

DIVIDE BY 12 COUNTER (2 and 6) — 7492

4 BIT BINARY COUNTER — 7493

4-BIT PARALLEL – IN PARALLEL – OUT SHIFT REGISTER — 7495

MONOSTABLE MULTIVIBRATOR — 74121

RETRIGGERABLE MONOSTABLE MULTIVIBRATOR WITH CLEAR — 74122

DUAL RETRIGGERABLE MULTIVIBRATOR WITH CLEAR — 74123

TTL-IC's

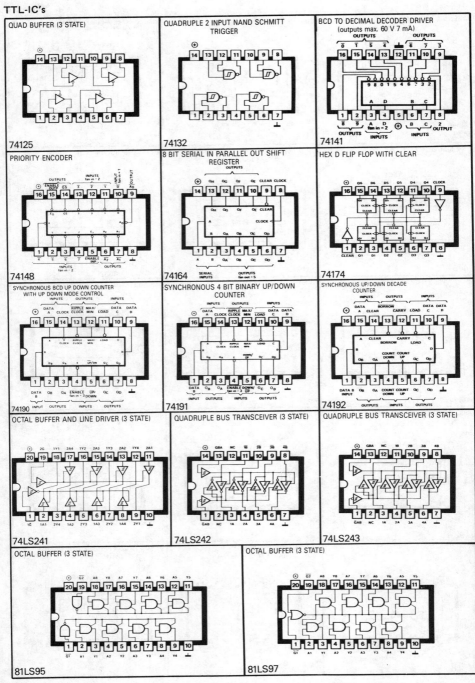

QUAD BUFFER (3 STATE)
74125

QUADRUPLE 2 INPUT NAND SCHMITT TRIGGER
74132

BCD TO DECIMAL DECODER DRIVER (outputs max. 60 V 7 mA)
74141

PRIORITY ENCODER
74148

8 BIT SERIAL IN PARALLEL OUT SHIFT REGISTER
74164

HEX D FLIP FLOP WITH CLEAR
74174

SYNCHRONOUS BCD UP DOWN COUNTER WITH UP DOWN MODE CONTROL
74190

SYNCHRONOUS 4 BIT BINARY UP/DOWN COUNTER
74191

SYNCHRONOUS UP/DOWN DECADE COUNTER
74192

OCTAL BUFFER AND LINE DRIVER (3 STATE)
74LS241

QUADRUPLE BUS TRANSCEIVER (3 STATE)
74LS242

QUADRUPLE BUS TRANSCEIVER (3 STATE)
74LS243

OCTAL BUFFER (3 STATE)
81LS95

OCTAL BUFFER (3 STATE)
81LS97

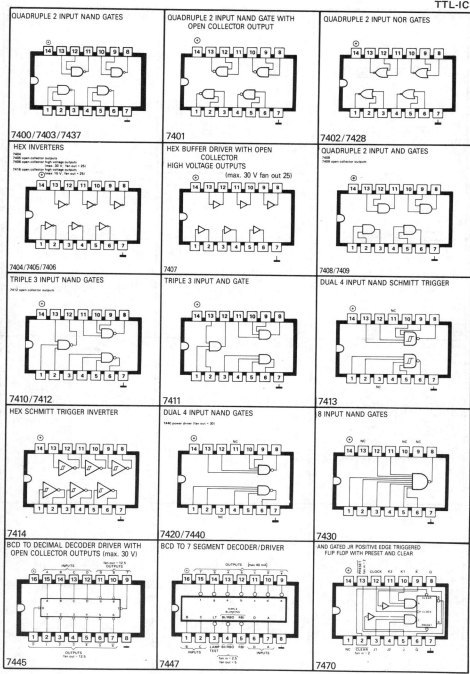

QUADRUPLE 2 INPUT NAND GATES

7400/7403/7437

QUADRUPLE 2 INPUT NAND GATE WITH
OPEN COLLECTOR OUTPUT

7401

QUADRUPLE 2 INPUT NOR GATES

7402/7428

HEX INVERTERS

7404
7405 open collector outputs
7406 open collector high voltage outputs
(max. 30 V, fan out = 25)
7416 open collector high voltage outputs
(max. 15 V, fan out = 25)

7404/7405/7406

HEX BUFFER DRIVER WITH OPEN
COLLECTOR
HIGH VOLTAGE OUTPUTS
(max. 30 V fan out 25)

7407

QUADRUPLE 2 INPUT AND GATES

7408
7409 open collector outputs

7408/7409

TRIPLE 3 INPUT NAND GATES

7412 open collector outputs

7410/7412

TRIPLE 3 INPUT AND GATE

7411

DUAL 4 INPUT NAND SCHMITT TRIGGER

7413

HEX SCHMITT TRIGGER INVERTER

7414

DUAL 4 INPUT NAND GATES

7440 power driver (fan out = 30)

7420/7440

8 INPUT NAND GATES

7430

BCD TO DECIMAL DECODER DRIVER WITH
OPEN COLLECTOR OUTPUTS (max. 30 V)

7445

BCD TO 7 SEGMENT DECODER/DRIVER

7447

AND GATED JK POSITIVE EDGE TRIGGERED
FLIP FLOP WITH PRESET AND CLEAR

7470

331

CMOS-IC's

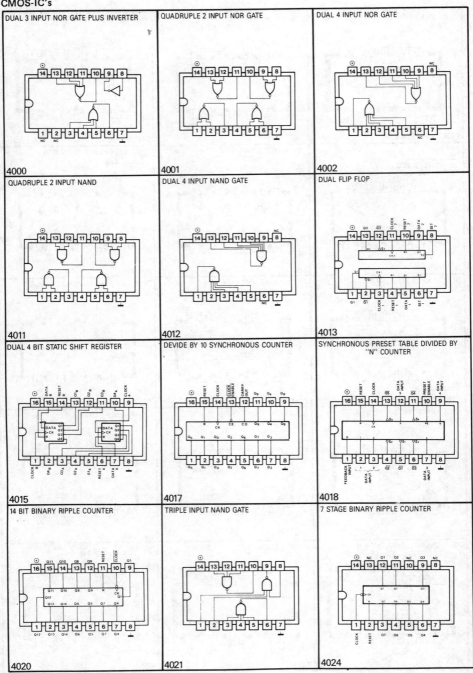

DUAL 3 INPUT NOR GATE PLUS INVERTER

4000

QUADRUPLE 2 INPUT NOR GATE

4001

DUAL 4 INPUT NOR GATE

4002

QUADRUPLE 2 INPUT NAND

4011

DUAL 4 INPUT NAND GATE

4012

DUAL FLIP FLOP

4013

DUAL 4 BIT STATIC SHIFT REGISTER

4015

DEVIDE BY 10 SYNCHRONOUS COUNTER

4017

SYNCHRONOUS PRESET TABLE DIVIDED BY "N" COUNTER

4018

14 BIT BINARY RIPPLE COUNTER

4020

TRIPLE INPUT NAND GATE

4021

7 STAGE BINARY RIPPLE COUNTER

4024

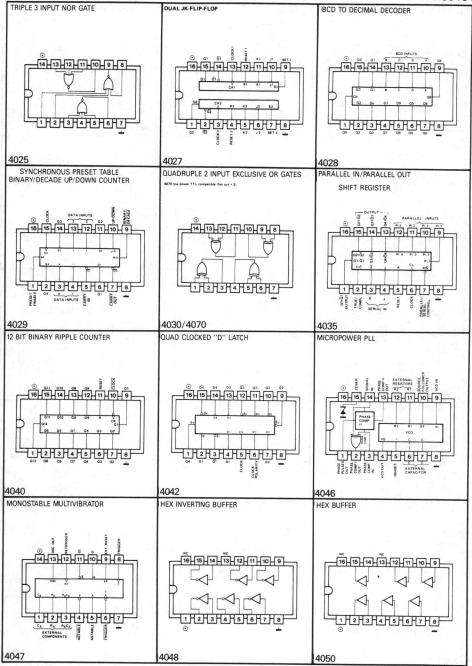

TRIPLE 3 INPUT NOR GATE

4025

DUAL JK-FLIP-FLOP

4027

BCD TO DECIMAL DECODER

4028

SYNCHRONOUS PRESET TABLE
BINARY/DECADE UP/DOWN COUNTER

4029

QUADRUPLE 2 INPUT EXCLUSIVE OR GATES

4070 low power TTL compatible (fan out = 2)

4030/4070

PARALLEL IN/PARALLEL OUT

SHIFT REGISTER

4035

12 BIT BINARY RIPPLE COUNTER

4040

QUAD CLOCKED "D" LATCH

4042

MICROPOWER PLL

4046

MONOSTABLE MULTIVIBRATOR

4047

HEX INVERTING BUFFER

4048

HEX BUFFER

4050

CMOS-IC's

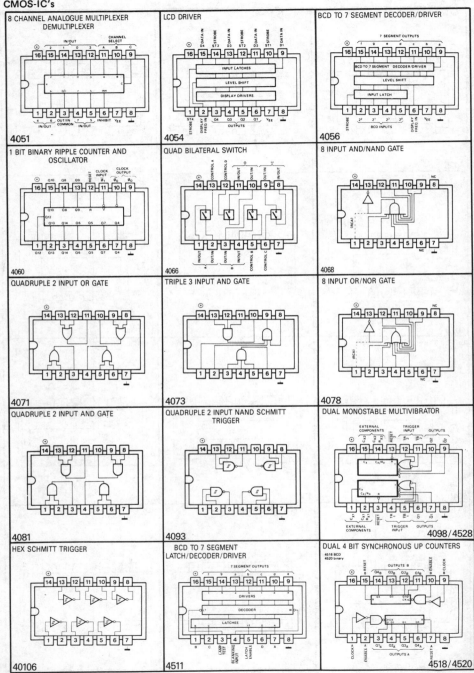

8 CHANNEL ANALOGUE MULTIPLEXER DEMULTIPLEXER
4051

LCD DRIVER
4054

BCD TO 7 SEGMENT DECODER/DRIVER
4056

1 BIT BINARY RIPPLE COUNTER AND OSCILLATOR
4060

QUAD BILATERAL SWITCH
4066

8 INPUT AND/NAND GATE
4068

QUADRUPLE 2 INPUT OR GATE
4071

TRIPLE 3 INPUT AND GATE
4073

8 INPUT OR/NOR GATE
4078

QUADRUPLE 2 INPUT AND GATE
4081

QUADRUPLE 2 INPUT NAND SCHMITT TRIGGER
4093

DUAL MONOSTABLE MULTIVIBRATOR
4098/4528

HEX SCHMITT TRIGGER
40106

BCD TO 7 SEGMENT LATCH/DECODER/DRIVER
4511

DUAL 4 BIT SYNCHRONOUS UP COUNTERS
4518/4520

334

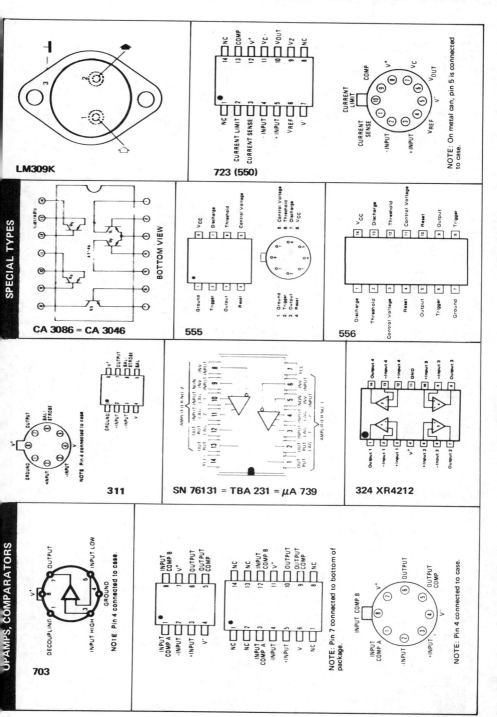

LM309K

723 (550)

NOTE: On metal can, pin 5 is connected to case.

CA 3086 = CA 3046

BOTTOM VIEW

555

556

311

NOTE: Pin 4 connected to case

SN 76131 = TBA 231 = µA 739

324 XR4212

703

NOTE: Pin 4 connected to case.

NOTE: Pin 7 connected to bottom of package.

NOTE: Pin 4 connected to case.

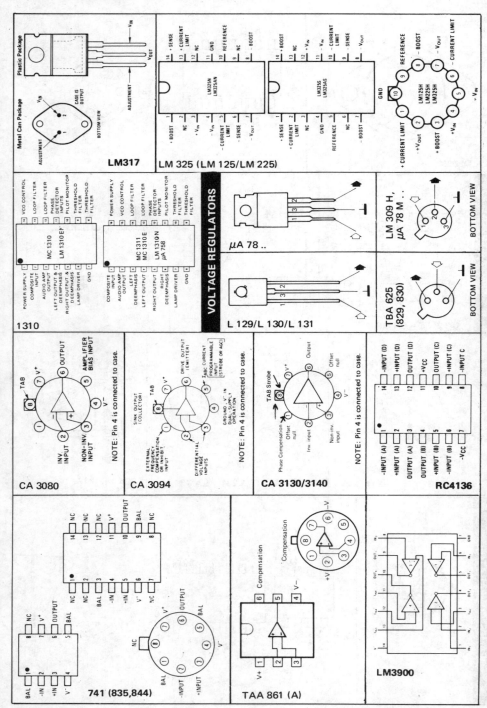

Plastic Package
V_{IN}
V_{OUT}
ADJUSTMENT

Metal Can Package
V_{IN}
2
1
ADJUSTMENT
CASE IS OUTPUT
BOTTOM VIEW

LM317

LM 325 (LM 125/LM 225)

LM325N
LM325AN
- SENSE / CURRENT LIMIT / NC / GND / REFERENCE / NC / - BOOST
+ BOOST / NC / + V_{IN} / - V_{IN} / - CURRENT LIMIT / - SENSE / - V_{OUT}

LM325S
LM325AS
+ BOOST / NC / + V_{IN} / + V_{IN} / - CURRENT LIMIT / - SENSE / - V_{OUT}
+ SENSE / + CURRENT LIMIT / NC / GND / REFERENCE / NC / - BOOST

LM125H
LM225H
LM325H
REFERENCE / BOOST / - CURRENT LIMIT / - V_{IN} / - BOOST / - V_{OUT} / + CURRENT LIMIT / GND / + V_{IN} / + BOOST / + V_{OUT} / + CURRENT LIMIT

1310

MC1310 / LM1310E
VCO CONTROL / LOOP FILTER / LOOP FILTER / PHASE DETECTOR INPUT / PILOT MONITOR / THRESHOLD FILTER / THRESHOLD FILTER
POWER SUPPLY / COMPOSITE INPUT / AUDIO AMP OUTPUT / LEFT OUTPUT / DE-EMPHASIS / RIGHT OUTPUT & DE-EMPHASIS / LAMP DRIVER / GND

MC1311 / MC1310E / LM1310N / μA758
POWER SUPPLY / VCO CONTROL / LOOP FILTER / LOOP FILTER / PHASE DETECTOR INPUT / PILOT MONITOR / THRESHOLD FILTER / THRESHOLD FILTER
COMPOSITE INPUT / AUDIO AMP OUTPUT / LEFT OUTPUT / DEEMPHASIS / RIGHT OUTPUT / DEEMPHASIS / LAMP DRIVER / GND

VOLTAGE REGULATORS

μA 78 ..

LM 309 H, μA 78 M ..
BOTTOM VIEW

L 129/L 130/L 131

TBA 625 (829, 830)
BOTTOM VIEW

CA 3080
TAB
V+
OUTPUT
AMPLIFIER BIAS INPUT
V-
INV INPUT
NON-INV INPUT
NOTE: Pin 4 is connected to case.

CA 3094
DRIVE OUTPUT (EMITTER)
AGC CURRENT (PROGRAMMABLE INPUT) (STROBE OR AGC)
V+
TAB
GROUND V- IN DUAL SUPPLY OPERATION
SINK OUTPUT (COLLECTOR)
EXTERNAL FREQUENCY COMPENSATION INPUT
DIFFERENTIAL VOLTAGE INPUTS
NOTE: Pin 4 is connected to case.

CA 3130/3140
TAB Strobe
V+
Output
Offset null
V-
Non.inv. input
Inv. input
Offset null
Phase Compensation
NOTE: Pin 4 is connected to case.

RC4136
-INPUT (D) / +INPUT (D) / OUTPUT (D) / +VCC / OUTPUT (C) / -INPUT (C) / +INPUT C
-INPUT (A) / +INPUT (A) / OUTPUT (A) / OUTPUT (B) / +INPUT (B) / -INPUT (B) / -VCC

NC / NC / NC / V+ / OUTPUT / BAL / NC
NC / NC / BAL / -IN / +IN / V- / V+

NC / V+ / OUTPUT / BAL
BAL / -IN / +IN / V-

NC / V+ / OUTPUT / BAL
BAL / -INPUT / +INPUT / V-

741 (835,844)

Compensation
-V
Compensation
+V
V-

Compensation
6 / 5 / 4
1 / 2 / 3
V+

TAA 861 (A)

LM3900